Adventure Guide

Tampa Bay

& Florida's West Coast

4th Edition

Chelle Koster Walton

HUNTER

HUNTER PUBLISHING, INC.
80 Northfield Avenue, Edison, NJ 08837
☎ 732-225-1900 / 800-255-0343 / fax 732-417-1744
www.hunterpublishing.com

IN CANADA:
Ulysses Travel Publications
4176 Saint-Denis, Montréal, Québec, Canada H2W 2M5
☎ 514-843-9882 ext. 2232 / fax 514-843-9448

IN THE UK & EUROPE:
Roundhouse Group
Millstone, Limers Lane, Northam
Devon EX39 2RG, England
☎ 01237-474474 / fax 01237-474774

ISBN 978-1-58843-645-0

© 2008 Chelle Koster Walton

*This and other Hunter travel guides are also available as
e-books through Amazon.com, NetLibrary.com and other
digital partners. For information, e-mail us at
comments@hunterpublishing.com.*

Cover: Great blue heron © Michael Thompson/iStockPhoto

Other images courtesy of the following: Brandenton Area CVB;
Citrus County TDC; Pasco County TD; Lee County VCB/The Beaches
of Fort Myers & Sanibel; Greater Naples, Marco Island & the
Everglades CVB; Sarasota CVB; Tampa Bay & Co.

Maps by Lissa K. Dailey & Kim André © 2008 Hunter Publishing, Inc.

Index by Nancy Wolff & Mary Ellen McGrath

4   3   2   1

ABOUT THE AUTHOR

Chelle Koster Walton began her greatest life adventure when she moved to Sanibel Island sight unseen in 1981. She's never looked back, except to wonder why she didn't move sooner. From her favorite island, the author travels around Florida and the Caribbean researching guidebooks, of which she has published eight, and writing articles for *Family Fun, National Geographic Traveler, Arthur Frommer's Budget Travel, Endless Vacation, The Miami Herald,* and other print and electronic media. Walton is co-founder of www.guide bookwriters.com and a member of the Society of American Travel Writers.

Author Chelle Walton. (Photo by Karen T. Bart-

ACKNOWLEDGMENTS

Many thanks to all who assisted me in the adventure of writing a Florida adventure guide, especially to these helpful souls: Alisa Bennett, Kelly Earnest, Nancy Hamilton, Lorraine Moore, and Wit Tuttell. I couldn't have done it without you.

DEDICATION

To Rob and his fabulous Walton Adventures.

HOW TO USE THIS BOOK

This book divides the West Coast into seven sections. It begins in the north with Citrus, Hernando, and Pasco counties, a region dubbed the Nature Coast. It then continues southward with St. Petersburg & Clearwater. The chapter encompasses Tarpon Springs, Clearwater, St. Petersburg, and the adjacent barrier island chain.

Tampa, as metropolitan core of the West Coast, has its own chapter; then we move south to Bradenton & Sarasota, with their islands and outlying towns.

The little-known Charlotte Harbor area has one chapter. Then we cover Lee County, promoted as The Beaches of Fort Myers & Sanibel.

Collier County, one of Florida's largest, includes its main town and governmental seat, Naples, as well as Marco Island, Ten Thousand Islands, Everglades City, the western half of the Florida Everglades, and its surrounding parks and preserves.

Each chapter begins with a brief overall history and information that will make finding your way around easier. Then it is divided by cities or areas within the sub-region, their adventure opportunities, sights, restaurants, hotels, and other attractions. Sprinkled amid the hard facts, you'll find budget tips, author recommendations, family-friendly choices, quirky Florida terms, and weekend adventure itineraries. Throughout, places that come highly recommended by the author are indicated by a star: ☆

Contents

MAPS

Introduction

For the purposes of this guide, the West Coast of Florida describes a slice of coastline along the Gulf of Mexico beginning in the quiet rural setting of Citrus County, north of the Tampa Bay area, and ending in the south at Naples and the utter wilderness of the Everglades. It encompasses the coastal portions of Citrus, Hernando, Pasco, Pinellas, Hillsborough, Manatee, Sarasota, Charlotte, Lee, and Collier counties. This region is cohesive in its types of vegetation and climate, yet it is infinitely diverse in culture and disposition.

THE HISTORY OF ADVENTURE

If you're looking for adventure, you're in the right place. West Coast Florida, as one of the nation's final frontiers, claims a history and heritage of rugged outdoorsmanship.

While the rest of the nation was busily traveling along paved roads and buying their supplies from general stores, in the farthest corners of Florida's Gulf Coast – down Naples way and in the Florida Everglades – folks were still trading with the natives for victuals and dredging enough land out of the swamps to build the **Tamiami Trail**. The West Coast of Florida was considered a wild, exotic place then, a place for safaris and catching giant silver fish; a place where prehistoric turtles, alligators, manatees, and horseshoe crabs thrived, where trees danced, birds dive-bombed, dolphins grinned, flowers bloomed at night, and winter never came.

■ THE FIRST VISITORS

The first white men traveled to western Florida for adventure. And they found it aplenty: half-naked natives, tricky waterways, impenetrable swamps, and enough fowl and fish to thicken seas, sky, and fire-brewed stews. In search of gold and youth, they chose to grumble, kill the natives, and curse the rest. They brought their own hogs, cows, and citrus to eat, then eventually left, discouraged by the persistent onslaughts from the resident Amerindian tribes – the **Calusa** in the south, the **Timucua** around today's Tampa and Sarasota. Evidence of important Amerindian centers of culture has been found in Marco Island, Mound Key, Pine Island, Useppa Island, Manasota Key, Terra Ceia, Safety Harbor, and Crystal River.

Anonymous 16th-century painting of Juan Ponce de León.

Juan Ponce de León was the first recorded European to set foot upon these shores, somewhere in Charlotte Harbor. **Hernando De Soto** landed at today's Fort Myers Beach or Bradenton, depending upon whom you believe. Ensuing parties established forts, missions, and colonies at Mound Key, Fort Myers Beach, Pine Island, and other strategic spots along the coast.

Legends fill the region's early timelines with dastardly pirates who came to prey upon ships sailing between the Caribbean and established towns in northern Florida. Much has been exaggerated, particularly the legend of Gasparilla, upon which a Tampa festival and a coastline attitude of devil-may-care thrive. The mottled backwaters of the West Coast undoubtedly harbored many a refugee from the law, but few as colorful as publicity agents have painted them.

More prevalent in the 17th through the 19th centuries were Spanish fishermen and gutsy farmers. Later, in the Charlotte Harbor area, commercial fishing developed into a thriving industry. Fishermen lived in stilt houses built on sand shoals from Placida to the Ten Thousand Islands. A handful of the historic shacks remain.

In many ways, **fishing** settled the West Coast. Farming proved less dependable, what with hurricanes and pests. Sugar plantations around Bradenton and Homosassa came and went with the wind. In later years, a reputation for great sportfishing brought well-heeled adventurers to the coast, which eventually put the region on the map of the socially connected.

THE 1800S

In the meantime, war introduced others to this balmy, palmy land. Florida, after being passed back and forth between Spain and England, became a **US territory** in the early 1820s. Shortly thereafter, Governor Andrew Jackson, to defend against the Seminole tribes he had angered, built forts on Lake Holathlikaha near today's Inverness, Tampa Bay, and the Caloosahatchee River at today's Fort Myers. Later, Civil and Spanish-American War fortifications were built on Egmont and Mullet keys, at the mouth of Tampa Bay. In the wake of war came ex-soldiers and their families. Then followed industry and tourism.

St. Petersburg was built in 1887 as a health resort, and **Tampa**, formerly Fort Brooke, gained a reputation as such. Railroads, cigar factories, and hotels started the twin cities down the path to becoming the region's metropolitan hub. Islands and coastal towns to the south remained the domain of the intrepid. It wasn't until big names such as Ringling and Edison became associated with the region that people sat up and took serious notice.

THE 1900S TO THE PRESENT

They came to fish. They came to swim in the warm, gentle Gulf waves. They came to hunt, to escape, to winter. They came to stay. Since the 1940s, the coast's population has built steadily. As more people came to reside permanently, cities developed along typical lines, adding services and culture to their slate of resorts, restaurants, and beachside facilities.

Adventure has always been a major part of what the coast offers. As eco-tourism came into fashion, emphasis shifted to this aspect of vacationing. To the fishing charters, tour boats, parasailing concessions, and Hobie Cat rentals were added bike trails, sea kayaking, and nature-oriented tours. The West Coast has firmly put its foot down about wanton development. This makes it especially desirable for adventurers seeking a return to what those first intrepid fishermen, hunters, and sailors found.

Largely gone are the untamed lands and rugged lifestyles that attracted adventurers a half-century ago. Development continually threatens some natural resources, but visitors can still find throughout the region areas and activities that retain the flavor and fervor of Florida's derring-do days.

THE PEOPLE & CULTURE

Western Florida has built its population in great part from tourists who came and never left. The result is a rich blend of cultures.

■ THE FIRST SETTLERS

The earliest tourists arrived before history books, probably first from Asia, later from South America and the Caribbean. The **Calusa** and **Timucua Amerindians** did not survive the next incursion of visitors. The **Spanish** eventually decimated their numbers with bows, arrows, and disease. Spanish influence persisted, and the area's oldest families have names such as Padilla and Menendez, familial survivors from a time when Cuban fishermen set up camps on the islands and Cuban cigar-makers migrated from Key West.

Most of the latter settled in Tampa's Ybor City. Germans, Italians, Jews, and other nationalities followed to work the cigar factories, making Ybor City still today one of the region's most colorful ethnic enclaves. The district is known for its restaurants, where a Cuban sandwich or bowl of rice and beans are culinarily symbolic.

Other early arrivals migrated from the north, among them the **Seminole Amerindians**, a branch of the Creek tribe, whose bloodlines reflected an intermingling of African and Spanish ancestry. The Seminole Wars forced them to Arkansas, except for those who took cover in the Everglades' forbidding wild lands. Seminoles and an offshoot tribe known as the **Miccosukee** still live in the Everglades and on tribal lands around Tampa. In the Everglades, many live in chickee huts, pole structures topped with intricately thatched roofs. The Native Americans subsist on fishing, farming, and tourism, selling their colorful weaving, and raking in the proceeds from bingo and gambling. The tribe runs casinos in Tampa, Miami, and Immokalee (in Collier County).

Osceola (1804-1838) was a war chief of the Seminole Indians in Florida. He led a small band of warriors (never more than 100) in the Seminole resistance during the Second Seminole War when the US tried to remove the Seminoles from their lands.

The Seminole Wars, and later the Civil War, further stocked the slowly growing population with American soldiers who fell in love with the pleasant climate and lush surroundings.

FLORIDIOM: Settlers from Georgia and Alabama came to be known as "Crackers," a term often associated with the region's early cattle drivers, who "cracked" their whips to herd wild cows. Others attribute the label to a Celtic word applied disparagingly to early Scotch-Irish plantation hands in the South. Whatever the origin, Crackers contributed to this region their Deep South cuisine, folk medicine, and a simple style of architecture known as the Cracker house, which has come back into fashion as "Old Florida" architecture. They settled and farmed mostly in the interior sections of the region, where to this day lifestyles whistle Dixie and folks speak with "South in the mouth."

■ THE POPULATION BOOM

Land booms of the pre- and post-Depression eras brought northerners from far reaches. First came the well-to-do in search of adventures in the untamed wilderness. Among them were President Teddy Roosevelt, Zane Grey, Shirley Temple, Hedy Lamarr, Charles Lindbergh, Thomas Edison, John Ringling, and Henry Ford. Giants from the industrial world followed, often buying up land to insure the exclusivity of the region. They left behind a standard for nature appreciation and beautiful architecture. Others, such as Henry Plant and Barron Collier, saw the opportunity to develop the land, and so built railroads, roads, ports, resorts, and hotels.

Once the word got out, another sort of adventurer, known then as the "Tin Can Tourist," arrived in motor homes. They, and those that followed, led to Florida's reputation as an RV heaven, a reputation recent hurricanes are dispelling.

Much of Southwest Florida's population in the past three decades came from the Midwest, bringing along its meat-and-potatoes cuisine and steady work ethics. Sarasota, for instance, harbors an Amish-Mennonite community that farms and operates home-style restaurants. At the onset of that era, retirees and seasonal residents dominated the population. The late 1980s and early 1990s saw the population homogenize somewhat, with folks coming from all parts of the United States, all age groups, and all walks of life.

The Hispanic and Haitian populations are growing, as immigrants move in to fill gaps in the agricultural workforce. Cape Coral, one pocket of Hispanic ethnicity, enjoys the celebrated cuisine and festivities indigenous to the culture. The town is also known for its German and Italian populations and restaurants.

Young families have found an ideal atmosphere for their children in West Coast Florida – a playground open all year 'round.

Today's West Coaster is said to have a calmer attitude than the East Coaster – more like the Gulf than the ocean. Laid-back is the term most commonly applied. The pace is slower, the surroundings more natural. That's where the generalities end. From the sophisticated Tampa metropolite to the Everglades backwoods Seminole, the West Coast embraces a range of people as diverse as its terrain.

NATURAL MAKEUP

With nearly 200 miles of Gulf coastline, more than 500 miles of freshwater river, thousands of acres of lakes, mangrove estuary, and untamed jungle, and the vast sawgrass plains of the Everglades, Florida's West Coast brims with opportunity for adventure on both land and water.

The diversity of its terrain and biological communities, when combined with the region's exotic, subtropical climate and ambiance, creates a destination that is both classroom and playground for outdoor enthusiasts. Where else can you camp on a warm, sand beach and canoe among roseate spoonbills and manatees?

Mangrove leaves.

MARINE LIFE

The island beach and marine communities, of course, are the most touted features of Gulf Coast Florida ecology. They introduce most visitors to the local environment with their shells, dolphins, pelicans, shorebirds, stingrays, tarpon, and loggerhead turtles; but they are only the beginning point.

STINGRAY SHUFFLE

In summer, stingrays nest along the shoreline in shallow waters. To avoid stepping on them and the excruciating pain that follows, locals do the "Stingray Shuffle." If you shuffle your feet as you enter the water, the stingrays will gladly avoid you. Punctures occur only when you step directly on the ray's barb.

MANGROVE ESTUARIES

Most intriguing to nature lovers are the undersung estuaries, the nurseries that build islands and nurture aquatic life. Haunting, steamy places, they harbor a species of tree that seems to dance on spindly legs – the mangrove. In its prop roots, dirt, barnacles, and other incrustations collect to build shorelines and islands. Its leaf fall provides rich and fertile muck; its branches, nests for local and migrating birds. Here the food chain begins with the tiniest crabs and ends with the birds, fish, and manatees that come to munch on seaweed or lunch on a half-shell. The cycle is ancient, and one can sense that in the quietly regenerating world of the mangrove estuary. Unfortunately, where the Caloosahatchee River empties in the bay, fragile estuaries are in serious trouble around Pine Island and Sanibel Island.

■ FLORA & FAUNA

© Gabriel Hurley

American alligator,
Everglades National Park

Less brackish and freshwater systems are the domain of another ancient component of Florida wildlife – the **alligator**. Gnarly and tyrannasaurish, the American alligator survives and thrives in coastal rivers and particularly in the Everglades. With it co-exist cypress trees, turtles, bass, river otters, and fabulous birds such as the wood stork and great blue heron.

Salt marshes, scrublands, flatwoods, and high pine lands occupy different elevations between sea level and ridge land. On hammocks, high and dry, hardwood forests harbor the rarest of all Florida creatures, the **panther**, seldom seen in the wild. Its cousin the **bobcat** is less reclusive, its numbers less depleted. **Black bears, white-tailed deer, squirrels, raccoons, opossums, armadillos**, and **gopher tortoises** roam the woodlands. Get closer and you'll find **indigo snakes, anole lizards, skinks, tree frogs, ant lions**, and **love bugs**.

Most native coastal plants are benign and serve to protect wildlife. Residents are becoming aware of that and there is a trend to plant wildlife-attracting gardens rather than exotic vegetation, which taxes the ecosystem. Cities, resorts, and commercial enterprises are using **sea oats, railroad vine**, and other maritime vegetation to keep sands anchored to the beaches. Native **grasses** attract gopher tortoises. Dead **tree trunks** provide homes for **kestrels** and other nesting birds, as well as food for **pileated woodpeckers. Butterflies** flock around certain native plants, to feed and lay their eggs.

> **CAUTION:** Some locals are less friendly than others. Those you want to avoid include rattlesnakes, pygmy rattlers, jellyfish, fire ants, and sand fleas ("no-see-ums"). There are also noxious plants that can pose danger, particularly the detested pepper plant, an introduced tree whose berries can cause allergic reaction. Poison ivy and oak grow in the wilds. A mystery novel set on Sanibel Island describes murder by a different plant, the oleander, a limb of which the murderer used to roast a marshmallow for his victim.

In 2002, the West Coast section of the **Great Florida Birding Trail**, ☎ 850-922-0664, www.floridabirdingtrail.com, opened, followed in 2006 by the South Florida leg. The trail strings together some of the great birding sites of the region along a flyway used for migrating species. It lists more than 60 sites within the Nature Coast and Sarasota area, and the South Florida section includes 42 birding spots in Charlotte, Lee, and Collier counties.

To further recommend the area to birders, *Birder's World* magazine lists three area sites among their top five. They include **J.N. "Ding" Darling National Wildlife Refuge** on Sanibel Island and **Corkscrew Swamp Sanctuary** and **Everglades National Park** in the Naples area.

On a larger scale, the region's many state and national parks and refuges began preserving habitat in its natural state back when land booms threatened Florida's fragile environment. Private enterprises have since joined the drive to save what is dwindling. Today, these preserves offer not only shelter to the threatened, but also recreation to those who appreciate the region's distinct environment.

ENDANGERED/THREATENED SPECIES

Florida is home to more than 100 fragile species. Close to 40 of these are listed on the US Fish and Wildlife Service list of endangered and threatened animals. Those found in West Florida include the **Florida panther, West Indian manatee, wood stork, bald eagle, red-cockaded woodpecker, Florida scrub jay, roseate tern, American crocodile, Atlantic loggerhead turtle, Eastern indigo snake,** and **sand skink**.

GUIDELINES FOR WILDLIFE PRESERVATION

While visiting Florida, take care to observe the following regulations and guidelines for the protection of wildlife and habitat.

SHELLING

- Live shelling is prohib-
ited in state and national
parks, in refuges, and on
all of Sanibel Island. In
these areas, do not keep
any shell with an animal
in it, whether or not you
believe the animal is
dead. Gently return a
live shell to the water; do
not fling it.

- Lee and Collier counties limit live shelling to two per species per person per day.

- Live shells must be cleaned properly or they will smell
like dead fish in a day or two. If you don't know what
you're doing, don't collect the shells only to toss them
from the car window down the road.

- A fishing license is required for collecting live shells in
Florida.

FEEDING WILDLIFE

- Don't feed wild animals. This includes everything from
those harmless seagulls on the beach to that very harm-
ful alligator behind the fence. Feeding alligators is illegal
in Florida and noncompliance is punishable by a hefty
fine. More importantly, by feeding an alligator, you are
training it to lose its fear of man. That's when toddlers get
grabbed off bank shores or fishermen's feet become
'gator bait.

- Feeding birds on the beach not only causes a nuisance,
it overrides their instincts and the birds forget how to
feed themselves.

- Do not throw fish to pelicans, no matter how much they
beg and how adorable they are. Large bony fish can
cause bill and throat punctures. Be careful when you
cast around gathered pelicans. They often swallow bait,
hook and all. If this happens, gently reel in the bird,
cover its head with a towel or shirt, and carefully clip and
extract the hook, trying to back it out rather than running the barb through the bird's skin.

- If you're camping or picnicking, you may find yourself in-
advertently feeding raccoons and squirrels. At night, put

all of your food, including supposedly sealed coolers and bags of garbage, inside a vehicle or trash bin.

HARMFUL LITTER

■ Discarded fishing filament, plastic shopping bags, and beverage six-pack rings can harm pelicans and marine life. Toss litter into a trash receptacle.

■ Be careful not to throw food or food wrappers out the car window. This attracts animals to roadways, where they can be run over.

SEA TURTLES

■ Loggerhead turtles come to nest on our beaches during the summer. Do not disturb their nests, which are marked by turtle night patrols. Turn off lights facing the beach; they disorient nesting and hatching turtles.

MANATEES

Watersports enthusiasts play a major role in the continued endangerment of the Florida manatee. To ensure the survival of these loveable creatures, please abide by these guidelines.

■ Use snorkel gear when diving with manatees. Scuba gear bubbles can frighten them.

■ Never feed a manatee in the wild.

■ Never approach or chase a manatee.

■ Never separate a cow from her calf.

■ Do not touch manatees. Never poke, prod, or stab a manatee with your hands, feet, or any object.

■ When boating, wear polarized glasses that permit you to see surfacing manatees better. Stay in the center of marked channels and out of seagrasses. Observe manatee speed zones and drive slowly enough to be able to see and avoid a manatee.

To report a manatee death, injury, harassment, or radio-tagged manatee, call ☎ 888-404-FWCC (3922). For more information, see the Florida Fish & Wildlife Conservation Commission's website at http://myfwc.com/manatee/ or floridamarine.org.

BOATING & FISHING

■ Observe manatee zone signs by slowing down to no-wake speed. Take the slack time to watch for the fascinating mammals as they surface for air.

- Stay in the marked channels when boating. This not only protects you and your vessel, but also the fragile grass flats that feed our fish.

Most local guides and fishermen practice catch-and-release, and will urge you to do so as well. Certain fish, such as tarpon, require a special permit to kill.

VEGETATION

- It is illegal to pick sea oats, which keep our beaches in place. Mangroves are also protected by the law; don't trim or cut them down.

GOVERNMENT-PROTECTED PARKS & REFUGES

The region's most extensive refuge lands, in Everglades National Park, were saved from disaster as they balanced on the brink, thanks to the efforts of **Marjory Stoneman Douglas**. Her 1947 book titled *The Everglades: River of Grass*, sparked a movement to convince the federal government to preserve the fragile wetlands.

Even after the creation of the national park – which protected only portions of the ecosystem, activists such as Douglas continued to work to preserve and protect the Everglades from further development.

■ EVERGLADES NATIONAL PARK

The Florida Everglades and its accompanying **Ten Thousand Islands National Wildlife Refuge** cover 2,100 square miles and claim 99 miles of canoe trails, 600 types of fish, 347 species of birds, 60 species of amphibians and reptiles, 43 species of mosquitoes, and 25 species of mammals. This guide covers the portion of the massive park that lies in Collier County and is accessible from the west – the part that borders Ten Thousand Islands.

Sharing the Everglades ecology, Florida Panther National Wildlife Refuge, Big Cypress National Preserve, Fakahatchee Strand State Preserve, and Collier Seminole State Park offer a score of eco-opportunities in the vicinity.

WILDLIFE & FOREST PRESERVES

Another national preserve in the region takes up half of Sanibel Island. **J.N. "Ding" Darling National Wildlife Refuge** is also Everglades-like in its wetlands makeup. **Egmont Key National Wildlife Refuge** occupies the entire 398 acres of Egmont Key, which is approachable only by boat. So is the **Pine Island National Wildlife Refuge**, comprising out-islands in Pine Island Sound. In the coast's northern reaches, **Chassahowitzka National Wildlife Refuge**, **Crystal River National Wildlife Refuge**, and **Withlacoochee State Forest** preserve the pristine waters and forests of Citrus and Hernando counties.

MARINE PRESERVES

Much of what attracts adventurers to the region lies off briny shores, in the Gulf of Mexico, the world's largest gulf, or in the Intracoastal Waterway of bays and harbors between mainland and barrier islands. Within the area we will be covering lie two of Florida's largest inlets: **Tampa Bay** and **Charlotte Harbor**. The 7,667-acre **Cape Haze Aquatic Preserve** in Charlotte Harbor protects precious marine resources. The long **Caloosahatchee River** provides watery passage between the Gulf and the great Lake Okeechobee, but unfortunately it was recently labeled among the nation's 10 most endangered rivers due to water releases from nutrient-rich Lake Okeechobee. The shoreline north of Tampa Bay is riddled with river deltas and marshlands that front them. Other West Coast sea preserves include the **Pine Island Sound Aquatic Preserve** and **Estero Bay Aquatic Preserve**.

STATE PARKS & HISTORIC SITES

Florida maintains an excellent system of state-operated parks, historic sites, and other recreational areas. This book covers several of the finest, from the unbridged island refuge of **Cayo Costa State Park** to the unusual slice of nature and history preserved at **Koreshan State Historic Site** and the 30-foot Indian mound in **Crystal River State Archaeological Site**. Many of the parks provide recreational opportunities that allow visitors to play while immersing themselves in nature and history.

> **MONEY-SAVER:** *If you plan on exploring the parks to any extent, consider purchasing an annual pass for $43.40 ($85.50 for families), available at the entrance booth to most of the parks or by calling ☎ 850-245-2157. Visit the Florida State Parks website at www.floridastateparks.org.*

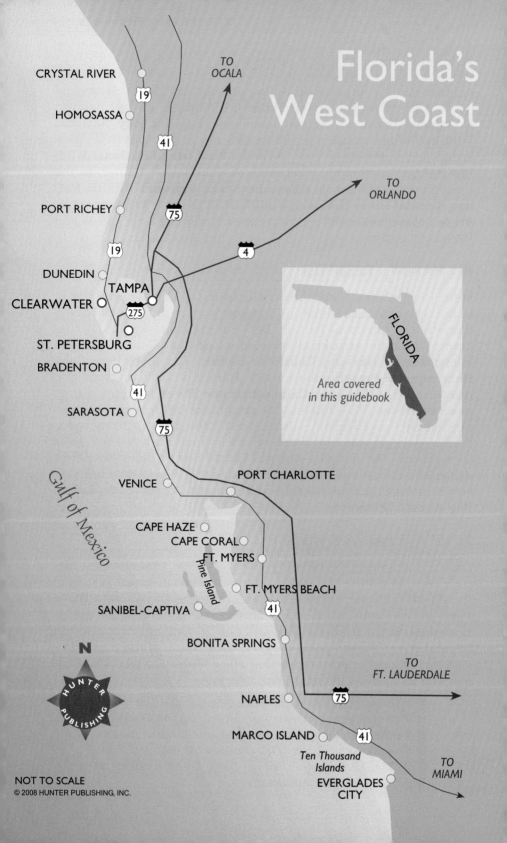

Practical Information

TRANSPORTATION

▓ BY AIR

If you are traveling by air, five international airports and various local runways serve your needs. **Tampa** has the largest international airport; others are located in **St. Petersburg, Sarasota-Bradenton**, and **Fort Myers. Orlando International Airport** is also convenient to the Nature Coast (Citrus and Hernando counties). Major domestic airlines serve all five. International flights arrive principally from Canada, Germany, and the United Kingdom. Each chapter gives specific airport and airline information.

▓ BY CAR

Motorists make inroads on **Interstate 75**, the coast's zippy north-south artery, and **Interstate 4**, which hits Tampa from the east, connecting it to Orlando. **Highway 41** (Tamiami Trail) and **Highway 98** provide more leisurely ways to explore the coast. **Florida's Turnpike** is the main artery between Orlando and the Nature Coast.

> **NOTE:** *In 2002, the numbering system for I-75 changed from sequential order to a system coordinating with mile markers. Most exit signs carry tags such as "Old 32," indicating the exit number before the change. Mile markers and exit numbers descend north to south.*

THE LAW: Florida has a seat belt law, so buckle up. The state also requires that children up to age four be restrained in an approved child safety seat. Children aged four and older can use the automobile manufacturer's installed restraint system, but booster seats are recommended for aged four through eight. The state recommends that all children age 12 and under should ride in the back seat of a vehicle.

In winter's high-season, traffic can get a bit frustrating through towns that seem to grow together at the seams, especially on "The Trail." Yet it, the coast's earliest land route, has a story to tell, if you take the time to stop, look, and listen.

SOUTHWEST FLORIDA DRIVING TIMES (approx, in hours)	CLEARWATER	CRYSTAL RIVER	FORT MYERS	NAPLES	ORLANDO	SARASOTA	ST. PETERSBURG	TAMPA
CLEARWATER		1½	2½	3¼	2¼	1	½	½
CRYSTAL RIVER	1½		3½	4	1½	2½	1¾	1½
FORT MYERS	2½	3½		¾	3	1½	2½	2½
NAPLES	3¼	4	¾		4	2	2¾	3¼
ORLANDO	2¼	1½	3	4		3¾	2½	1¾
SARASOTA	1	2½	1½	2	2¾		¾	1
ST. PETERSBURG	½	1¾	2¼	2¾	2½	¾		½
TAMPA	½	1½	2½	3¼	1¾	1	½	

Actual driving time may vary based on traffic and road construction.
Source: Visit Florida

ON THE WATER

Before folks traveled from town to coastal town on the **Tamiami Trail**, they followed water routes – rivers, bays, and the Gulf. Water transportation is still the preferred mode for adventurous West Coasters. The **Intracoastal Waterway** runs between the mainland and the islands from Pinellas County to the Everglades. These shoal-ridden waters can be tricky, particularly the skinny waters around Ten Thousand Islands and in the Everglades; in fact, the natives had to invent new means of transportation to get around. The **swamp buggy** was Naples-born and remains a symbol of frontier adventure. The shallow-draft airboat, described on page 381, is another invention mothered by necessity.

WEATHER/WHAT TO PACK

Weather is one of the region's top selling points, particularly in winter when you can celebrate the great outdoors free from fear of freezing. Temperatures along the entire subtropical coast are generally balmy throughout the winter months, although snow has been sighted as far south as Fort Myers. The average winter temperature north of Tampa is around 60°; in the southern extremes, the average is 67.5°. From November through February, definitely pack your swimsuit (Gulf temperatures rarely dip below 60°), but don't forget a warm jacket, long-sleeved shirts, and slacks. If you'll be traveling by water, gloves, hats, and scarves may prove valuable.

Those who don't know better believe the weather skips right over spring, but residents have learned otherwise. In spring, as in fall, changes are subtle. No spring showers here, generally; a torrent of flower blossoms is more indicative of the season. Fall brings crispness to the normally moist air and a long-awaited reprieve from summer swelter.

Hibiscus flower.

© Pratheepps

TIP: *During March, April, October, and November, you won't need heavy clothes, but you should still pack shirts with long sleeves, sweaters, sweatshirts, jeans, and slacks.*

Summer comes early to the Gulf Coast, and is a great time for watersports. Hiking, biking, and other dry activities are best planned for early morning. Work into exercise gradually if you're not used to the heat and humidity. Drink plenty of water before, during, and after. Average summer temperatures range from 80° in the northern reaches covered in this book to around 82° in the south. Gulf temperatures reach 86°.

When planning your summer trip to Florida's West Coast, take into account that **hurricane season** officially begins in June. Warnings come well in advance of a major storm. Afternoon summer storms are the norm, so schedule your activities accordingly.

Pack your coolest duds for the summer months, May through September. Plan on living in a swimsuit or shorts during daylight hours, and in light cotton shorts, shirts, skirts, and dresses at night. If you'll be hiking in wooded areas, or even on the beach at sunset, bring something light to protect your arms and legs against mosquitoes and no-see-ums. A hat with a brim will protect your face and scalp from the sun. In Tampa, St. Petersburg, Sarasota, and Naples, you may have occasion to dress formally for theater or dinner, but in general, restaurants declare a casual dress code. For the adventurer, surf walkers, sneakers, and deck shoes are more essential than high heels or wing tips.

> TIP: *Don't forget to pack some common sense. No matter what time of year you visit, bug repellent and sunscreen are necessities. Keep a level head about potential crime, sunburn, over-exertion, over-exposure, and dehydration, and your vacation to West Coast Florida will be a happy one.*

SIGHTS & ATTRACTIONS

Although this book focuses on adventure and outdoor activities, it gives visitors alternatives for sightseeing and playing indoors. I pay particular attention to those attractions that lean on nature, and note them under *Eco-Adventures*. Beaches and parks that offer a wide variety of open-air fun are listed under *Sights & Attractions*, and may also be profiled under specific activities.

West Coast beaches and state parks are centers of regional adventure. Beaches have restrooms unless otherwise noted. Most prohibit alcohol, pets, open fires, and glass containers. State parks also prohibit pets.

> NOTE: *Admission fees and hours change constantly at Florida attractions, often according to seasons. Call ahead to confirm.*

ADVENTURES

ON WATER

FISHING

Since the days of Teddy Roosevelt and before, fishing has been the lure for adventure-seekers on Florida's West Coast. For early residents, it was a way of life, and commercial fishing, due to net banning, is just beginning to die out in the last hold-out fishing communities, such as Pine Island and Cortez.

Recreational fishing still thrives; many once-commercial fishermen have turned to guiding. To make sure it continues to thrive, the state enforces licensing, season, number, and size regulations.

FISHING LICENSES

Non-Florida residents age 16 or older must obtain a saltwater license to cast from shore or any pier or vessel not covered by its own license. (Most charter boats carry vessel licenses that cover all passengers.) Florida residents under age 65 fishing from a non-licensed boat also are required to have a license. Inexpensive short-term licenses are available for non-residents, as are lifetime licenses and combination fishing and hunting licenses. Separate licenses are required for freshwater and saltwater fishing.

You can purchase licenses by credit card ($3.95 surcharge), ☎ 888-347-4356, online ($2.25 plus 2.5 surcharge), www.floridaconservation.org/license, or at the county tax collectors' offices and some local bait shops, K-Marts, Wal-Marts, and marinas (surcharges may be charged).

For more information, contact the Florida Fish & Wildlife Conservation Commission, ☎ 850-488-4676; www.florida conservation.org.

SALTWATER FISHING LICENSE FEES		
NON-RESIDENTS	three-day	$6.50
	seven-day	$16.50
	one-year	$31.50
RESIDENTS	one-year	$13.50
	five-year	$61.50
Separate $2 permits are required for those wanting to catch snook or crawfish, and a $51.50 tag is needed for tarpon fishing. Combination saltwater-freshwater licenses for residents cost $25.50 per year.		
FRESHWATER FISHING LICENSE FEES		
NON-RESIDENTS	seven-day	$16.50
	one-year	$31.50
RESIDENTS	one-year	$13.50
	five-year	$61.50

The West Coast offers several types of fishing. In saltwater, where some 300 species of fish live, there is **backwater fishing**, also known as flats fishing. It takes place around bays, estuaries, mangrove areas, oyster bars, and Intracoastal waters near shore. The region's excellent backwater fishing has spawned a recent interest in fly fishing. Most backwater fishing uses light tackle. Backwater catches include tarpon, mangrove snapper, sheepshead, ladyfish, nurse sharks, sea trout, snook, and redfish. You can do this kind of fishing from piers, docks, seawalls, and leeside shores, or by boat. Backwater fishing charters are numerous throughout the coastal region, and are generally cheaper than deep-water excursions, about $300 per half-day for two to four people.

> TIP: *For guidelines on species size and season, visit local bait shops (see listings for bait shops in each chapter, under Fishing).*

Open water fishing can be intimidating for the first-timer. If you're serious about catching fish, hire a guide. If you set out on your own, look for fast-moving waters in passes and rivers, and for shady spots, mangroves, and bridges, where fish lay up in the heat of the day. Seek advice at the local bait shop concerning tides, type of bait, and prescribed line weight.

Charters and party boats take you **offshore fishing** to catch grouper, red snapper, king mackerel, and other whoppers that lurk in deep seas. Party boats, also called head boats, are an affordable option, costing about $40 per person. The fee normally includes bait, tackle, license, and cleaning. It is customary to tip the crew.

Surf fishing is another option and can be done from most beaches – again, with the best success in passes between islands or at the end of islands.

Freshwater fishing yields bass, perch, catfish, and other catches. The West Coast has its share of rivers and small lakes for fishermen, particularly in the northern Nature Coast region.

> TIP: *To receive a free copy of* **Florida Fishing & Boating**, *an official publication of the State of Florida, call the Florida Sports Foundation at* ☎ *850-488-8347, or visit www.flasports.com and click "Florida Fishing & Boating" under "Golf & Fishing."*

Schools of fish are abundant in Florida's clear waters.

BOATING

Whether you own or are renting a boat, you should use a chart of local waters. Many rental concessions provide them. West Coast waters are challenging, riddled with shoals, oyster beds, and grass flats. If you're not practiced at boating and chart reading, consider hiring a guide with local knowledge to take you out for the first time or two.

> BOATING LAW: All motor-powered boats used in Florida must be registered at the local county tax collector's office. Boats currently registered out-of-state need not be registered in Florida for stays of 90 days or less.

Island-hopping along the coast is one of the region's greatest adventures and pleasures. From Tarpon Springs south, the islands are edged in the sand of recreationists' dreams. To the north, you'll find more mangroves and less sandy shores. Unbridged islands from Anclote (*St. Petersburg & Clearwater* chapter) in the north to the Ten Thousand Islands in the south (*Naples & Everglades* chapter) offer beaches, restaurants, bird watching, shelling, and other activities enhanced by the thrill of being cut loose from mainland bustle and tempos.

> TIP: *For help in locating area boat ramp, visit* **www. boatUS.com** *and click on "Boating Info."*

CHARTER BOATS

You won't have any problem finding charters along the coast, for everything from island-hopping and fishing to sightseeing, shelling, and dolphin-spotting. Private charters by motor or sail can be easily tailored to your interests, and vessels usually hold four to six people. For a half-day, that will typically run you $300 to $450.

TOUR BOATS

Larger tour boats have a set agenda and hold a party of people for sunset, mansion-gazing, island lunching, manatee-spotting, and other special interests. In some places, you'll find huge cruise ships or showboats with dinner, shows, gambling, and dancing. Prices vary greatly. Every chapter offers several options. In the Everglades and other shallow-water areas, airboat tours make it easier to get around. Rates start at about $15 per person for a sunset or two-hour tour without meals. Reservations are usually required for charters and tours.

A flat-bottomed river boat has plenty of seating for tourists.

RENTALS

Powerboat rentals will cost you anywhere from $50 for a Jon boat to $400 for a deck boat for a half-day, which amounts to four hours, either morning or afternoon. Daily rates usually cover eight hours. Some places will rent vessels by the hour, some by the week. Rental rates vary according to boat and engine size. This book gives a range of rates as a guideline to renters. Be sure to ask whether quoted rates include gas, oil, and tax. They usually don't, with the exception of pontoons and Jet Skis or WaveRunners.

The most popular type of boat, especially for open water fishermen, has a center console. Freshwater anglers often use flat-bottomed bass boats, skiffs, or small Jon boats. Bowriders are better suited to passenger travel. Pontoon and deck boats are flat boats set aboard floats and are practical for large groups and for use in shallow waters, such as around Ten Thousand Islands.

Sailboats for rent are scarcer. Many resorts and some beach concessions have small Hobie Cats and Sunfish, which run about $60 for a half-day. Lessons are available in some locales, as part of a rental or part of a cruise.

CANOEING & KAYAKING

The best way to get close to nature while on the water is by canoe or kayak. Sea kayaking is enjoying a surge in popularity off Florida shores. Confined water kayaking is usually less strenuous. You're likely to find rentals, lessons, sales, and tours available no matter where you land. You can rent a single or tandem. Rates run around $20 for two hours.

The Everglades, Peace River, Myakka River, Hillsborough and Alafia rivers, and Homosassa, Chassahowitzka, Withlacoochee, and Crystal rivers provide excellent canoeing and kayaking trails. Many state parks rent canoes for use in their waterways.

BOATING INFORMATION

■ To receive a free copy of *Florida Fishing & Boating*, an official publication of the State of Florida, call the Florida Sports Foundation, ☎ 850-488-8347, or visit www. flasports.com and click "Florida Fishing & Boating" under "Golf & Fishing."

■ For more information on canoeing and kayaking, contact the Florida Department of Environmental Protection, Office of Greenways and Trails, 3900 Commonwealth Ave., Mail Station 795, Tallahassee, FL 32399-2400, ☎ 877-822-5208 or 850-245-2053. Visit www.floridagreenwaysandtrails.com for an online version of *Florida Greenways & Trail Guide* and for listings of outfitters.

■ Visit www.adventuresportsonline.com/canoeing.htm for links to canoe outfitters and other paddling resources.

For information on recreational access for the physically disabled, order Wheelchairs on the Go: Accessible Fun in Florida by Michelle Stigleman and Deborah Van Brunt, www.wheelchairsonthego.com.

OTHER WATERSPORTS

WaveRunners and **Jet Skis**, known under the umbrella of personal watercraft, are usually rented by the half-hour for $55-$65 and charge an extra fee for passengers. Concessions often offer tours.

Sailboarding (windsurfing), **para-sailing**, and **water-biking** are all part of the resort water scene. The larger resorts and some beaches offer these and other rentals. **Kiteboarding**, shown here, is the newest and most extreme on the scene and often requires extensive training.

© Jim Semlor

Surfing, **snorkeling**, and **scuba diving** are found on the West Coast, but are generally better and more popular on Florida's East Coast. Approaching storm fronts make for the occasional good day of surfing, but for the experienced only. The springs, caves, and rivers of the Nature Coast constitute this book's most popular diving destinations. Crystal River is the region's scuba mecca.

ON FOOT

HIKING

Nature trails in state and other parks provide opportunity for short, scenic hiking in the sunshine. The chapters on the Nature Coast and St. Petersburg & Clearwater contain longer, paved **rails-to-trails paths** shared by cyclists and inline skaters. Visit www.floridagreenwaysandtrails.com for an online guide to hiking.

> TIP: When hiking here, be sure to take drinking water. Plan for the heat and, if you're hiking on the beach, the soft surface. Hiking parts of the coast can be strenuous.

HUNTING

Florida's days as the great hunting ground are gone. But hunters will be kept happy in the **Everglades**, or at **Fred C. Babcock-Cecil M. Webb Wildlife Management Area**, in the Charlotte Harbor area, and **Withlacoochee State Forest**. For information about hunting licenses, visit http://myfwc.com/license/.

Opposite: A forested shoreline is best explored by kayak.

ON WHEELS

Bike paths and lanes accommodate casual cyclists; more serious bikers take to quiet back roads throughout the region. Bike paths are separated from traffic by distance and, ideally, by a vegetation buffer. The best ones leave the roadside altogether to penetrate natural environments unreachable by motor vehicles. Lanes, on the other hand, are a part of the roadway designated for bike traffic.

In resort communities, you can usually rent a bike at your hotel or at bike shops. Some have only basic equipment, others carry a variety of bikes and paraphernalia. Rates are usually offered by the hour, half-day, day, and week.

ROAD RULES: Where neither lanes nor paths exist, bikers must share the road with vehicular traffic. Florida law considers a bicycle a vehicle, so its operator must follow all the rules of the road upon entering the flow of traffic. Florida law requires that bike riders and passengers under age 16 wear helmets.

WHERE TO STAY

The West Coast of Florida is the land of resorts in all shapes, sizes, and price ranges. Some areas are more expensive than others. You'll find the best bargains along the Nature Coast, and in St. Petersburg & Clearwater, and Charlotte Harbor.

RATES

Rates throughout the area change seasonally. Some resort rate cards reflect as many as six different seasons: Christmas (high), January, February-Easter (high), Easter-May, Summer, and Fall (low). Smaller places stick to two or three seasons: high (mid-December-Easter), low (Easter-September or mid-December), and possibly shoulder (summer). Always ask about specials, packages, and about corporate, AAA, or other discounts that may apply.

> **NOTE:** *Most counties add a 5%-7% bed tax to rooms, revenue that goes toward maintaining and improving beaches, parks, and other tourist-impacted areas.*

There is usually a room charge for more than two persons; not always for children, however. Most accommodation rates are based on the European Plan, with no meals, except for B&Bs and certain others noted within their description. Many of the listed accommodations have kitchen facilities, whether basic or full, which can save you on dining bills.

ACCOMMODATIONS PRICE KEY		
Rates are per room, per night, double occupancy. Price ranges described for each property often do not take into account penthouses and other exceptional, high-priced accommodations.	$	Up to $75
	$$	$75 to $150
	$$$	$151 to $250
	$$$$	$251 and up

■ CAMPING

The best wilderness camping is found in the coast's state parks. See individual chapters for particulars or contact the **Florida State Parks Information Center**, 3900 Commonwealth Blvd., Tallahassee, FL 32399, ☎ 850-245-2157, www.floridastateparks.org. Reserve your state park campsite or cabin by calling ☎ 800-326-3521 or visiting www.reserveamerica.com. For more information on camping, ☎ 850-562-7151 to request a *Florida Camping Directory*, or visit www.floridacamping.com.

> **TIP:** *The* **Florida RV Trade Association** *at 10510 Gibsonton Dr., Riverview, FL 33569,* ☎ *813-741-0488, www.frvta.org, can help you locate campgrounds, resorts, and dealers.*

WHERE TO EAT

■ CUISINE

Seafood is the pride of West Coast Florida cuisine. Influenced by Deep South, Cajun, Caribbean, Latin, Midwestern, Pacific Rim, Mediterranean, and continental styles, restaurants dish up infinite variety and creativity.

In the fish houses you'll find classic Florida cuisine – raw oysters, steamed clams, fried grouper and shrimp, broiled snapper, and chilled stone crab claws. At the other end of the scale, fine restaurants create masterpieces in the art of cultural mix-and-match. Most *au courant* are fusion styles that stew together global foodways, mixing local fresh produce with exotic preparations. Modern bistros and tapas bars keep on the cutting-edge of dining trends, particularly in Naples, Sarasota, and Tampa. Ethnic eateries from northern Italian to East Indian demonstrate the cultural influences that make up the West Coast's melting pot.

Dining outside is almost always an option.

■ DINING CHOICES

The dining sections give a quick overview of that area's restaurant scene, then short descriptions of a few favorites in different categories. Since this is an adventure guide, my preferences reflect adventures in dining, whether that translates into exciting cuisine or a location near the water or the action. In each, I give a price range for the meals served, rounding off prices to the nearest dollar. I leave out dishes that stray too far up or down from the average. Nightly specials and that one expensive surf-and-turf platter, for instance, do not figure into the range.

NIGHTLIFE

West Coast Florida pales in comparison to its East Coast counterparts when it comes to culture and nightlife. Don't despair, however, if you're an adventurer who likes to use the night-time hours to test the good-time waters. If nightlife is a priority, plan your destination along the coast's metropolitan sections – in **Tampa**, **St. Petersburg** and vicinity, and **Sarasota**. These, along with **Fort Myers Beach** and **Naples**, are the hot spots, and you'll find plenty of after-dark action.

Sarasota's and Naples' brand of nightlife appeals to a highbrow crowd as well as pub-crawlers. Sarasota is known for its theater; Naples for its upscale clubs. Tampa and St. Petersburg have something for everyone. Fort Myers Beach is strictly for bar-hopping, and there's plenty of that.

TOURIST INFORMATION

For general travel information about Florida, contact **Visit Florida**, 661 E. Jefferson St., Ste. 300, Tallahassee, FL 32301, www. visitflorida.com, ☎ 888-7FLA-USA. Ask for the official *Florida Vacation Guide* and subscribe to the *Great Florida Getaways* electronic magazine.

Practical Information

The Nature Coast

Florida is fond of assigning pet names to different parcels of its shoreline. This is more true on the East Coast, where you find the Gold Coast, the Treasure Coast, the Space Coast and so on.

Lacking an identity for many years, as the coastal regions to its south stole the tourism spotlight, the land north soon coined Nature Coast for its personality handle. An apt handle it is at that. Because the coastline north of Tarpon Springs is missing the barrier islands and beaches of its southern neighbors, tourism has left it more naturally intact. Instead of sand aprons, marshes line the shores of the Nature Coast, where wild rivers gush into the Gulf of Mexico.

While this spells bad news for beach-loving tourists, it means top conditions for wildlife. Most noted for its wintering manatee herd (there's even an AM radio station – 1640 on the dial – you can tune into for the latest manatee information), the Nature Coast is also home to hundreds of bird species, including egrets (shown at right), fish that most anglers only dream about, and an environment made for kayaking, hiking, biking, and enjoying nature.

Ironically, the largely undiscovered Nature Coast holds some of Florida's oldest tourist attractions, built long before travelers dared south, back when railroads passed through. These remain within a framework of hometown

neighborliness. At one, you can watch mermaids swim in an underwater springs theater. At another you'll find a 30-foot-high ancient Amerindian mound.

The Nature Coast is definitely not for the amusement park crowd (although it does claim one water park). It's a hideaway spot made for those who prefer back yards over curbside appeal. Tourists who come these days are looking for nature, a preserved way of life, and the region's affordability. High tourist season for this region is set by the visiting manatees, who come to winter September through April. (They are most concentrated in warm pockets of water created by natural springs and power company run-off January-March.) Although some predict that urban sprawl from Tampa and Orlando is bound to overtake this preserved nugget of coastline, much of the Nature Coast will always remain wildlife-possessed, thanks to government foresight: one-third of Hernando County and 40% of Citrus County constitute protected land. Watersports enthusiasts will be happy to find more than 25,000 surface acres of lakes and rivers in addition to the Gulf of Mexico in Citrus County alone.

This chapter covers **Hernando** and **Citrus** counties entirely, including the adventurer's wild haven of Withlacoochee State Forest, and the towns of Crystal River, Inverness, Homosassa, Brooksville, and Weeki Wachee.

WHAT'S IN A NAME?

Hernando County was named after that rascal explorer who left his fingerprints all over the West Coast of Florida – Hernando de Soto. His suspected route through this neighborhood is marked along existing highways.

One needn't guess too long to figure out how **Citrus County** was named. Citrus was once the county's mainstay, until Mother Nature put the freeze on the industry in the winter of 1894-95. Now there's little citrus in Citrus County. It's been suggested that Manatee County (see the *Bradenton/Sarasota* chapter), which has fewer manatees than citrus fields, and Citrus County, which is thick with manatees, should swap names.

TRANSPORTATION

■ AIRPORTS

Two major Florida airports lie within an hour's drive of the Nature Coast. **Tampa International Airport** (TPA), ☎ 800-767-8882 or 813-870-8700, www.tampaairport.com, lies to the south. **Orlando**

International Airport (MCO), ☎ 800-626-6244 or 407-825-3896, www.orlandoairports.net, is also convenient to the Nature Coast. The major domestic and international airlines that service each facility are listed in the chart below.

DOMESTIC & INT'L AIRLINES SERVING TAMPA INT'L AIRPORT (TPA) & ORLANDO INT'L AIRPORT (MCO)	TPA	MCO
Aero Mexico.............. ☎ 800-237-6639		✔
Air Canada .... ☎ 888-247-2262	✔	✔
Air France.............. ☎ 800-247-2262		✔
Air Jamaica .... ☎ 800-247-2262		✔
AirTran Airways.......... ☎ 800-247-8726	✔	
Air Transat .... ☎ 877-872-6728		✔
Alaska Airlines .... ☎ 800-252-7522		✔
Alitalia................. ☎ 800-223-5730		✔
American/American Eagle.... ☎ 800-433-7300		✔
America West Airlines...... ☎ 800-235-9292	✔	✔
ANA.................. ☎ 800-235-9262		✔
ATA.................. ☎ 800-225-2995		✔
Austrian................ ☎ 800-843-0002		✔
Bahamasair .... ☎ 800-222-4262		✔
BMI................... ☎ 800-788-0555		✔
British Airways .... ☎ 800-247-9297	✔	✔
Canjet.................. ☎ 800-809-7777		✔
Cayman Airways.......... ☎ 800-422-9626	✔	✔
Champion Air............ ☎ 888-225-5658		✔
China Airlines .... ☎ 800-227-5118		✔
Comair .... ☎ 800-354-9822		✔
Condor................. ☎ 800-524-6975		✔
Continental Airlines........ ☎ 800-525-0280	✔	
Copa Airlines .... ☎ 800-359-2672		✔
Delta Air Lines .... ☎ 800-221-1212	✔	✔
Frontier................. ☎ 800-432-1359	✔	✔
Gulfstream International..... ☎ 800-525-0280	✔	✔
Iberia.................. ☎ 800-772-4642		✔

DOMESTIC & INT'L AIRLINES SERVING TAMPA INT'L AIRPORT (TPA) & ORLANDO INT'L AIRPORT (MCO)	TPA	MCO
Icelandair............... ☎ 800-223-5500		✔
JAL.................... ☎ 800-585-3663		✔
JetBlue................. ☎ 800-538-2583	✔	✔
Korean Air .... ☎ 800-438-5000		✔
LAN................... ☎ 866-435-9526		✔
LOT................... ☎ 800-223-0593		✔
Lufthansa............... ☎ 800-645-3880		✔
Martinair............... ☎ 800-627-8462		✔
Mexicana............... ☎ 800-531-7921		✔
Midwest................ ☎ 800-452-2022		✔
Northwest/KLM .... ☎ 800-225-2525	✔	✔
Pace.................. ☎ 336-776-4100		✔
Royal Air Maroc .... ☎ 800-344-6726		✔
Scandanavian Airlines ...... ☎ 800-221-2350		✔
Singapore Airlines......... ☎ 800-742-3333		✔
Song.................. ☎ 800-359-7664	✔	✔
Southwest.............. ☎ 800-435-9792	✔	✔
South African Airlines...... ☎ 800-772-9675		✔
Spirit.................. ☎ 800-772-7117	✔	✔
Sun Country Airlines ...... ☎ 800-359-6786		✔
Sun Wing............... ☎ 800-671-1711		✔
Swiss.................. ☎ 877-359-7947		✔
TACA .... ☎ 800-400-8222		✔
TAP Portugal............ ☎ 800-221-7370		✔
Ted .... ☎ 800-225-5833	✔	✔
United................. ☎ 800-241-6522	✔	✔
USA 3000 .... ☎ 800-895-3000		✔
US Airways .... ☎ 800-428-4322	✔	✔
Virgin Atlantic........... ☎ 800-862-8621		✔

■ TRAIN SERVICE

Amtrak, ☎ 800-872-7245, offers passenger train service into Tampa and Orlando.

■ RENTAL CARS

Rental cars are available at the airports, including **Alamo**, ☎ 800-327-9633, **Avis**, ☎ 800-331-1212 or 813-396-3500 (Tampa), **Hertz**, ☎ 800-654-3131, and **Budget**, ☎ 800-527-0700 or 813-877-6051 (Tampa). **Enterprise**, ☎ 800-736-8222, rents cars from locations in Crystal River, 622 NE First Terrace, ☎ 352-563-5511, and Inverness, 3730 E. Gulf to Lake Hwy., ☎ 352-637-6632.

■ GETTING AROUND

Highway 19 (known as Commercial Way in Hernando County and Suncoast Blvd. in Citrus County) is the thread that pulls the Nature Coast together and connects it to northern Pinellas County (see the *St. Petersburg & Clearwater* chapter).

Highway 41 (also called Florida Ave. and Broad Ave. in parts) heads out of Tampa and through the center of the two counties at Brooksville and Inverness.

Interstate 75 swings clear of Hernando and Citrus counties. To cross from the interstate to Hwy. 19, take northernmost Exit 329 (Rte. 44 through Inverness); Exit 321 to the Jumper Creek Tract of the Withlacoochee State Forest; Exit 309 to Withlacoochee's Croom Tract; Exit 301 (Hwy. 98 through Brooksville – a.k.a. Ponce de Leon Blvd.); or Exit 293 (Rte. 52) to the south of Hernando County.

From Orlando, the **Florida Turnpike** delivers you directly to I-75, just miles south of Exit 328 to Inverness. From anywhere in the Tampa Bay area (Sarasota to Hernando County), dial 511 or log on to www.511tampabay.com for up-to-date traffic and route information.

INFORMATION

For information on Hernando County, contact the **Hernando County Tourist Development Council**, 30305 Cortez Blvd., Brooksville, ☎ 800-601-4580 or 352-754-4405, www.co.hernando.fl.us/visit. Hours are 8-5, Monday-Friday.

The **Citrus County Visitors & Convention Bureau**, ☎ 800-587-6667 or 352-628-0703, www.visitcitrus.com, disseminates information.

The Nature Coast

FESTIVALS & EVENTS

★ **JANUARY** – The **Brooksville Raid Festival**, ☎ 352-796-6766, re-enacts a Civil War battle during two days of festivities. Admission. The **Florida Manatee Festival**, ☎ 352-726-2801, takes place in Crystal River the second weekend in January, featuring fine arts and entertainment. $2 donation requested for adult admission.

★ **MARCH – Weeki Wachee Swamp Festival**, ☎ 352-596-2567, www.wwswampfest.com, features local culture and traditional rural craftsmanship in a two-day celebration. Relive Seminole War days at reenactments during **Fort Cooper Days,** ☎ 352-726-0315, held at Fort Cooper State Park one weekend mid-month.

Queen of the Swamp Festival.

★ **APRIL** – Cast for a $4,500 first prize in the **Citrus County Bass Challenge**, ☎ 352-527-8828. **Hernando County Fair**, ☎ 352-796-4552, www.hernandocountyfair.com, lasts 10 days in late April.

★ **OCTOBER** – The big event this month is the **Hernando County Rodeo & Barbecue Festival**, ☎ 352-796-2290, www.brooksvillerodeo.com, a three-day extravaganza. Admission. **A Rails to Trails Bike Ride**, ☎ 352-527-3263, takes place on Withlacoochee State Trail, departing from Inverness.

★ **NOVEMBER** – Inverness hosts the **Citrus Stampede Rodeo**, ☎ 352-564-4525, for two days mid-month. Admission. **Homosassa Arts, Crafts & Seafood Festival**, ☎ 352-628-2666, runs for two days in Old Homosassa at the corner of Yulee Dr. and Mason Creek Rd. Live entertainment does back-up to mounds of fresh seafood. $2 donation requested.

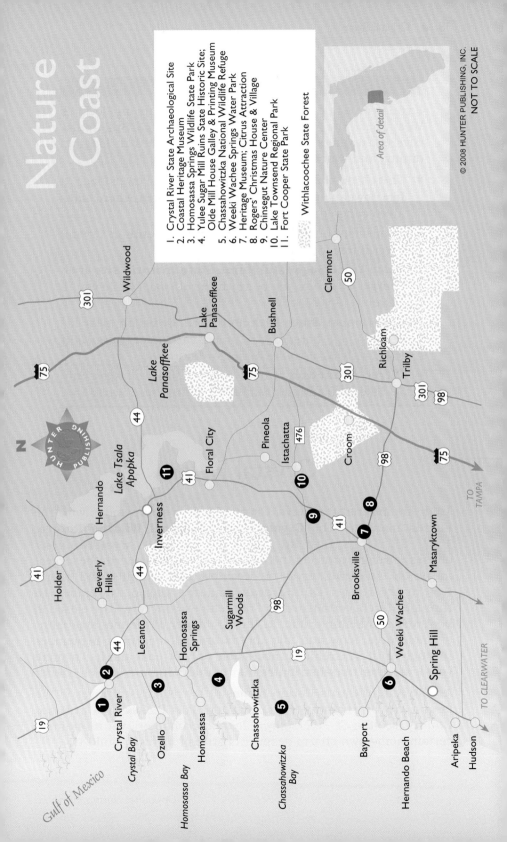

Nature Coast

1. Crystal River State Archaeological Site
2. Coastal Heritage Museum
3. Homosassa Springs Wildlife State Park
4. Yulee Sugar Mill Ruins State Historic Site;
   Olde Mill House Galley & Printing Museum
5. Chassahowitzka National Wildlife Refuge
6. Weeki Wachee Springs Water Park
7. Heritage Museum; Citrus Attraction
8. Rogers' Christmas House & Village
9. Chinsegut Nature Center
10. Lake Townsend Regional Park
11. Fort Cooper State Park

Withlacoochee State Forest

Area of detail

© 2008 HUNTER PUBLISHING, INC.
NOT TO SCALE

HUNTER PUBLISHING

Gulf of Mexico

Crystal Bay

Homosassa Bay

Chassahowitzka Bay

TO CLEARWATER

TO TAMPA

Wildwood

Lake Panasoffkee

Lake Panasoffkee

Bushnell

Clermont

Richloam

Trilby

Croom

Pineola

Istachatta

Floral City

Lake Tsala Apopka

Hernando

Inverness

Beverly Hills

Holder

Lecanto

Homosassa Springs

Sugarmill Woods

Brooksville

Masaryktown

Weeki Wachee

Spring Hill

Hernando Beach

Aripeka

Hudson

Bayport

Chassahowitzka

Homosassa

Ozello

Crystal River

301

75

44

41

50

301

98

75

98

476

41

41

44

44

19

98

50

19

41

75

301

BUDGET TIPS

If you're on a budget and looking for adventure on Florida's West Coast, the Nature Coast is the place to go. Still undiscovered, it offers the region's greatest values in lodging, dining, and watersports.

- There's no charge to get a charge out of Power Place, a free power plant attraction in **Crystal River**, where manatees congregate.

- Admission to the **Coastal Heritage Museum** in Crystal River if free; donations are accepted.

- Roam **Yulee Sugar Mill Ruins State Historic Site** at no charge. Have a picnic beneath the old oaks while you're there.

- **Fort Cooper State Park** and its sandy beach, near Inverness, is a bargain at $2 for a carload of up to eight folks, only $1 if you're hiking or biking.

- **Citrus Attraction** outside of Brooksville charges only $3.59 each for adults; $2.59 for children aged two to 15.

Crystal River

To divers and nature-lovers, Crystal River is synonymous with the Florida manatee. The **Crystal River National Wildlife Refuge**, 1502 SE Kings Bay Rd., ☎ 352-563-2088, www.fws.gov/chassahowitzka, protects the waterway's wintering herd, the largest in the US. An aerial survey in December 2006 counted 363 manatees in the refuge. During peak manatee season, November 15 through March, certain areas of the refuge's waterways are closed to boat and snorkeling traffic. In the remainder of the manatee management area, slow and idle speeds are enforced from September through April. The refuge is accessible only by boat and has a small visitor's center that distributes information on tours and charters.

As the hub of Citrus County's coastal towns, Crystal River is the largest city on Highway 91 north of the Port Richey area in Pasco County (see the *St. Petersburg/Clearwater* chapter), yet it retains a certain hometown charm despite its strip of highway build-up.

Opposite: Spring manatee.

GETTING HERE

Highway 19 is the major thoroughfare through Crystal River. Rte. 44 (Gulf to Lake Highway) connects it to Inverness in the east and, eventually, I-75. Downtown, **Citrus Avenue** is the heart of Crystal River's historic district.

INFORMATION

For more information, contact **Citrus County Chamber of Commerce**, 28 NW Hwy. 19, Crystal River, 34428, ☎ 352-795-3149, 8:30-4:30, Monday-Friday, www.citruscountychamber.com or Citrus County Visitors & Convention Bureau, www.visitcitrus.com.

WEEKEND ADVENTURE ITINERARY

■ **FRIDAY:** Go snorkeling or diving in Crystal River in the morning. Have lunch at Café on the Avenue and tour and shop Crystal River's historic district in the afternoon. Visit Crystal River State Archaeological Site. Have dinner at Cracker's. Spend the night in Crystal River.

■ **SATURDAY:** Drive to Homosassa for a half-day kayak or boat tour of the river. Drive to Inverness and hike or bike the Withlacoochee State Trail. Have dinner at Fisherman's Restaurant. Spend the night in Inverness.

■ **SUNDAY:** Drive through Floral City to Fort Cooper State Park. Relax and have a picnic on the beach. Visit Weeki Wachee Springs in the afternoon. Have dinner at Backwaters in Ozello. Watch the sunset from Hernando Beach Park or Bayport Park. Spend the night in the Weeki Wachee area.

SIGHTS & ATTRACTIONS

 Author favorites are indicated with a star.

■ OF HISTORIC OR CULTURAL INTEREST

 Archaeologists believe that Crystal River and environs served as an important center of Amerindian culture. At **Crystal River State Archaeological Site** at the north end of town off State Park Street at 3400 N. Museum Point, ☎ 352-795-3817, burial, temple, and midden mounds plus a museum provide evidence of a series of native cultures dating back to 500 BC. The tallest mound rises 28 feet, overlooking Crystal River. An observation deck is provided for visitors who climb the 55 steps to the top. The 14-acre park is open daily, 8 to sunset. The museum, which shows an eight-minute video about local ancient civilizations, is open 9-5. Admission to the park is $2 per car.

Indian Mounds,
Crystal River Archeological Park

Hometown and small, **Coastal Heritage Museum**, 532 Citrus Ave., ☎ 352-795-1755, provides an insightful tour into local history, spiced with tidbits of gossip and legend. Get to know the characters who made this town grow through fishing, turpentine, pencil-making, and Spanish moss-processing eras. The museum occupies the old city hall, which has an Alamo-style appearance. Open 11-3 Tuesday-Friday; 9-2 Saturday; closed July. Admission is free; donations are accepted.

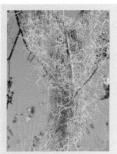

Spanish moss is actually not a moss at all, but an epiphyte related to the orchid and pineapple. It drapes its curly tendrils over oaks and other trees. Back when county residents harvested the spongy matter, Henry Ford and others were using it to stuff car seats and furniture. The plant feeds off nutrients in the air and causes no direct damage to its host tree.

■ BEACHES, PARKS & NATURAL AREAS

One of the best beaches of the Nature Coast lies off the beaten path. **Fort Island Gulf Beach**, 16000 W. Fort Island Trail, ☎ 352-795-1478, is a well-maintained park with volleyball, a boat launch, picnic tables, and a newly renovated sandy beach. In summer, lifeguards supervise.

Fort Island Trail Park, 12073 W. Fort Island Trail, nearby, has a T-dock, boat launch, and picnic ground.

ADVENTURES

■ ON WATER

Citrus County boasts 52 miles of Gulf shoreline, 106 miles of river, and 19,111 acres of lakes. It's an adventurer's paradise, unspoiled still by wheelers, dealers, and big-time developers.

> **TIP:** For a complete list of fishing guides, charters, and guidelines, contact the **Citrus County Visitors Bureau** (see Information, above).

FISHING

Sports Afield once named the area around Crystal River as one of the "12 Best Fishing Spots in North America." With its variety of salt and fresh water, the region offers a wealth of species.

Fish into the Gulf from the pier at **Fort Island Trail Park** (see Sights & Attractions, above), 12073 W. Fort Island Trail.

For live or frozen bait and all your fishing gear needs, stop at **Ed's Tackle Shop**, 983 N. Suncoast Blvd., ☎ 352-795-4178. It's open daily 5:30 a.m. to 5:30 p.m.

Scalloping is a sport everyone can enjoy.

Apollo Deep Sea Fishing, 1340 NW 20th Ave., ☎ 352-795-3757, is a party boat that loads up all-day excursions at a cost of $65 per person.

SCALLOPING

In 2002, the government reopened recreational scallop harvesting as far down as Weeki Wachee. In 1994, it had closed along the Nature Coast due to diminished populations. Now that the species has restored itself, harvesting is legal July through Sept. 10. A fishing license is required. The tasty shellfish is easy to collect in shallow water with little more than a pair of hands and a mesh bag.

Snorkelers look deeper in grass flats. Harvesting is limited to two gallons of in-shell scallops or one pint of scallop meat per day.

BOAT RAMPS

For access to the Gulf, you can put in at Fort Island Gulf Beach, 16000 W. Fort Island Trail, Fort Island Trail Park, 12073 W. Fort Island Trail, or Pete's Pier, SW First Place.

BOAT CHARTERS & TOURS

Dayjammer Cruises, 3940 N. Apalachee Point, ☎ 352-795-0553, conducts one-hour tours of local rivers and bay on a daily basis, maximum of 10 to a boat. Cost is $10 per person, with a three-person minimum. Manatee and other specialty tours are also available.

PADDLING

The 27-mile **Nature Coast Canoe and Kayak Trail** starts on the Salt River off Fort Island Trail and travels into the Homosassa and Chassahowitzka rivers. Trail markers help paddlers along the twisty trail.

Kayaking on the Chassahowitzka River.

For kayak rentals, call **Manatee Tour & Dive**, at Third St. on the river, ☎ 352-795-3337. Single kayaks rent for $35 a half-day and $45 full; doubles for $45 and $55.

SNORKELING & DIVING

Crystal River is a scuba hot spot. Not only does it draw the tanked crowd with its clear spring waters and amiable manatee population, but also with its caves and variety. Tour boat operators and dive instructors and charters put you into the water with ease.

© American Pro Diving Center

Go snorkeling or diving with **American Pro Diving Center**, 821 SE Hwy. 19, www.americanprodi ving.com, ☎ 800-291-DIVE or 352-563-0041. Guided tours are offered in the Crystal, Homosassa, or Rainbow rivers. A snorkel trip on the Crystal River costs $29.50, plus equipment. A snorkel-and-dive excursion costs $39.50, and dive-only tours range from $29 to $50. Two- to four-day vacation packages and instruction are available – including a special Manatee Awareness Course.

Bird's Underwater at 300 NW Hwy. 19, ☎ 800-771-2763 or 352-563-2763, www.birdsunderwater.com, conducts manatee snorkel tours October through March. Trips cost $29.50 per person, and the outstanding wildlife encounter is well worth it. Tours depart early morning and include hot beverages and donuts to help you warm up. Snorkel equipment (quality ScubaPro brand) rental is extra: $8 for mask, fins, and snorkel, $12 for wet suit. Bird's Underwater also teaches PADI scuba, guides dives, and rents kayaks.

> NOTE: *Use snorkel gear when diving with manatees; bubbles from Scuba tanks can scare them. See page 11 for information on protecting these loveable creatures.*

ON WHEELS

The **Fort Island Bicycle Trail** runs for 18 miles adjacent to Fort Island Trail, ending at Fort Island Beach.

■ IN THE AIR

Crystal Aero Group at the Crystal River Airport on Hwy. 19, 718 N. Lindbergh Dr., ☎ 352-795-6868, supplies bird's-eye views of the area's divinely patterned mesh of water and land. Glider rides cost $40 per person. Air/photo tours are $150 an hour (up to three persons) with a half-hour minimum. Flight instructions and charters are also available.

SHOPPING

Downtown Crystal River has arranged itself into a cozy little shopping district with historic Cracker charm. Within the Heritage Village, you can shop for antiques and gifts. **Manatee Toy Company**, ☎ 352-795-6126, http://manateeville.com, is popular for its plentiful supply of playthings and gifts that represent Crystal River's town icon. It's open daily.

WHERE TO STAY

ACCOMMODATIONS PRICE KEY		
Rates are per room, per night, double occupancy. Price ranges described for each property often do not take into account penthouses and other exceptional, high-priced accommodations.	$	Up to $75
	$$	$75 to $150
	$$$	$151 to $250
	$$$$	$251 and up

■ HOTELS

Divers like the **Best Western Crystal River**, 614 NW Hwy. 19, ☎ 800-435-4409 or 352-795-3171, www.crystalriverresort. com, for its convenience to the river and its manatees. The on-site dive shop is full-service, plus the resort offers manatee tours, boat and canoe rentals, a ramp, and docking. There's also a pool, restaurant, and tiki bar. A new boardwalk leads along the river to nearby restaurants. Rooms and efficiencies are available. $$

High end in budget-priced Crystal River, **Plantation Inn**, 9301 W. Fort Island Trail just off Hwy. 19, ☎ 800-632-6262 or 352-795-4211, www.plantationinn.com, appeals to the golf crowd with 27 holes and a golf school. It also has its own dive shop and Southern-style restaurant. Accommodations ensconced in colonial revival architecture include rooms, suites, junior suites, and two-story villas. $$-$$$

■ CAMPING

East of Crystal River at 9835 N. Citrus Ave., **Quail Roost RV Campground**, ☎ 352-563-0404, www.quailroostcampground. com, has tent and RV sites, as well as recreational facilities. RV sites cost $29 a day, including electricity.

Camp among age-old oak trees with easy access to fishing and boating at **Lake Rousseau Campground**, 10811 N. Coveview Terrace off Rte. 488, six miles north of Crystal River, ☎ 800-561-CAMP or 352-795-6336, www.lakerousseaurvpark.com. RV guests pay $28 per night and have access to a pool, shuffleboard, billiards, general store, boat rentals, and bait shop. Furnished rentals are also available.

WHERE TO EAT

 Author favorites are indicated with a star.

In Heritage Village, **Café on the Avenue** in the Florida Hearth & Home décor shop at 631 N. Citrus Ave., ☎ 352-795-3656, presents a pleasant indoor-outdoor venue. It serves casual, creative fare such as pecan chicken salad and a BBT (bacon, basil, and tomato) sandwich. It's open daily for lunch and dinner on the weekends. Entrée salads and sandwiches range from $6 to $9. Dinner entrées such as veal Marsala, grouper Rockefeller, and filet mignon run $14-$24.

With seating right on King's Bay and a boardwalk that is being built at its rim, **Cracker's Bar, Grill & Tiki** at 502 NW Sixth St., ☎ 352-795-3999, www.crackersbar grillandtiki.com, is a favorite for sandwiches and seafood platters. Prices on the all-day menu range from a $6 for a tuna melt or hot turkey and bacon sandwich to $15 for combo seafood platters.

To get your fill of home-cooked, Old Florida-style eating, go to **Oysters**, 606 NE Hwy. 19, ☎ 352-795-2633, where breakfast, lunch, and dinner are served daily. Breakfast prices range from $2 to $6. The lunch menu has everything from down-home country-fried steak to oyster burgers and grouper, $6-$8. The soup tastes homemade. At dinner, offerings such as chicken and dumplings, mullet, and shrimp and crab Alfredo range from $10 to $16.

For a special occasion, make a reservation at the **Savannah Room** at the Plantation Inn, 9301 W. Fort Island Trail just off Hwy. 19, ☎ 800-632-6262 or 352-795-4211, www.plantationinn.com, and feel like you've drifted off to Tara. Breakfast ($7-$11), lunch ($7-$14), and dinner ($15-$32) are served in a genteel Old South setting with a white-brick fireplace and a view of the pool. Dinner specialties include tournedos of beef with a blue cheese-red wine glaze, duck à l'orange, Floribbean grouper, Texas rib-eye steak, and mango-bourbon bananas foster.

Inverness

The rolling hills and lakeside pose of a town named Tompkinsville reminded settlers of Inverness, Scotland, and so it was named in 1889. Lined with old oaks waving lacy Spanish moss hankies, Lake Tsala Apopka, Inverness's sprawling waters, drew settlers here and continues to contribute to its attraction. The town lists 25 sites dating back to the turn of the century. Many of the commercial buildings are found in the downtown streets that edge Inverness's lovely central park at Courthouse Square, which was the site of filming for Elvis Presley's 1961 movie *Follow That Dream.*

GETTING HERE

Inverness lies at the crossroads of **Highway 41** (Florida Ave.) and **Rte. 44** (a.k.a. Gulf to Lake Highway). Take Exit 328 from I-75 and head west on Rte. 44.

INFORMATION

Contact the **Citrus County Chamber of Commerce**, 401 W. Tompkins St., Inverness 34450, ☎ 352-726-2801, www.citrus countychamber.com. The office is open Monday-Friday, 8:30-4:30.

The Nature Coast

SIGHTS & ATTRACTIONS

■ OF HISTORIC OR CULTURAL INTEREST

Named for a Seminole War camp built in 1836, **Fort Cooper State Park**, 3100 S. Old Floral City Rd., ☎ 352-726-0315, is today headquarters for recreation on spring-fed Lake Holathlikaha. The lake's sandy beach is more inviting than swimming the marshy lake waters. Nature trails, canoeing, paddleboating, volleyball, a playground, and picnicking offer recreation within the park's 710 acres. Wildlife inhabitants include deer, fox, rabbits, owls, lots of squirrels, and cardinals. Recently, the park completed a 2,300-foot/ half-mile multi-use paved trail that connects with the Withlacoochee State Trail. In March, the park stages Seminole War re-enactments ($5 fee for adults that day, $1 for youths aged six-17. Admission to the park is $2 per vehicle (up to eight passengers), $1 for cyclists. It's open daily, 8-sunset.

Fort Cooper Re-Enactment Days

On the scenic shores of the Lake Tsala Apopka chain, **Floral City** first bloomed in 1883. By the late 1890s, population had grown to more than 10,000, fueled by rock phosphate mining. Today listed on the National Register of Historic Places, Floral City is a small, quiet wayside town that makes for a pleasant return to yesteryear, just seven miles south of Inverness on Hwy. 41. Along E. Orange Ave. lines up a slew of historic buildings in a quaint country farm town setting. The town's Avenue of Oaks, shown at left, is a popular cycling destination.

> **TIP:** *To learn more about Floral City's surviving past, pick up a copy of* **Floral City: A Guide to Historic Architecture** *from the local visitors bureau.*

ADVENTURES

Kneeboarding on Lake Tsala Apopka.

■ ON WATER

The extensive **Lake Tsala Apopka** chain provides ample opportunity to cast for freshwater fish. For a complete list of fishing guides, charters, and guidelines, contact the Citrus County Chamber of Commerce (see *Information*, page 47).

■ ON FOOT

Five miles of self-guided nature trails traverse **Fort Cooper State Park**, 3100 S. Old Floral City Rd., ☎ 352-726-0315 (see *Sights & Attractions*, above). Strollers and hikers also hit the connecting Withlacoochee Trail State Park (see below).

■ ON WHEELS

Withlacoochee State Trail, ☎ 352-726-0357, www.railstotrailsonline. com, comes straight through town, where it provides a lovely, well-maintained thoroughfare for hikers, bikers, and 'bladers. Florida's longest paved rails-to-trails path, it runs 46 miles and has six trailheads, the one in Inverness being its major one.

To ride the trail, rent from **Suncoast Bicycles Plus**, located right at one of the trailheads, 322 N. Pine St., ☎ 800-296-1010 or 352-637-5757, www.suncoastbikes.com. Rentals cost $10 for the first hour, $4 per each additional hour, and $25 a day. Discounts apply to groups of three or more.

A family cycling on the Withlacoochie State Trail.

WHERE TO STAY

Inverness accommodations tend toward the very individual and strikingly unusual.

 Author favorites are indicated with a star.

■ HOTELS & RESORTS

 For the best view for your buck, rent a cabin at **Moonrise Resort**, at 8801 E. Moonrise Ln., off Hwy. 41 on Old Floral City Rd., ☎ 800-665-6701 or 352-726-2553, www. moon riseresort.com. Also an RV park, it has 10 comfortable, homey cabins (with handmade quilts on the beds) right on Lake Tsala Apopka in a beautiful, sporty setting. Canoe and boat rentals are available on property. $-$$

© Moonrise Resort

■ INNS/BED & BREAKFASTS

© The Lake House B&B

In Inverness's land of lakes, **The Lake House Bed & Breakfast**, 8604 E. Gospel Island Rd. off Route 44, ☎ 352-344-3586, www. thelakehouse.org, takes a lovely, plantation-like waterside stance. Five guest rooms lie off the house's magnificent, high-ceilinged great room with a stone fireplace; each room has its own homey personality and private bath. $-$$.

Convenient for cyclists to the **Withlacoochee State Trail** 1¼ miles away, Magnolia Glen, 7702 E. Allen Dr., ☎ 800-881-4366 or 352-726-1832, www.magnoliaglen.com, has some quirks, including its slightly eccentric innkeeper, Bonnie Kuntz, a former sailing champion who has a passion for Admiral Nelson. Situated on an oak-framed lakefront in a residential neighborhood a couple of miles from downtown, the English Tudor home offers use of canoes, along with gourmet breakfast. Its three rooms exude personality. $$

WHERE TO EAT

In downtown Inverness, a few restaurants intersperse with shops around Courthouse Square. One of these, **Coach's Pub & Eatery** at 114 W. Main St. ☎ 352-344-3333, satisfies casual appetites in a sports bar atmosphere of corrugated tin walls, pool tables, and TVs. Finger food runs the range from pot stickers, nachos, and asiago-stuffed olives to fried pickle spears. Sandwiches and entrées include a wide selection of wraps, burgers, ribs, and steaks and cost $5 to $17.

Ironically, they claim to make the "world's best hamburger" at **Fisherman's Restaurant**, outside of Inverness at 12311 E. Gulf to Lake Hwy. (Rte. 44), ☎ 352-637-5888. They also serve grouper, shrimp, 'gator, and lobster. The unpretentious country-style but popular spot also specializes in barbecue. The world's best hamburger costs only $3. Other sandwiches and entrées range from $2 to $25. It's open for lunch and dinner, Wednesday-Sunday.

Homosassa Area

Homosassa Springs sprung up around its wildlife park attraction, shown below, on Highway 19, and the park is what most people zooming through identify as Homosassa. But the town's roots reach back to frontier days, sugar plantations, and Old Homosassa, which lies west of 19 on Rte. 490. It and Ozello, another out-of-the-way old

community on Homosassa backroads, grew up on the waterfront, where pioneers made their living, and old fish-camp-style lodging and restaurants survive as souvenirs of an earlier, simpler era. On the other hand, Homosassa Springs shapes up as a modern suburb with the typical chain trademarks of shapeless development.

GETTING HERE

Hwy. 19 is the main thoroughfare through Homosassa Springs. To get to Old Homosassa, turn west on Rte. 490. Rte. 494 takes you to Ozello.

INFORMATION

The **Citrus County Chamber of Commerce** is located at 3495 S. Suncoast Blvd., Homosassa Springs 34448, ☎ 352-628-2666, www. citruscountychamber.com (mailing address: PO Box 709, Homosassa Springs 34447). It's open 8:30-4:30, Monday-Friday.

Citrus County Visitors & Convention Bureau at 9225 W. Fishbowl Dr., near Homosassa Springs Wildlife State Park, ☎ 352-628-9305, www.visitcitrus.com, is open 8-5 Monday through Friday, 10-4 on Saturday.

SIGHTS & ATTRACTIONS

■ OF HISTORIC OR CULTURAL INTEREST

Roam the past and enjoy a picnic at the oak-shaded grounds of **Yulee Sugar Mill Ruins State Historic Site**, W. Yulee Dr. in Old Homosassa, ☎ 352-795-3817. A paved path winds around ancient rock ruins and machinery, with signs that explain the history of sugar processing and the site – the erstwhile plantation of Florida's first US Senator, David Yulee. Admission is free.

Across the street from the Yulee Sugar Mill Ruins is the **Olde Mill House Gallery & Printing Museum**, 10466 W. Yulee Dr. (Hwy. 490), ☎ 888-248-6672 or 352-628-9411, www.chronicle-online. com/printmuseum.htm. It may seem like an odd, narrow-niched type attraction in a town like Old Homosassa, but don't miss an opportunity to meet Jim Anderson, whose tours are lively, entertaining, and hands-on. There's a café on-site, open Tuesday-Saturday for lunch. Call ahead for tours, available Monday-Saturday. Admission is $5 for adults, $2 for students.

Yulee Sugarmill Ruins State Historic Site.

■ NATURAL AREAS

South of Homosassa, including a portion of the Homosassa River, **Chassahowitzka National Wildlife Refuge**, ☎ 352-563-2088, www.fws.gov/chassahowitzka/, covers more than 31,000 acres of mangrove islands, estuaries, saltwater marshland, and hardwood swamp. The refuge is accessible only by boat and has become a popular canoe and kayak destination with an established canoe trail. Besides the Homosassa, the Chassahowitzka River – both listed among Florida's designated Outstanding Waters – empties into the refuge's bays. More concerned with wildlife than human life, Chassahowitzka is refuge to white-tailed deer, black bear, bald eagles, manatees, woodstorks, green sea turtles, indigo snakes, and migrating whooping cranes, which follow ultralight aircraft down to the refuge each year from Wisconsin. Airboat use within the refuge is by per-

Deer are just one of many animals you might see.

mit only in designated areas. April-August posted speed restrictions protect wintering manatees.

The town's greatest attraction, **Homosassa Springs Wildlife State Park**, 4150 S. Suncoast Blvd., off Highway 19, ☎ 352-628-5343, www.homosassasprings.org, began as a private enterprise some 50 years ago. In recent times, the state has taken over and guided it from honky-tonk into a modern, ecologically correct stature. Its centerpiece has always been its manatee population, which is kept in a semi-captive state in spring waters. Visitors can view and hear all nine via an underwater floating observatory or

© Thomas M Anderson

Red Hawk, Homosassa Springs.

during three daily presentations that are the best I've seen – liberally sprinkled with facts, lore, and humor. (The Manatee Education Center here is run in conjunction with Crystal River National Wildlife Refuge.) Daily educational programs demonstrate also the habits of alligators, manatees, and other animals. In the 168-acre park's virgin Florida forest, you'll see local fauna both caged and roaming free: turtles, bobcats, black bears, deer, ospreys, and other birds. A 20-minute boat ride tours visitors around the mix of saltwater and freshwater habitat. The park is open 9-5:30 daily (ticket sales close at 4). If you arrive before 1, you can see all the programs. Admission is $9 plus tax for visitors aged 13 and older, $5 for children aged three-12.

ADVENTURES

■ ON WATER

FISHING

For expert inshore saltwater fishing, who you gonna get? **Fish Buster**, ☎ 352-400-1766, charges $350 for half-day charter and $400 for full-day for one or two people. Extras cost $50 each, up to four. Guides promise speckled trout, redfish, jack crevalle, pompano, snapper, and sheepshead.

You can fish into the Gulf from the pier in Ozello on John Brown Rd.

Charter boats for fishing and cruising are widely available.

SCALLOPING

Capt. Mike's Sunshine River Tours, www.sunshinerivertours. com, ☎ 866-645-5727 or 352-628-7397, runs seven-hour scalloping boat excursions leaving from Crystal River at 7 am July 1 through Sept. 10. The $50 fee includes license and use of snorkeling equipment.

BOAT RAMPS

To launch into the Chassahowitzka River to the Gulf, you'll find ramps at **Chassahowitzka River Campground**, 8600 W. Miss Maggie Dr. The ramps at **Mason Creek**, 6891 S. Mason Creek Rd., and **Mac Rae's**, 5290 S. Cherokee Way, provide access to the Homosassa River.

Ozello Community Park, 410 N. Pirate Point, has launching into the Gulf. Homosassa Riverside Resort at 5297 S. Cherokee Way, ☎ 352-628-2474 or 800-442-2040, www.riversideresorts.com, charges $5 for use of its ramp.

BOAT RENTALS

Pontoon and Jon boats are for rent at **River Safaris & Gulf Charters**, 10823 Yulee Dr., ☎ 800-758-FISH or 352-628-5222, www.riversafaris.com. A Jon boat holds five people and costs $75 for a half-day, $90 for a full day. Pontoons vary in capacity from five to 14 people; in cost from $85-$145 half-day, $130-$215 full day. Tax and fuel are extra.

Homosassa Riverside Resort at 5297 S. Cherokee Way, ☎ 352-628-2474 or 800-442-2040, www.river sideresorts.com, rents pontoon boats ($90 half-day, $135-$155 full day), Jon boats ($40/$50-$60), and kayaks and canoes ($30/ $40).

Long-established and respected in these parts, **MacRae's Bait House** at 5300 S. Cherokee Way, ☎ 352-628-2602, rents Jon boats for $55 a half-day, $65 full day. Pontoon rentals run $100-$140.

BOAT CHARTERS & TOURS

River Safaris & Gulf Charters, 10823 Yulee Dr., ☎ 800-758-FISH or 352-628-5222, www.riversafaris.com, conducts a variety of tours lasting one to two hours. Choose from a Springs tour, backwater tour, combination tour, sunset cruise, manatee tour, or airboat ride. Prices are $16-$60 per person.

To see and learn about what's above and below the water at Chassahowitzka National Wildlife Refuge, book a scenic eco-tour with **Glass Bottom Boat**, 8501 Miss Maggie Dr., ☎ 352-382-3698, www.captainkaren.com. Rates for a two-hour trip are $25 per person with a four-person minimum and six-person maximum. Three-hour trips are $35 each.

PADDLING

Chassahowitza National Wildlife Refuge, ☎ 352-563-2088, is an oarsman's dream-come-true. The exploring range is endless, given the number of rivers that flow into Gulf waters here, and the maze of mangroves and estuaries near shore. A variety of tours focuses on manatee-watching, snorkeling, picnics on a private island, history lessons, and stargazing.

Riversport Kayaks, ☎ 877-660-0929 or 352-621-4972, www. flakayak.com, on the Homosassa River at Riverside Resort, 5297 S. Cherokee Way, rents single kayaks starting at $10 an hour and tandem kayaks and canoes for $15 an hour. Kayaking tours are available.

■ ON FOOT

HUNTING

Chassahowitzka National Wildlife Refuge at 1502 SE Kings Bay Dr., ☎ 352-563-2088, allows the hunting of ducks, coots, wild hogs, deer, and other overpopulated animals under restricted conditions. Access is by boat only. Contact the refuge for regulations.

WHERE TO STAY

Like the rest of the county, Homosassa area lodgings are incredibly affordable. They range from chain-name places to no-nonsense fishing lodges, all instilled with plenty of character.

ACCOMMODATIONS PRICE KEY		
Rates are per room, per night, double occupancy. Price ranges described for each property often do not take into account penthouses and other exceptional, high-priced accommodations.	$ $$ $$$ $$$$	Up to $75 $75 to $150 $151 to $250 $251 and up

■ MOTELS & HOTELS

Right in the Homosassa Springs Wildlife Park's backyard (see *Sights & Attractions*, above), you can stay at the **Bella Oasis Hotel & Spa**, 4076 S. Suncoast Blvd., ☎ 352-628-4311, www.bellaoasis.com, and take a walkway to the attraction. It has a fitness center, day spa, pool, restaurant, and comedy club on the premises. Continental breakfast is included. $$

Right on the Homosassa River with its own marina, **Homosassa Riverside Resort**, 5297 S. Cherokee Way, ☎ 352-628-2474 or 800-442-2040, www.riversideresorts.com, is a happening place to stay. It has shuffleboard, a pool, a restaurant and lounge with a view of Monkey Island, rooms and efficiencies, canoeing, kayaking, tours, a boat ramp, a bait shop, and fishing charters. If you're a true adventurer, you'll be happy here in a standard room or suite with full kitchen. $-$$

The Nature Coast

For a taste of Old Homosassa and a solid fishing fix, drive down to **MacRae's** at 5300 S. Cherokee Way, ☎ 352-628-2602. Run by a longtime local family on the Homosassa River, it has a marina and rents log cabins and efficiencies by the night and week. $$

■ CAMPING

RV parks are plentiful in this neck of the woods. Some also offer tent sites.

On the edge of the national wildlife preserve, **Chassahowitzka River Campground and Recreation Area**, 8600 W. Miss Maggie Dr., ☎ 352-382-2200, has 36 RV ($20 per night for full hookup) and 46 tent sites ($15 a night). The location on the river is ideal for canoeists and boaters. Launching facilities are provided.

WHERE TO EAT

If you're looking to hang out with the local fishing crowd and bikers on the banks of a river, **The Shed** at MacRae's, ☎ 352-628-2602, fills the prescription. The open-air bar serves cold beer and fried seafood and chicken baskets at budget prices, $5-$8.

Nearby at Homosassa Riverside Resort, **Riverside Crab House** at 5297 S. Cherokee Way, ☎ 352-628-2474 or 800-442-2040, www.riversideresorts.com, gives you an elevated and entertaining view of an island that's populated by monkeys and sits in the middle of the river. The lunch and dinner menu concentrates on local seafood and country fare such as barbecue pork sandwich, steamed blue crab, fried or broiled catfish, scallops, and pasta. Sandwiches and entrées range from $8 to $21. Closed Monday.

Way off the beaten path between Homosassa Springs and Crystal River in the backroads fishing resort community of Ozello, **Pecks Old Port Cove** on Ozello Trail, nine miles off Hwy 19, ☎ 352-795-2806, has been feeding appetites for seafood and rural riverside peace for decades. The owners farm their own soft-shell crabs on the premises, so you know they're fresh. Pound-and-eat garlic crabs are another specialty. The menu lists 48 selections of appetizers, sides, seafood baskets and dinners, sandwiches, and desserts, plus all-you-can-eat feasts that change daily. Order sandwiches and entrées in the $4-$16 range (market price for some items) for lunch or dinner daily.

Withlacoochee State Forest

Native Americans bestowed upon the region its name, meaning "crooked waters." The tannic-tinted river that shares its name with today's 157,469-acre state forest borders the territory to the east, runs into the Gulf of Mexico in the north, and reaches the Green Swamp to the southeast. Thirteen miles of the 70-mile-long river flow through the preserved forestlands, along with two other Outstanding Florida Waters – Jumper Creek and Little Withlacoochee River.

FLORIDIOM: Many of Florida's rivers have a rusty-brown tint to them. In the case of the most pristine of them, such as the Withlacoochee, this comes not from pollution or mud, but from the tannic acid produced by cypress trees. These waterways are known as blackwater rivers.

The forest itself is scattered throughout Hernando and Citrus counties in five sections, or tracts: Forest Headquarters, Citrus, Croom, Richloam, and Jumper Creek. Once the home of turn-of-the-century pioneers and site of boom-time phosphate mining, the tracts have since been developed for outdoor recreational opportunities, from bird watching to all-terrain cycling. Withlacoochee's vast reaches embrace a

Flocks of birds gather in the area.

number of biological communities – low-lying sand to cypress swamps. The forest hosts creatures of rare and endangered status, including the bald eagle, Eastern indigo snake, black bear, and red-cockaded woodpecker. Alligators, wild boar, bobcats, rabbits, deer, and quail also find shelter. Declared by the World Wildlife Fund as one of the "10 Coolest Places You've Never Been in North America," it is also part of the Great Florida Birding Trail (see page 9).

GETTING HERE

Different parts of the Withlacoochee are spread out all over Hernando and Citrus counties, on both sides of **I-75**. Exit 301 takes you to the Richloam Tract to the east and the southern entrance of Croom Tract to the west. Exit 309 lies smack dab at the eastern entrance to Croom. **Rte. 480** (Croom Rd.) runs east-west through the tract. At Exit 321, take Rte. 470 north, then Rte. 479 west to get to Jumper Creek Tract. **Hwy. 41** runs through the Forest Headquarters. Citrus Tract lies west of Hwy. 41 along Rte. 480 or 44. **Rte. 581** runs north-south along the tract's eastern border with access to Mutual Mine and Holder Mine recreation areas.

SIGHTS & ATTRACTIONS

Recreational opportunities here begin at **Withlacoochee State Forest Headquarters,** 15003 Broad Street, Brooksville, ☎ 352-754-6896, www.fl-dof.com/state_forests/withlacoochee.html. The 1,230-acre area on Highway 41, about seven miles north of Brooksville, is centered around **McKethan Lake**, which is popular with fishermen, and a nature trail circles it for hiking enthusiasts (see *On Foot*, below). Facilities also include a fitness course and picnic tables. The forest is divided into separate tracts, each with trails and forest roads. The visitor's center is open Monday-Friday, 8-5, and Saturday, 8-noon and 12:30-4:30.

To the southeast, **Croom Tract** offers the most to recreationists within its 21,359 acres, including **Silver Lake Recreation Area**, a day-use and camping grounds suited to boating, fishing, and picnicking. Overnight campgrounds comprise more than 90 sites and hiking trails keep the on-the-hoof crowd busy. The tract also includes an off-road motorcycling area (see *On Wheels*, below) that makes use of an old mine pit. Three other recreation areas provide camping, fishing, boating, canoe launching, hiking trails, and picnic grounds.

Richloam Tract, 49,200 acres, is named for its fertile soil, responsible for vital cypress growth and resultant controlled timbering. Here, to the southeast of Croom, ponies and cattle thrive as they have for centuries. They run wild, descendants of horses and cows left by early Spanish explorers.

Richloam's main activity is nature hiking through pine flatwoods, pine plantations, cypress ponds, and hardwood hammocks. It connects to the **Green Swamp Hiking Trail** for extra mileage. In summer, rainfall makes the trail muddy. It has a canoe launch that marks the beginning of the 83-mile Withlacoochee Canoe Trail (see *Paddling*, below).

Northwest of Forest Headquarters, **Citrus Tract** occupies 42,613 acres of sandhill scrub and pine uplands. It is known for its large deer population and horse trails. Deer-hunting is open to archers. Picnicking and camping are also available.

Jumper Creek Tract lies to the northeast with 10,068 acres and is the least developed. Hunting, fishing, birding, horseback riding, and hiking are popular. Only primitive day-use facilities exist.

ADVENTURES

■ ON WATER

FISHING

Within the forest, fishing is best in **Croom Tract**, where the Withlacoochee River squiggles its way through. It is permitted at **Silver**

Lake Recreation Area, River Junction Recreation Area, Hog Island Recreation Area, and **Iron Bridge Day Use Recreation Area.** Fishing is also popular and fruitful at the **McKethan Lake State Recreation Area** near Forest Headquarters on Hwy. 41.

BOAT RAMPS

You can launch your boat into the Withlacoochee River from any of the recreation areas in Croom Tract: **Silver Lake Recreation Area, Hog Island Recreation Area**, and **Iron Bridge Day Use Recreation Area**.

BOAT RENTALS

Nobleton Canoe Rental, off I-75 at Exit 309, 29196 Lake Lindsey Rd. in Nobleton, ☎ 800-783-5284 or 352-796-7176, www.nobleton canoes.com, rents pontoon boats for two to eight people for use in the Withlacoochee River. Rates are $100 for a half-day, $140 all day. Fishing boats cost $40 for four hours, $60 all day.

PADDLING

The black waters of the **Withlacoochee River** – a designated Florida Outstanding Water – take you into the quiet of Florida gone by via an 83-mile canoe trail that begins in **Richloam Tract** at Coulter Hammock launch, flows northward through **Croom Tract** and the western boundary of **Jumper Creek Tract**, then continues on to the Gulf of Mexico.

For canoe outfitting and shuttle service on the Withlacoochee River, visit **Nobleton Canoe Rental**, off I-75 at Exit 309, 29196 Lake Lindsey Rd. in Nobleton, ☎ 800-783-5284 or 352-796-7176, www.nobletonoutpost.com. Canoe trips range from five-13 miles with a float time of two-5½ hours. The 5½-hour trip costs $40 for two people, $45 for three. The rest are $35 and $40. Overnight trips, kayaks, and trolling motors are available. The black river runs south to north, and a shuttle takes you to your starting point, after which time you're on your own. Explore the offshoot waterways and bays to discover the richest wildlife. Parks along the way provide pit stops.

Watch for blue herons as you paddle the forest's waterways.

ON FOOT

A number of hiking trails – nearly 150 mile's worth total – in and around Withlacoochee State Forest provide rich opportunities to commune with unspoiled nature. Picnic areas are convenient to each of the trails. For information on the state's **Trailwalker Program**, ☎ 850-414-0871.

There are hiking trails at all of the recreation areas within Croom and Citrus tracts. Recreation areas in Citrus Tract include **Holder Mine Recreation Area**, **Mutual Mine Campground**, and **Tillis Hill Recreation Area**. In Croom Tract, these include **Silver Lake Recreation Area**, **River Junction Recreation Area**, **Hog Island Recreation Area**, and **Iron Bridge Day Use Recreation Area**.

East of Brooksville and I-75, **Richloam Hiking Trail**, off Rte. 50 on Clay Sink Rd., travels 31½ miles and is open to foot traffic only. Primitive and established camping sites are available. The trail is closed during the first nine days of the general hunting season. In summer's rainy season, trails get muddy.

> **NOTE:** *Hiking, biking, and horse trails are closed at certain times during hunting season. To receive a copy of the schedule, contact the forest recreation center at ☎ 352-754-6898.*

To the northeast, the two miles of **McKethan Lake Nature Trail** off Hwy. 41 in Withlacoochee Forest, ☎ 352-754-6896, circle the lake and penetrate hardwood hammock habitat where longleaf pine and turkey oak proliferate. Other flora and fauna include squirrel, rabbit, white-tailed deer, resurrection fern, magnolia, and cabbage palm. Picnic facilities are provided. For all-day use, there's a $1 per person admission fee into the McKethan Lake Recreation Area.

Three loop trails comprise 2½ miles for exploring Withlacoochee Forest along **Colonel Robins Nature Trail**, off Hwy. 41. Deer, gopher tortoises, gray squirrels, and foxes inhabit the upland habitat along the trails. A self-guiding brochure helps you identify flora along the way.

FLORIDIOM: Cabbage palm, also known as sabal palm, is Florida's state tree and the hardiest of the infinite varieties of palms the state hosts. The bud of the tree was eaten by natives and Florida Crackers as "swamp cabbage," but today it is protected. In trendier circles, it's known as hearts of palm.

Withlacoochee Trail State Park, ☎ 352-726-2251, www.dep.state. fl.us/gwt/guide/regions/crossflorida/trails/with_state.htm, is the major recreational path for hikers, cyclists, and skaters. Formerly a railroad track, it runs 46 miles from Hwy. 301 south of Brooksville, through parts of the state forest and Citrus County (see more at Inverness, page 49). Benches, restrooms, parks, sights, and other conveniences accommodate users along the paved trail. It provides access to the Florida Trail in the Croom Tract of the Withlacoochee Forest (see *Sights & Attractions,* above). Parking for the trail is provided at Silver Lake Recreation Area and Townsend Lake Regional Park.

> **HUNTING RULES:** Hunting seasons for hogs, turkey, and small game are listed in Withlacoochee's Wildlife Harvest Guide, ☎ 352-754-6896. Dates for archery, muzzleloading gun, modern gun, and general gun hunting are given.

■ ON WHEELS

BICYCLING

The 46-mile **Withlacoochee Trail State Park**, ☎ 352-726-2251, is a rails-to-trails path for hikers, cyclists, and skaters. It intersects with **Croom Off-Road Bicycle Trails**, two trails of more than 40 miles.

MOTORCYCLING

An off-road track accommodates motorcyclists at 2,600-acre **Croom Motorcycle Area** in Withlacoochee State Forest, ☎ 352-754-6896. Permits are required. The area includes an inexperienced rider zone, training pit, day-use picnic area, and campground. The entrance is off Rte. 50, just east of I-75, Exit 61.

■ ON HORSEBACK

Withlacoochee Trail State Park and **Withlacoochee State Forest** provide endless opportunities for equestrians with their own ride.

WHERE TO STAY

■ CAMPING

Withlacoochee State Forest provides primitive camping for the backpacker as well as established facilities. Camping time limit is 14 days. Charge at established campgrounds is $12 without electricity, $15 with. Sites accommodate tents and RVs. Call ☎ 352-754-6896 for information on all the campgrounds below.

For facilities with a few conveniences – bathrooms, water, and grills – try **Holder Mine Recreation Area**, **Mutual Mine Campground**, and **Tillis Hill Recreation Area** in Citrus Tract. Tillis Mine has 37 sites and Holder Mine has 27 sites with electrical hookups. Tillis is the only one in Citrus Tract with a dump station and is popular with equestrians. Mutual Mine is the only campground without hot showers.

In Croom Tract, **Silver Lake Recreation Area**, **River Junction Recreation Area**, and **Hog Island Recreation Area** all have camping sites. Silver Lake is largest with 77 sites, 57 of them with electrical hookups. All have dump stations and hot showers. River Junction is the most secluded.

Brooksville

Brooksville is Hernando's county seat and a bit of a historic show-off. It was established in 1856, but most of its oldest buildings were constructed around 1912. It has an old-fashioned, small-town allure despite a tendency to sprawl into chain fast-food and department store syndrome.

GETTING HERE

Highways 41 (Broad Ave.) and **98** (Jefferson St.) meet in Brooksville. To reach the town from I-75, take Exit 301 and head west.

INFORMATION

The **Hernando Chamber of Commerce**, ☎ 352-796-0697, www. hernandochamber.com, disseminates information at two locations. One close to the interstate at Exit 314, the other downtown Brooksville at 101 E. Fort Dade Ave. Or contact **Hernando County Tourist Development** at 30305 Cortez Blvd., ☎ 800-601-4580 or 352-754-4405, www.co.hernando.fl.us/visit.

SIGHTS & ATTRACTIONS

■ OF HISTORIC OR CULTURAL INTEREST

Downtown Brooksville holds a cache of **historic buildings** along brick-paved streets, some dating back to the 1880s. The largest concentration lies along Main St., Liberty St., and Brooksville Ave.

One of the town's oldest and proudest Victorian architectural gems was built in 1856 and holds the **Hernando Heritage Museum** at 601 Museum Ct., ☎ 352-799-0129, www.hernandoheritage museum.com. A guided tour through the four-story mansion spills tales of old Brooksville, including legends that the museum's house is haunted. It's open noon-3, Tuesday-Saturday. Requested donation is $3 for adults, $1 for children.

■ FAMILY FUN

An unusual find, **Citrus Attraction** at Boyett's Groves, 4355 Spring Lake Hwy. (1½ miles south of Hwy. 98, east of Brooksville), ☎ 352-796-2289 or 800-780-2296, www.boyettsgrove.com, offers a small zoo, a dinosaur cave, a 14,000-gallon saltwater reef tank, and other

Bobcat © Dan Banister/Dreamstime.com

aquariums, in addition to a look at a working citrus packinghouse (mid-November-April only). Admission is $3.59 for adults; $2.59 for children aged two-15. Hours are 9-5, daily.

ADVENTURES

■ ON WATER

Lake Townsend Regional Park at 28011 Lake Lindsay Rd. (Rte. 476) has a fishing pier and boat ramp into the lake at the edge of Withlacoochee Forest, as well as extensive park facilities.

■ ON FOOT

Suncoast Trail, ☎ 352-754-4027, www.dep.state.fl.us/gwt/guide/ regions/westcentral/trails/suncoast.htm, runs south for 41 miles to Tampa's outskirts. Biking and hiking are allowed along the paved surface, which will eventually extend to connect to the Pinellas Trail (see *St. Petersburg & Clearwater* chapter). Trailheads in the Brooksville area are located on Suncoast Parkway, west of town on Route 50 and at Anderson Snow Regional Park/Sports Complex, southwest of Brooksville off County Line Rd.

A system of nature trails forms the heart of **Chinsegut Nature Center**, off Hwy. 41 at 23212 Lake Lindsey Rd. (Rte. 476), seven miles north of Brooksville, ☎ 352-754-6722, http://myfwc.com/recreation/chinsegut/ or http://myfwc.com/chinsegut/. The trails explore uplands and wetlands habitats that attract a myriad endangered species. The small nature center is open Friday and Saturday, 8-2. Ask for a schedule of walks and talks.

SHOPPING

Downtown Brooksville provides a charming ambiance for antique and specialty shopping. Its most famous shop is actually five in one, and something of a tourist attraction. **Rogers' Christmas House &**

Village, 103 S. Saxon Ave., ☎ 877-312-5046 or 352-796-2415, www. rogerschristmashouse.com, spreads a tantalizing array of themed gifts in its Storybook Land, Country Cottage, Magnolia House, Christmas House, and other shops with gardens interspersed. It's open daily, 9:30-5.

WHERE TO STAY

■ CAMPING

The countryside around Brooksville holds many campgrounds for RVs and tents alike. **Brentwood Lake Camping**, 11089 Ancient Trail, ☎ 352-796-5760, charges $19 per night. Nightly rates for Frontier Campground, 15549 Cortez Blvd., ☎ 352-796-9988, are $28.

WHERE TO EAT

Downtown has a lot of interesting eateries that are open only for weekday lunch. One that has survived since 1940, but with different owners today, is the **Main Street Eatery**, 101 N. Main St., ☎ 352-799-2789, which touts its "Famous Pressed Cuban" sandwich and 97% fat-free deli meats. Try the Buzzard Breath Chili or the Greek salad. It's open for lunch only (closed Sunday). Salads and sandwiches cost around $5. If you're there beyond banker's hours, go where the locals do, **Papa Joe's**, east of town at the juncture of routes 41 and 50, ☎ 352-799-3904. Cliché in décor, this Italian favorite serves uncommonly good food, from pizza to pasta topped with fresh sauces to veal parmigiana and seafood jambalaya. It opens daily for lunch ($6-$9) and dinner ($10-$17).

Weeki Wachee

Mermaids made Weeki Wachee famous. The mermaids of Weeki Wachee Springs, an attraction that dates back to the 40s, wear silver-tailed costumes and take breaths of piped-in air to perform their classic – if somewhat hokey – underwater extravaganza. Around the transparent springs and its mermaids grew up a touristy little community whose back roads still hold uncontrived Florida fishing camps and towns. Explore the neighboring communities of Spring Hill, Bayport, and Pine Island (see page 287) to find doorways to on-the-water adventure.

The Nature Coast

GETTING HERE

Arriving from **I-75** via Brooksville, follow Rte. 50 (Cortez Blvd.) west to get to Weeki Wachee. From the north, **Highway 19**, here known as Commercial Way, plunges into the heart of Weeki Wachee. Spring Hill lies to the north, east of Highway 19 on Spring Hill Drive. **Cortez Blvd.** (Rte. 50/550) to the west goes to the small waterfront communities of Pine Island and Bayport. **Shoal Line Blvd.** (Rte. 597) runs north-south off Cortez and takes you to the local beaches and other park attractions. Rte. 595 (Aripeka Rd.) takes you into Aripeka.

SIGHTS & ATTRACTIONS

■ PERFORMING ARTS

In Spring Hill, the musical and non-musical classics come to stage at **Stage West Community Playhouse**, 8390 Forest Oaks Blvd., ☎ 352-683-5113, www.stagewest.net. Individual regular season tickets in its two theaters cost $10-$18.

■ BEACHES, PARKS & NATURAL AREAS

Although you don't find beaches along the Nature Coast like you do, say, along the St. Petersburg/Clearwater area, they are here. One of the most popular in these parts, **Alfred McKethan Pine Island Park**, ☎ 352-754-4031, lies on Rte. 495 off 550 and works well for families or anyone interested in swimming in the river, playing a little volleyball, swinging, and relaxing on the waterfront. Entry fee is $2 per vehicle.

Hernando Beach Park, 6400 Shoal Line Blvd. (Rte. 597) also lays down a sand blanket for visitors, and has an observation tower.

■ FAMILY FUN

One of the region's prime attractions is **Weeki Wachee Springs Waterpark**, at the intersection of Hwy.19 and Rte. 50, ☎ 877-GO-WEEKI or 352-596-2062, www.weekiwachee.com. Its underwater mermaid show is a classic, appealing to kids with stories of Pocahontas, the Little Mermaid, and other kid heroes. Spectators watch from an underwater theater as the pretty young mermaids perform in the natural setting of clear spring waters. Other shows around the park involve exotic birds and birds of prey. A river wilderness cruise, a petting zoo, springs beach swimming, bumper boat rides, and flume slides complete the many ways to have fun at Weeki Wachee (just saying the name is fun!). Hours vary, so call or check the website in advance. Admission for the springs and water park is $22.95 for adults, $15.95 for children aged three to 10, plus tax. When the water park is closed (November-mid-March), prices are $13.95 and $10.95. Parking is $3. The get-wet portion of the park, known as Buccaneer Bay, is open only in summer and on weekends and holidays in the spring.

The Mermaid Theater is the only one of its kind in the world.

ADVENTURES

■ ON WATER

FISHING

Fishing is fertile along the coast and in inland waters. Prize catches are tarpon and shark, which are released. In the Spring Hill area, there are fishing piers at **Hernando Beach Park**, 6400 Shoal Line Blvd. (Rte. 597), **Bayport Park**, 4140 Cortez Blvd. (Rte. 550), and **Jenkins Creek Park**, 6401 Shoal Line Blvd. (Rte. 597).

The Nature Coast

For $4 (kids under age 16, $3) you can shore-fish all day on the Mud River at **Mary's Fish Camp**, 8092 Mary's Fish Camp Rd., four miles west of Weeki Wachee on Rte. 550, ☎ 352-596-2359. Pole rental, RV sites, and cabins are available. It's open for fishing daily 8-10.

FLORIDIOM: Central Florida has fish camps, huddles of fish frenzy that grew up in the early days of tourism and watersports. They're a good place to find a cheap, spartan place to stay close to the water. Most have bait and tackle shops, some have little barebones restaurants where the fish is as fresh as it gets.

For fishing gear and bait, visit **Hernando Beach Bait & Tackle**, 4211 Shoal Line Blvd. in Hernando Beach, ☎ 352-596-3375.

BOAT RAMPS

You can find ramps into the Gulf in Spring Hill at **Bayport Park**, 4140 Cortez Blvd. (Rte. 550) and **Hernando Beach Park**, 6400 Shoal Line Blvd. (Rte. 597). **Rogers Park**, 7244 Shoal Line Blvd. in Spring Hill provides access to Weeki Wachee River and charges a $2 per vehicle entrance fee in season.

BOAT RENTALS

Weeki Wachee Marina, 7154 Shoal Line Blvd. in Spring Hill, ☎ 352-596-2852, rents 14-foot Jon boats with 6hp motors for use in the river. They hold up to four people and cost $60 for a half-day and $75 for a full day.

PADDLING

For canoeing and kayaking, you can't beat the Nature Coast. Sea kayakers favor the **estuaries** around Bayport and Pine Island.

Conveniently located in the parking lot at Weeki Wachee Springs (see *Sights & Attractions*, above), **Weeki Wachee Canoe Rental**, 6131 Commercial Way (Hwy. 19), ☎ 352-597-0360, www. floridacanoe.com, rents canoes and two-person kayaks for $38 a day, single-seat kayaks for $30.

Paddlers can head to **Rogers Park** (see *Boat Ramps*, above) to put into Weeki Wachee River, which leads to a spring six miles upriver.

Weekiwachee Preserve, accessible from Shoal Line Blvd. and Rte. 595, offers terrific kayaking in confined water.

SNORKELING & DIVING

Hernando County offers freshwater and Gulf diving for divers of all levels. For beginners, 20-foot dives into the **Weeki Wachee River** and at artificial reefs offshore eight-13 nautical miles supply a variety of underwater scenery. Caves and sinkholes challenge advanced divers at **Hospital Hole**, **Eagle's Nest** and other locales. For more information, contact local dive shops.

ON FOOT

Weekiwachee Preserve, ☎ 800-423-1476 or 352-796-7211 ext. 4470, www.swf wmd.state.fl.us/recreation/areas/weekiwachee.html, is accessible from Shoal Line Blvd. and Rte. 595. Marking 10 miles of biking and hiking trails through the hardwood swamps, limestone lakes, and hammocks along Weeki Wachee River, it is home to black bears and other rare critters.

Neighborhood Park at 14755 Coronado Drive in Spring Hill offers a 2/3-mile walking trail through its more than eight acres.

ON WHEELS

Weekiwachee Preserve, accessible from Shoal Line Blvd. and Rte. 595 (see above), provides 5½ miles of paved and limerock biking trails into lowland and upland vegetation.

WHERE TO STAY

MOTELS

Convenient to Weeki Wachee Springs, **Comfort Inn**, 9373 Cortez Blvd., ☎ 352-596-9000, offers free continental breakfast, in-room coffeemaker, an exercise room, and a pool. Some of its 68 tidy rooms have whirlpool bathtubs. $$

■ CAMPING

Cody's Catfish Pond, 8588 Ostrom Way, ☎ 352-596-6010, www.
codyscatfishpond.com, lies west of Hwy. 19 and offers standard facilities for $24 a night.

WHERE TO EAT

Head off the main highway along Route 50 to find the funky and fun
in seafood restaurants. **Backwaters**, 6024 Cortez Blvd., ☎ 352-597-
5457, has splashes of Caribbean color outside, glass-encased sea
charts for tables, and an ambitious menu that flexes beyond seafood. Sandwiches and burgers at lunchtime range from $5 to $8.
Come dinner, grouper specials, crab legs, pasta, prime rib, and
pages full of other entrées are $8 to $17. Dine early for sunset specials, priced $5 to $8.

St. Petersburg & Clearwater

The West Coast's largest and most popular sun-spotlit playground is contained in Pinellas County and has been dubbed Florida's Beach. From Anclote Key in the north to St. Pete Beach in the south, it is one long fling – 35 mile's worth – of sand-lined islands where fun-in-the-sun and full-speed adventure reign.

The not-a-care-in-the-world beaches give the region a playful, somewhat boisterous reputation but, as you will find in this chapter, there's something for everyone here. Far flung, remote islands offer the flip side to all that action. These are hide-outs for wildlife and reclusive beachers.

In its far north reaches, Pinellas boasts two cultural enclaves: Greek Tarpon Springs and Scottish Dunedin. The Clearwater area holds all sorts of pleasant surprises: a 34-miles-and-growing bike trail, a natural mineral spa, one of the state's oldest surviving wooden hotels, a marina-full of high sea adventures, and a highly respected marine biology facility.

St. Petersburg, the region's metropolitan center, along with its environs, has long been the destination for winter refugees seeking restored health. Downtown became known for its population of retirees, but in more recent years has injected youthful life into its withering reputation. With its Dali and other museums and trendy clubs, it satisfies high-brow vacation requirements. Its sling of islands, conversely, built an early and lasting reputation for frivolity, even back when Scott and Zelda danced at the landmark Don CeSar Hotel. Because the islands have been hosting beachers for so many years, they have a faded-glory feeling. That too is changing, as the county pumps more and more dollars into beautifying park and beach areas.

Huge centers of water recreation, most notably Clearwater Beach Marina and John's Pass Village at Madeira Beach, make this sunshiny land legendary for its boating, fishing, and beaching. The sum total of Pinellas County covered in this chapter begins in the north at Tarpon Springs and neighboring (to the north) Port Richey, then continues to the fat peninsula separated from mainland and the city of Tampa by deep, wide Tampa Bay. Sandwiched between it and the Gulf of Mexico, the region is all but surrounded by on-the-water opportunities. Despite its metropolitan and developed beach nature, it has plenty of wild spaces and recreational adventures to offer landlubbers as well.

FLORIDIOM: The name Pinellas endures from the era of Spanish conquest. Punta pinal, or "point of pines," described land features for early mapmakers and explorers.

Anclote Palm Beach

© Amanda Martin

TRANSPORTATION

■ AIRLINES

Two international airports serve the Tampa Bay area, one in Tampa, the other in Clearwater. **Tampa International Airport**, ☎ 800-767-8882 or 813-870-8700, www.tampaairport.com, receives more flights, especially from international destinations. **St. Petersburg/ Clearwater International** (PIE), ☎ 727-531-1451, www.fly2pie. com, principally serves charters and shuttles.

DOMESTIC & INTERNATIONAL AIRLINES SERVING TAMPA INT'L AIRPORT (TPA)

Air Canada	☎ 888-247-2262	www.aircanada.com
AirTran Airways	☎ 800-247-8726	www.airtran.com
American Airlines	☎ 800-433-7300	www.aa.com
British Airways	☎ 800-247-9297	www.ba.com
Cayman Airways	☎ 800-422-9626	www.caymanairways.com
Continental	☎ 800-525-0280	www.continental.com
Delta Air Lines/Comair	☎ 800-221-1212	www.delta.com
Frontier	☎ 800-432-1359	
Continental	☎ 800-525-0280	
Delta Air Lines / Comair	☎ 800-221-1212	
Delta Express	☎ 866-235-9359	
Frontier	☎ 800-432-1359	www.frontierairlines.com
Gulfstream	☎ 800-992-8532	www.gulfstreamair.com
JetBlue	☎ 800-538-2583	www.jetblue.com
Midwest	☎ 800-452-2022	www.midwestairlines.com
Northwest/KLM	☎ 800-225-2525	www.nwa.com
Southwest	☎ 800-435-9792	www.southwest.com
Spirit	☎ 800-772-7117	www.spiritair.com
Ted	☎ 800-225-5833	www.flyted.com
United	☎ 800-241-6522	www.united.com
US Airways	☎ 800-428-4322	www.usairways.com
USA3000	☎ 877-872-3000	www.usa3000airlines.com
WestJet	☎ 800-538-5696	www.westjet.com
Gulfstream International	☎ 800-525-0280	
JetBlue	☎ 800-538-2583	
Midwest Express	☎ 800-452-2022	
Northwest KLM	☎ 800-255-2525	

▨ BUS & TAXI SERVICE

Pinellas Suncoast Transit Authority (PSTA), ☎ 727-530-9911, www. psta.net, provides bus service to St. Petersburg and the rest of the county. It runs a trolley to the beaches at $3.50 a person for the entire day. Ask about PSTA's Bikes on Buses program.

Several taxi companies provide transportation to and from the airport, including **Yellow Cab**, ☎ 727-797-2230 or 727-799-2222; and **Super Shuttle**, ☎ 800-282-6817, 727-572-1111, www.supershuttle.com.

▨ RENTAL CARS

Rental cars are available at the airport and other locations throughout the area. Companies include **Avis**, ☎ 800-331-1212 or 727-530-1406; **Hertz**, ☎ 800-654-3131; **National**, ☎ 800-227-7368 or 727-530-5491; **Thrifty**, ☎ 800-847-4389; and **Budget**, ☎ 800-527-0700 or 727-530-0441.

■ GETTING AROUND

I-275, which merges into I-75 from the north and south and into I-4 (and Orlando) from the east, is the major thoroughfare of the area. At its south end lies the dramatic **Sunshine Skyway Bridge** (shown here); at its north, **Howard Frankland Bridge** (I-275) crosses to Tampa. To the south, the **Gandy Bridge** (Highway 92), connects St. Petersburg to downtown Tampa. **Courtney Campbell Causeway** (Rte. 60/Memorial Highway), north of I-275, connects Clearwater to north Tampa.

Skyway Bridge

Highway 19 runs north-south on the east side of the Pinellas County peninsula. Nearer to the islands, **Alternate Highway 19** takes you along the county's northern shores. A new toll road, **Suncoast Parkway**, runs north between highways 19 and 41, beginning east of Tarpon Springs.

> **TIP:** *From anywhere in the Tampa Bay area (Sarasota to Hernando County), dial 511 or log on to www.511tampabay.com for up-to-date traffic info.*

INFORMATION

For information on Pinellas County, contact **St. Petersburg/ Clearwater Convention & Visitors Bureau**, 13805 58th Street N., Suite 2-200, Clearwater, FL 33760; ☎ 877-FL-BEACH (toll free) or 727-464-7200, www.FloridasBeach.com.

BUDGET TIPS

■ Pick up the red "Welcome" guide-map at local visitors information centers and retail outlets. It contains coupons for many local attractions.

■ The region's small historical sites and museums generally don't charge admission. Some request a small donation. They include: **West Pasco Historical Museum** and **Baker House** in Holiday, **Indian Rocks Area Historical Museum**, and **Gulf Beaches Historical Museum** in Pass-A-Grille.

■ In Tarpon Springs, you can tour **Spongeorama** and **St. Nicholas Greek Orthodox Church** free of charge.

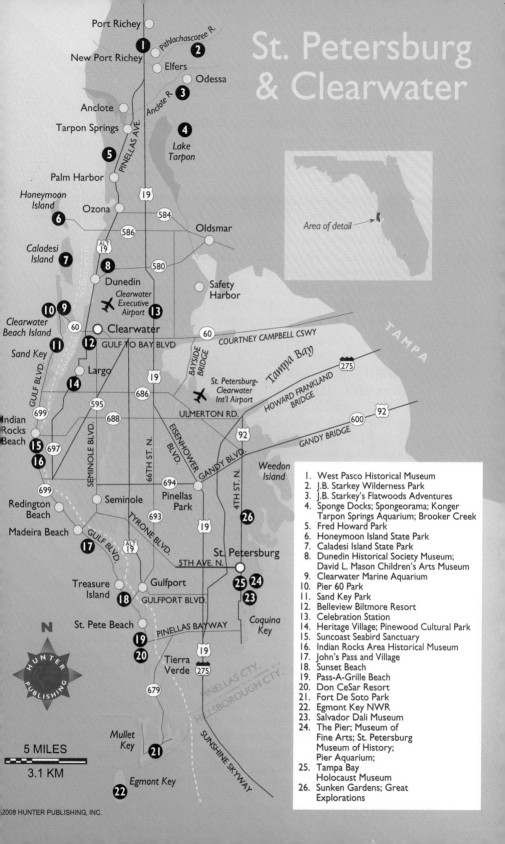

St. Petersburg & Clearwater

Port Richey

New Port Richey

Elfers

Odessa

Pithlachascotee R.

Anclote R.

Anclote

Tarpon Springs

PINELLAS AVE.

Lake Tarpon

Palm Harbor

Honeymoon Island

Ozona

584

586

ALT 19

Oldsmar

Caladesi Island

580

Dunedin

Clearwater Executive Airport

Safety Harbor

Clearwater Beach Island

Clearwater

60

COURTNEY CAMPBELL CSWY

Sand Key

GULF TO BAY BLVD

BAYSIDE BRIDGE

TAMPA

Largo

19

St. Petersburg-Clearwater Int'l Airport

Tampa Bay

275

HOWARD FRANKLAND BRIDGE

686

Indian Rocks Beach

699

697

595

688

SEMINOLE BLVD.

66TH ST. N.

EISENHOWER BLVD.

ULMERTON RD.

92

GANDY BLVD.

600

92

GANDY BRIDGE

Redington Beach

699

Seminole

694

Pinellas Park

Weedon Island

4TH ST. N.

26

Madeira Beach

693

TYRONE BLVD.

19

St. Petersburg

GULF BLVD.

ALT 19

5TH AVE. N.

25

24

23

Treasure Island

Gulfport

GULFPORT BLVD.

Coquina Key

St. Pete Beach

PINELLAS BAYWAY

19

19

Tierra Verde

275

20

679

N

HUNTER PUBLISHING

Mullet Key

21

5 MILES

3.1 KM

Egmont Key

22

PINELLAS CTY.

HILLSBOROUGH CTY.

SUNSHINE SKYWAY

Area of detail

1. West Pasco Historical Museum
2. J.B. Starkey Wilderness Park
3. J.B. Starkey's Flatwoods Adventures
4. Sponge Docks; Spongeorama; Konger Tarpon Springs Aquarium; Brooker Creek
5. Fred Howard Park
6. Honeymoon Island State Park
7. Caladesi Island State Park
8. Dunedin Historical Society Museum; David L. Mason Children's Arts Museum
9. Clearwater Marine Aquarium
10. Pier 60 Park
11. Sand Key Park
12. Belleview Biltmore Resort
13. Celebration Station
14. Heritage Village; Pinewood Cultural Park
15. Suncoast Seabird Sanctuary
16. Indian Rocks Area Historical Museum
17. John's Pass and Village
18. Sunset Beach
19. Pass-A-Grille Beach
20. Don CeSar Resort
21. Fort De Soto Park
22. Egmont Key NWR
23. Salvador Dali Museum
24. The Pier; Museum of Fine Arts; St. Petersburg Museum of History; Pier Aquarium;
25. Tampa Bay Holocaust Museum
26. Sunken Gardens; Great Explorations

2008 HUNTER PUBLISHING, INC.

■ Enter by donation at one of the Suncoast's most famous attractions: **Suncoast Seabird Sanctuary**.

■ In Largo, you can tour two fine attractions for free: **Heritage Village** and **Pinewood Cultural Park**.

■ Downtown St. Petersburg's **Pier Aquarium** requests a mere $2 donation.

FESTIVALS & EVENTS

★ **JANUARY** – Tarpon Springs celebrates its Greek heritage most fervently during its **Epiphany celebration** on January 6. For almost 80 years, the festivities have been capped by a tradition known as "diving for the cross," where boys aged 16-18 dive into chilly waters to retrieve a white wooden cross in hopes of a blessed year. Greek food, dancing, and music follow the event. ☎ 727-937-3540 or www.epiphanycity.org for information.

★ **APRIL** – April ushers in a tradition nearly 40 years old: **Dunedin Highland Games & Festival**, ☎ 727-733-3197, www.dunedinhighlandgames.com. Highlights include kilted bagpipe bands, Scottish storytelling, dancing, and feats of skill such as tossing the caber and throwing the hammer. Safety Harbor Marina hosts **Safety Harbor Kayak Races & Boat Day**, ☎ 727-724-1572, with races, live entertainment, food, and more. Downtown St. Petersburg goes all-out to celebrate its annual **Festival of States**, ☎ 727-321-9888, www.festivalofstates.com, for two weeks beginning in April – everything from fireworks to clown school. **Tarpon Springs Fine Arts Festival**, ☎ 727-937-6109, features more than 200 artists and live entertainment for two days early in the month.

★ **OCTOBER** – **Clearwater Jazz Holiday**, ☎ 888-4-CLEAR WATER or 727-461-5200, www.clearwaterjazz.com, one of the longest-running and hugest free jazz festival in the Southeastern US, brings music-loving crowds to Clearwater for four days and nights.

Look to the sky for exhilarating aerobatic performances by nationally famous pilots during two days at **St. Petersburg Airfest** at Albert Whitted Airport, ☎ 727-204-6282, www.albertwhittedairfest.com. Live music, vintage and military aircraft exhibits, and a food court happen on the ground.

★ **NOVEMBER – Strictly Sail St. Petersburg**, ☎ 800-817-SAIL, www.strictlysail.com/shows/stpete.asp?, is the only all-sail boat show on Florida's Gulf Coast and features free sailboat rides, live music, and seminars every day during the four-day event.

The **Central Florida Pirate Festival** in Coachman Park, downtown Clearwater, ☎ 727-520-4926, www.piratefair. com, presents a weekend of interactive stage shows, arts and crafts, games, rides, grub, and grog.

★ **DECEMBER** – Downtown St. Petersburg has its own **Lighted Boat Parade**, ☎ 727-821-6443, at The Pier, along with a month-long **Snowfest** and **Holiday Fantasy**, ☎ 727-893-7441.

New Port Richey

The thickly suburban towns of Port Richey and New Port Richey run into Tarpon Springs from the north, along Highway 19. Not much of a resort area, their residential neighborhoods do hold a few attractions for visitors, nonetheless. New Port Richey itself claims an interesting downtown area arranged around a central park along the Pithlachascotee River (mercifully shortened to Cotee in local jargon). Inland, natural areas survive amid Tampa's urban sprawl and county seat Dade City merits a visit for its historic district, historical museum, and antique shops.

GETTING HERE

Highway 19 along the coast is Pasco County's main thoroughfare. Between it and I-75, **Suncoast Parkway** provides a speedy, toll-fee route from Brooksville in the north to metropolitan outskirts.

INFORMATION

For information on the Port Richey area, contact the **Pasco County Office of Tourism** at 7530 Little Rd., New Port Richey, 34654; ☎ 800-842-1873 or 727-847-8990, www.visitpasco.net.

SIGHTS & ATTRACTIONS

OF HISTORIC OR CULTURAL INTEREST

Memorabilia, photographs, antiques, and Amerindian artifacts fill **West Pasco Historical Museum**, 6431 Circle Blvd. in New Port Richey, ☎ 727-846-0680. Admission is free and hours of operation are 10-1 Tuesday and Saturday, 1-4 on Friday and Saturday.

> *FLORIDIOM: "Cracker" refers to Florida pioneers and their lifestyles. Some say the term comes from the way Cracker cowboys sounded their whips to call cattle. Others attribute it to cracked corn, a pioneer staple. The square, wooden, tin-roofed homes of the Crackers continue to influence architectural style in Florida. Built for the sub-tropical climate, they have been reinvented into what is termed "Old Florida style."*

BEACHES, PARKS & NATURAL AREAS

At the twin parks of **Anclote Gulf Park** and **Anclote River Park** on Anclote Blvd., folks gather to swim off a small sand beach, fish on a 24-hour pier (shown at right), picnic, and explore a Timucua Amerindian midden mound. Admission is free.

PERFORMING ARTS

For Broadway hits, head to the longstanding **Show Palace Dinner Theatre**, 16128 Hwy. 19, in Hudson, ☎ 888-655-7469 or 727-863-7949, www.showpalace.net.

ADVENTURES

ON WATER

FISHING

From New Port Richey, **Bounty Hunter**, ☎ 800-833-0489 or 727-843-0489, www.gianttarpon.com, takes two passengers for $600 for six-hour tarpon trips and eight-hour flats boat fishing. Extra persons up to four are charged $75 on the tarpon trips, $50 on the flats boat.

BOAT RENTALS

Rent a pontoon for a day of island-hopping along the coast from **Anclote Adventure Boat Rentals** at 5015 Hwy. 19, ☎ 727-505-3274, www.ancloteadventure.com. Rentals start at $30 an hour, $125 for four hours, $225 for eight hours. Picnic, fishing, and snorkeling rental packages are available.

BOAT CHARTERS & TOURS

Fly with the wind on a cruise with **Windsong Sailing Charters**, departing from 4927 Hwy. 19 in New Port Richey, ☎ 727-859-0213, www.windsongcharters.com. Cruises start at $225 for a half-day, $345 for a full day. Snorkel rental is $5 per person per day. Meal options are available.

© Windsong Charters

ON FOOT

The 8,300-acre **J.B. Starkey Wilderness Park**, 10500 Wilderness Park Rd., New Port Richey, ☎ 727-834-3247, is east of New Port Richey via Route 587. It has a 1.3-mile self-guided nature trail and 13 miles of hiking trails through a wide variety of Florida terrain, from wet to high and dry flatlands. In addition, there are paved biking trails, camping, and cabins. Nature programs and guided tours are also available; call for details and schedule. A day use area, open dawn to dusk, provides picnic facilities and restrooms.

St. Petersburg & Clearwater

FLORIDIOM: Flatwoods refers to a type of habitat common in Tampa environs. It is dominated by longleaf pines and saw palmetto scrub and is home to rattlesnakes, white-tailed deer, and the endangered red-cockaded woodpecker. Lightning fires are common occurrences and necessary for the survival of the flatwoods.

ON WHEELS

Opened in 2001, the **Suncoast Trail**, ☎ 813-929-1260, runs south for 42 miles from Brooksville to Tampa, paralleling Suncoast Parkway. Biking and hiking are allowed along the paved surface, which will eventually extend another 10 miles and connect to the Pinellas Trail. One trailhead lies east of New Port Richey on Route 54. A spur from J.B. Starkey Wilderness Park (see above) connects to its biking trail.

WHERE TO STAY

Along Hwy. 19, you'll find mostly economy chain motels.

HOTELS, MOTELS & RESORTS

The interior towns of Land O' Lakes and Lutz have developed a reputation for nudist and clothing-optional resorts. **Paradise Lakes Resort** at 2001 Brinson Rd. in Lutz, ☎ 866-SWIMNUDE or 813-949-9327, www.paradiselakes.com, is one of the nicer, more complete resorts of the handful you can find in these parts. Couples and families have the option to stay clothed and accommodations range from RVs to individually owned condos. The friendly community is heavily gated and encompasses five swimming pools, a heated conversation pool, a bar and nightclub, a restaurant, a fitness center, a lake, and a spa that should be open by the time you visit. Accommodations start at $75 for a lakeside studio and go up to $140 for a two-bedroom condo.

CAMPING

J.B. Starkey Wilderness Park, 10500 Wilderness Park Rd., New Port Richey, ☎ 727-834-3247 (see *On Foot*, above) rents nine cabins accommodating up to eight persons for $15 per cabin, per night. Cabins are shaded, well-spaced, and provided with a barbecue grill (cooking inside is prohibited). Sixteen primitive tent sites cost $5 per night for one family or up to five unrelated persons. Reservations for tent sites and cabins are recommended.

WHERE TO EAT

Pull up a bar stool or grab a picnic table next to the Cotee River for a taste of local color and seafood at the **Crab Shack**, 5430 Baylea Ave., ☎ 727-847-6300. Pay $6 to $12 for burgers, wraps, salads (try the gator on the green salad – a Caesar with blackened, grilled, or fried gator tail), seafood baskets, and other dinners. Or splurge on a $17 helping of crab legs. Crab cakes are a specialty – tasty and very crabby. Stay for the live evening entertainment, in case the locals and airbrushed buildings aren't entertaining enough.

Tarpon Springs & Dunedin

Sponges for sale, Tarpon Springs.

In its northern extremes, Pinellas County starts off in another world. It's a world far from the sybaritic beaches below, a world whose character was formed in the Old World lands of Greece and Scotland. Greeks arrived in fledgling, turn-of-the-century Tarpon Springs to harvest its fertile sponge crops, 30 feet below. Their influence remains strong in the town's sponge market, Greek pastry shops, onion-domed Greek Orthodox Church, and annual Epiphany Day dive for the cross.

Between Tarpon Springs and Dunedin lie small, out-of-the-way resort communities. Dunedin, named "Best Walking Town in America" by *Walking* magazine, brings another culture shock, though not as severe as Tarpon Springs. The town's Scottish heritage is most evident in its annual Highland Games and Festival, and Scottish American Society. Today, the quiet little outré-suburban town is known more for its island beaches and downtown antique shops.

Traditional Scottish dance is performed at the Highland Games.

> **FUN FACT:** Named in 1882, Dunedin means "castle on the rock" in Scottish. The town is sister city to Stirling, Scotland.

GETTING HERE

Highway 19 and its offspring that starts between New Port Richey and Tarpon Springs, **Alternate Highway 19**, provide the main routes of transportation through the region in a north-south direction. In Tarpon Springs, **Dodecanese Blvd.** and **Tarpon Ave.** are the main streets that are of interest to visitors. In Dunedin, **Main Street** takes motorists off Alternate Highway 19 and into its downtown heart.

WEEKEND ADVENTURE ITINERARY

- **FRIDAY:** Arrive at Tarpon Springs in the morning. Visit the sponge docks, Konger Tarpon Springs Aquarium, St. Nicholas Greek Orthodox Church, and the historic district. Have lunch at Costa's. In the afternoon, head south to Dunedin to visit Honeymoon Island State Recreation Area and Caladesi Island State Park. Drive to Clearwater Beach for dinner at Bob Heilman's Beachcomber. Catch sunset at Pier 60. Spend the night in Clearwater Beach.

- **SATURDAY:** Spend the morning on the beach. Have lunch at Frenchy's Rockaway Grill. Tour Clearwater Marine Aquarium in the afternoon and take the Sea Life Safari. Drive to Redington Beach for dinner at The Lobster Pot. Spend the night in Clearwater Beach or Sand Key.

Frenchy's, Clearwater Beach

- **SUNDAY:** Drive to downtown St. Petersburg. Tour the Salvador Dali Museum or Florida International Museum, and The Pier. Have lunch at Baywalk. Drive to Fort De Soto Park in the afternoon or hop aboard a charter to Egmont Key. Spend time on the beach, fishing, hiking, snorkeling on Egmont Key, or touring the fort. Drive to Pass-A-Grille for dinner at The Wharf or Hurricane Restaurant. Spend the night camping at Fort De Soto Park or in history-tinged luxury at the Don CeSar Resort.

INFORMATION

The **Tarpon Springs Chamber of Commerce** distributes information on the area at 11 E. Orange St., Tarpon Springs, 34689, ☎ 727-937-6109, www.tarponsprings.com. It's open Tuesday-Saturday, 10:30-4:30, Sunday, 11-5.

The **Dunedin Chamber of Commerce** is located at 301 Main St, Dunedin, 34698, ☎ 727-733-3197, www.dunedin-fl.com. It is open 8:30-4:30 on weekdays.

SIGHTS & ATTRACTIONS

Tarpon Springs

BEACHES, PARKS & NATURAL AREAS

A popular destination for boating beach-lovers, **Anclote Key Preserve State Park**, ☎ 727-469-5942, has no road connections to the mainland, which keeps it pristine and removed from the masses. In 2003, thanks to fundraising efforts, its historic lighthouse was re-lit. Sandbars north and south attract snorkelers and beachcombers.

East of town, **Lake Tarpon** is headquarters for watersports. **Anderson Park** on Hwy. 19, ☎ 727-943-4085, provides access for bass fishermen and other water-lovers. There are also picnic grounds and a nature trail. Open daily, 7-sunset.

Fred Howard Park, 1700 Sunset Dr., ☎ 727-943-4081, hides far from the mainstream in Tarpon Springs, but is the best beach in these parts that is accessible from the mainland. The beautifully canopied grounds are a favorite for picnickers. A mile-long causeway, popular with windsurfers, delivers you to sand. The park opens daily at sunrise and closes at 9 pm.

The beach at Fred Howard Park.

Brooker Creek Preserve, ☎ 727-453-6900, www.friendsofbrooker creekpreserve.org, www.pinellascounty.org/environment/, on Route 582, sets aside 8,500 acres for wildlife and environmental education. You can see the preserve along a series of trails. A hands-on Environmental Education Center contains awesome video and interactive exhibits, including a super-sized gopher tortoise you can climb through and a holographic film about the lands' history.

St. Petersburg & Clearwater

FAMILY FUN

Konger Tarpon Springs Aquarium, 850 Dodecanese Blvd., ☎ 727-938-5378, www. tarponspringsaquarium.com, is small but intriguing. The centerpiece is a 120,000-gallon reef-shark tank where divers do feeding demonstrations. Other tanks and exhibits deal with moray eels, seahorses, octopuses, alligators, and baby sharks, and include a touch tank. Hours are 10-5, Monday-Saturday; noon-5, Sunday. Admission is $5.25 for adults, $4.50 for seniors, $3.25 for children aged three-11, and free for toddlers under age three.

Stingray feeding.

© Konger Tarpon Springs Aquarium

LOCAL COLOR

The true measure of Greek influence in Tarpon Springs rises above the skyline with onion domes of **St. Nicholas Greek Orthodox Church**, 36 N. Pinellas Ave., ☎ 727-937-3540. Visitors are allowed in when services are not in session. It's a stunning example of Greek ecclesiastical architecture and baroque excess, styled after St. Sofia's in Istanbul.

Mural of sponge diver at Tarpon Springs Sponge Exchange.

Soak up some local Greek culture at the **Sponge Docks** on Dodecanese Blvd. Here, along narrow European-style streets, you'll find a somewhat touristy scene of charter boats, souvenir and sponge shops, Greek eateries, and other sights.

The slightly decrepit **Sponge-orama**, 510 Dodecanese Blvd., ☎ 727-943-2164, gives an interesting overview of sponging and local Greek heritage. Exhibits explain the different kinds of sponges, the dangers of sponging, and the role of religion in the Greek community. A free 26-minute film presentation tells about sponge-diving. Admission is free.

St. Petersburg & Clearwater

View from Anclote Key Beach © Amanda Martin

Dunedin

 Author favorites are indicated with a star.

■ OF HISTORIC OR CULTURAL INTEREST

Housed in the 1920s town train depot, **Dunedin Historical Society Museum**, 349 Main St, ☎ 727-736-1176, www.dunedinmuseum. org, is open 10-4, Tuesday-Saturday. It features railroad and historical displays and rotating Florida exhibits. Admission is $2 for anyone over age 12.

■ BEACHES, PARKS & NATURAL AREAS

Dunedin's most popular attractions are its two barrier island state parks. **Honeymoon Island State Park**, Causeway Blvd., ☎ 727-469-5942, www. floridastateparks.org/honey moonisland, the second most-visited state park in Florida in 2005-2006, is accessible by car and is well-loved by bird watchers and other nature lovers for its trails and populations of res-

ident and migrant feathered friends. It has a beach where you can swim and fish, as well as a separate pet beach. Café Honeymoon feeds the hungry, and a nature center is in the park's future. Admission is $5 per car of eight persons or fewer, $3 for one person in a car, and $1 for pedestrians, cyclists, and extra person. It's open daily, 8-sunset.

 The beach at nearby **Caladesi Island State Park**, ☎ 727-469-5918, www. floridastateparks.org/ caladesiisland, is far superior, however, but accessible mainly by boat. Three miles long, it is powdery and sheer white. On the mangroves side of the island, picnic grounds, bathhouses, a food concession, a play-ground, and docks accommodate visitors, who arrive by private boat or public ferry. Between the shores, you can explore barrier island ecology via sand paths and boardwalks. The park is open every day, 8-sunset. A ferry departs hourly from Honeymoon Island (see *On Water*, below). Maximum stay on the island for ferry arrivals is four hours. Admission by private boat is $4 for up to eight people; kayakers $1 each; overnight boat fee is $20.

FAMILY FUN

Kids are urged to explore contemporary art with all the senses and their parents at **David L. Mason Children's Arts Museum** in the Dunedin Fine Arts Center, 1143 Michigan Blvd., ☎ 727-298-3322, www.dfac.org. Exhibit themes change annually. Hours are Monday-Friday, 10-5; Saturday, 10-2; and Sunday, 1-4. Summer hours may vary. Admission is $4; seniors pay $3.50; free for children aged two and under.

Dunedin Stadium's Grant Field is spring training grounds for the Toronto Blue Jays in March. Call ☎ 727-733-9302, http://toronto.bluejays.mlb.com, for ticket and schedule information.

ADVENTURES

ON WATER

At Tarpon Springs, being out on the water has constituted a way of life for more than a century. Fishing, sponging, and boating remain a means of livelihood as well as a means for recreation.

FISHING

South of Tarpon Springs, Crystal Beach's **fishing pier** reaches out from an old-fashioned park on Gulf Drive N.

Capt. Dave Graham, Tarpon Springs City Marina, ☎ 727-938-7371, www.florida-fishing-trips.com, will take you out after snook, tarpon, redfish, trout, and cobia for $300 for four hours, $400 for six hours, $500 eight hours. Tarpon fishing tours are $700. Prices apply to up to three persons. Fourth passenger pays $100.

Stop at **Dunedin Fishing Center**, 2436 Bayshore Blvd., ☎ 727-738-5628, www.igfa.org/ws.asp, for bait, tackle, and supplies before you hit the state parks.

BOAT RAMPS

Boaters can launch into **Lake Tarpon** at **Anderson Park** (see *Sights & Attractions*, above) for freshwater fishing.

BOAT RENTALS

Rent a kayak or sailboat at **Sail Honeymoon** on the Dunedin Causeway, ☎ 727-734-0392, www.sailhoneymoon.com. Paddle an ocean kayak to the 3¼-mile kayak nature trail that leads through the interior of Caladesi Island. Rates start at $25 for two hours for one-person vessels, $35 for two-person craft. Rates for trimarans, catamarans, and other sailboats start at $50 for two hours. Instruction is available with rentals.

BOAT CHARTERS & TOURS

Learn the history and methods of sponge-diving on a half-hour trip with **St. Nicholas Boat Line**, departing from the Tarpon Springs Sponge Docks, 693 Dodecanese Blvd., ☎ 727-942-6425. A diver dons traditional diving suit and helmet to demonstrate sponge harvesting. Rates are $8 for adults, $4 for children aged six-12.

The **Honeymoon Island Ferry** to Caladesi Island, ☎ 727-734-1501, costs $9 for adults and $5.50 for children aged four-12. The ferry runs every hour (every half-hour on busy weekends) between 10 and 5. Maximum stay on the island is four hours.

PADDLING

Simply Kayaking, ☎ 727-481-0184, www.simplykayaking.com, runs daily guided tours of Tarpon Springs' Sponge Docks and bayous, the Anclote River, and local estuaries. Cost for a two-hour or sunset tour is $49 per person, for a half-day trip it's $69.

© Sharon Sagnella

SNORKELING & DIVING

Specializing in manatee trips, **Narcosis Scuba Center** at 926 N. Pinellas Ave. in Tarpon Springs, ☎ 727-934-6474, www.narcosis scuba.com, is a full-service dive center offering charters, rentals, and PADI certification courses. A maximum of six divers goes out on each boat. Manatee trips cost $55 for a one-tank dive and guide.

Sunny Seas Scuba, 6615 Hwy. 19 S. in New Port Richey, ☎ 727-849-2478, charges $95 for a two-tank dive.

ON WHEELS

The Energy Conservatory, 745 Main St., Dunedin, ☎ 727-736-4432, http://energybicycle.com/index.cfm, claims to be Florida's biggest bicycle shop. It's close to the Pinellas Trail and rents bikes for $15 a day. Hours are 10-6, Tuesday-Friday; 9-4:30, Saturday; 11-4 on Sunday.

ON FOOT

Caladesi Island has a three-mile trail through scrub and beach communities. Paved with soft sand, it takes longer than you'd think and can be hard on leg muscles. Wear shoes with support.

ECO-ADVENTURES

Learn how cow hunters once dominated central Florida and intriguing details about local flora on a two-hour open-bus tour with **J.B. Starkey's Flatwoods Adventures**, northeast of Tarpon Springs in Odessa at 12959 Rte. 54, just west of Gunn Hwy., ☎ 877-734-WILD, www.flatwoodsadventures.com. On a good day, you'll see wild turkeys and boars. You're guaranteed a 'gator sighting; they've rounded one up in a pen just for your camera. Still a working ranch, Flatwoods Adventures gives eco-tours of its pasturelands, alligator caves, cypress swamp, and palmetto flatwoods. The guide does hands-on talks about the medicinal and other uses of local plants and life on a ranch, then and now. Admission is $16.70 for adults, $9.28 for children aged three-12, and $15.64 for seniors, including tax.

SHOPPING

Tarpon Springs and, even more so, Dunedin are recognized for antiques shopping. Tarpon Springs' historic **antiques district** is centered around **Tarpon Ave**.

In Dunedin, the majority of antiques shops are found on **Main Street** and side streets. The town holds **antiques fairs** every spring and fall.

An Olde Feedstore at 735 Railroad Ave., Dunedin, ☎ 727-736-8115, is something of a museum, with store displays in period settings. Open Monday-Saturday, 10-5; Sunday, noon-5.

WHERE TO STAY

 Author favorites are indicated with a star.

ACCOMMODATIONS PRICE KEY		
Rates are per room, per night, double occupancy. Price ranges described for each property often do not take into account penthouses and other exceptional, high-priced accommodations.	$	Up to $75
	$$	$75 to $150
	$$$	$151 to $250
	$$$$	$251 and up

▨ HOTELS, MOTELS & RESORTS

Tops for golfing and family fun in this area, **Innisbrook Resort & Golf Club**, 36750 US Hwy. 19 North, Palm Harbor, ☎ 800-456-2000 or 727-942-2000, www.innisbrook golfresort.com, boasts its own Loch Ness water theme park. Its rooms and suites look out onto lush links containing 72 holes of top-rated golf. A fitness center, kids' playground and program, and 11 Har-Tru tennis courts round out Innisbrook's athletic facilities. $$$$

Water adventurers will enjoy the location of **Best Western Yacht Harbor Inn**, next to the Dunedin's city marina and its coterie of deep-sea fishing charters at 150 Marina Plaza, ☎ 800-447-4728 or 727-733-4121, www.advantus corp.com. Also on the property is a fine restaurant and lounge, a casual café, and pool. Rooms have a coffee machine, microwave, and small refrigerator; studios have a kitchenette. $$-$$$$

INNS/BED & BREAKFASTS

Gracious and handsome, the **Spring Bayou Inn**, 32 W. Tarpon Ave., Tarpon Springs, ☎ 727-938-9333, www.springbayouinn.com, occupies one of Tarpon Springs' first homes, built around the turn of the century. From its wraparound porch you can watch the goings-on in the town's historic district. Seven rooms (one with shared bath) are rentable by the day, week, or month. $-$$

New and pretty next to the Dunedin RV Resort (see below), **The Blue Moon Inn** at 2910 Alt. 19 N. in Dunedin, ☎ 800-345-7504 or 727-784-3719, rents roomy suites with kitchenettes for reasonable prices. Besides breakfast, amenities include a swimming pool, Internet access, and a lovely patio view. $$.

Just off downtown's Main Street in Dunedin, **Meranova Guest Inn** at 458 Virginia Ln., ☎ 727-733-9248, www.meranova.com, feels

homey yet designer-artsy. Its eight cottage suites each have their own private entrances and efficiency kitchens. Rates include a three-course breakfast served to your room each morning. Children must be older than 14 to stay at Meranova. $$-$$$

© Meranova Inn

CAMPING

Clean and pretty **Dunedin RV Resort**, 2920 Alt. Hwy. 19 N., Dunedin, ☎ 800-345-7504 or 727-784-3719, www.campingfriend.com/dunedinrvresort, charges $42-$50 for a two-person RV site and a full complement of facilities: heated pool, rec room, playground, shuffleboard, horseshoes, and complete utility hookups. Weekly and monthly rates are available.

WHERE TO EAT

TARPON SPRINGS

Somewhat less tourist-ridden than the restaurants on Dodecanese Blvd., **Costa's Restaurant**, 521 Athens St., ☎ 727-938-6890, advertises "Mama's Greek style." In the simple lunchroom setting, it dishes up Hellenic authenticity, along with some American concessions. Pickled octopus, fried smelt, gyro sandwiches, *dolmades*, and lamb shanks are a few of the oddities and specialties. Try the marinated chicken or pork grilled with peppers and onions and topped with feta and tomato sauce. Lunch ($5-$13) and dinner ($8-$14) are served daily.

South of Tarpon Springs just off the highway in Palm Harbor, **Thirsty Marlin**, 1023 Florida Ave., ☎ 727-784-3469, www.thirstymarlincom.verizonsupersite.com/location, reels 'em in with a carefree attitude, Bahamian influence, indoor and outdoor seating, and casual eats of the fin and hoof variety. Start with the nicely spiced conch chowder or a fried green tomato salad topped with Gorgonzola, then go for a Grand Slam two-pound burger, cracked conch, ribs, or fried grouper cheeks. Sandwiches and entrées on the all-day menu run $7-$20.

Between Tarpon Springs and Dunedin, west of Alt. Hwy. 19, (and 1, 150 miles from New York City, according to a signpost) lies the tiny, free-spirited town of Ozona. **Molly Goodheads Raw Bar & Seafood**, Orange St. at Tampa Rd., ☎ 727-786-6255, www.mollygoodheads.com, puts the town on the map with its idiosyncratic Cracker house décor and great eats. Guests can sit outdoors on the porch or indoors where it's a combination of country home, with walls covered in flowered wallpaper, and casual bar, with walls covered in license plates and photos. Sandwiches, pasta, steak, and seafood platters run $6-$15 and are served at lunch and dinner daily. Recommendable: the grouper sandwich, and Key lime pie (the real thing!).

DUNEDIN

Dunedin's definitive fine dining experience sits downtown at 315 Main St. **Black Pearl**, ☎ 727-734-DINE, is open daily for dinner. It dabbles in Continental style with such offerings as duck liver pâté, butternut squash ravioli, wild mushroom ragout, shrimp and roasted red pepper scampi, and rack of lamb. Entrées range from $20 to $30.

In the setting of an old Dunedin home, diners dig in to seafood specialties such as Coco Cabana shrimp and cornmeal fried catfish, along with pasta, salads, and sandwiches at **Sea Sea Riders**, 221 Main St., ☎ 727-734-1445. It opens daily for lunch, Sunday brunch, and dinner. Luncheon sandwiches and entrées range from $6 to $9; dinner entrées, $13 to $17.

Clearwater's famous beach.

Clearwater & Clearwater Beach

Often overshadowed by the more household names of St. Petersburg and St. Pete Beach, the Clearwater area is the place to head if you're serious about spending days on and in the water. Its beach facilities are top-notch and its marinas are beehives of sail-away activity.

Clearwater itself is principally big-city. Its main concession to tourism is a 100-year-old grande dame wooden hotel, the Belleview Biltmore Resort & Spa (see page 104). On its eastern coast, fronting Tampa Bay, the community of **Safety Harbor** is the county's birthplace – a quiet spot for boaters, picnickers, and spa-goers.

Clearwater Beach occupies all of Clearwater Beach Island, as well as part of neighboring Sand Key. Extensive upgrade work is underway centering around a Beach Walk and including new high-end resort-and-spa complexes.

GETTING HERE

Gulf to Bay Blvd. (Rte. 60) is the major road running east-west. It connects to the **Courtney Campbell Causeway** and Tampa at its eastern extreme, penetrates downtown Clearwater (where its name changes to Cleveland St.) and, at its western extreme, crosses Memorial Causeway to the new roundabout at Clearwater Beach. It intersects with **Gulfview Blvd.** (Rte. 699), the island's major road. South of the Clearwater Pass Bridge, the road's name changes to Gulf Blvd. **Mandalay Ave.** is the northern extension to Gulfview Blvd., where you'll find most of the shopping.

> **TIP:** *The Clearwater area is closely policed. Mind the speed limit signs (25 mph at the beach), and be sure to feed your meter.*

Clearwater Yellow Cab, ☎ 727-799-2222, provides transportation to and from the Tampa and St. Petersburg/Clearwater airports.

■ AROUND TOWN

The Jolley Trolley, office at 483 Mandalay Ave., #213, ☎ 727-445-1200, www.thejolleytrolley. com, travels around Clearwater Beach and downtown Clearwater. Tours begin and end at the trolley office on Mandalay Ave., with pickups every 30 minutes, daily. Fare is $1.25 (tokens available at office) each, 60¢ for children aged four to 10.

INFORMATION

For more information on the area, contact the **Clearwater Regional Chamber of Commerce**, 1130 Cleveland St., Clearwater, 33755, ☎ 800-425-3279 or 727-461-0011, www.visitclearwaterflorida.com, open 8:30-5, Monday-Friday; or visit the Clearwater/Pinellas Suncoast Welcome Center at 3350 Courtney Campbell Causeway., ☎ 727-726-1547, open from 9 to 5 Monday-Saturday, 10-5 Sunday.

You can reach the **Clearwater Beach Chamber of Commerce Welcome Center** at 333C South Gulfview Blvd, Clearwater Beach, 33767, ☎ 888-799-3199 or 727-447-7600, www.beachchamber. com. Hours are 9-3, Monday-Friday, 9-2 Saturday.

SIGHTS & ATTRACTIONS

BEACHES, PARKS & NATURAL AREAS

Pier 60 entrance

Clearwater Beach has some of the widest, most gorgeous beaches in the area, offering outdoor entertainment in a variety just as broad. **Pier 60 Park**, at the intersection of Causeway and Gulfview boulevards, is most active, with its fishing pier (see *On Water*, below), ☎ 727-462-6466, and continuous volleyball, for which Clearwater Beach has a reputation (national play-offs are often held there). You'll also find lifeguards, concessions for food, beach supplies, watersports rentals, and a sheltered playground with very cool equipment. City renovation plans include a playground expansion project with interactive fountains. Each night around sunset, artisans, musicians, clowns, and performers put on a show (☎ 727-449-1036 for updated recorded info about this event). You pay $1.50-$2.50 an hour to park in large lots at each end of the beach.

Across the south-end bridge to Sand Key lies Clearwater Beach's most highly rated recreational area, **Sand Key Park**, 1060 Gulf Blvd., ☎ 727-588-4852. Its 95 acres contain lots of green spaces with picnic areas and playgrounds (one for dogs!). The wide, sugar-sand beach is patrolled by lifeguards. Parking: $1 an hour.

FAMILY FUN

Clearwater Marine Aquarium, 249 Windward Passage, off Memorial Cause-way, ☎ 888-239-9414, ext. 31 or 727-441-1790, www.CMAquarium.org, conducts research and rehabili-

© Carol Buchanan/Dreamstime

tates marine mammals, river otters, and sea turtles. A touch tank, aquariums, and other tanks hold local and exotic sealife, including mangroves, seahorses, baby sharks, dolphins, playful otters, Kemp's ridley sea turtles, and a loggerhead turtle. Be sure to catch some of the educational presentations, especially the one about dolphins. The center offers on-the-water sealife encounters (see *Eco-Adventures*, below). Admission is $9 for adults, $6.50 for kids aged three-12. Hours are Monday-Friday, 9-5; Saturday, 9-4; and Sunday, 11-4.

FLORIDIOM: Loggerhead sea turtles, mammoth sea turtles as prehistoric as the sea itself, bulldoze ashore local beaches from late April to September to paddle-fin holes in the sand where they drop their hundred-or-so eggs. Adult loggerheads weigh in at up to 300 pounds.

From Pac-Man to virtual reality boxing, **Beach Gameland** at 483 Mandalay Ave. on Clearwater Beach, ☎ 727-444-4494, www.beachgameland.com, sells digital keys in varying value increments to use in its games.

Send the older ones off to race go-carts or bumper boats, take the tots to Playland, and round 'em all up for pizza afterward. **Celebration Station**, 2½ miles north of Rte. 60 at 24546 Hwy. 19, ☎ 727-791-1799, www.celebrationstation.com, also has batting cages, miniature golf, and video games. Open Monday-Thursday, 10 am-11 pm; Friday-Saturday, 10 am-midnight; Sunday, noon-11 pm. Fees are per activity; packages available.

© Celebration Station

Besides putt-putt, **Congo River Mini-Golf**, 20060 Hwy. 19 N., ☎ 727-797-4222, has a live iguana exhibit, a game arcade, and (shamefully – it's a bad idea to teach kids they can feed alligators) a 'gator-feeding attraction. Admission is $10 for 18 holes. Open Sunday-Thursday from 10am-11pm, Friday and Saturday from 10am-midnight. Unlimited golf costs $13 all day.

On Clearwater Beach, **Captain Bligh's Landing Mini-Golf**, 630 S. Gulfview Blvd., ☎ 727-443-6348, has a pirate ship theme and large game room. Open 10am-midnight daily. Cost is $9 for adults, $8 for children under age 12, including tax.

ADVENTURES

ON WATER

The possibilities for on-the-sea adventure are practically endless on Clearwater Beach.

FISHING

Fishing enthusiasts dangle their bait from **Pier 60** on Gulfview Beach (see *Sights & Attractions*, above), at the intersection of Causeway Blvd. and Gulfview Blvd., ☎ 727-462-6466. It contains all the shops and facilities necessary for a successful day of fishing; you provide the catches. Admission for fishing from the pier runs $5-$6.30; 50¢ just for walking. You can rent rods for $17 per day.

For half- and full-day fishing charters, check at the **Clearwater Marina**, 25 Causeway Blvd., ☎ 727-462-6954. Guides and party boats line the dock; you can just walk around and "shop" for the one that fits your needs. A bait house, shops, and a restaurant complete the complex.

Two C's II at Clearwater Marina slip #27, ☎ 888-234-7435 or 727-797-0784, www.fishtwocs.com, takes parties of up to six persons aboard a 37-foot custom fast cat for deep-sea and offshore fishing. Cost starts at $400 for four hours.

Ride aboard modern, comfortable catamarans on the **Double Eagle III** and **II** at Clearwater Marina, ☎ 727-446-1653. Cost is $43 for adults and $27 for children 13 and under for a half-day of deep-sea fishing; for all day, it's $63 and $50.

BOAT RAMPS

There's a boat ramp into Clearwater Harbor at Clearwater Beach Recreation Center on **Bay Esplanade**, and into Tampa Bay in Safety Harbor at **Phillippe Park**, 2525 Phillippe Pkwy., ☎ 727-669-1947,

St. Petersburg & Clearwater

which has extensive picnic facilities. Another ramp, at **Marina Park**, has limited picnic facilities and docking.

BOAT CHARTERS & TOURS

Many day-boating trips launch from Clearwater Beach Marina, headed to Caladesi Island (see *Sights & Attractions*, above), Sarasota, and points beyond. One popular thing is cruises offering dolphin encounters. You are not allowed to feed dolphins on these trips, however.

The **Original Dolphin Encounter Cruise** departs from Clearwater Beach Marina, ☎ 727-442-7433, www.dolphinencounter.org, and guarantees sightings or the next trip is free. The 75-minute tours cost $19.85 for adults and $11.45 for children aged four to 12, and

includes unlimited beverages. The double-decker *Clearwater Express* does several tours throughout the day. Call or visit their website for times.

For something much faster, **Sea Screamer** at marina slip 15, ☎ 727-447-7200, www.SeaScreamer.com, charges $20 for adults, $15 for children aged 12 and under, tax included. The hour-long tour takes in dolphins, the beaches, and open Gulf waters. Rides aboard the 73-foot speedboat depart daily at noon, 2, and 4, with an extra tour at 6 in summer.

The **Show Queen** at Clearwater Beach Marina, ☎ 800-772-4479 or 727-461-3113, www.showqueen.com, hosts narrated daily lunch, sightseeing, tropical party, and dinner sunset cruises aboard a 65-foot three-deck riverboat. Lunch fares are $19.95 adults, $9.95 children; sightseeing, $10.95/$6.95 days, and $12.95/$8.95 evenings; sunset and party, $29.95 and $14.95. Tax and gratuities are extra.

BOAT RENTALS

KID-FRIENDLY: *Your best bet for kids is* **Captain Memo's Pirate Cruise at the marina,** *Dock 3,* ☎ *727-446-2587, www.captainmemo.com. Dressing as pirates, face-painting, water-pistol battles, storytelling, and cannon-shooting are part of the regime. The boat sets sail for two hours at 10 (except on Sundays) and 2. Cruises cost $32 for adults, $27 for seniors and those aged 13-17, and $22 for children under 13. Adults pay $35 for the evening champagne cruises. Complimentary soft drinks, beer, and wine.*

Clearwater Boat Rentals, ☎ 727-442-8601, rents pontoons for $249 for four hours, $349 for eight; and fishing boats for $199-$269 four hours, $299-$369 eight hours.

Starlite Majesty at the marina, ☎ 800-444-4814 or 727-462-2628, www.starlitecruises.com, hosts luncheon, sightseeing, entertainment, and dinner and dance cruises aboard a modern, three-deck yacht. Tickets cost $11.90-$17.55 for adults for lunch and dinner cruises; meal is extra. Tax is not included.

With a fleet of more than 40 boats available to the public, the **Clearwater Community Sailing Center** at 1001 Gulf Blvd., ☎ 727-517-7776, www.clearwatercommunity sailing.org, offers sailing programs to people of all abilities, including individual and family rates and 12-hour packages, which can be used over several days. It is open Tuesday through Sunday, 9-6.

© Kai Lani

Take a two-hour dolphin or sunset sail aboard a 50-foot catamaran with **Kai Lani** at slip #49, ☎ 727-446-6778, www. kailanicat.com, for $40 each adult, $15 per child.

SNORKELING & DIVING

Rock ledges, underwater sinkholes, artificial reefs, and submerged vessels provide variety for divers, and visibility can reach 60 feet. Most sites are well offshore. The Clearwater Reef is one of the area's largest and most popular artificial reefs.

WAVERUNNERS & PARASAILING

Parasails are a gay and common sight along Clearwater's beaches. You'll find concessions at the Clearwater Marina (see *On Water*, above). They generally charge according to height of ride, something like $50 for 600 feet, $60 for 800 feet, and $80 for 1,000-1,200 feet. Some include an optional free fall, for the ultimate thrill. Try **Parasail City** at slip #2, ☎ 727-449-0566, or **Sky Screamer Parasail** at slips 8 and 9, ☎ 727-449-2454.

For WaveRunner tours, check with **Gulfside Watercraft Adventurers** at slip #25, ☎ 727-485-4544. Cost is $95 for one hour.

ON WHEELS

Joggers, inline skaters, and cyclists take to the 34-mile (and growing) **Pinellas Trail**, ☎ 727-464-8200, www.pinellascounty.org/trailgd, which begins in downtown St. Petersburg and heads north

St. Petersburg & Clearwater

through Clearwater and beyond along an old railroad route through the historic districts of Dunedin and Tarpon Springs.

For your extreme kids, **Central Skate Park**, 6140 Ulmerton Rd. in Clearwater, ☎ 727-523-0785, www.skateboardpark.com, offers indoor ramps and an outdoor street course. The indoor arena has a cool foam pit where they can practice their skateboard and inline-skate jumps. Cost is $10 per session, which is about three hours, or $15 a day.

ECO-ADVENTURES

Sea Life Safari Cruises, ☎ 800-444-4814 or 727-462-2628, www. CMAquarium.org, visits a barrier island and bird sanctuary and puts guests "in touch" with creatures retrieved by trawl net. The two-hour tour costs $17.75 for adults, $11.45 for children aged three-12. There's a discount for passengers who pay to visit the aquarium in conjunction with the cruise. Tour boats depart three times daily from the aquarium and Clearwater Marina slip 58.

SHOPPING

Largo Mall, Ulmerton Rd. and Seminole Blvd., ☎ 727-587-0100, offers numerous discount stores.

Countryside Mall is located at the corner of Hwy. 19 and Rte. 580, ☎ 727-796-1079. It has stores, restaurants, and movie theaters.

WHERE TO STAY

ACCOMMODATIONS PRICE KEY

Rates are per room, per night, double occupancy. Price ranges described for each property often do not take into account penthouses and other exceptional, high-priced accommodations.		
	$	Up to $75
	$$	$75 to $150
	$$$	$151 to $250
	$$$$	$251 and up

CLEARWATER

HOTELS & RESORTS

To stay in grand style, revel in the Old-Florida aristocracy of the **Belleview Biltmore Resort & Spa** at 25 Belleview Blvd. in Clearwater, ☎ 800-237-8947 or 727-373-3000, www.belleviewbiltmore.com. One of the state's few surviving wooden hotels, it was

© Belleview Biltmore

built in the 1890s with wide verandas, distinctive gables, nearly two miles of hallways, and Victorian airs. 244 rooms, swimming pool with waterfalls, spa, and gracious lobby and dining areas. Packages are available. $$$$

Across the peninsula on Tampa Bay, **Safety Harbor Resort and Spa** at 104 N. Bayshore Dr., ☎ 888-237-8772 or 727-726-1161, www.safetyharborspa.com, is the historic pride of the bay coast. The low-slung, Mediterranean villa-style property boasts one of Florida's best spa and gym facilities. Packages available. $$$-$$$$

CLEARWATER BEACH

Clearwater Beach is evolving in an upward pattern as work on the boardwalk means tearing down some of the old and building luxury resorts. But affordable places remain, especially on the bayside.

HOTELS & MOTELS

Hilton Clearwater Beach Resort, 400 Mandalay Ave., ☎ 800-753-3954 or 727-461-3222, www.hiltonclearwaterbeachresort.com, purveys all the luxury and service the name implies. Rooms and suites in tropical colors are plush and equipped with coffeemakers (microwaves in suites only). Besides beachfront recreation, its amenities include two pools, restaurants, bars, a kid's program, volleyball, soccer nets, watersports rentals, and a tiki bar on the beach. It's next to Pier 60, suitable for those who love beach bustle. $$-$$$$

High-rising **Marriott Suites** at 1201 Gulf Blvd., ☎ 800-228-9290 or 727-596-1100, www.clearwaterbeachmarriottsuites.com, across from Sand Key Park on the bay, has taken the old Radisson hotel a step up. It offers 220 roomy bay-view two-room suites, as well as cabanas. Each suite contains a refrigerator, wireless Internet access, microwave, coffeemaker, and wet bar. There's a day spa and a waterfront restaurant named **Watercolour**. Waterfalls give the hotel's pool an exotic feel. A kid's clubhouse, watersports, and daily scheduled activities make this a popular family choice. $$$

© Marriott Suites

St. Petersburg & Clearwater

WHERE TO EAT

When compared to prices in Tampa and on islands to the south, restaurants in Pinellas are refreshingly reasonable. And the seafood is about as fresh as it gets, short of catching it yourself.

Beachgoers will find **Frenchy's Rockaway Grill**, 7 Rockaway St., ☎ 727-446-4844, www.frenchyson line.com, convenient, tropical, and lively. Seafood again, and the very freshest, prepared grilled, blackened, and jerk-style. Grouper rules. Seating is outdoors on the beach with a view of waves or a volleyball game, or inside where it's cooler and equally colorful. The attitude is at the same time old-island and fresh. There is live music Thursday-Sunday nights. It's open daily for lunch and dinner; prices for sandwiches, salads, and dinners run $7-$16.

Near Clearwater Marine Aquarium, **Island Way Grill** at 20 Island Way, ☎ 727-461-6617, www.islandwaygrill.com, is the popular choice for Pacific Rim-style grilled meats and seafood in a busy, ultra-modern designer setting. Start with the Thai mussels in coconut milk broth or sushi, enjoy the refreshing house salad with entrées such as the excellent citrus-seared scallops with sweet and sour glaze over sesame-lime noodles, meatloaf with wasabi mashed potatoes, or Korean BBQ T-Bone. Open daily for dinner, its entrées range from $10 to $30. Also open for Sunday brunch.

For something more classic, try **Bob Heilman's Beachcomber** at 447 Mandalay Ave., ☎ 727-442-4144. It's a popular choice for American cuisine. Back-to-the-farm chicken with all the fixings is an all-time favorite. Seafood and prime meat dishes run a gamut from Everglades frog legs to Wisconsin veal piccata. A large variety of specials are offered daily. People dress up and the setting is on the elegant side – a refined respite from the beach bustle. Prices are surprisingly affordable. Lunches are $7-$17 for sandwiches and salads; Dinners are $9-$30. Open for lunch and dinner daily. Dinner reservations recommended.

NIGHTLIFE

Whether you're on spring break, enjoying retirement, or somewhere in-between, Clearwater offers entertainment for your evening hours.

Ruth Eckerd Hall at 1111 McMullen Booth Rd., Clearwater, ☎ 800-875-8682 or 727-791-7400, www.rutheckerdhall.com, presents the top traveling entertainment in an acoustically sound environment – from Broadway shows to country singers and comedians. It is home to the Florida Orchestra and often hosts the Florida Opera. Call for schedule and ticket prices.

Several restaurants and bars keep the beach hopping with live music, especially in spring and summer. **Frenchy's Rockaway Grill** (see *Where to Eat*, above), 7 Rockaway St., Clearwater Beach, ☎ 727-446-4844, features a beach setting and live music Thursday-Sunday.

The best party appears at **Pier 60 Park**, (see *Sights & Attractions*, above) 10 Pier 60 Dr., Clearwater Beach, ☎ 727-449-1036, www.sunsetsatpier60.com, every evening two hours before and after sunset. In addition to live music, artisans, clowns, and other performers entertain.

Sand Key Communities

Twelve-mile-long Sand Key begins in the north at the bridge to Clearwater Beach, which occupies a few miles at the island's top. South from there, a series of communities in varying degrees of commercial development stretch to John's Pass and Sand Key's most developed and water-adventuresome town, Madeira Beach. A few of the towns through which you pass, such as Belleair Beach, are blink-of-an-eye residential settlements. Others, such as Redington Beach, Redington Shores, Indian Shores, and Indian Rocks Beach, offer visitors beach and old-island character, as well as a slew of fun-time activities, particularly fishing.

This stretch of island isn't among the best beaches in Pinellas County. On the private communities, there are no public accesses. In Madeira Beach, beaches have a distinctly metropolitan feel.

GETTING HERE

Gulf Blvd. (Rte. 699) runs down the middle of 12-mile-long Sand Key. Four bridges cross from Sand Key to the mainland. They are located (from north to south) in Belleair Shores at West Bay Drive (Rte. 686), in Indian Rocks Beach at Walsingham/Ulmerton Rd. (Rte. 688), in Indian Shores at Park Blvd. (Rte. 694), and in Madeira Beach at 150th Ave., which intersects with Seminole Blvd. (Rte. 595) and Alternate Highway 19 on the mainland.

INFORMATION

Stop by or call the local offices of **Tampa Bay Beaches Chamber of Commerce**. You can also check their website for information, www.tampabaybeaches.com or ☎ 800-944-1847. **The Madeira Beach/John's Pass Village office**, 12902 Village Blvd, ☎ 727-397-1667, is open Monday-Friday, 10-4.

SIGHTS & ATTRACTIONS

INDIAN ROCKS BEACH

OF HISTORIC OR CULTURAL INTEREST

A collection of local historical memorabilia is found in a vintage home known as the Indian **Rocks Beach Historical Museum** at 203 Fourth Ave., ☎ 727-593-3861, www.indian-rocks-beach.com/historical_society.html. It is open Wednesday-Saturday 10-2. Admission is free or by donation.

BEACHES, PARKS & NATURAL AREAS

In **Indian Rocks Beach**, between 15th and 27th avenues and First and Eighth avenues, you'll see public beach accesses about every block or so. This is a good spot for surfers and surf-fishers. The county maintains a large lot and facilities at 18th St.

At Indian Shores, **Tiki Gardens Beach Access**, 19601 Gulf Blvd., ☎ 727-549-6165, provides ample parking spaces in a lot across the street.

MAINLAND ATTRACTIONS

OF HISTORIC/CULTURAL INTEREST

From the Indian Rocks Bridge (Walsingham Rd), head east to the town of Largo, where you can explore the history of Pinellas County in a 21-acre historic village known as **Heritage Village** at 11909 125th St. N., ☎ 727-582-2123, www.pinellascounty.org/heritage. The park holds 25 of the county's oldest existing structures and replicas, including family homes, a one-room schoolhouse, a railroad depot, a blacksmith shop, a log house dating back to 1852, and a

St. Petersburg & Clearwater

circa-1915 neighborhood mercantile, complete with garage and barber shop. Tour guides and artisans dress the part of turn-of-the-century pioneers and demonstrate period crafts. Visit for free Tuesday-Saturday, 10-4, or Sunday, 1-4. Docent tours of some building interiors are available.

Florida Botanical Gardens

Next door to Heritage Village is **Pinewood Cultural Park**, 12175 125th St. N., ☎ 727-582-2200, www.pinewoodculturalpark.org. This combination cultural-historical-botanical attraction contains the Gulf Coast Museum of Art, ☎ 727-518-6833, www.gulfcoastmuseum.org. Its galleries feature Florida artists on a permanent, rotating basis and other temporary exhibits. They are open Tuesday-Saturday, 10-4, and Sunday, noon-4. Admission is $8 for adults, $7 for seniors, $4 for students, free for children under age seven. Florida Botanical Gardens, also at 12175 125th St. N., ☎ 727-582-2200, www.flbg.org, encompasses 150 acres, growing everything from palm trees to kitchen vegetables, and a botanical learning center. Admission is free. The gardens are open daily, 7-7.

PERFORMING ARTS

Largo Cultural Center, at 105 Central Park Dr., ☎ 727-587-6793, has concerts, children's theater, and shows.

■ MADEIRA BEACH

At Sand Key's south end, Madeira Beach, also known as Mad Beach, is where the action happens, but more so in and around marinas than on the town's claustrophobic beaches. Most of the activity centers around John's Pass and Village, where a fishing charter industry has grown into a shopping and restaurant district with a shanty fish house motif.

FAMILY FUN

The Gulf beaches and mini-golf go together. **Smugglers Cove Adventure Golf**, 15395 Gulf Blvd., Madeira Beach, ☎ 727-398-7008, www.smugglersgolf.com, uses the ever-popular pirate's theme for its 18 holes of putt-putt. Adults pay $9.49; children aged 12 and under, $8.49, plus tax. Additional rounds are $1.49 each.

ADVENTURES

■ ON WATER

FISHING

Grouper is the password here. **John's Pass** claims it is the grouper-catchingest place in the world. Try your luck on a deep-sea fishing charter. Other favored catches include pompano, snapper, snook, redfish, and tarpon.

> *FLORIDIOM: Grouper is a large, deepwater fish with mild meat that lends itself to culinary versatility. Fried grouper sandwiches are a Florida restaurant staple. In recent years, supplies have become depleted, meaning higher price tags and limited seasonal availability.*

Locals recommend the **Redington Long Pier** at 17490 Gulf Blvd. in Redington Shores, ☎ 727-391-9398, for the best fish action onshore. It extends more than 1,000 feet into the Gulf and offers a snack bar, bait and tackle, shelters, and restrooms. It costs $10 for adults and $9 for children under age 10 to fish off the pier, $2 to walk on. There's a two-pole maximum and no shark fishing is allowed. Rod rentals are available. The pier is open 6 am to midnight Sunday-Thursday, and 24 hours on weekends.

Across the street, you'll find a more extensive stock of fishing supplies and bait at the **Dogfish Tackle Company**, 17477 Gulf Blvd., ☎ 727-392-6644.

Head to **Hubbard's Marina** at 150 John's Pass Boardwalk, ☎ 800-755-0677 or 727-393-1947, www.hubbardsmarina.com, and embark on a deep-water trip aboard 72- to 75-foot vessels. The excursions last anywhere from five to 34 hours. Rates begin at $42 for adults, half-price for kids under age 12. Trips are offered daily. Rod rental available.

For bait, fuel, fishing licenses, rod rentals or sales, and other fishing accessories, stop by **Don's Dock** at 215 Boardwalk Place E., John's Pass, ☎ 727-391-3223.

BOAT RAMPS

Boating access is provided at the **Belleair Boat Ramp**, 3900 W. Bay Drive in Bellair Bluffs.

You can launch your own craft at **Park Blvd. Boat Ramp**, near the Indian Shores Causeway. There's free parking across the street.

BOAT CHARTERS & TOURS

Hubbard's Sea Adventures, ☎ 800-755-0677 or 727-398-6577, www.hubbardsmarina.com, departs out of Hubbard's Marina (see above) at John's Pass Village for five-hour beach cruises to unbridged Shell Island. Cost for cruise is $26.90 for adults, $13.45 for children aged 11 and under. The Egmont Key Snorkel Tour costs $15 and $7.50. Two-hour dolphin and sunset cruises cost $16.82 and $8.41. The boats have restrooms and covered seating. Reservations are suggested.

SNORKELING & DIVING

Thirteen offshore and nearly 30 inshore artificial reefs line Sand Key. The inshore reefs, accessible from the beach, lie anywhere from 100 to 900 yards offshore in about 15 feet of water. Offshore, depths reach up to 80 feet and reefs consist of various wrecks, including 10 army tanks and a 110-foot Coast Guard cutter.

© Get Wet Watersports

Indian Rocks Tackle & Dive Center at 1301 N. Gulf Blvd., ☎ 727-595-3196, offers PADI instruction and has complete diving services. It's open 9-6 Tuesday-Saturday.

WAVERUNNERS & PARASAILING

Try **Get Wet Watersports** at John's Pass Village, www.getwetwatersports.com, ☎ 727-320-8320, for WaveRunner rentals ($60-$80 an hour) and parasailing.

ON WHEELS

MOTORCYCLE RENTALS

Get your motor running with **Street Eagle Harley** rentals, 12529 66th St. N. in Largo, ☎ 866-479-2453 or 727-536-8900, www.streeteagletampabay.com. Rides are priced for one day, three days, and one week. One-day rentals range from $130 to $175. Reservations are highly recommended. Street Eagle is open Monday-Saturday, 9-5; Sunday, 9-3.

ECO-ADVENTURES

Suncoast Seabird Sanctuary at 18328 Gulf Blvd. in Indian Shores, ☎ 727-391-6211, www.seabirdsanctuary.org, is one of the largest wild bird hospitals in North America. In a zoological setting on the Gulf, it nurses more than 40 species – owls, hawks, sandhill cranes, pileated woodpeckers (shown at right), wood storks, and lots of pelicans. It is open daily, 9 am-dark. One-hour tours are conducted every Wednesday and Sunday at 2. Look for the big pelican sculpture out front. Admission is free, but donations are appreciated.

WHERE TO STAY

There are numerous places to stay along the stretch of Sand Key, in unlimited variety. Most have their own distinct personality and are not part of any chain. Rates are relatively low.

ACCOMMODATIONS PRICE KEY		
Rates are per room, per night, double occupancy. Price ranges described for each property often do not take into account penthouses and other exceptional, high-priced accommodations.	$ $$ $$$ $$$$	Up to $75 $75 to $150 $151 to $250 $251 and up

© Great Heron Inn

HOTELS & COTTAGES

Cottages, rental homes, and mom-pop motels line Gulf Boulevard in Indian Rocks Beach. Most, including **Great Heron Inn** at 68 Gulf Blvd., ☎ 727-595-2589, www.heroninn.com, are nicely affordable. This is a barefoot beach place with two stories of well-maintained one-bedroom apartments with fully equipped kitchens. The swimming pool and barbecue grills sit at the edge of the beach. $$

Top-end is the **Doubletree Beach Resort** at 17120 Gulf Blvd., North Redington Beach, ☎ 727-391-4000, www.doubletreebeachresort. com. High-rise in style, its 125 rooms are set on the beach, where a pool, restaurant, and tiki bar complete the amenities. $$$-$$$$

▨ RENTAL AGENCIES

For condo and apartment rentals, contact **Best Beach Rentals**, 18610 Gulf Blvd., Indian Shores, ☎ 727-577-9404, www.floridabest. com; **Florida Lifestyle Vacation Rentals**, 19713 Gulf Blvd., Indian Shores, ☎ 800-487-8953 or 727-593-2000, www.ourcondo.com; or **Travel Resort Services**, 16401 Gulf Blvd., Redington Beach, ☎ 800-237-6586 or 727-393-3425, www.trsinc.com/trs.

WHERE TO EAT

The Sand Key area has some of the best seafood you'll ever find, and at tasty prices. Check out the fish markets for do-it-yourself seafood feasts.

For fresh seafood at reasonable prices in a relaxed setting, **P.J.'s Oyster Bar & Seafood Restaurant** at 500 First St. on Indian Rocks Beach, ☎ 239-596-5898, has the right attitude. The all-day menu gives you a multitude of options from seafood gumbo to fried catfish or Key West Delight grouper topped with pimento garlic cream. For landlubbers, burgers, ribs, steaks, and more please. Save room for the Key lime or bourbon pecan pie. Entrées range from $6.25 to $20.

Smack on the water, **Salt Rock Grill**, 19235 Gulf Blvd. in Indian Shores, ☎ 727-593-ROCK, www.saltrockgrill.com, makes a splash

© Salt Rock Grill

with its new-age fish motif and cuisine. Sample such inspired oak-grilled specialties as cioppino or crusted seven-bone rack of lamb. It's open daily for dinner, with entrées ranging from $10 for early-bird items to $40 for fire-roasted lobster tail. Specialty martinis are served in a stylish cigar bar. Reservations are suggested.

For something special, **The Lobster Pot Restaurant**, 17814 Gulf Blvd. in Redington Shores, ☎ 727-391-8592, www.lobsterpot.com, combines fish-house casual ambiance with finely executed cuisine. Lobster dominates in varieties undreamed-of, followed in eminence by other forms of seafood. It's open daily for dinner, priced at $14-$38. Reservations recommended.

Friendly Fisherman Seafood Restaurant at 150 John's Pass Boardwalk on Madeira Beach, ☎ 727-391-6025, should be the Florida fish-house prototype, with its casual attitude, water view, and just-caught fish. You can even bring in your own catch to be cleaned and cooked to your specifications. It's open daily for breakfast, lunch, and dinner. Breakfast ranges from $4 to $8; try the Benedicts, the hollandaise is fresh and fluffy. Luncheon sandwiches and platters range from $7 to $12, dinners run $12 to $30.

Treasure Island, St. Pete Beach & the Islands

Treasure Island, despite its rich-sounding name, is the coast's best value. It's low on character, except for its Sunset Beach district, yet offers the same white sand beaches and watersports thrills as its neighbors.

St. Pete Beach occupies a 7½-mile island known as **Long Key**. Of all the area's islands, Long Key's intriguing history is the best preserved. Its greatest landmark is the fantasy-pink **Don CeSar Resort**, playground of 1920s glitterati such as F. Scott Fitzgerald and Al Capone. It majestically crowns St. Pete Beach's southern threshold. The island's southernmost community of **Pass-A-Grille** fills its history pages with adventuresome tales of French fishermen and 20th-century drug smugglers.

Shell Key

South of Long Key, the islands get smaller and more remote. **Tierra Verde** holds a marina community at the doorstep to Fort De Soto County Park, which occupies five small keys, where once war strategies were planned. Unreachable by land, **Egmont Key** was the site of Fort De Soto's sister fortifications. Today it is a refuge for wildlife and weekenders. **Shell Key Preserve** has its namesake shells and birds on its pristine 1,755 acres.

FLORIDIOM: A key is a small (generally under 10 acres), low-lying island. According to the US Geological Survey, there are 882 keys in Florida. Anything smaller is classified a shoal, reef, or sandbar. The word derives from the Spanish cayo, which has been shortened to cay in the Bahamas and Caribbean, and is pronounced "key."

GETTING HERE

Central Ave. connects Treasure Island to Highway 19 and downtown St. Petersburg. There's a toll to cross the Treasure Island Causeway, which becomes 107th Avenue on the island. **Gulf Blvd.** (Rte. 699) runs the length of the island, connecting it to Sand Key in the north. At the south end, **Blind Pass Rd.** leads to Long Key/St. Pete Beach.

To get to St. Pete Beach from the south, take **I-275** off I-75 to the **Sunshine Skyway**. Turn east on **Pinellas Bayway** (54th Ave./Rte. 682), toll 50¢, which goes directly to St. Pete Beach. Pinellas Bayway (Rte. 679) splits off at Isla Del Sol to take you to Tierra Verde and Fort De Soto County Park. Roadways are well marked. Toll to Fort De Soto Park is 35¢.

From downtown St. Petersburg, take **Central Ave**. west about nine miles, turn south on **Pasadena Ave**. and proceed to the St. Pete Beach Causeway/75th Ave. Follow **Rte. 699** down from the islands to the north. **Blind Pass Rd.** crosses from Treasure Island to St. Pete Beach, and connects to Gulf Blvd., which runs the island's length as the major thoroughfare. In Pass-A-Grille, Gulf Blvd. splits into Gulf Way and Pass-A-Grille Way, the bayfront route. Eighth Street is the historic section's main drag.

You can reach Egmont and Shell keys via shuttles, charters, and boat rentals (see *On Water*, below).

INFORMATION

For more information, contact the **Tampa Bay Beaches Chamber of Commerce**, 6990 Gulf Blvd., St. Petersburg Beach, 33706, ☎ 800-944-1847 or 727-360-6957, www.tampabaybeaches. com. Open Monday-Friday, 9-5. The Treasure Island office is located at 113½ 107th Ave., Treasure Island, 33706, ☎ 727-363-6184, and is open Tuesday-Saturday, 9-5.

SIGHTS & ATTRACTIONS

 Author favorites are indicated with a star.

OF HISTORIC OR CULTURAL INTEREST

South of the majestic Don CeSar Resort, you'll discover historic **Pass-A-Grille**. Browse between Eighth and 10th avenues, where old-island homes, and galleries and shops occupying historic buildings take you back to yesteryear. Of special interest, **Evander Preston Contemporary Jewelry** at 106 Eighth Ave., ☎ 727-367-7894, www.evanderpreston.com, is the studio and gallery of a local character. Besides his own artistic jewelry, you can see his private eclectic collection of art, which ranges from bison-skin rugs to an 1830 Russian motorcycle. The store is open daily.

Nearby, **Gulf Beaches Historical Museum** at 115 10th Ave., ☎ 727-552-1610, resides in a historic church near the beach. Through pictures and artifacts, it tells the story of settlement in these parts. Admission is free or by donation. The hours are Friday and Saturday, 10-4; Sunday, 1-4; and, mid-September to June, Thursday, 10-4.

Fort De Soto, ☎ 727-582-2267, www.pinellascounty.org/park/05_Ft_DeSoto.htm, is the centerpiece of Fort De Soto County Park, located in the Lower Islands at 3500 Pinellas Bayway S. in Tierra Verde.

Part of the fortifications are preserved: gun and ammunition rooms, 12-inch mortar cannons, and other features. Forty-five steps take you up to the fort's battery embankment, where the view of the now peaceful waterfront scene is the best part.

■ BEACHES, PARKS & NATURAL AREAS

Treasure Island is perhaps the blandest of the region's beaches – behind the times but not far enough to have a lot of character. The exception is Sunset Beach on the island's south end, where you'll find a mish-mash of architectural styles, from historic cottages to funky bars to majestic modern homes, of which more are becoming the rule. Its beach bars are fun to visit day or night. Beach parking is metered on Treasure Island.

Egmont Key, in the Lower Islands area, is less than two miles long and covers 398 acres. It is a national wildlife preserve where visitors can explore history and nature. The ruins of Fort Dade occupy the northwest end of the island. The ruins have eroded into the water to provide sea life and snorkelers with an artificial reef. Nature trails lead to gopher tortoise nests and a historic lighthouse.

Egmont Key

The beach at **Pass-A-Grille**, and along St. Pete Beach, is quite lovely – a wide apron of clean sand with enticingly gentle seas. Parking is metered ($1.25 an hour, $5 a day) and closely monitored.

Shell Key is a narrow strip of island with mostly sand, shells, and birds to see.

ADVENTURES

ON WATER

You won't lack for water-oriented activities in St. Pete Beach. Fishing and boating are a way of life here, and have been since human history was first recorded in these parts.

FISHING

John's Pass Bait & Charter, ☎ 727-367-5772, on the south side of John's Pass at John's Pass Marina on Treasure Island, sells bait and fishing supplies.

A small sea-walled patch of park on Blind Pass at Sunset Way and Corey Ave. is designated **Fisherman's Park**. Restaurants are conveniently located at both ends.

Two exits off the Skyway Bridge take you to the north and south adjuncts of the **Skyway State Fishing Pier**, ☎ 727-865-0668 for North Pier; 941-729-0117 for South Pier; www.skywaypiers.com. There are picnic and rest areas at the same exits. The piers were created from the remains of an old bridge and are the state's only drive-on piers. Admission fees for each pier are $3 per vehicle ($10 per RV), plus $2 per person aged 12 and older, $1.50 for seniors, $1 for children aged six-11. Both piers have bait and tackle concessions and are open 24 hours daily.

In Pass-A-Grille, **Merry Pier** at Eighth Ave. and Pass-A-Grille Way, ☎ 727-360-6606, is the focus of south-end water adventures. You can fish free from the pier, which has bait and tackle and rod and reel rentals ($10 for a half-day, $15 for full day). It's also a good place to catch a fishing charter. The 51-foot ***Miss Pass-A-Grille***, ☎ 727-367-

9833, goes deep-sea fishing. Half-day trips cost $44 for adults and $34 for children 12 and under. On Wednesdays and Saturdays, a full-day trip costs $64 (adults) and $44 (children).

Fort de Soto Park (see *Sights & Attractions*, above), ☎ 727-864-9937 or 727-864-3345, has a 1,000-foot pier projecting into the gulf and a 500-foot pier into the bay, both equipped with bait, tackle, and food concessions.

BOAT RAMPS

Treasure Island has two free boat ramp locations on **Gulf Blvd.**, one at 84th Ave. and one at 100th Ave.

St. Pete Beach's free boat ramps are located at **E. 33rd Ave.** and at **Egan Park**, 9101 Blind Pass Rd.

Across from the Don CeSar Resort, there's a boat ramp with limited metered parking at **West Maritana & Casa Blanca**. Launching facilities are also available at **Blind Pass Marina**, 9555 Blind Pass Rd., ☎ 727-360-4281.

In Tierra Verde, you can launch your boat and do your other boat-related business at **Tierra Verde Marine Center**, 100 Pinellas Bayway, ☎ 727-866-0255.

Fort De Soto County Park (see *Sights & Attractions*, above), has a free boat ramp.

BOAT RENTALS

Tierra Verde Boat Rentals, located at the marina, ☎ 727-867-0077, www.tvboatrentals.com, rents bowriders, deck boats, and three-seat WaveRunners by the hour (except deck boats), half-day, six hours, and full day. Hourly rates are $60-$70; half-day rates, $195-$225; full day, $259-$299.

Island Marine at 11045 Gulf Blvd., ☎ 727-367-2132, www.island marinerentals.com, rents boats, deck boats, and personal watercraft. Half-day boat rental rates range from $125-$300; full-day $89-$300. Tax and gas are extra. Two- and three-person WaveRunners rent for $50-$60 per hour.

BOAT CHARTERS & TOURS

A new **Fort De Soto Ferry**, ☎ 727-867-6569, www.hubbardsmarina. com, runs twice-daily shuttles from Fort De Soto County Park to Egmont Key National Wildlife Refuge for $15 round trip ($7.50 for children). Optional snorkel gear rental is $5 and a ferry ride to snorkel the fort's sunken ruins is $10. The ferry departs Fort De Soto at 10 and 11 am, returning at 2 and 3 pm. The schedule may be limited September to February.

Mid-island, **Dolphin Landings**, 4737 Gulf Blvd. (behind Dolphin Village Shopping Center), ☎ 727-360-7411 or 727-367-4488, www. dolphinlandings.com, is a good place to look for charters, especially for trips to Shell Island and dolphin watching. Sailboat cruises are $30 each. Excursions last two to three-and-a-half hours.

The **_Starlite Princess_** riverboat shoves off from the Corey Causeway at St. Pete Beach, ☎ 800-444-4814 or 727-462-2628, www.starlite-cruises.com. Prices begin at $11.90 for adults for an afternoon cruise; lunch is extra. Adults pay $17.75 for a three-hour dinner and entertainment cruise, plus $11.75 and up for the meal.

The Shell Key Shuttle, ☎ 727-360-1348, www.shellkeyshuttle.com, departs from Merry Pier (see _Fishing_, above) three times daily for $22 adult fare, $11 for children aged 12 and under, plus tax. Sunset cruises are the same price.

PADDLING

To paddle your way around the 2.25-mile self-guided trail in Fort De Soto Park, rent from **Topwater Kayak** inside the park, ☎ 727-864-1991. Single and double kayaks go for $23-$30 for one hour and $55-$70 for the day.

SNORKELING & DIVING

Treasure Island Artificial Reef and a barge wreck provide places of interest for divers.

The **St. Petersburg Beach Artificial Reef** and a wreck are popular dive destinations in less than 30 feet of water.

Many charter boats to Egmont Key provide snorkeling equipment so you can explore the fort ruins and their coral formations. Visibility is about 30 feet.

ON FOOT

The hike around **Fort De Soto** (see _Sights & Attractions_, above), and up and down its steps, provides solid exercise with your history lesson. A one-mile interpretive nature trail takes you through scrub and mangrove terrain at the **Arrowhead Picnic Area** near North Beach at Fort De Soto County Park.

Paths, some of them still brick-paved from when the island was a thriving military settlement, cross **Egmont Key**. One leads from the fort to the lighthouse; others meander.

ON WHEELS

Biking is popular in **Fort De Soto County Park** (see page 118), which has 10 miles of wide paths, and in the campground there. Topwater Kayak, ☎ 727-864-1991, rents bikes starting at $8 for one hour, $25 for four hours, and $40 for the day. Two-seater bikes and Surreys are available.

Beach Cyclist Sports Center, 7517 Blind Pass Rd., ☎ 727-367-5001, rents bikes and inline skates for $6 an hour; $25 for 24 hours.

WHERE TO STAY

In the St. Pete Beach area, there are as many different kinds of lodging as there are different kinds of visitors. A lot of these places are beach-front and geared to activity in the waves.

ACCOMMODATIONS PRICE KEY		
Rates are per room, per night, double occupancy. Price ranges described for each property often do not take into account penthouses and other exceptional, high-priced accommodations.	$	Up to $75
	$$	$75 to $150
	$$$	$151 to $250
	$$$$	$251 and up

HOTELS & MOTELS

Families will love **TradeWinds Island Resorts** at 5500 Gulf Blvd., ☎ 800-360-4016 or 727-367-6461, www.justletgo. com, where there are paddleboats to navigate the property's canals, a pizza parlor, a putting area, swimming lessons, a terrific kids' program, pools of all sizes, and a game room. Rooms occupy two hotels within walking distance of one another. $$$-$$$$

The 80-year-old **Loew's Don CeSar Beach Resort & Spa** at 3400 Gulf Blvd., ☎ 866-728-2206 or 727-360-1881, www.doncesar.com,

© Loews Hotels

is the doyenne of local beach resorts. Palatial, yet playful, it houses amenities from dual swim pools and a kids' program, to watersports rentals and a small spa that will have moved to a new, stand-alone, larger facility by the time you visit. $$$-$$$$

Inn on the Beach at 1401 Gulf Way in Pass-A-Grille, ☎ 727-360-8844, www.innonbeach.com, has 12 cozy, clean, comfortable, and nicely appointed rooms with tile floors, kitchens, and views of the beach. Relax and grill dinner in the garden courtyard. $$-$$$

CAMPING

 The region's best campground occupies St. Christopher Key in **Fort De Soto County Park**, ☎ 727-582-2267. The 238-site campground is spotless, surrounded by water, and perfect for fishermen, hikers, and bike riders. Rates are $28 per night, including tax. You can make reservations in person or at www.pinellascounty.org.

WHERE TO EAT

For beach casual with style on Treasure Island, try **Caddy's Waterfront Beach BBQ**, 9000 W. Gulf Blvd. on Sunset Beach, ☎ 727-360-4993. Open for lunch and dinner daily, it sets picnic tables out on the open deck and patio tables inside where it's still open, but there's sports TV to entertain instead of waves and shorebirds. Sandwiches, seafood dinners, and barbecue dinners range from $5 to $12.

St. Pete Beach is perfect for the hungry adventurer with a limited pocketbook. Seafood restaurants up and down the strip serve fresh seafood, often in old fish-house style, meaning breaded and fried, or simply broiled or steamed.

For something off the beaten path, casual, waterfront, and locally loved, head to **Woody's Waterfront Café & Beach Bar** at Corey Ave. and Sunset Way, ☎ 727-360-9165. You sit in the open air, beneath a ceiling of hanging surfboards, or under umbrellas on the patio overlooking the pass between Treasure Island and Long Key. The fare is burgers and seafood baskets for $5-$11. Dinner entrées include grouper Oscar, stuffed mahi-mahi, and filet mignon. By the way, the "beach" part of the name is misleading; the beach is long gone. Open daily.

When you do get ready to spend a lot of cash for a culinary splurge, head to **The Maritana Grille** at the Don CeSar Resort, 3400 Gulf

Blvd., ☎ 727-360-1882. Dishes such as marmalade-roasted red snapper and garlic-roasted lamb chop are executed in fine new Florida style and are priced à la carte in the $31-$44 range. Booths and tables sit in an atmosphere of aquariums and refined tropicalia. Reservations recommended.

On the bayfront with docking space, **Wharf Seafood Restaurant**, at 2001 Pass-A-Grille Way, ☎ 727-367-9469, is a local's kind of place occupying a 1912 fish processing plant and serving unpretentiously prepared fish, shrimp, crab cakes, and crab claws. Open non-stop for lunch and dinner daily. Prices run $4-$15. Tuesday is fish fry all day for $6.50.

Hurricane Seafood Restaurant, Ninth Ave. and Gulf Way in Pass-A-Grille, ☎ 727-360-9558, www.thehurricane.com, is the island's best-known and most imposing restaurant. The three-story Victorian building overlooks the beach and historic district. I find the food

and service overrated, but it's worth at least one visit. The ground floor features a casual menu ($4-$23) with specialty drinks such as Hurricane Alley and shots of Banana Bomb. Upstairs serves finer fare, entrées $15-$26. Grouper sandwich is the specialty on both menus. The restaurant is open daily for lunch and dinner.

NIGHTLIFE

Gators Café & Saloon, 12754 Kingfish Dr., ☎ 727-367-8951, www.gatorscafe.com, is decorated with alligator and Florida Gator team paraphernalia. It hosts live entertainment daily, and boasts the world's largest waterfront bar, overlooking John's Pass on Treasure Island.

Party-down day and night at **St. Pete Beach**. You'll be in good company. Many party places are located within resorts. Watch local papers for what band is playing where and at what time.

Stormy's at the Hurricane at Ninth Ave. and Gulf Way in Pass-A-Grille, ☎ 727-360-9558, creates a Caribbean atmosphere where you can enjoy DJ music Thursday through Sunday.

St. Petersburg

Downtown St. Petersburg is an old city previously known for its aging population. Since the 1880s, when Peter Demens gave the city a railroad and the name of his Russian hometown, St. Petersburg has been associated with healthful climes and restorative waters. In its early days, retirees and convalescents flooded the peninsular town looking for rest and rejuvenation. This took its toll on St. Petersburg. For many years it looked like a worn-out rest home waiting room.

But new blood has been transfused into the city in recent decades, making its waterfront district a happening place for lovers of the outdoors and for other visitors. The rejuvenation is ongoing, turning St. Petersburg into a thriving metropolis with its own college, major-league baseball arena, world-class museums, and fashionable shopping districts. But it still retains a yesteryear patina: A scenic drive along the bayfront takes in 32 historic sites. Sophisticated and savvy, it presents the flip side of the barrier islands' swimsuit-and-suntan-oil attitude.

Explore the neighborhoods around St. Petersburg, particularly the waterfront towns of Gulfport, for a different, homey perspective on the big city.

TRANSPORTATION

From I-275, take **I-175** or **375** to get downtown. Numbered streets run north-south, numbered avenues run east-west. Second Street is closest to the waterfront. Beach Drive is where First Street logically would be, at bay's edge. Fourth Street North is **Highway 92**, which takes you to Tampa Bay bridges. **Central Avenue** is the dividing point between avenues north and avenues south. It also connects downtown to the beaches.

AROUND TOWN

Tour downtown on the **Looper Trolley**, which runs 11-5 every day. Tours begin at The Pier (see *Sights & Attractions*, below), 800 Second Ave. NE, ☎ 727-892-5700 or 727-821-5166, www.loopertrolley.com, and cost 25¢, 10¢ for seniors. Exact change is required.

INFORMATION

St. Petersburg Area of Commerce is at 100 Second Ave. N., Ste. 150, ☎ 727-821-4715, www.stpete.com, open Monday-Friday, 8-5. Or visit **The Pier Visitor Information Center** at 800 Second Ave. NE, ☎ 727-821-6164, open 10-8, Monday-Saturday; 11-6 on Sunday.

SIGHTS & ATTRACTIONS

DOWNTOWN

OF HISTORIC OR CULTURAL INTEREST

Explore art through the ages at the **Museum of Fine Arts**, 255 Beach Dr. NE, ☎ 727-896-2667, www.fine-arts.org. Gallery rooms and gardens display the works of major artists, including Georgia O'Keeffe, Edgar Degas, and Paul Gauguin. Admission is $8 for adults, $7 for seniors, $4 for students older than six. Sunday admission is by donation. Hours are 10-5, Tuesday-Saturday; 1-5 on Sunday.

St. Petersburg Museum of History at 335 Second Ave. NE, ☎ 727-894-1052, www.spmoh.org, is not your normal, stuffy historical museum. Light and airy, it features a circa-1910 Benoist airboat hanging from the ceiling – the first recorded airplane to fly a commercial route by crossing from Tampa to St. Petersburg – and costumes you can "try on" by standing behind glass pull-out displays and looking in the mirror. Other vignettes realistically depict life throughout the history of St. Petersburg. Adult admission is $5, $4 for seniors and college students, and $2 for children aged seven to 17. Hours are Tuesday-Saturday, 10-5; Sunday, noon-5, Monday noon-7.

Florida International Museum, 244 Second Ave. N., ☎ 727-341-7900, www.floridamuseum.org, open in 1995. Exhibits of international stature, such as "800 Years of Russian Art, Culture, and History" from the State Russian Museum, circulate in and out. The museum is open Monday through Saturday, 9-6, and Sunday, noon-6. Admission is $17 for adults, $15 for seniors, and $5 for students aged seven and older.

The world's fourth-largest of its kind, **Florida Holocaust Museum**, 55 Fifth St. S., www.flholocaustmuseum.org, ☎ 727-820-0100 or 800-960-7448, displays Holocaust art and other related permanent and rotating exhibits. Continuous exhibits include a film and original boxcar used for transporting prisoners in Poland. Hours are daily 10-5; last admission is at 4. Adult admission is $8; seniors and college students $7; students aged 18 and under $4.

One of downtown's most impressive treasures, the **Salvador Dali Museum** at 1000 Third St. S., ☎ 727-823-3767 or 800-442-3254, www.salvadordalimuseum.org, houses the world's largest collection of original works by the renowned surrealist, with melting clocks, men hatching from eggs, and more. Exhibits span Dali's works from 1904 and his "formative years" to his entrée into the cinematic world with a film of his dream sequence in Hitchcock's *Spellbound* in 1947. An entirely new facility being built to house the collection is slated for completion in 2009. Browse the museum store for something unusual. The museum is open Monday-Saturday, 9:30-5:30 (until 8 on Thursday, 6:30 on Friday), and on Sunday, noon-5:30. Cost for adults is $15; for seniors, $13.50; for students, $10; for children aged five-nine, $4. One-hour tours are free.

PERFORMING ARTS

American Stage, 211 Third St. S., ☎ 727-823-7529, www.americanstage.org, performs professional theater in an intimate 135-seat setting. Tickets range from $21 to $31 for adults, $7.50 to $10 for children and students.

Mahaffey Theater, 400 First St. S., ☎ 727-892-5767, hosts the Florida Orchestra, Tampa Bay Symphony, celebrity entertainment, athletic events, and other performances. Call for schedule and ticket prices.

FAMILY FUN

The Pier, 800 Second Ave. NE, ☎ 727-821-6443, www.stpete-pier.com, a futuristic structure in the shape of an upside-down pyramid at the end of a long wharf, is the core of downtown action. It's the place to shop, dine, party, fish, or catch a tour. It's open 10-9, Monday-Thursday; 10-10 on Friday and Saturday; 11-7 on Sunday. Parking is $3 ($5 during special events), which includes trolley transportation from the lots to The Pier.

On the second floor of The Pier, you'll find the **Pier Aquarium**, ☎ 727-895-7437, www.pieraquarium.org, filled with environmental exhibits and huge tanks. Admission is $2 for guests older than age 12. Hours are 10-8, Monday-Saturday; noon-6, Sunday. Daily events include a touch tank presentation at 2 pm and fish feeding at 3 pm.

The city of St. Petersburg has resurrected one of the area's oldest attractions. **Sunken Gardens**, 1825 Fourth St. N., ☎ 727-551-3100, www.stpete.org/sunken.htm, had sunk into disrepair in decades past. Now it's back up, functioning, and flowering in its cool depths of 15 feet below street level. New additions to the botanicals and wildlife shows include a butterfly garden, rainforest information center, and Great Explorations (see below). It opens Monday-Saturday, 10-4:30, and Sunday, noon-4:30. Admission is $8 for adults, $6 for seniors, and $4 for children.

A self-animation lab, climbing wall, moving music, lie detector, fire house, pizza parlor, build-your-own-car race track, and other interactive play areas make up the new **Great Explorations, the Hands**

On Museum at Sunken Gardens, 1925 Fourth St. N., ☎ 727-821-8992, www.greatexplorations.org. Designed for the toddler and early elementary school set, its hours are the same as those for Sunken Gardens. Admission is $9 for adults and children older than 11 months, $8 for seniors.

SPECTATOR SPORTS

Major league baseball has hit Tampa Bay hard. St. Petersburg's amazing **Tropicana Field** at 16th St. and First Ave. S., ☎ 888-FAN-RAYS or 727-825-3250, www.devilrays.com, hosts the young Tampa Bay Devil Rays team. And the fans have gone wild. This is the only way to enjoy summer baseball in Florida – in air-conditioned

comfort. More like a small city than a stadium, Tropicana holds a sit-down restaurant, lots and lots of food stands, video games and a play area for kids, a cigar bar, and even a hot-tub somewhere up there in the stands. General, reserved and box admission runs $5-$195 ($2 for kids), plus you'll pay about $7 for parking. Field and home plate seating is also available. The concessions aren't cheap, either – the price of air-conditioned comfort. Tours of the stadium are offered Monday-Friday and cost $3 for seniors and children aged four and under, $5 for adults. The **Ted Williams Museum & Hitters Hall of Fame** (www.twmuseum.com) moved in 2006 from its Citrus County home to Tropicana Field. It opens two hours before home games and remains open through the last inning. The "D Rays" spring-train right in town at Al Lang Stadium, 822 Second Ave., ☎ 727-898-RAYS, where you can see them play for $4-$15.

TAMPA BAY BASEBALL TRIVIA

Although Tampa-St. Petersburg didn't get its first major league baseball team until 1998, the region has scored a few claims to baseball fame in its past.

- On April 4, 1919, **Babe Ruth** hit his longest home run at Tampa's Plant Field. His 587-foot hit set a record in a pre-season game.
- Ybor City native **Al Lopez**, known as "El Señor," was elected to the Baseball Hall of Fame in 1977. Lopez spent 18 years as a catcher with the Pittsburgh Pirates, Brook-

lyn Dodgers, and Boston Braves and 17 years as manager of the Chicago White Sox and Cleveland Indians.

▪ The New York Yankees hold their spring training in Tampa. Their facility is named **Legends Field**, and designed after their stadium in New York (see page 164).

▪ The **Philadelphia Phillies** held spring training at Jack Russell Memorial Stadium in Clearwater until 2004 when the city built the new Bright House Networks Field, ☎ 727-441-8638.

▪ The **International Softball Federation** maintains its Hall of Fame, training and competition center, and international headquarters in Plant City, in eastern Hillsborough County. It occupies the stadium once used for spring training by the **Cincinnati Reds**.

GULFPORT

OF HISTORIC OR CULTURAL INTEREST

Originally built in the early 1900s and twice rebuilt, the **Gulfport Casino Ballroom**, on the waterfront at 5500 Shore Blvd. S., ☎ 727-893-1070, keeps it classic with ballroom, swing, and salsa dance lessons four days a week – Tuesday through Thursday and Sunday. Following the lessons, there's open dancing, on Sundays with a live band. Lessons are included in a cover fee of $4-$6.

Gulfport is known largely for its charming galleries, gift shops, and restaurants. To experience it at its liveliest, hit the **Gulfport Art Walk**, ☎ 727-893-1070, www.ci.gulfport.fl.us, every first Friday and third Saturday of the month.

Catherine A. Hickman Theater of Gulfport at 5501 27th Ave. S., ☎ 727-893-1070, www.ci.gulfport.fl.us, hosts community cultural events.

OUTLYING AREAS

SPECTATOR SPORTS

At Derby Lane, 10490 Gandy Blvd., ☎ 727-812-3339, www.derbylane.com, greyhound races are held at 12:30, Monday, Wednesday, and Saturday, with evening races Monday-Saturday at 7:30. General admission is $1.

NATURAL AREAS

Just south of the Gandy Bridge that takes you to Tampa lies an oasis of green known as **Weedon Island Preserve**, 1800 Weedon Dr. NE, ☎ 727-453-6500, www.pinellascounty.org/environment. The developing 3,100-acre bayside plot offers a 45-foot observation tower, two paddling trails and launch, a fishing pier, and more than eight miles of boardwalk and hiking trails along two small lakes jumping with mullet. The still-developing, state-of-the art Cultural & Natural History Center uses special effects and hands-on delivery to teach about Weedon Island's 1,800-year past, the native culture for which it is named, its archaeological excavations, and its fauna and flora. The preserve is open daily dawn to sunset, the center hours are 10-4 Wednesday-Sunday. Saturday guided hikes travel two miles in two hours starting at 9 am. Call ahead to reserve a spot.

ADVENTURES

■ ON WATER

FISHING

Since 1889, **The Pier** (see *Sights & Attractions*, above) at 800 Second Ave. NE, ☎ 727-821-6443, www.stpete-pier.com, in its various incarnations, has lured fishermen. A **bait house** on the south side takes care of tackle and bait needs daily. Two catwalks accommodate fishermen. Rods and reels rent for $10 a day.

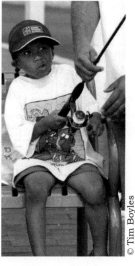

© Tim Boyles

There's another modern, free fishing pier at **Weedon Island Preserve** (see above).

Friendship TrailBridge (see *On Foot*, below), ☎ 727-549-6099, is a 2.6-mile trail on the old Gandy Bridge designated for fishing as well as bike and foot traffic.

Across from Veterans Memorial Park, **Ultimate Fishing Center**, 9385 Bay Pines Blvd., ☎ 727-320-9032, offers bait and equipment rental and repair.

> FUN FACT: Ranked eighth on Old Spice deodorant's list of "America's Sweatiest Cities," St. Petersburg offers a plethora of opportunities to work up a sweat and to cool down.

St. Petersburg & Clearwater

BOAT RAMPS

St. Petersburg has several free boat access points throughout the city. They include **Coffee Pot Park**, First St. at 31st Ave. NE; **Demens Landing South**, Bayshore Drive at First Ave. S.; and **War Veterans Memorial Park**, 9600 Bay Pines Blvd.

ON FOOT

Completed in December, 1999, the **Friendship TrailBridge**, ☎ 727-549-6099, www.friend shiptrail.org, is the longest over-the-water recreation trail (2.6 miles) in the US. It transformed the Old Gandy Bridge over Tampa Bay into a trail for biking, walking, running, inline skating, and fishing.

For a peaceful brush with nature and hiking and biking trails through varied habitat from swamp woodlands to oak pine hammock, head to **Boyd Hill Nature Center** at 1101 Country Club Way S., ☎ 727-893-7326. Beneath oak canopies you can picnic, play on the playground, see caged birds, spot butterflies, visit the new nature center with interactive displays and an aviary, and stroll in quietude around Lake Maggiore. Admission to the center is free; use of the trails costs $2 for adults, $1 for children aged three-16. Hours are 9-8 Tuesday, Wednesday, and Thursday; 9-6 Friday-Saturday; 11-6 Sunday.

ON WHEELS

BICYCLING & INLINE SKATING

The 34-mile **Pinellas Trail**, ☎ 727-464-8200, www.pinellas county.org/trailgd, begins near downtown St. Petersburg at 34th St. and Eighth Ave. S., then heads north through city, town, and country following an old railroad route to Tarpon Springs. You can hike, bike, jog, or skate it. Parking for the trail is at Leach Park, 7111 Old Oakhurst Rd., in Seminole.

The **Friendship TrailBridge** (see *On Foot*, above) is also used for biking and skating.

You can rent bikes at **The Pier** (see *Attractions*, above) starting at $7 per hour for a beach cruiser, $10 for reclining bikes, and $18-$25 for multi-person Surreys.

Save your energy and two-wheel it around the downtown area on a Segway Human Transporter with **Tampa Bay Segs** at Baywalk, ☎ 727-772-3639, www.tampabaysegs.com. Ninety-minute tours cost $45 each.

MOTORCYCLING

Get your motor running with a rental from **Jim's Harley-Davidson** of St. Petersburg, 2805 54th Ave. N. (at 28th St. N.), www.jimshd.com, ☎ 866-228-6188 or 727-527-9672. Rates on a variety of models are $110-$135 for 24 hours, $255-$270 for three-day weekend, and $525-$595 a week.

IN THE AIR

At **Biplane Rides**, Albert Whitted Airport off I-275 at Exit 22, ☎ 727-895-6266, www.biplanerides.com, your air taxi is a 1933 WACO UIC originally owned by William Randolph Hearst. Three passengers pay $120 per flight and up for short to extensive tours.

SHOPPING

The Pier, 800 Second Ave. NE, ☎ 727-821-6443, holds a gamut of specialty souvenir shops, including one devoted entirely to hot peppers complete with a tasting bar, and another to cartoon memorabilia.

Downtown's latest shopping and entertainment sensation, **BayWalk**, 153 Second Ave. N., holds a 20-theater movie complex, lively bars and restaurants, and fun shops – both chain and one-of-a-kind. The downtown celebrates on the first Friday of the month. Gallery Walks take place the second Saturday.

Gulfport is known for its **artists' galleries** and other fun shops. Plan to visit on the first Friday or third Saturday for extra activity.

Book-lovers should head to block-long **Haslam's Book Store**, 2025 Central Ave., ☎ 727-822-8616, www.haslams.com, Florida's largest bookseller.

For mall-sized shopping, try **Tyrone Square**, 66th St. and 22nd Ave. N., ☎ 727-347-3889, www.simon.com.

WHERE TO STAY

 Author favorites are indicated with a star.

Other than business travelers, most people head to the beaches to stay. Lodging downtown tends to be priced slightly higher than on the beaches, but is quieter and more sophisticated.

ACCOMMODATIONS PRICE KEY		
Rates are per room, per night, double occupancy. Price ranges described for each property often do not take into account penthouses and other exceptional, high-priced accommodations.	$	Up to $75
	$$	$75 to $150
	$$$	$151 to $250
	$$$$	$251 and up

HOTELS, MOTELS & RESORTS

 To luxuriate totally, do what the rich folk did back in the '20s: check into the Vinoy. The **Renaissance Vinoy Resort and Golf Club**, 501 Fifth Ave. NE, ☎ 727-894-1000 or 800-HOTELS-1, www.vinoyrenai

ssanceresort.com, is a renovated vision of roaring twenties with long, arched hallways, plush rooms (some with whirlpools), pampered dining, and a convenient location on downtown's waterfront. The marina, tennis courts, golf course, and fitness center cater to active types. Ask about packages. $$$$

INNS/BED & BREAKFASTS

Downtown St. Petersburg has a number of bed-and-breakfasts and small accommodations. **Inn at the Bay** at 126 Fourth Ave. NE, ☎ 727-822-1700 or 888-873-2122, www.innatthebay. com, is among the former, its 12 rooms ensconced in a lovely 1910 Victorian house decorated with Florida

themes. It is steps away from downtown's shopping district, and features a romantic dining room and garden. $$$-$$$$

Another historic presence downtown, **The Pier Hotel** at 253 Second Ave. N., ☎ 800-735-6607 or 727-822-7500, www. thepierhotel.com, serves a deluxe Continental breakfast to guests of its 32 rooms. Happy hour takes place in the warm common room with its fireplace and grand piano. Rooms and suites are decorated with a touch of elegance; many retain the claw-footed tubs from the hotel's early days in the 1920s. $$-$$$

The Peninsula Historic Inn & Spa at 2937 Beach Blvd. in Gulfport, ☎ 888-9000-INN or 727-346-9800, www.thepeninsulainnspa.com, provides a fitting place to lay your head in this artsy town. Its 10 rooms are named and themed for places in Africa, and all have private bathrooms and lots of character. Expanded Continental breakfast is included in the rates and the grill is open for lunch and dinner, plus there's an intimate fine-dining room call Six Tables. $$-$$$

▨ RENTAL AGENCIES

Florida Vacation Condos & Homes, 4700 34th St., ☎ 800-237-5960 or 727-866-2494, www.capalborental.com, lists short-term rental properties throughout the St. Petersburg, Clearwater, and the islands.

▨ CAMPING

Close to the beaches, **St. Petersburg/Madeira Beach KOA** at 5400 95th St. N., ☎ 800-562-7714 or 727-392-2233, www.koa.com/where/fl/09144.htm, gives you the option of tent, RV, or air-conditioned cabin camping on lovely, oak-shaded grounds. It's great for outdoors enthusiasts, providing bike and canoe rentals, boat slips, a fishing dock, a swimming pool, three hot tubs, bike trails, miniature golf, shuffleboard, volleyball, bocci ball, and children's playground. Rates for two adults are $37-$51 for tent, $50-$75 for RV, and $73-$78 for a cabin.

WHERE TO EAT

Downtown St. Petersburg has fine choices for dining out. Easiest for visitors are the many options at **The Pier** (see *Sights & Attractions*, page 100), 800 Second Ave. NE, ☎ 727-821-6443, www. stpete-pier. com. The food court has a bakery, coffee and tea, pizza, Chinese food, steaks, burgers, and ice cream, all reasonably priced and above standard fast-food fare. Often you're entertained by minstrels.

On the fifth floor of The Pier, ChaCha Coconuts, ☎ 727-822-6655, is a fun place to eat, sky-high, panoramic, and all done up in bright, Caribbean colors. It serves lunch and dinner daily; sandwiches and entrées, such as Yucatán chicken (spicy with peppers and tortillas), voodoo ribs (brushed with guava barbecue sauce), and coconut shrimp, run $7-$14.

The most elegant among the crowd at BayWalk is **Gratzzi Ristorante**, ☎ 727-822-7769. On the second level with indoor and outdoor dining, Gratzzi serves a long list of Italian classics daily. Luncheon salads, sandwiches, and entrées include an excellent grilled vegetable salad, oak-grilled portobello pressed panini sandwich, veal parmesan, and mostaccioli pesto in a price range from $8 to $12. Meat or fish off the wood grill is the dinner specialty, along with tempting pasta, lobster, and veal delights, ranging from $13 to $27.

North of downtown, head to **Fourth Street Shrimp Store** at 1006 Fourth St. N., ☎ 727-822-0325, for a taste of old Florida seafood and casual, kooky and slightly rickety ambiance. Open daily for lunch and dinner, it does all-you-can-eat clams on Monday, snow crab on Tuesday, and shrimp on Wednesday. Catfish sandwich, shrimp hoagie, crab coquette sandwich, clam roll, and seafood entrées prepared fried, broiled, or blackened range from $4 to $15. For the best deals, order the Express Lunch weekdays 11-3 or the Early Bird Special 3-6 any day but Sunday.

En route to the islands, stop at **Ted Peter's Famous Smoked Fish**, an enigmatic little spot at 1350 Pasadena Ave. S., ☎ 727-381-7931. Locals crowd the outdoor counter and picnic tables along a busy street. There's also air-conditioned, uncrowded indoor seating, but for some reason this is usually second-choice, even on hot summer days. The menu contains a handful of items centered around its famous smoked mullet, mackerel, and salmon, and Manhatten [sic] clam chowder and German potato salad. Sandwiches and platters range from $2.50 to $17.50. It's open for lunch and early dinner every day but Tuesday. Cash only.

Away from downtown, **Skyway Jack's** at 2795 34th St. S., ☎ 727-866-3217, is legendary. A colorful version of passé funk, it's popular with fishermen, businessmen, and all sorts. The food is homemade, Southern style, and plain cheap. Open daily, it prices its popular breakfasts at $3-$6, lunches $3-$5, and dinners $5-$7. No credit cards. Look for the big chicken out front.

Watch the world go by from the veranda while you munch on a grilled salmon wrap or black walnut-crusted grouper at The Peninsula Inn's **Palm Terrace Grill** (2937 Beach Blvd. in Gulfport, ☎ 888-9000-INN or 727-346-9800). You can opt for an inside table around set around the bar. There's a variety of sandwiches, salads, pasta, and grilled specialties at lunch ($6-$20) or grilled meats and seafood at dinner ($14-$25).

NIGHTLIFE

Downtown St. Petersburg is hopping, from The Pier and waterfront on down Central Ave. toward Tropicana Field, in an area being developed as **The Dome District**. Hit downtown on the first Friday of the month for a lively **street fair**.

BayWalk Complex, 151 Second Ave. N., www.baywalkstpete.com, holds 20 cinema screens, dozens of dining and drinking spots, and retail shops. Wet Willie's hops and jives with the energy of youth. The Martini Bar is a bit more sedate and sophisticated.

ChaCha Coconuts (see *Where to Eat,* above) at The Pier, ☎ 727-822-6655, and other Pier businesses sponsor indoor and outdoor events with live rock or reggae, and often with mobs of people.

Jannus Landing at 687 Central Ave., ☎ 727-895-3045, www.jannuslandingconcerts.com, is downtown St. Pete's ultimate concert venue, with live groups performing everything from belly dancing to hard rock in the courtyard.

Fans of big band dancing or the movie *Cocoon* should visit the classic big-band **Coliseum Ballroom** at 535 Fourth Ave. N., ☎ 727-892-5202, www.stpete.org/coliseum, where part of the above-mentioned flick was filmed. It's open for afternoon Tea Dance sessions on Wednesdays at 12:30 pm. Cover charge is $5. A dance lesson before the session is $2.

St. Petersburg & Clearwater

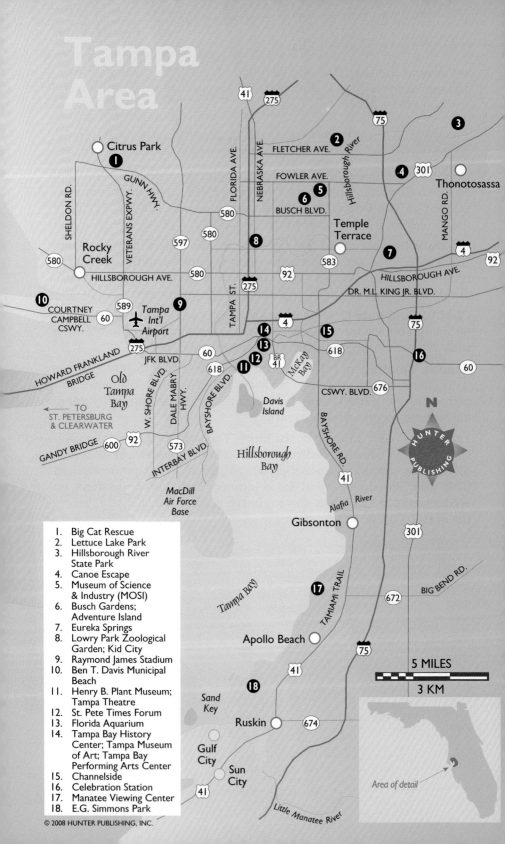

Tampa Area

1. Big Cat Rescue
2. Lettuce Lake Park
3. Hillsborough River State Park
4. Canoe Escape
5. Museum of Science & Industry (MOSI)
6. Busch Gardens; Adventure Island
7. Eureka Springs
8. Lowry Park Zoological Garden; Kid City
9. Raymond James Stadium
10. Ben T. Davis Municipal Beach
11. Henry B. Plant Museum; Tampa Theatre
12. St. Pete Times Forum
13. Florida Aquarium
14. Tampa Bay History Center; Tampa Museum of Art; Tampa Bay Performing Arts Center
15. Channelside
16. Celebration Station
17. Manatee Viewing Center
18. E.G. Simmons Park

© 2008 HUNTER PUBLISHING, INC.

Tampa

ampa is big city – skyscrapers, industry, traffic jams, the whole bit. Known as "The Big Guava," the city alone has a population of 303,000 plus. Many of its guests come on business. Tourists and adventurers are more likely to head to the islands of St. Petersburg/Clearwater.

FLORIDIOM: A round, yellow fruit, the guava grows around Tampa and is popular in Latin cuisine. It is used to make jelly, paste, and juice. To some, the fleshy guava has an offensive odor. Others find its scent sweet and appealing.

Still, Tampa has its vacation appeal, especially for the cultural traveler, and has since the 1880s, when **Henry Plant** brought his railroad to town and built an elaborate hotel designed after the Alhambra in Spain. With its deep port and easy water accesses, Tampa thrived. **Cigars** constituted one of its earliest big money-making industries and built an entire city named for industry magnate Don Vicente Martinez Ybor. Today, upwardly evolving **Ybor City** retains the essence of the Cuban cigar-makers and their immigrant workforce and is the city's best cultural attraction. Teddy Roosevelt added to Ybor City's historic allure. Stationed with his Rough Riders in the vicinity during the Spanish-American War, he frequented a local club.

Busch Gardens is Tampa's major attraction. It, along with the **Florida Aquarium**, a number of museums, professional sports, and parks, gives Tampa a lot to offer the sightseer. Outdoor enthusiasts fare less well, but they will find a lot of indoor activities or attractions that deal with nature. In the great wide open, **Tampa Bay** (the largest harbor in the US between Norfolk and New Orleans), **Hillsborough** Bay, and the **Hillsborough River**, which wends its way from civilization to sheer wilderness, generate some recreational excitement. Most adventure is sought on the water and away from city lights. This chapter generally covers Tampa and its Hillsborough County outskirts as far north as to what spills into eastern Pasco County.

The chapter is divided into three parts: Downtown; Ybor City; and Northwest, Northeast & South of Tampa. The latter covers the area around the airport and north, Busch Gardens, and southern Hillsborough County between Tampa and Bradenton.

TRANSPORTATION

■ AIRLINES

Tampa International Airport (TPA), ☎ 800-767-8882 or 813-870-8700, www.tampaairport.com, is the West Coast's largest and Florida's third busiest. The table below shows domestic and international airlines that land in Tampa.

DOMESTIC & INTERNATIONAL AIRLINES SERVING TAMPA INT'L AIRPORT (TPA)		
Air Canada . . . . ☎ 888-247-2262 . . . . www.aircanada.com		
AirTran Airways . . . . ☎ 800-247-8726 . . . . www.airtran.com		
American Airlines . . . . ☎ 800-433-7300. . . . . www.aa.com		
British Airways . . . . ☎ 800-247-9297. . . . . www.ba.com		
Cayman Airways . . . . ☎ 800-422-9626 . . . . www.caymanairways.com		
Continental . . . . ☎ 800-525-0280 . . . . www.continental.com		
Delta Air Lines/Comair . . . . . ☎ 800-221-1212 . . . . www.delta.com		
Frontier. . . . . ☎ 800-432-1359 . . . . www.frontierairlines.com		
Gulfstream . . . . ☎ 800-992-8532. . . . . . www.gulfstreamair.com		
JetBlue. . . . . ☎ 800-538-2583 . . . . www.jetblue.com		
Midwest. . . . . ☎ 800-452-2022 . . . www.midwestairlines.com		
Northwest/KLM . . . . ☎ 800-225-2525 . . . . www.nwa.com		
Southwest . . . . ☎ 800-435-9792 . . . . www.southwest.com		
Spirit . . . . ☎ 800-772-7117 . . . . www.spiritair.com		
Ted . . . . ☎ 800-225-5833 . . . . www.flyted.com		
United . . . . ☎ 800-241-6522 . . . . www.united.com		
US Airways . . . . ☎ 800-428-4322. . . . . www.usairways.com		
USA3000. . . . . ☎ 877-872-3000 . . . . www.usa3000airlines.com		
WestJet. . . . . ☎ 800-538-5696 . . . . www.westjet.com		

■ RENTAL CARS

Rental cars are available at the airport and other locations throughout the area. Companies include all **Alamo**, ☎ 800-327-9633; **Avis**, ☎ 800-331-1212 or 813-396-3500; **Hertz**, ☎ 800-654-3131; and **Budget**, ☎ 800-527-0700 or 813-877-6051.

■ BUS, TRAIN & TAXI SERVICE

HARTline (Hillsborough Area Regional Transit), ☎ 813-254-HART, www.hartline.org, runs buses through the city. By permit, bike riders are allowed to transport bicycles on special bus bike racks. Fares are 50¢-$2.50; exact change is required.

Amtrak, ☎ 800-872-7245, offers passenger train service into Tampa.

For ground transportation to and from the airport, contact **United Cab**, ☎ 813-253-2424; **Yellow Cab**, ☎ 813-253-0121; or **Alpha Limousines**, ☎ 813-247-6190.

■ GETTING AROUND

Tampa lies at the crossroads of interstates 75, 275, and 4. **I-275** rushes east-west north of downtown, then veers north. It connects St. Petersburg to I-75. **I-4** branches off I-275, crosses I-75 farther south, then heads to Orlando. **I-75** forms an eastern border to the metropolitan area. **Hwy. 41** (Nebraska Avenue) pierces the city limits on the east side of town. The fastest route through town is **Cross-**

town Expressway (Rte. 618), a toll road that runs north-south from Hwy. 92 to downtown, then squiggles east-west to I-75, with limited exits. Three bridges cross Tampa Bay from St. Petersburg/Clearwater. North to south, they are Courtney Campbell Causeway (Rte. 60/Memorial Highway), Howard Frankland Bridge (I-275), and Gandy Bridge (Hwy. 92).

From anywhere in the Tampa Bay area (Sarasota to Hernando County), dial 511 or log into www.511tampabay.com for up-to-date traffic and route information.

> FUN FACT: I-4 is the lowest numbered interstate in the United States.

INFORMATION

An automated **information line** and attraction/accommodation reservation system is available 24 hours a day at ☎ 888-224-1733, 813-223-2752, or 800-36-TAMPA.

For additional information, contact **Tampa/Hillsborough Convention and Visitors Association**, 401 E. Jackson St., Suite 2100, Tampa, 33602, ☎ 800-44TAMPA or 813-223-1111, www.visittampabay.com. The **Visitor Information Center for the Greater Tampa Chamber of Commerce** is located at 615 Channelside Dr., Tampa, 33602, in the downtown area, ☎ 813-228-7777 or 800-448-2672, www.tampachamber.com. It's open Monday-Saturday, 9:30-5, and Sunday, 11-5.

FESTIVALS & EVENTS

★ **FEBRUARY** – Tampa's most celebrated event takes place in February. **Gasparilla Pirate Fest**, ☎ 813-353-8108, www.gasparillapiratefest.com, re-creating the legend of a local hero, pirate Gasparilla. On Invasion Day hundreds of swashbuckling pirates raid the city aboard the three-masted *Jose Gasparilla* pirate ship and lead a boisterous parade along Bayshore Blvd. Month-long festivities include street dances, foot races, and art shows.

Ybor City's **Fiesta Day**, ☎ 813-241-8838, a street festival and illuminated night parade, runs concurrently with Gasparilla Days, as does the **Florida State Fair** at Florida State Fairgrounds, ☎ 813-621-7821 or 800-345-FAIR (FL). Admission is $10 for adults, $5 for children aged six to 11.

★ **OCTOBER** – Ybor City's liveliest event is **Guavaween**, ☎ 813-248-0721, www.ybortimes.com/guavaween. html, a Latin-flavored celebration. It features a satirical night parade known as the Mama Guava Stumble, costumed street party, and Family FunFest. Admission is $5 during the day, $15 after 3.

★ **DECEMBER** – Ybor City's Cuban version of Christmas is celebrated early in the month, with **Santa Fest and Krewe of Venus Holiday Parade**. In store are tons of snow, an outdoor ice-skating rink, live entertainment on five stages, Santa Claus, kids games, crafts, and more. For information, contact the Ybor City Chamber of Commerce, ☎ 813-242-8838.

BUDGET TIPS

■ **Busch Gardens** offers a free day's admission when you purchase a ticket, as long as you use it within 13 days. Check out www.buschgardens.com for details on it and on two-day ticket-transportation packages for Busch Gardens and SeaWorld in Orlando.

■ Admission to **Ybor State Museum** and a tour of its La Casita cigar-worker's home cost only $3 each.

■ To save money on a day at Busch Gardens, pack your own snacks and beverages, or leave for lunch and walk across the street to a fast-food restaurant and return later. To make beverages stay cooler in Florida heat, freeze them first. Bring your own towels and rain ponchos so you won't be forced to buy them at highly inflated theme-park prices.

■ **Tampa Bay History Center** is open free to the public (see page 146).

■ There's no charge for seeing the manatees and touring the exhibits at Tampa Electric's **Manatee Viewing Center** (page 172).

Downtown Tampa

Downtown Tampa, a hub of business activity, is restructuring to widen its appeal to tourists, particularly cruise-ship passengers. Each year, a new attraction increases the area's tourism opportunities. Scored into segments by waterways and channels, Tampa's downtown is also the center of shipping and cruise ship activity.

Tampa

Much of the restoration takes place in the once unsightly shipping zones of the **Channel District**, where a 10-screen theater and dining complex is a big attraction.

Sights are basically divided between the neighborhoods of **Hyde Park** and **Davis Islands** on the west side, downtown/Harbour Island in the center, and the still-developing Channel District on the east side.

WEEKEND ADVENTURE ITINERARY

- **FRIDAY:** Arrive in north Tampa. Go canoeing on the Hillsborough River with Canoe Escape in the morning. Have a picnic lunch at Hillsborough River State Park. Visit Museum of Science and Industry or Lowry Park Zoo in the afternoon. Eat dinner at Oystercatchers or Armani's and spend the night in the Westshore region; try the Grand Hyatt, DoubleTree Guest Suites, Renaissance International Plaza, or Hampton Inn.
- **SATURDAY:** Go to Busch Gardens or take a hot-air balloon ride with Big Red Balloon in the morning. Have lunch at Mel's Hot Dogs. Spend the afternoon back at Busch Gardens or at Adventure Island. Spend the night in north Tampa.

■ **SUNDAY:** Head downtown and visit the Florida Aquarium in the morning. Take the streetcar to Ybor City for lunch at Columbia Restaurant. Tour Ybor City Museum and Centro Ybor in the afternoon. Return downtown for dinner at Channelside District. Stay for a movie or see what's happening at St. Pete Times Forum. Spend the night in downtown Tampa.

TRANSPORTATION

From I-75, the **Crosstown Expressway** (Rte. 618, Exit 256), a toll road, is the quickest way to downtown. From St. Petersburg, cross Gandy Bridge (Hwy. 92) and hop on the expressway. From I-4, take Exit 1 and head south on 22nd St.

■ AROUND TOWN

In Hyde Park, **Swann Ave**. is the main through-street. **Kennedy Blvd**., to the north, forms one border for the neighborhood, and leads into downtown. **Bayshore Blvd**. is Hyde Park's 4½-mile show-off promenade, where visions of the deep blue intermingle with the grandeur of old homes. It connects with the new Riverwalk in the Channel District.

Main downtown streets running north and south are **Ashley**, **Tampa**, and **Florida** streets. **Channelside Dr**. takes you into the Channel District. To get to Ybor City, follow **Nebraska Ave**. north to Nick Nuccio Pkwy.

Look for blue directional signs in the downtown area. They point out your way to major attractions along twisting, intertwining, confusing streets.

The **TECO Ybor Streetcar**, ☎ 813-254-4278, www.tecolinestreetcar. org, runs replicas of Tampa's original transportation cars to carry cruise ship passengers and other visitors between downtown and Ybor City. Trolleys make 11 stops and run daily

every 15 to 20 minutes. Cost is $2 each way (exact change required), $4 for an all-day pass. Call for schedule. **Uptown-Downtown Connector buses**, run free-of-charge by HARTline (☎ 813-254-4278), travel through the heart of downtown east-west with dozens of stopping points.

SIGHTS & ATTRACTIONS

■ OF HISTORIC OR CULTURAL INTEREST

The minarets of the Henry B Plant Museum.

Downtown Tampa brims with artistic and historical opportunities. To learn all about Tampa's history, visit the bizarre structure you can't help but notice. The **Henry B. Plant Museum** at 401 W. Kennedy Blvd., ☎ 813-254-1891, www.plantmuseum.com, was built in the 1890s to lodge rich railroad arrivals. With its onion domes and minarets, it looks like a set from *Arabian Nights*. Dazzling, period-furnished rooms and priceless art treasures explore the hotel's fate and portray the times. Hours are Tuesday-Saturday, 10-4; Sunday, noon-4. Admission is by donation, suggested as $5 per adult, $2 for children under age 12. During the month-long Victorian Christmas Stroll, admission is higher.

The Tampa Bay History Center, downtown in the Tampa Convention Center Annex at 225 S. Franklin, ☎ 813-228-0097, www.tampabayhistorycenter.org, is a storehouse for Tampa's past, with drawers and showcases full of artifacts. Admission is free; donations accepted. It's open Tuesday-Saturday, 10-5.

The six galleries at **Tampa Museum of Art**, 600 N. Ashley Dr., ☎ 813-274-8130, www.tampamuseum.com, host five changing and one permanent exhibit of classic antiquities. Admission is $8 for adults, $6 for seniors, and $3 for students with ID. Everyone enters free (or by donation) from

5-8pm the third Thursday of each month and 10-noon every Saturday. Normal hours are 10-5, Tuesday-Saturday (10-8 on the third Thursday of each month); and 11-5 on Sunday. The third Friday of the month is **Art After Dark**, when the museum also opens 8-11.

Cross a bridge just off Bayshore Boulevard to reach the Davis Islands historic district, a fun place to shop and especially to dine. Restaurants range from a popular pizza sports bar hangout to new upscale eateries.

■ PERFORMING ARTS

Tampa Bay Performing Arts Center at 1010 N. MacInnes Place, ☎ 813-222-1000 or 800-955-1045, www.tbpac.org, is home to 12 performing arts groups and hosts operas, ballets, Broadway musicals, the Spanish Lyric Theatre, and more in its three theaters. Call for schedule and ticket prices. Every Wednesday and Saturday at 110 am, the center welcomes visitors for a free tour.

Downtown also has its classic treasures, including the gothically embellished **Tampa Theatre** at 711 Franklin St., ☎ 813-274-8981, www.tampa-theatre.org. Restored to its 1926 grandeur, it stages films, concerts, and other special events. One-hour tours every Wednesday include a concert with a pipe organ once used in the silent movie era. Suggested donation: $5 each.

© Tampa Theatre Archives

Photo of Tampa Theatre, 1926

Climb aboard the ***American Victory*** to see what life was like aboard a 455-foot merchant marine ship between the years of WWII and the

Vietnam War. American Victory Mariners Memorial & Museum Ship at 705 Channelside Dr., ☎ 813-228-8766, www.american victory.org, lets you self-tour the ship's nine decks. The ship conducts six-hour living history cruises on weekends, complete with food and entertainment. Admission is $8 for adults, $7 for se-

Tampa

niors, and $4 for children aged six to 12. Cruises cost around $100 each.

■ FAMILY FUN

The **Florida Aquarium** at 701 Channelside Dr., www.flaquarium. org, ☎ 813-273-4000, is the jewel of downtown redevelopment, part of the Channelside District. Beneath a seashell-shaped glass dome, exhibit areas replicate the state's different watery environments: mangrove estuary, freshwater, beach, marine, and coral reef – the most popular with its sharks, angelfish, and other intriguing creatures of the deep.

Exhibits examine Florida's unwanted exotic species with hands-on learning, and the sea's predators – jellyfish, sharks, octopuses. At the end, a touch tank holds small sharks and rays that are safe to pet. Behind-the-scenes tours and swim with the fishes programs are available for an extra charge. The latest addition is an outdoor wet and dry playground with a Caribbean motif. An animal show takes the stage adjacent to the area.

Admission for adults is $17.95; for seniors, $14.95; for children aged three-12, $12.95. Parking is $5. Hours are 9:30-5, daily.

■ SPECTATOR SPORTS

Nearby, the **Tampa Bay Lightning** hockey team plays October-April in the huge St. Pete Times Forum (formerly the Ice Palace), near the Florida Aquarium at 401 Channelside Dr., ☎ 813-223-4919, www.tampabaylightning.com. Individual game tickets range from $20 to $300. ☎ 813-301-6600 to order tickets.

ADVENTURES

■ ON WATER

You're never far from water in Tampa, even in the middle of downtown. Its variety of water bodies gives saltwater and freshwater fishermen their due. From downtown, it's easy to hook up with a charter headed for deep waters. For a fuller menu of fishing and boating opportunities, head to the beaches around St. Petersburg. Some outlying areas (see below) offer better access to canoeing and freshwater pursuits.

FISHING

Ballast Point Pier at 5300 Interbay Blvd. on the south end of Bayshore Blvd., extends 1,000 feet into Hillsborough Bay at a park with a boat ramp, bait shop, waterfront restaurant, and playground.

Capt Dave Markett, ☎ 813-962-1435, charges $350-$500 to take two fishermen out to the flats for four to eight hours, covering territory as far as Boca Grande to the south and Homosassa to the north. Dave also offers alligator hunting and eagle observation airboat tours.

En route to the ramp on Davis Islands, pick up supplies at **Davis Islands Bait & Tackle**, 241 E. Davis, ☎ 813-514-4133.

BOAT RAMPS

You'll find boat ramps at these four locations: on the east side of the **Gandy Bridge**; at **Ballast Point Park**, 5300 Interbay Blvd.; on **Bayshore Blvd**. near Platt St.; at **Marjorie Park** on Davis Islands' south end; and on the 22nd St. Causeway.

BOAT CHARTERS & TOURS

Florida Aquarium (see page 148) conducts eco-tours from 701 Channelside Dr., ☎ 813-273-4000 or 373-4020, www.flaquarium. org, aboard a 64-foot, 49-passenger catamaran. Cost is $19.95 for adults, $18.95 for seniors, and $14.95 for children under age 12. Combination tickets with Florida Aquarium are available.

Nearby at 603 Channelside Dr., ***StarShip* Dining Yacht**, ☎ 813-223-

7999 or 877-744-7999, www. yachtstarship.com, departs on lunch, brunch, and dinner cruises into Tampa Bay, entertainment provided by a five-piece band. Lunch and brunch cruises are $39.95; dinner cruise, $69.95 to $79.95. Children's and special Floridian rates are available.

■ ON FOOT

NATURE WALKS

For a quiet nature walk in the city, head to **McKay Nature Park** at Crosstown Expressway and 34th St., a 150-acre refuge for more than 180 species of birds and other wildlife. Trails head into uplands habitat.

JOGGING & SKATING

Bayshore Blvd., billed as the world's longest continuous sidewalk (4½ miles), is perfect for inline skating and jogging. It runs between Hillsborough Bay and some of the town's loveliest old homes.

SHOPPING

Hyde Park Village at Swann and Dakota avenues, ☎ 813-251-3500, www.hydeparkvillage.net, is hip, trendy, and scenic, with lots going on besides the upscale, name-brand and one-of-a-kind stores that line old streets. Free parking. Shops are open Monday-Saturday, 10-7, and on Sunday from noon-5.

The **Channelside** entertainment district (shown here) at 615 Channelside Dr., ☎ 813-223-4250, www.channelsidetampa.com, put downtown's waterfront revitalization on the fast track. Mostly designed for movie-, restaurant-, and club-goers, it has some shopping to go with it all.

WHERE TO STAY

Tampa Bay area visitors with a yearning for adventure typically park themselves in Tampa's northern regions or out on St. Petersburg's beaches. If

Tampa

you want to (or must) stay in the inner city, downtown has plenty of rooms in all price categories.

ACCOMMODATIONS PRICE KEY		
Rates are per room, per night, double occupancy. Price ranges described for each property often do not take into account penthouses and other exceptional, high-priced accommodations.	$	Up to $75
	$$	$75 to $150
	$$$	$151 to $250
	$$$$	$251 and up

© Marriott Hotels

Occupying one of downtown's most enviable locations, **Marriott Tampa Waterside** at 700 S. Florida Ave., ☎ 813-221-4900 or 888-268-1616, www.tampawaterside.com, has convenience and view on its side. A 32-slip marina, three restaurants, and a complete spa make a stay in one of the resort's 717 guest rooms a self-contained prospect. Should you want to get out, everything happening about downtown lies within footsteps, including the convention center, which means it's popular with business clientele and well as leisure travelers. $$$$

Handy to downtown attractions, **Sheraton Tampa Riverwalk Hotel**, at 200 N. Ashley Dr., ☎ 813-223-2222 or 800-325-3535, www.tampariverwalkhotel.com, gives you handsomely decorated, spacious rooms and suites. If you score a river view, you often can see scullers in training at one of the nation's leading collegiate sculling locations. The award-winning Ashley Street Grille takes care of hunger pangs. The pool sits above the river. $$$-$$$$

© Marriott Hotels

WHERE TO EAT

Tampa stays on the cutting edge of cuisine trends and has carved out a reputation for its fine and eclectic dining. Some of the classics still remain favorites, however, in this town of old and new. Many of the most popular collect in a pocket dubbed the Soho District, because it is centered around South Howard Ave. Channelside, downtown, provides casual options in a party atmosphere.

⭐ *Author favorites are indicated with a star.*

For that special night out, there is no other choice than **Bern's Steak House** at 1208 S. Howard Ave., ☎ 800-282-1547 (FL) or 813-251-2421, www.bernssteakhouse.com, where steaks are cut, aged, and prepared to perfection. All of the meal's other ingredients get at least as much attention: Bern's has its own live fish tank, organic garden, bakery, and coffee roaster. The main menu diversifies into meats other than steak, with seafood dishes as well. The wine selection is renowned (Bern's boasts the

largest working wine cellar in the world), as is the upstairs dessert parlor, with cozy booths and some 40 dessert selections. Count on a slow, enjoyable evening of fine dining in a setting of baroque elegance. Entrée prices start at $21 and go up to three figures for large cuts to share among many. It's open daily for dinner. Reservations are required.

What it lacks in atmosphere, **Gourmet Pizza Company** at 610 S. Armenia Ave., ☎ 813-258-1999, www.gourmetpizza-company.com, more than compensates in quality of food. There's no matching its pizza crust and sauce. Choose from an outstanding and unusual variety of classic, specialty (such as steak gorgonzola and chicken smoked gouda), regional (Thai chicken and Cajun crawfish), and meatless pizzas (portobello gorgonzola and pesto vegan). Or create your own from a list of veggies, sauces, cheeses, and meats. The menu also offers pastas, calzones, salads, and soft drinks. You can eat in, but most people take out.

Sip Mad Dog 20/20, munch "Southern caviar" (pimento cheese dip), get down on some grilled meatloaf covered with ham cream gravy or pulled pork barbecue, and dance it all off at Stumps Supper Club, ☎ 813-226-2261, www.stumpssupperclub.com, located at the new Channelside complex downtown. Save room for the fruit cobbler dessert. If you're not all

Tampa

that inclined toward "Southern cooking & deep-fried dancing," try a key lime martini and filet mignon. The décor is pure flea market, down to terry cloth hand towels for napkins. It opens daily for dinner. Entrées range from $12 to $19.

On Davis Islands, **Estela's Mexican Restaurant** at 209 E. Davis Blvd., ☎ 813-251-0558, www.estelas.com, has been around a long time, spinning off into four more locations in the area. Its huge lunches ($6-$15) and dinners ($8-$15) cover the realm of Hispanic foods from tacos to shrimp à la Diablo, *pollo ranchero*, and combination dinners. Sit inside the inviting cantina or bright dining room, or outdoors on the sidewalk with plastic chairs and tables.

NIGHTLIFE

Music – live, cutting-edge, and celebrity – happens here on a regular basis. Check current listings in *Creative Loafing*, an edgy entertainment giveaway publication available on newsstands throughout the area. Or visit http://tampa.creativeloafing.com.

Channelside entertainment complex at 615 Channelside Dr., ☎ 813-223-4250, www.channelsidetampa.com, holds a 10-screen movie and IMAX theater, an upscale bowling alley, and trendy restaurants and shops in a festive open-air venue.

Nearby, the **St. Pete Times Forum** (shown below) at 401 E. Channelside Dr., hosts major musicians in concert; ☎ 813-223-1000 for events, 813-287-8844 for tickets, www.icepalace.com.

Ybor City

Ybor (pronounced EE-bore) City emerged out of a puff of smoke in the 1850s. Here, Cuban immigrants from Key West settled to make a name for Tampa in the burgeoning cigar industry, following the lead of namesake Don Vicente Martinez Ybor. Germans, Italians, Spaniards, and other nationalities came to work the factories and give the neighborhood a boom-time aura and distinctive flavor. In its heyday, the cigar industry employed 12,000 *tabaqueros* (cigar-makers) in 200 factories and produced 700 million cigars a year.

Centro Ybor.

The district and its cobbled streets have been trying for a couple of decades to recover from a slump that left Ybor City looking rundown. The emergence is slow, but sure. It's gradually growing into a trendy shopping, nightclub, and dining zone, greatly boosted in recent years by the opening of Centro Ybor entertainment complex in the historic Spanish social club. Much of what's new is oriented toward upscale dining and frenzied nightlife. A few old Ybor-style restaurants still persist, with their *café con leche* and Cuban sandwiches, along with the tradition of hand-rolled cigars.

> **TAMPA TRIVIA:** In the cigar factories of yore, one of the more educated workers was elected **"El Lector."** His role was to read the day's news, passages from the classics, and political treatises to the *tabaqueros* as they worked. The tradition began in Cuba and spread to Key West and Tampa.

GETTING HERE

Ybor City lies basically within a rectangle created by **I-4**, **Nebraska Ave.**, **Adamo Drive**, and **22nd St. Seventh** (aka "La Séptima") is "main street." Nebraska or 22nd will take you between Ybor and downtown. From I-4 west, take Exit 1.

INFORMATION

Contact the **Ybor City Chamber of Commerce** at 1800 E. Ninth Ave., ☎ 813-248-3712, www.ybor.org. It's open Monday-Friday, 9-5.

The **Chamber's Visitor Information Center** at Centro Ybor, 1600 E. Eighth Ave., Ste. B104, ☎ 813-241-8838, is open Monday-Saturday, 10-6 pm, and Sunday, noon-6. It contains a small cigar museum.

SIGHTS & ATTRACTIONS

■ OF HISTORIC OR CULTURAL INTEREST

Historic cigar factories, social clubs, and workers' homes, many of them reborn as shops, art galleries, and restaurants, fill the 110-block Ybor City district. Pick up a *Walking Map & Guide* from the Visitor Information Center (see above).

The **Ybor City Museum State Park** at 1818 E. Ninth Ave., ☎ 813-247-6323, www.ybormuseum.org, surveys the political, social, and cultural factors in Spain, Cuba, and the US that influenced the district's boom era. It occupies a handsome old yellow-brick bakery building where Cuban bread was made until 1973. Displays dwell on the history of cigar- and bread-making and the lives of the workers.

> *FLORIDIOM: Traditional Cuban bread is formed by hand into 36-inch-long loaves and baked to a golden crispiness with a single palm frond laid down the middle. The frond splits the crust, causing it to "bloom" down the center.*

The museum is open daily, 10-6. Admission is $3 for anyone older than six and includes a tour of La Casita House Museum at 1804 E. Ninth Ave., which sits among a row of "shotgun" cottages (named for their straight-through design), typical of those where cigar factory workers lived circa 1896. This one is furnished as it would have been. You'll find it in **Centennial Park**, a period reconstructed streetscape that hosts Ybor City **Saturday Market**, ☎ 813-241-2442, http://yborfreshmarket.ypguides.net. Tours of La Casita generally begin every 30 minutes between 10 and 3. The museum also conducts one-hour tours of Ybor City at 10:30 every Saturday for $6 each. For a look at more typical immigrant homes, visit Historic Ybor Village on Fifth Ave.

The Cuban government holds title to **El Parque de Amigos de José Martí** at 13th St. and Eighth Ave. This small park contains a statue of Cuban revolutionary hero José Martí and soil from each Cuban province.

Casitas, *Centennial Park*

GUIDED TOURS OF YBOR CITY

Historic Tours and Events, 4520 Swann Ave., ☎ 813-286-1636, organizes customized tours by an Ybor City native, whose mother once worked as a *tabaquero* (cigar roller). Sites include Centro Ybore, a Cuban bread bakery, Ybor City State Museum, and Columbia Restaurant.

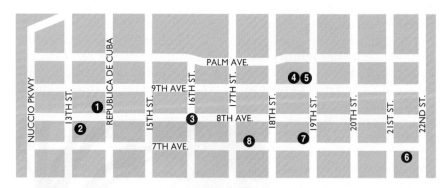

Ybor City

N

1. Centro Ybor Visitors Information
2. El Parque de Amigos de José Martí
3. Ybor City Chamber of Commerce
4. La Casita House Museum / Centennial Park
5. Ybor City State Museum
6. Columbia Restaurant
7. La Tropicana Café
8. Hilton Garden Inn

© 2008 HUNTER PUBLISHING, INC.

ADVENTURES

■ ON FOOT

Stop at Ybor City's **Visitor Information Center**, 1600 E. Eighth Ave., ☎ 813-241-8838, if you're interested in a self-guided walking tour; a brochure with a map and site descriptions is available.

WHERE TO STAY

Ybor City's first hotel, **Hilton Garden Inn**, 1700 E. Ninth Ave., ☎ 813-769-9267 or 800-STAY-HGI, www.tampaybor.stayhgi.com, was built to blend with local architecture in Mediterranean style, with a low skyline. The 95-room inn has a pool, fitness center, and complimentary shuttle to downtown and the cruise port. $$$-$$$$

Don Vicente de Ybor Historic Inn, 1915 Republica de Cuba, ☎ 813-241-4545, www.donvicenteinn.com, is set in the circa-1895 headquarters for the eponymous founder of the cigar industry. It recalls the era with gilded elegance, rich décor, and the original sweeping marble staircase. The restaurant serves free continental breakfast, lunch, and occasional live jazz. $$$

WHERE TO EAT

Once an enclave of inexpensive Cuban sandwiches, black bean soup, Cuban coffee, and other ethnic staples, Ybor City is watching its dining scene turn yuppy. But there are a few hold-outs where the past is still palpable and delicious.

Ybor's most renowned dining establishment, **Columbia Restaurant**, survives in rare form at 2117 E. Seventh Ave., ☎ 813-248-4961, www.columbiarestaurant.com. You can't miss it: gaily tiled and Mediterranean in style, it takes up a full city block. Inside, the rooms go on and on, each with its specific character. The main dining room is high ceilinged, with balconies and fountains. The Columbia, founded here in 1905, has spun off into locations throughout Florida, but this is the flagship. Along with its authentic Spanish-Cuban cuisine, it serves up live flamenco dancers Monday-Saturday. The restaurant is open daily for lunch and dinner. Dishes such as paella, *boliche* (eye round of beef stuffed with chorizo), *ropa vieja* (shredded beef), Spanish-style seafood, and chicken with yellow rice cost $16-$25. Tapas, sandwiches, and lunch entrées are $6-$16.

© Columbia Restaurant

La Tropicana at 1822 E. Seventh Ave., ☎ 813-247-4040, hangs on to old Ybor traditions, with Cuban sandwiches, black beans and rice, and Cuban coffee. Sandwiches and specialties cost $4.25-$6.50 It's open for breakfast and lunch, Monday-Saturday.

FLORIDIOM: A Cuban sandwich, Tampa style, not to be confused with a Miami-style Cubano, uses Cuban bread stuffed with roast pork, baked ham, Genoa salami, and cheese. If you have it dressed, you'll get mustard and pickles. If you have it pressed, the traditional way, it will be heated and squashed in a special press called a plancha. Some restaurants refer to this as "dresst and presst."

Another long-timer featuring authentic Spanish cuisine, **Carmine's Restaurant** at 1802 E. Seventh Ave., ☎ 813-248-3834, occupies a handsome red-brick building with a pressed-tin ceiling. Go Latin with the Spanish bean (garbanzo) soup and half a Cuban sandwich

Tampa

or deviled crabs, a local delicacy resembling a big, crab-stuffed hush puppy. Italian specialties also figure importantly on the all-day menu. Sandwiches, pasta, and entrées range from $4 for a half of a Cuban, to $16 for a grouper or sirloin dinner.

The menu at **Fresh Mouth**, ☎ 813-241-8845, at the Centro Ybor entertainment complex, 1600 E. Eighth Ave., reveals a slate of burgers and sandwiches with clever names such as Lock Jaw (double burger), Hey, Fish Face (tuna salad sandwich), and Open Mouth, Insert Foot (a foot-long hot dog). It serves daily, all-day in a bright diner-like atmosphere. Sandwiches range from $4.25 to $8.

NIGHTLIFE

From flamenco dancers to hot disco, you'll find the full extent of music in Ybor City's thriving clubs, the heart of Tampa's nightlife. The **Columbia Restaurant** (see *Where to Eat*, above) at 2117 E. Seventh Ave., ☎ 813-248-4961, features authentic flamenco dancers Monday-Saturday.

Centro Ybor, www.centro ybor. com, took over a historic social club, where Spanish cigar workers once partied on Saturday nights, to become Ybor City's premier entertainment complex. Restaurants, nightclubs, and **GameWorks**, ☎ 813-241-9675, a Steven Spielberg virtual reality creation, fill the open-air courtyard with music and laughter well into the wee hours. The movie complex (www.muvico.com) has 20 theaters. **Improv Comedy Theater & Restaurant**, ☎ 813-864-4000, www.tampaimprov. com, contributes to the laughter factor. Reservations are recommended.

Balcony seats at the Tampa Improv.

© Tampa Improv LLC

Northeast, Northwest & South of Tampa

GETTING HERE

Interstates 275 and **4** zip you across Tampa's northern reaches. The northwest quadrant, part of Westshore, is home to Tampa International Airport and professional sports teams. **Dale Mabry Highway** (Highway 92) and **Veterans Memorial Expressway** are the major north-south arteries.

The northeast quadrant lies across I-275 on its way north. Nebraska Ave. (Highway 41) parallels it to the east. **Hillsborough Ave.** (Highway 92), **Busch Blvd.**, **Fowler Ave.**, and **Fletcher Ave.** are roads you'll no doubt be spending time on in this part of town. They run east-west.

To reach the small towns south of Tampa – Gibsonton, Apollo Beach, Ruskin, and Sun City – take either Highway 41 or I-75, Exits 246 and 240.

INFORMATION

For information on Tampa's northeast and northwest districts, contact the **Tampa/Hillsborough Convention and Visitors Association**, 401 E. Jackson St., Suite 2100, Tampa, 33602, ☎ 800-44TAMPA or 813-223-1111, www.visittampabay.com..

For specific information about Ruskin and environs, contact the **Ruskin Chamber of Commerce** at 315 South Tamiami Trail, Ruskin, 33570, ☎ 813-645-3808, www.ruskinchamber.org, open Monday-Friday, 9-4.

For Apollo Beach information, write or call the **Apollo Beach Chamber of Commerce**, PO Box 3686, Apollo Beach, 33572, ☎ 813-645-1366, www.apollobeachchamber.com.

SIGHTS & ATTRACTIONS

■ NORTHWEST TAMPA

BEACHES, PARKS & NATURAL AREAS

Tampa's one saltwater beach, **Ben T. Davis Municipal Beach**, lies on the Courtney Campbell Causeway, ☎ 813-274-7719. Lifeguards are on duty during busy times along the slim stretch of sands. There's also picnicking and fishing.

To the north on Old Tampa Bay, **Upper Tampa Bay Park** at 8001 Double Branch Rd., off Rte. 580, ☎ 813-855-1765, offers nature-lovers a peek into many biological communities, from oyster bars to freshwater ponds and oak hammocks. Its nature center has a saltwater aquarium and exhibits on snakes and other indigenous critters. A boardwalk runs along a bay view. The park is open daily, 8-6.

FAMILY FUN

Tampa is second only to Orlando for kid-designed attractions. Kids and animal-lovers especially like Tampa's oldest attraction, **Lowry Park Zoo**, 7530 North Blvd., ☎ 813-935-8552, www.lowryparkzoo. com. Its 56 acres hold 1,600 animals from around the world – manatees, Florida panthers, Komodo dragons, Sumatran tigers, an Indian rhinoceros, red pandas, lorikeets, and other exotic animals, plus native creatures in their natural habitat. Newest is Safari Africa, where guests can feed a giraffe, ride a camel, or touch a white rhinoceros. Stingray Bay is another hands-on exhibit, and at Australian-themed Wallaroo Station, there's a petting zoo and pony rides. Toddlers and young kids will enjoy the manatee splash fountains in which to cool off on hot days, a carousel ride ($1), and a discovery center with a video kaleidoscope, a puppet theater, and creepy crawly creatures. The park is open daily, 9:30-5. Admission is $14.95 for adults, $13.95 for seniors, and $10.50 for children aged three-11. Mechanical and animal rides are extra and you can purchase an "unlimited-rides" armband for $18. A one-hour River Odyssey Eco-Tour by boat Wednesday through Sunday costs an extra $14, $13, and $10, or there are combo tickets.

Next door to the park, **Kid City, The Children's Museum of Tampa**, ☎ 813-935-8441, www.flachildrensmuseum.com, has indoor hands-on exhibits and a miniature outdoor city geared toward teaching safety. Admission is $5 for aged one and older. Hours are 9-5:30, Tuesday-Friday; 9-2, Monday; 10-5, Saturday; noon-5, Sunday.

Besides go-cart racing, **Tampa Grand Prix**, 14320 N. Nebraska Ave. , ☎ 813-977-6272, www.grandprixtampa.com, keeps kids busy with miniature golf courses, batting cages, and game rooms. Hours are noon-9, Sunday-Thursday; noon-midnight on Friday and Saturday. Go-cart rides cost $5.75 for two-seaters. Golfing fees are $5.95 for children aged 12 and under, $6.95 for others. Hours are Sunday-Thursday, 10 am-11pm; Friday and Saturday, 10 am-1 am.

Opposite: Wallabies at Lowry Park Zoo

SPECTATOR SPORTS

Sports fans head in this direction. At 3501 W. Tampa Bay Blvd., the **Raymond James Stadium** hosts the National Football League's Tampa Bay Buccaneers, ☎ 800-282-0683 or 813-879-BUCS, www. buccaneers.com, in winter. The state-of-the-art stadium features lounges, sports bars, luxury suites, and a 20,000-square-foot replica of a 19th-century seaport village with a 103-foot-long pirate ship. Single-game Buccaneer tickets for the September-December season cost $45-$74, but are nearly impossible to obtain.

Pirate ship, Raymond James Stadium

Nearby, the Yanks play March's spring exhibition games at the **Legends Field**, ☎ 800-96-YANKS, 813-879-2244, or 813-875-7753, www.legendsfieldtampa.com, which replicates the team's home field. In the off-season, there's rookie and semi-professional baseball. Call for ticket prices.

■ NORTHEAST TAMPA

FAMILY FUN

Tampa's number one attraction, **Busch Gardens** at 3605 E. Bougainvillea Ave., ☎ 813-987-5000 or 813-987-5082, www.buschgardens.com, requires a whole day to experience all of its 300 acres and various African lands, such as Egypt, Morocco, and Timbuktu. The lands contain theme adventure rides, shops, shows, and restaurants. More than 2,000 animals from around the world wander freely; you swoop over them by skyride or pass them on a chug-along train. The Myombe Reserve features a gorilla area with plexiglass where visitors can "rub noses" with the beasts. There's free beer in the beer gardens, to steel your nerves for such roller-coasting terrors as the 60 mph, just-try-to-breathe SheiKra dive coaster, and Montu – the tallest and longest of its kind with a lot of topsy-turvy action. Some of the rides will get you soaked, so bring extra clothes and rent a locker. Land of the Dragons provides less scary entertainment for pre-schoolers. Edge of Africa allows visitors a close-up and personal wildlife experience, where lions, hyenas, and other beasts can be viewed through plexiglass barriers. Interactive adventure tours, such as the Serengeti Safari, allow participants aboard a flat-bed truck to feed and pet ostriches, bongos, and giraffes, while getting close to zebras, African cranes, and other native and exotic animals. The Rhino Rally combines elements of a wildlife safari and a competitive raging river thrill ride. The new KaTonga show takes the park's entertainment to a

Rhino Ralley, Busch Gardens

new level with African-inspired dance, original music, and magnificent costumes and puppetry. Adult admission is $57.95; for children aged three-nine, $47.95 (plus tax). Second-day admission is discounted. Online and Florida resident discounts are available.

Parking costs $9 for cars. Normal operation hours are 10-6 daily, but are extended during summer and other select times. The 30-minute Serengeti Safari costs an extra $33.99 plus tax per person (adults and children). Participants must be at least five years old to take the tour. Call ☎ 813-984-4043 for advance reservations.

Next door's **Adventure Island** at 10001 Malcolm McKinley Dr., ☎ 813-987-5600 or 888-800-5447, www.adventureisland.com, is also owned by Busch. It's one of Florida's best water parks, with a

Key West theme and attractions like the new Riptide, the Splash Attack maze, the Endless Surf pool, Caribbean Corkscrew, and Tampa Typhoon. It's open daily, mid-March to September, from 10 to 5 or longer; weekends only September and October; and closed the rest of the year. Admission is $34.95 for adults, $32.95 for children aged three-nine (tax extra). Online and Florida resident discounts are available. Parking costs $5 per car or camper. Combination Busch Gardens and Adventure Island tickets costs $72.95 and $62.95, plus tax.

ADVENTURE ISLAND TIPS

Adventure Island is a great place to spend a hot summer day. Here are some tips for getting the most out of your wet adventure:

- To save money, bring a picnic lunch and arrive early to grab a picnic table.
- Put surf shoes on the kids to prevent hot feet between water attractions.
- Rent a locker to stash towels and extra sunscreen.

The Museum of Science & Industry (MOSI) at 4801 E. Fowler Ave., ☎ 813-987-6000, 800-995-MOSI, www.mosi.org, tops the list of discovery attractions. In addition to its four floors of interactive exhibits, planetarium, and IMAX Theater, in 2005 it opened a separate building, Kids In Charge!, the largest children's science center in the country. Four exhibit areas challenge young kids and inspire them to learn with hands-on puzzles and changing exhibits. In the original building, kids can experience a high-wire bike ride, a motion simulator, and exhibits devoted to flight, the body, and more. Disasterville opened in 2006 and deals with hurricanes, earthquakes, and other epic natural phenomena. Outside are nature trails, a butterfly garden, and a hurricane simulator. Special exhibits cycle through in addition. Admission is $23.95 for adults, $21.95 for seniors, and $19.95 for kids aged two-12. Admission includes one IMAX film. The museum opens daily at 9. Closing hours vary according to season.

SPECTATOR SPORTS

Tampa Bay Downs, at Rte. 580 and Race Track Rd., ☎ 866-823-6967 or 813-855-4401, www.tampabaydowns.com, is the only thoroughbred race track on Florida's West Coast. Season runs December-May, with year-round simulcast wagering. The track is open daily except Monday and Wednesday. Admission is $2-$3 for adults, children free.

On the east side of I-275 at the Bird St. exit, **Tampa Greyhound Track**, ☎ 813-932-4313, www.tampadogs.com, holds evening races at 7:30, Monday-Saturday, July-December. Matinees are at 12:30 Wednesday, Saturday, and Sunday. More than 130 TV monitors enhance race viewing. Admission is $1-$2.50. No live racing takes place from January-June, but it remains open for simulcast wagering.

GAMBLING

Poker and bingo are the names of the games at the **Seminole Hard Rock Casino**, 5223 N. Orient Rd., ☎ 866-502-PLAY or 813-627-7625, www.hardrockhotelcasinotampa.com. Stakes are high, but admission is free. It has more than 2,200 games, a cafeteria, and lounge. The casino is open 24 hours.

■ SOUTH HILLSBOROUGH

A few steps south of the big city, rural agricultural communities are evolving into winter retirement enclaves. Quiet towns such as Apollo Beach, Ruskin, and Sun City, away from the mobile home parks and tomato fields, are fine places to launch a canoe or cast a rod into Hillsborough Bay. Save time to explore these quiet gems.

BEACHES, PARKS & NATURAL AREAS

You can find good access to adventure at **E.G. Simmons Park** on 19th St. NW in Ruskin, two miles west of Hwy. 41, ☎ 813-671-7655. It has picnic facilities, a boat ramp, a sandy beach in the bay with roped-off swimming area, a campground, and wildlife areas. Open daily, 8-6.

Tampa

ADVENTURES

 Author favorites are indicated with a star.

■ ON WATER

BOAT RAMPS

E.G. Simmons Park (see above) has a boat ramp into Hillsborough Bay.

To launch your craft into the lower Hillsborough River, use the ramp at **Lowry Park** (see page 148), for a nominal fee. There are also areas for fishing and picnicking there.

PADDLING

Canoe and kayak owners can launch at several county parks along the upper Hillsborough River, including **Sargeant Park, Morris Bridge Park, Trout Creek Park, Lettuce Lake Park**, and **Rotary Park**.

 Twelve miles from downtown Tampa is **Canoe Escape**, just east of I-75 on Fowler Ave. (Exit 265) in Thonotosassa, ☎ 800-44-TAMPA ext. 6 or 813-986-2067, www.canoe-escape.com. The company offers excursions into the upper Hillsborough River, where wildlife abounds close to city limits. Alligators, water snakes, ibises, river otters, turtles, and feral hogs are common sights on this quiet, natural extension of Tampa's Hillsborough River. Here, it reaches into wilderness preserve and conces-

White ibis

sion owners ensure peace by discouraging the beer-drinking crowd. No radios, dogs, or glass are allowed. Canoe Escape provides outfitting and shuttle service for two-hour to full-day excursions, priced at $39-$55 for two paddlers in a double canoe or kayak (passenger $8-$10 or free if under age 12). Solo kayak or canoe prices are $35-$45. Tours and shuttle service fees are available to canoe and kayak owners. Reservations for rentals and tours recommended.

Hillsborough River State Park, 15402 Hwy. 301 N. in Thonotosassa, east of I-75 (Exit 265), ☎ 813-987-6771, www. floridastateparks.org, rents canoes for use in the park. Cost is $8 per hour, including tax. Rangers lead a free guided canoe tour every Friday at 2 pm, limited to five canoes on a first-come basis.

The scenic **Alafia River** runs along the northern edge of south Hillsborough and is suited mainly to small crafts and canoes. A narrow, 13-mile canoe trail runs under a canopy of oak, cypress and cedar. The waterway runs east-west from Hillsborough Bay at Gibsonton. Alafia Marine at 9810 Vaughn in Gibsonton has a boat ramp you can use for a fee.

The **Little Manatee River** south of Ruskin is a designated canoe trail, accessed from paved ramps off Hwy. 41, three miles east of Ruskin.

Canoe Outpost on Hwy. 301 in Wimauma, ☎ 813-634-2228, outfits canoeists and kayakers for two- to four-hour excursions on the Little Manatee, priced at $25-$38, including equipment.

■ ON FOOT

CLIMBING

Vertical Ventures, near the Tampa International Airport at 5404 Pioneer Park Blvd., ☎ 813-884-7625, www. verticalventures.com, offers the thrill of rock climbing at an indoor gym. It caters to all levels of learners, from beginners to experts. A pro shop rents and sells equipment, and visitors can watch from a viewing deck. The gym is open Tuesday-Thursday, 2-10; Friday, 2-midnight; Saturday-Sunday, 10-6. Daily rate is $14; 20-minute classes for beginners cost $30, including gear.

© Vertical Adventures

HIKING

The Museum of Science & Industry (MOSI), 4801 E. Fowler Ave., ☎ 813-987-6300 or 800-995-MOSI, has three miles of backwoods trails where you can hike and experience local habitat. See page 166 for details about the museum.

The various trails at **Hillsborough River State Park**, 15402 Hwy. 301 N. in Thonotosassa, east of I-75, Exit 265, ☎ 813-987-6771, www.floridastateparks.org, cover more than seven miles. A favorite takes in the rapids tripping over rocks in the river.

You can take a leisurely hike around the cypress swamp wildlife boardwalk at **Lettuce Lake Park** (see below), 6920 Fletcher Ave., ☎ 813-987-6204. It also has a bike path and fitness course. $1 donation per car suggested.

Eureka Springs Park on Eureka Springs Rd., near the junction of I-4 and Hwy. 301, ☎ 813-744-5536, has trails and boardwalks to hike, as well as a lovely botanical garden, greenhouse, and picnic area. Open 8-6, daily.

■ ON HORSEBACK

Beginners through advanced riders aged seven and older can take the reins at **In the Breeze Horseback Riding Ranch and Children's Camp**, 7514 Gardner Rd., ☎ 813-264-1919, www. inthebreezeranch.com. Trail rides range from $29 to $45 for 60-90 minutes. Reservations are requested. The ranch holds day camp for children whenever there's no school, plus it offers pony rides and group events.

■ IN THE AIR

BALLOON RIDES

Big Red Balloon, ☎ 813-969-1518, www.bigredballoon. com, lifts off at sunrise for a 1, 000-foot-high view of Tampa's outlying wildlife and skyline. Guests meet at Mimi's Café, 11702 N. Dale Mabry Hwy. Prices begin at $160 for children aged five to 10, $185 for adults, $500 for couples flying alone, plus tax. Sunrise flights include sit-down champagne breakfast. It operates daily, 10-8.

SKYDIVING

Take the ultimate rush-adventure plunge at **Skydive City**, 4241 Skydive Lane in Zephyrhills (northeast of Tampa), ☎ 800-404-9399 or 813-783-9399, www.skydivecity.com. Facilities include training, a pro shop, and camping. First-time tandem dives cost $184, which requires only about 20 minutes of training.

ON WHEELS

Lower Hillsborough Wilderness Park (see *Eco-Adventures*, below) has a network of more than 35 miles of off-road biking trails between Morris Bridge Park, Flatwoods Park, and Trout Creek Park. A seven-mile loop of the Flatwoods trail is paved and suitable for inline skating.

ECO-ADVENTURES

More than 140 exotic and endangered big cats live at **Big Cat Rescue**, 12801 Easy St., ☎ 813-920-4130, www.bigcatrescue.org. The non-profit refuge is located just off Gunn Highway. Tours cost $22 per person, and are offered Monday-Friday at 9 and 3; Saturday at 9:30, 11:30 and 1:30. Feeding, night, private, and all-day tours are also available.

As you travel farther from city center, opportunity for adventure in a natural setting increases. **Lettuce Lake Park** at 6920 E. Fletcher Ave., a quarter-mile west of I-75, ☎ 813-987-6204, occupies 240 acres with an Audubon Center open on weekends, a cypress swamp, alligators, birds, a wildlife boardwalk, an observation tower, a bike path, a playground, a fitness course, and picnic areas. Donation of $1 per car suggested.

Lower Hilleborough Wilderness Park, www.swfwmd.state.fl.us/recreation/areas/lowerhillsborough.html, is a system of county-operated recreational areas along

Boardwalk, Lettuce Lake Park

the upper Hillsborough River (hardly recognizable as the origin of what flows through downtown Tampa). It lies east of Interstate 75 off Morris Bridge Rd. and along Hwy. 301. Its four main components are **John B Sargeant** Park, ☎ 813-987-6208, **Trout Creek Park**, ☎ 813-987-6200; **Morris Bridge Park**, ☎ 813-987-6209; and **Flatwoods Park**, ☎ 813-987-6211. They offer picnic facilities, canoe launches, horse trails, and, combined, 30 miles of lopped off-road biking trails.

Hillsborough River State Park, 15402 Hwy. 301 N., east of I-75 Exit 265, ☎ 813-987-6771, www.floridastateparks.org/hillsborough river, sits prettily among a 16,000-acre preserve. It's one of Florida's oldest state parks, and wears its age gracefully. Here, the Hillsborough River frolics around limestone upcroppings, providing rapids for experienced canoeists. A reconstructed Seminole War historic site, **Fort Foster**, is open for touring at 2 pm on Saturdays and 11 am on Sundays. The park has two campgrounds, a swimming pool, a playground, canoe rentals, nature trails, and oak-shaded picnic grounds. Admission to the park is $4 per car of two to eight persons or less, $3 per single driver, $1 per pedestrian, cyclist, or additional persons in vehicle. Admission to the fort is $2 for adults, $1 or children aged six-12. Pool admission is $2; children aged five and younger are admitted free (included in camping fees).

In Apollo Beach, you can see manatees as they migrate to warmer waters in winter at Tampa Electric's **Manatee Viewing Center**, Big Bend and Dickman roads, off I-75 at Exit 246, ☎ 813-228-4289, www.manatee-teco.com. An observation platform, educational displays, a 900-foot "tidal walkway" into a saltmarsh, and a video familiarize visitors with the behavior of Florida's "gentle giants" and the history and workings of the power plant. It's open daily, 10-5, from November to mid-April. Admission is free.

SHOPPING

Near Tampa's major attractions, **University Mall**, 2200 E. Fowler Ave., ☎ 813-971-3465, www.universitymalltampa.com, is open daily with more than 150 department stores and shops, a movie complex, and a food court. In the Westshore region, **WestShore Plaza**, at the intersection of Westshore and Kennedy boulevards, ☎ 813-286-0790, www.westshoreplaza.com, claims the area's only Saks Fifth Avenue, plus an upscale variety of name-brand stores and shops. **International Plaza**, near the airport at 2223 N. Westshore Blvd., ☎ 877-883-1770, www.shopinternationalplaza.com, counts Neiman Marcus among its 200 merchants.

One of the newer additions to the major mall scene, **Citrus Park Town Center**, ☎ 813-926-4644, lies at the northwest edge of town, just west of Veterans Expressway on Gunn Hwy. Department stores, 120 shops, 20 cinema screens, a food court, and restaurants occupy the mall's American nostalgic architecture.

WHERE TO STAY

ACCOMMODATIONS PRICE KEY		
Rates are per room, per night, double occupancy. Price ranges described for each property often do not take into account penthouses and other exceptional, high-priced accommodations.	$	Up to $75
	$$	$75 to $150
	$$$	$151 to $250
	$$$$	$251 and up

■ HOTELS & MOTELS

Hotels cluster near the airport on Tampa Bay at Courtney Campbell Causeway and around Busch Gardens. Most are the chain variety, with everything from budget to luxury.

Near the airport, **Hampton Inn** at 4817 W. Laurel St., ☎ 813-287-0778 or 800-HAMPTON, www.zmchotels.com, is a good value, with complimentary breakfast bar, a heated swimming pool, and free local airport and local restaurant shuttle. $$-$$$

Shoppers especially will enjoying dropping in at **Renaissance Tampa Hotel International Plaza** at 4200 Jim Walter Blvd., ☎ 800-HOTELS-1 or 813-877-9200, www.renaissancetampa.com. Located on the campus of an upscale shopping mall just next door to Nieman Marcus, it is geared toward business clientele, yet leisure guests don't get the sense of being mobbed by conventioneers. Its 293 rooms are spacious enough, but the hotel's elegance lies in its public areas, particularly its acclaimed Pelagia Trattoria restaurant (see *Restaurants*, below). $$$-$$$$

© Marriott Hotels

Tampa

Doubletree Guest Suites at 3050 N. Rocky Point Dr. W., ☎ 800-222-TREE or 813-888-8800, gives you a water view for your money. Located at the Courtney Campbell Causeway, amenities include airport shuttle, pool, whirlpool, sauna, exercise room, and business center. Its 203 suites are designed with separate bedroom and living areas and contain wet bar and coffeemaker. $$-$$$$

Top chic in the Westshore neighborhood, **Grand Hyatt Tampa Bay**, 6200 Courtney Campbell Causeway, ☎ 800-233-1234 or 813-874-1234, http//:grandtampabay.hyatt.com, towers over bay waters

and its own 35-acre wildlife refuge. Within the spread-out complex are 377 rooms, 45 "casitas," 23 suites, three restaurants (see Armani's and Oystercatchers under *Where to Eat*, below), and a pool. $$$$

© Marriott Hotels

Near Busch Gardens and MOSI, **DoubleTree Guest Suites Busch Gardens**, 11310 N. 30th St., ☎ 813-971-7690, is made of suites, lush gardens, a pool and whirlpool. It offers a complimentary shuttle to Busch. The two-room suites are stocked with microwave, fridge, and coffeemaker. Rates include complimentary breakfast. $$-$$$

Adventurers headed out on the trails of Lower Hillsborough Wilderness Park can find convenient and inexpensive beds at **Ramada Inn**, 11714 Morris Bridge Rd, just off I-75 Exit 265, ☎ 813-985-8525. Some of the red brick hotel's 122 rooms have microwave ovens, mini-fridges, and flat-panel TVs. Free high-speed Internet in the rooms, Wi-Fi in the lobby, a pool, a small fitness center, and complimentary Continental breakfast add to the value. $-$$

■ RESORTS

Outside of Tampa to the north, **Saddlebrook Resort** at 5700 Saddlebrook Resort, Wesley Chapel, ☎ 813-973-1111 or 800-729-8383, www.saddlebrookresort.com, is a destination in itself, especially for golfers and sports-lovers. Around a central "Superpool" hub, it clusters 36 Arnold Palmer-designed holes of golf, a golf academy, 45 tennis courts (including one Wimbledon-grass surfaced), volleyball, basketball, lawn games, a fitness center, and a spa, along with a kids' program. Breakfast and dinner are included in the rates. Ask about packages. $$$$

■ CAMPING

Northeast of Tampa, around Zephyrhills, RV resorts are plentiful.

Hillsborough River State Park
(see page 172), 15402 Hwy. 301
N., east of I-75 Exit 265, ☎ 813-
987-6771, www.floridastate
parks.org, has two camp-
grounds – one riverside, the
other in hammock vegetation –
with 115 sites, playgrounds,
laundry facilities, and showers.
Cost is $22.40 per night.
Leashed pets are allowed. To reserve a campsite, call 800-326-
3521 or visit www.reserveamerica.com.

E.G. Simmons Park (see page 167) on 19th Ave. NE, two miles west
of Hwy. 41, ☎ 813-671-7655, has an open campground with a view
of the bay. Fees are $12 a night with water and electricity, $10 for seniors.

WHERE TO EAT

Many of the best, non-chain restaurants around the airport are located within the area's hotels. **Pelagia Trattoria** at the Renaissance,
4200 Jim Walter Boulevard, ☎ 813-313-3235, www.pelagiatrattoria.
com, is an example of dining way above the typical hotel food. Modern and Mediterranean in style, its specialties include grilled cala-
mari salad, lobster ravioli, saffron tagliatelle, pizza, and cappuccino
crème brulée. Open daily for breakfast ($9-$15), lunch ($7-$14),
and dinner ($15-$35).

For top-shelf dining, make your reservations at **Armani's** in the
Grand Hyatt Tampa Bay at 6200 Courtney Campbell Causeway,
☎ 813-207-6800. Exquisite 14th-floor views and superb northern
Italian-style seafood and other specialties, including a large anti-
pasto bar, are the draws. A jacket is required. It's open for dinner every day but Sunday. Entrées are $20-$35. Reservations are
recommended.

Also on the Hyatt property, **Oystercatchers**, ☎ 813-207-6815, overlooks the property's 35-acre bayfront nature preserve. In a bright,
open, polished setting, it serves new American-style cuisine. It is
open weekdays for lunch and daily for dinner. Luncheon salads,
sandwiches, seafood, and signature items such as seafood pasta
and grouper tacos range from $13 to $18. A la carte dinner entrées

such as monkfish "osso bucco" and crab cakes range from $19 to $30.

If your idea of atmosphere is junkyard chic, you'll love **Skipper's Smoke House** at Skipper Rd. and Nebraska Ave., ☎ 813-971-0666, www.skipperssmokehouse.com. Particularly if you favor plain, ungarnished seafood. Slurp "sliders" in the oyster bar or relish the black bean 'gator chili, crab cakes with black bean salsa, and other Florida and Cajun specialties, ranging in price from $7 to $15. It's open for lunch and dinner daily, except Monday.

Wieners are an artform at **Mel's Hot Dogs**, 4136 E. Busch Blvd., ☎ 813-985-8000. Select from a classic Chicago-style dog, a bagel dog, bacon-cheddar dog, corn dog, and others. Or be rebellious and order a burger or Italian steak sandwich. Wash it down with a beer, wine, or soda. Prices run $3-$9. Open for lunch and dinner daily.

NIGHTLIFE

Skipper's Smoke House (see above) at Skipper Rd. and Nebraska Ave., ☎ 813-971-0666, has established itself as the place for alternative music in the Tampa Bay area. Live reggae, zydeco, and blues bands play open-air in the backyard of the ramshackle restaurant, nightly except Sunday. Cover charge varies.

Bradenton & Sarasota

Though distinctly individual in character, the metropolitan areas of Bradenton and Sarasota often get lumped together. The two do sort of melt into one another geographically, but anyone who has gotten to know the cities can feel immediately when they've crossed the boundaries. This is demonstrated most dramatically on Longboat Key, a 12-mile island split between Sarasota County and Bradenton's Manatee County. In Bradenton's northern half, you find an old fishing village with easygoing seafood restaurants and beach cottages. In the Sarasota portion, everything climbs several steps upscale, and manicured landscaping exalts the island's prima donna status.

FLORIDIOM: Manatee County gets its name from one of Florida's most loveable animals. The ancient manatee, or sea cow, used to confuse sailors into believing they'd sighted a mermaid. The sailors had obviously been into the rum rations, as the manatee, with its burlap-like skin and 3,000-pound ungirlish figure, more closely resembles its cousin, the elephant. The gentle manatees fall victim only to man and red tide, which sadly bring their numbers to the brink of extinction.

So while northern Bradenton and its islands of **Anna Maria** and **Longboat Key** exude something more casually Old Florida, Sarasota and its string of island pearls affect utter sophistication, save for **Siesta Key**, with its strains of beachy, subtropic island behavior.

Bradenton and Sarasota each trace their identity back to a male historic figure. In Bradenton, it's none other than **Hernando De Soto**, whom historians claim made his first New World landfall on local shores. As a result, Bradenton has a propensity for preserving history. Its Manatee River, Gulf front, and Intracoastal bays offer ample scope for watersports.

Sarasota owes its development and artistic reputation to, ironically, the circus, which wintered there beginning in the late 1800s. In contrast to circus raucousness, however, **John Ringling** was a man swayed by esthetics. The art he loved had a bit of three-ring showiness to it, nonetheless, as demonstrated by the baroque Italianate palace that he built here. It comprises, along with his art museum complex, Sarasota's most renowned attraction. Ringling is also responsible for building bridges – with his circus elephants, it is told – to Sarasota's cherished islands, some of the West Coast's most exclusive. On Sarasota's islands, you'll find world-class shopping, the coast's whitest beach, a premium marine laboratory, nature parks and beaches, and a love for the sea and its pleasures. The islands and the mainland put every bit of waterfront to use, much of it sea-walled and commercially developed. This affords heavy opportunity for boating, fishing, and other watersports.

John Ringling

At the southern reaches of Sarasota County, **Venice** hides in the shadow of its neighbor. Along with nearby communities of Osprey, Casey Key, Nokomis, and Nokomis Beach, it has much to offer seafarers and adventurous landlubbers on its Myakka River and Gulf front, and in its non-exploited parks and beaches.

North Jetty, Casey Ket

TRANSPORTATION

■ AIRPORTS

Sarasota-Bradenton International Airport (SRQ), www.srq-airport.com, ☎ 941-359-2770 or 941-359-2777, is in Bradenton, three miles north of Sarasota.

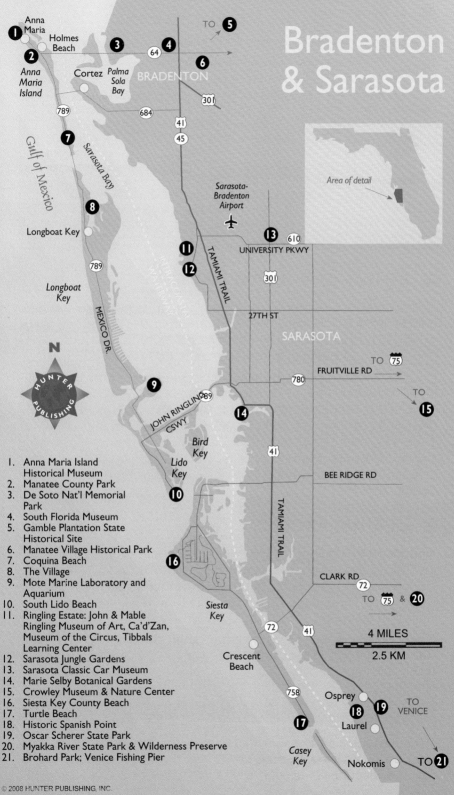

Bradenton
& Sarasota

Anna Maria
Holmes Beach
Anna Maria Island
Cortez
Palma Sola Bay
BRADENTON
789
Gulf of Mexico
Sarasota Bay
Longboat Key
Longboat Key
MEXICO DR.
64
684
41
45
301
Sarasota-Bradenton Airport
UNIVERSITY PKWY
610
301
27TH ST
SARASOTA
TAMIAMI TRAIL
RINGLING CAUSEWAY
JOHN RINGLING CSWY
789
Bird Key
Lido Key
41
BEE RIDGE RD
FRUITVILLE RD
TO 75
TO
780
Siesta Key
Crescent Beach
Casey Key
CLARK RD
TAMIAMI TRAIL
72
758
Osprey
Laurel
Nokomis
TO VENICE
41
72
4 MILES
2.5 KM
TO 75 &
Area of detail

N
HUNTER PUBLISHING

1. Anna Maria Island Historical Museum
2. Manatee County Park
3. De Soto Nat'l Memorial Park
4. South Florida Museum
5. Gamble Plantation State Historical Site
6. Manatee Village Historical Park
7. Coquina Beach
8. The Village
9. Mote Marine Laboratory and Aquarium
10. South Lido Beach
11. Ringling Estate: John & Mable Ringling Museum of Art, Ca'd'Zan, Museum of the Circus, Tibbals Learning Center
12. Sarasota Jungle Gardens
13. Sarasota Classic Car Museum
14. Marie Selby Botanical Gardens
15. Crowley Museum & Nature Center
16. Siesta Key County Beach
17. Turtle Beach
18. Historic Spanish Point
19. Oscar Scherer State Park
20. Myakka River State Park & Wilderness Preserve
21. Brohard Park; Venice Fishing Pier

MAJOR AIRLINES & SHUTTLES SERVING SARASOTA-BRADENTON (SRQ) INT'L AIRPORT

Air Canada	☎ 888-247-2262	www.aircanada.com
Air France	☎ 800-237-2747	www.airfrance.us
AirTran Airways	☎ 800-247-8726	www.airtran.com
Alitalia	☎ 800-223-5730	www.alitalia.it
American Airlines	☎ 800-433-7300	www.aa.com
Cape Air	☎ 800-352-0714	www.flycapeair.com
Continental	☎ 800-525-0280	www.continental.com
Delta Air Lines / Comair	☎ 800-221-1212	www.delta.com
JetBlue	☎ 800-538-2583	www.jetblue.com
Northwest/KLM	☎ 800-225-2525	www.nwa.com
US Airways	☎ 800-428-4322	www.usairways.com

■ RENTAL CARS & TAXI SERVICE

Rental cars are available at the airport and other locations throughout the area. Try **Alamo**, ☎ 800-327-9633 or 941-359-5540; **Avis**, ☎ 800-331-1212 or 941-359-5240; **Hertz**, ☎ 800-654-3131 or 941-355-8848; and **Budget**, ☎ 800-763-2999, or 941-359-5353.

Companies that provide transportation to and from the airport include **Checker Cab of Bradento**n, ☎ 941-755-9339; **Diplomat Taxi**, ☎ 941-355-5155; **West Coast Executive Sedans**, ☎ 941-355-9645 or 941-359-8600; and **Longboat Limousine**, ☎ 800-LB-LIMO-1 or 941-383-1235, www.longboatlimousine.com. Vans from **Sarasota/Tampa Express**, ☎ 800-326-2800 or 941-355-8400 (reservations), www.stexps.com, service the Sarasota/Bradenton and Tampa airports.

■ GETTING AROUND

Highway 41 (Tamiami Trail) cuts close to the coastline in Bradenton and Sarasota, and takes you straight into downtown Sarasota. **Highway 301** parallels 41 to the east through Bradenton. The two converge in Sarasota. I-75 swings wide from the coast here, to the east of Highway 41.

From anywhere in the Tampa Bay area (Sarasota to Hernando County), dial 511 or log into www.511tampabay.com for up-to-date traffic and route information.

INFORMATION

For information on the area, call or write the **Bradenton Area Convention & Visitors Bureau** at PO Box 1000, Bradenton, 34206, www.floridagulfislands.com, ☎ 941-729-9177 or 800-4 MANATEE.

It operates a tourist information kiosk at Prime Outlets shopping mall in Ellenton, ☎ 941-729-7040.

Or contact the **Sarasota Convention & Visitors Bureau** at 655 N. Tamiami Trail, Sarasota, 34236, www.sarasotafl.org, ☎ 800-800-3906 or 941-957-1877, open Monday-Saturday from 9-5.

BUDGET TIPS

■ Find discount coupons in "SEE" booklets and the orange "Welcome" guide map to Sarasota/Bradenton. Both are readily available from area establishments.

■ **Gamble Plantation Historic State Park's** visitor's center (see page 187) has museum exhibits and is open free to the public. Admission to and tours of the mansion are only $4 for adults, $2 for children aged six-12.

■ Sarasota area dining has a reputation for being pricey, but you can save money without having to hit the fast-food chains at several fine restaurants, including a number of Amish ones, such as **Sugar & Spice** (see page 223) in Sarasota. Other budget restaurants include **Gulf Drive Café** (see page 201) in Bradenton Beach, and **Old Salty Dog** on Lido Key (page 211) and Siesta Key.

■ Bradenton's best free attractions are **Manatee Village Historical Park** (page 184), **Manatee County Agricultural Museum**, and **De Soto National Memorial Park** (page 185).

■ You can watch the **Pittsburgh Pirates** (page 187) practice for free at Pirate City during spring training in March.

■ Admission to **Anna Maria Island Historical Museum** (page 195) is free or by donation.

■ Admission to the **Ringling Estate** (page 214), by decree of John Ringling's will, is free on Mondays.

■ At **City Island** (page 209), between Lido Key and Longboat Key, you'll find a couple of things to do without opening up your wallet: **Sarasota Bay Walk** and **Sarasota Ski-A-Rees Show**.

FESTIVALS & EVENTS

★ **FEBRUARY/MARCH** –The **Cortez Fishing Festival** on Rte. 684 in Cortez, ☎ 941-794-1249, http://cortez fishingfestival.org, takes place over two days in late Feb-

Sign, Cortez Fishing Festival

ruary, and consists of food vendors, country music, arts and crafts with a nautical theme, net-mending demonstrations, and environmental exhibits describing Cortez's 100-year-old fishing industry. For four days in February, the Ringling Estate (see page 164) hosts the wildly popular and artistically done **Ringling Medieval Fair**, ☎ 877-334-3377, www.renaissancefest. com, at the Sarasota County Fairgrounds.

★ **APRIL** –Bradenton's entire Manatee County celebrates its past during **DeSoto Heritage Festival**, ☎ 941-747-1998. A plastic bottle boat regatta on Palma Sola Causeway, a seafood festival, and a lighted night parade highlight month. April also brings **Siesta Fiesta**, ☎ 954-472-3755. In Venice, the big event is the **Sharks Tooth Festival**, ☎ 941-412-0402, which means music, seafood, a shark tooth scramble, and marine life displays. Admission is charged.

★ **JUNE** –Kayak races, classes, clinics, and demonstrations fill two days at the end of the month during the **Kayak & Outdoor Festival**, ☎ 941-729-9177 ext. 233, www.floridasgulfislands.com.

★ **JULY** – Head to Sarasota's islands to watch **The Suncoast Offshore Grand Prix**, ☎ 941-371-8820 ext. 1800, www.suncoastoffshore.org, a charity event that draws powerboat racers from around the world for Fourth of July week. Golf and fishing tournaments and entertainment are part of the festivities.

★ **AUGUST** – The **De Soto Fishing Tournament**, ☎ 941-747-1998, takes place at Bradenton Yacht Club in Palmetto the second week of the month. Entry fees.

★ **DECEMBER** – For three evenings the first weekend of the month, downtown Bradenton turns into **Winter Wonderland**, ☎ 941-708-6200 ext. 288, with mountains of snow, a holiday boat parade, the Jingle Bell Run along the Riverwalk, and a lively street festival. Sarasota celebrates its holidays with a **Christmas Boat Parade**, ☎ 941-371-8820 ext. 1800, through the town's canals and bays on a Saturday early in the month.

WEEKEND ADVENTURE ITINERARY

▪ **FRIDAY:** Tour Gamble Plantation Historic State Park and Manatee Village Historical Park in the morning. Have lunch in downtown Bradenton at Twin Dolphin Marina Grill. Spend the afternoon at Anna Maria Island beach or out on the water on a boat rental. Have dinner at Beach Bistro in Anna Maria. Spend the night on the island.

▪ **SATURDAY:** Begin with breakfast at Gulf Drive Café. Tour Mote Marine Aquarium and board a Sarasota Bay Explorers excursion. Have lunch at St. Armands Circle. Visit the Ringling Estate in the afternoon. Do dinner and theater in downtown Sarasota in the evening. Stay in downtown Sarasota.

▪ **SUNDAY:** Drive to Venice for canoeing and lunch at Snook Haven. Go to Brohard Park for shark-tooth collecting or fishing on the pier. Have dinner at Crow's Nest. Spend the night in Venice.

Bradenton

After Spanish explorer Hernando De Soto left his mark here in 1539, then continued on his way to discover the Mississippi River, Bradenton remained wild and unsettled until the sugar plantations of the 1840s and the cattle industry of the 1880s established themselves.

Some find Bradenton too sleepy to be fun. If you're a history buff, you'll refute that. But if you're looking for action, head to the beaches or Sarasota.

Bradenton's outlying towns, particularly Palmetto and Ellenton, are more suited to adventure than Bradenton itself. Both of the above-mentioned lie north of Bradenton, on the opposite bank of the Manatee River.

Cortez juts into bay waters southwest of town. Its peninsular location catalyzed its development as a fishing town with lots of flavor and local color.

GETTING HERE

From **I-75**, Exit 224 takes you along the north side of the Manatee River via **Highway 30**. From Exit 220, **Rte. 64** travels straight into downtown and out to Anna Maria Island. From Exit 217, **Rte. 70** runs through the south part of town. Highway 41 and Business 41 stab through town's center. Highways 301 and 41 merge in the north, then split south of town.

The **Manatee County Area Transit** (MCAT) system, ☎ 941-749-7116, www.co.manatee.fl.us (click on MCAT) travels around Bradenton, Palmetto, Cortez, and Longboat Key. Basic fare is $1 for adults, 50¢ for seniors and children. Its **Manatee Trolley** services Anna Maria Island free of charge, with connecting service to MCAT.

INFORMATION

Call or write for more information: **Manatee Chamber of Commerce**, 222 10th St. W., Bradenton, 34205, www.manateechamber.com, ☎ 941-748-4842. It's open Monday-Friday, 9-5.

SIGHTS & ATTRACTIONS

In Town

▦ OF HISTORIC OR CULTURAL INTEREST

Bradenton bygones are preserved in a shady park setting at **Manatee Village Historical Park**, 15th St. E. and Manatee Ave., ☎ 941-749-7165. Buildings of local historical significance include a circa 1860 county courthouse, church, Cracker farmhouse, one-room schoolhouse, smokehouse, and general store. Staff members don period dress. Admission is free. Open Monday-Friday, 9-4:30, and Sunday (except July and August), 1:30-4:30. This is a great place for a cool picnic.

Downtown's devotion to history is evident in its rejuvenating streets and old buildings, and at the **South Florida Museum**, 201 10th St. W., www.southfloridamuseum.org, ☎ 941-746-4131. Displays cover local history through the eras of native Americans, Spanish conquistadors, and space exploration. Kids like the resident manatees at Parker Manatee Aquarium and hands-on activity center. The Bishop Planetarium, which suffered fire damage in 2001, reopened all state-of-the-art in 2005 and hosts a full schedule of star-studded programs. From January through April and in July, the museum is open Monday-Saturday 10-5 and Sunday noon-5; from May through December, except July, the museum is closed on Mondays. It also closes Thanksgiving, Christmas, New Year's Day, and the last two weeks in August. Admission for adults is $16; for seniors, $14; and for children aged four-12, $12.

Snooty, the aquariums' friendly manattee.

To honor Bradenton's trademark historical event, **De Soto National Memorial Park** at 75th St. NW, ☎ 941-792-0458, www.nps.gov/deso, recalls the life and times of explorer Hernando De Soto – who is

said to have made first New World landfall here – through displays, a film, a half-mile shell and boardwalk nature trail, old trees like the one shown on the previous page, and living history guides (in season only). The park also offers a lovely, out-of-the-way view of Old Florida and the Manatee River. Admission is free; visitor center hours are 9-5, daily. Grounds are also open daily, sunrise to sunset.

> **TIP:** *The **Sarasota Bay National Estuary Program,** ☎ 941-359-5841, www.sarasotabay.org, has organized a map of The Gulf Coast Heritage Trail, locating more than 100 sights of historical, cultural, and environmental interest in Manatee and Sarasota counties.*

■ PERFORMING ARTS

One of Florida's longest running community theaters, **Riverfront Theatre**, 102 Old Main St., ☎ 941-748-5875, hosts the Manatee Players, www.manateeplayers.com, which performs its main season September-May, plus a summer series and family productions. Tickets cost $23 for adults, $11 for students.

■ FAMILY FUN

A video arcade, go-cart track, burger stand, and laser tag add to the fun of miniature golf at **Pirates Cove Fun Park**, 5410 Hwy. 41, ☎ 941-755-4608, www.piratescovefunpark.com. Golf prices are $4 for 18 holes; laser tag costs $7. It's $6.25 for go-cart rides. The park opens daily; hours vary according to season and day of the week, generally 10-10.

Smugglers Cove Adventure Golf, 2000 Cortez Rd. W., www.smugglersgolf.com, ☎ 941-756-0043 (also at 3815 N. Tamiami Tr. in Sarasota, ☎ 941-351-6620), charges $10 for adults, $9 for children aged four to 12, and $3 for aged three and younger. It is open daily, 9-11.

■ TOURS

Here's a juicy attraction: **Mixon Fruit Farms** at 2712 26th Ave. E., ☎ 800-608-2525 (seasonal) or 941-748-5829; www.mixon.com. A tram tour takes you through orange groves and Mixon's processing plant in the height of the producing season (November-April). Sample the fruit and juice and buy citrus by the bagful. For the family, there's a maze and wildlife rescue center. Hours are Monday-Saturday, 8:30-5:30. Admission is $7 for adults and $3 for children aged 12 and younger.

■ SPECTATOR SPORTS

Baseball fans can watch a professional team in action in March when the **Pittsburgh Pirates** play their spring exhibition season at McKechnie Field, Ninth St. and 17th Ave. W., ☎ 941-748-4610. While in town, they practice from 10-1:30 at Pirate City, 1701 27th St. E., ☎ 941-747-3031.

 Author favorites are indicated with a star.

Outlying Areas

■ OF HISTORIC OR CULTURAL INTEREST

To explore the region's sugar-coated past, visit a masterfully restored sugar manor north of Bradenton at **Gamble Plantation Historic State Park**, on Rte. 301 west of I-75, ☎ 941-723-4536, www.floridastateparks.org/gambleplantation. Besides learning about its former life as home for a sugar lord and the town's social center, you'll hear how the Greek-revival mansion, built in

1840, sheltered the Confederate Secretary of State as he fled for his life after the Civil War. The grounds are open daily, 8-sunset. The house is open Thursday-Monday and may be viewed by tour only. Tour times are 9:30, 10:30, 1, 2, 3, and 4. Admission is $4 for adults, $2 for children aged six-12. A museum in the visitor's center tells the plantation's story through the eras and can be enjoyed for free. It is open daily, 8-5 (closed 11:45-12:45).

To the west, facing downtown Bradenton across the Manatee River, the tomato processing town of Palmetto works at recycling the historic value of its downtown. In **Palmetto Historical Park**, Sixth St. W. and 10th Ave. W., ☎ 941-723-4991, www.manateeclerk.com/ClerkServices/HisVill/village.htm, clusters some old pioneer buildings, including a circa 1929 one-room schoolhouse and an 1880 post office. To tour the buildings, stop in at the Carnegie Library historical museum in the complex, Tuesday-Friday and the first and third Saturday of the month,

10-noon and 1-4. Within the park, Manatee County Agricultural Museum (shown here) at 1015 Sixth St. W., ☎ 941-721-2034, commemorates the town's farm heritage in a barn-like setting (without the smell). Exhibits on farming and commercial fishing include tools, photos, equipment, a growers hall of fame, and hands-on activities such as lassoing a cow. It opens the same hours as the historical park. Admission to both is free.

To tour more of Palmetto's **historic district**, contact the Manatee Chamber of Commerce for Manatee Riverwalk tour brochures.

■ PARKS & NATURAL AREAS

Take a hike at **Emerson Point Preserve** at 5801 17th St. W. in Palmetto, ☎ 941-721-6885, and you'll find yourself atop an ancient Indian shell mound overlooking bay water vistas and their rampant bird life. Paths delve into thick woods populated heavily with mosquitoes in summer, so be prepared.

On the water, **Riverside Park** and the neighboring **Regatta Pointe Marina** on Riverside Drive provide a milieu for boating, fishing, and dining enthusiasts (see more under *Adventures* and *Where to Eat*, below). From there, the so-called Green Bridge (Hwy. 41), takes you to the heart of downtown Bradenton.

East of I-75, **Lake Manatee State Park** at 20007 Rte. 64, ☎ 941-741-3028, www.floridastateparks.org/lakemanatee, provides an opportunity for communing with nature in 556 acres of wildlife habitat. You can swim in the freshwater lake (but beware of alligators), launch or rent a boat, fish, and picnic on grounds with a play

area. Admission is $4 per vehicle of up to eight people, $1 for pedestrians and bicyclists. The park is open daily, 8-sunset.

■ SPECTATOR SPORTS

Desoto Super Speedway, eight miles east of the interstate on Rte. 64, www.desotosuperspeedway.com, ☎ 941-748-3171, hosts Saturday night stock car racing February through November on a paved oval track. Tickets are $15 for aged 13 and older, $5 for children aged six through 12, and $25 for pit entry.

ADVENTURES

■ ON WATER

FISHING

You can fish for 50¢ (kids free) from the **Bradenton City Pier** on Bridge St. Hunt Memorial Pier at Riverside Park (see *Sights & Attractions*, above), and the **Green Bridge Pier** in Palmetto, are other popular spots.

Otherwise, most fishing and boating activity takes place on the islands or on the mainland at a fishing village named **Cortez**. Land and wading fishermen favor **Palma Sola Causeway** at Palma Sola Bay and Rte. 64, which heads from the mainland to Anna Maria Island.

For freshwater fishing, try **Lake Manatee State Park** (see *Sights & Attractions*, above) at 20007 Rte. 64, ☎ 941-741-3028, www.floridastateparks.org/lakemanatee. Huge Lake Manatee, a dammed portion of the Manatee River, yields bass, perch, catfish, and other freshwater species. It has a boat ramp and fishing dock. Boat motors are restricted to 20hp or less. You can rent kayaks and canoes (with motors) nearby (see *Paddling*, below). Admission is $4 per vehicle.

Fishing charters depart from **Green Bridge Tackle** and **Regatta Pointe Marina** in Palmetto.

Captain Allen Engle, ☎ 941-812-6369, specializes in backwater and light tackle strategies. He accommodates up to four on his 26-foot boat, at a cost of $350 for a half-day, $550 for all day.

Annie's Bait & Tackle, open daily at 4334 127th St. W. in Cortez, ☎ 941-794-3580, supplies bait, rents tackle, and arranges fishing charters.

BOAT RAMPS

To launch your own boat, proceed to **Palma Sola Causeway** at Palma Sola Bay and Rte. 64, where you'll find plenty of watersports activity.

BOAT CHARTERS & TOURS

On **Captain Kim's Charters**, 12306 46th Ave. W in Cortez, ☎ 941-920-3307, www.kimscharters.com, Kim will skim the grass flats for interesting marine creatures to show and tell. She'll take you fishing, island-hopping, birding, snorkeling – whatever you have in mind. She charges $15 per person, per hour.

Sail aboard the 36-foot catamaran **Mahina La**, departing from the Seafood Shack Restaurant at the bridge in Cortez, ☎ 941-713-8000. Cruises start at $30 per person for a two-hour dolphin excursion to $90 for a day on Egmont Key (see page 118) lunching, shelling, hiking, and snorkeling. Longer trips to Cayo Costa (see page 290) and Key West are also offered. Wannabe sailors can take lessons.

PERSONAL WATERCRAFT

On the Palma Sola Causeway to Anna Maria Island, **Ultimate Power Sports of Bradenton**, 12310 Manatee Ave. W., ☎ 941-761-7433, www.bradentonjetski.com, rents Jet Skis for $85 per hour. It also offers beach cats, pontoon boats, fishing charters, and parasailing.

WINDSURFING

Palma Sola Causeway Beach, on Rte. 64 heading to Anna Maria Island, is popular with windsurfers and WaveRunner operators, who can launch from the causeway's boat ramp. There are also rentals, restrooms, and a picnic area.

PADDLING

For getting around Lake Manatee, rent a canoe or kayak at **Lake Manatee Fish Camp**, the corner of Rtes. 64 and 675 near Lake Manatee State Park ☎ 941-322-8500. Canoes and kayak rentals run $15 per person, per day.

Canoeing adventures can last a half-day, whole day, or overnight at **Ray's Canoe Hideaway**, 1247 Hagle Park Rd., ☎ 941-747-3909 or 888-57-CANOE, www.rayscanoehideaway.com. Canoe rentals run $25 for a half-day, $30 for a full day, and $39 overnight. Kayak rentals cost $25-$40 a half-day, and $35-$50 all day. Launching your own boat costs $6. Expeditions follow the Upper Manatee River, rich with lore, fish, and birdlife. Tours and fishing pole rental are available. The facility closes on Wednesdays. Call ahead for reservations.

ON WHEELS

Emerson Point Preserve on Snead Island in Palmetto (see *Parks & Natural Areas*, above), gives you waterside vistas along its 2.7-mile partially paved trail.

IN THE AIR

At **Gulfside Ultralight Tours**, 9915B Manatee Ave. W., ☎ 941-761-3597, you can learn to fly with lessons lasting from 10 minutes to an hour. The two-person Ultralight is equipped with floats.

SHOPPING

Off I-75 at Exit 224, **Prime Outlets of Ellenton**, ☎ 888-260-7608, www.primeoutlets.com, boasts a Caribbean setting and 135 stores full of factory merchandise.

The Bradenton **Farmers' Market** brings artisans, antiques dealers, and performers to downtown Bradenton every Saturday, 7:30 am-12:30 pm, on 13th St. between 6th Ave. and 8th Ave.; ☎ 941-747-2498.

WHERE TO STAY

ACCOMMODATIONS PRICE KEY		
Rates are per room, per night, double occupancy. Price ranges described for each property often do not take into account penthouses and other exceptional, high-priced accommodations.	$	Up to $75
	$$	$75 to $150
	$$$	$151 to $250
	$$$$	$251 and up

■ HOTELS & MOTELS

As for lodging on the mainland, Bradenton offers nothing spectacular. Near the airport, you'll find the usual business-chain array. If you want something close to downtown, try the 150-room **Rodeway Inn** at 2303 First St. E., ☎ 941-747-6465. $$

Holiday Inn Riverfront at Hwy. 41 and Manatee Ave., ☎ 800-HOLIDAY or 941-747-3727, www.bradentonholidayinn.com, has more atmosphere: Mission-style architecture, a river view, a courtyard pool with gardens and waterfalls. Amenities include a restaurant and bar, fitness room, and whirlpool. $$-$$$

■ CAMPING

Many of the area's private campgrounds are designed for retired winter residents and don't allow children, except as visitors. If you have kids, call first and ask if they are welcome.

Lake Manatee State Park (see page 188) at 20007 Rte. 64, ☎ 941-741-3028, www.floridastateparks.org/lakemanatee, has 60 scrubland habitat campsites and does accept families. Campsites cost $18 a night. Call ☎ 800-326-3521 or visit www.reserveamerica.com for reservations (required).

Sarasota Bay Travel Trailer Park at 10777 44th Ave. W., ☎ 800-247-8361 or 941-794-1200, www.paradisebay-sarasotabayrvpark.com, is a retiree camp, located on the bay with full RV hookups, a boat ramp and dock, fishing, horseshoes, exercise room, recreation hall, and entertainment. Daily rates for full hookup are $30-$40.

You'll find several campgrounds in and around Palmetto, including **Frog Creek Campground** at 8515 Bayshore Rd. in Palmetto, ☎ 800-771-FROG or 941-722-6154, www.frogcreekrv.com. You can fish the creek (shown at right) or play shuffleboard and horseshoes. Tent camping is allowed. Year-round rate for RVs with full hookup is $32 a day for two persons, plus electricity. Weekly and monthly rates are available. Pets are allowed for an additional $1 per day, per pet. Wireless Internet access is available.

Bradenton & Sarasota

WHERE TO EAT

In undiscovered Palmetto, **Riverside Café** at Regatta Pointe Marina, 955 Riverside Dr., ☎ 941-729-4402, www.riversidecaferpm.com, overlooks a yacht harbor on the Manatee River. Seating is pleasant inside or out for breakfast, lunch, or dinner every day (no dinner Sunday or Monday). The extensive menu is priced $5-$7 for breakfast, and anywhere from $7 for a luncheon salad or sandwich to a $16 seafood sampler or plate of ribs for dinner.

Reflecting Palmetto's agricultural and Hispanic heritage, **Alvarez Mexican Food** at 143 Eighth Ave. W., ☎ 941-729-2232, has been offering a full spread of south-of-the-border specialties to a range of clientele since 1976. Besides the classic breakfast, lunch, and dinner mainstays, it specializes in camarones al Diablo (spicy shrimp), Mexican barbecue, pork or chicken mole-style, and combination dinners. Grab a $4.99 "speedie" combo weekdays. Other meals range from $4 to $13.

Situated on the town's historic pier, **Mattison's**, 1200 First Ave. W., ☎ 941-748-8087, www. mattisons.com, features large windows looking onto the river and al fresco dining. The lunch menu offers sandwiches, pasta, and seafood entrées for $9-$12. The dinner menu, which concen-

© Mattison's Riverside

trates on seafood with a Caribbean flair, has items costing $13-$22. It's open daily for lunch and dinner.

Anna Maria Island

The largest of the Bradenton-Sarasota islands, Anna Maria has three distinct communities. Northernmost Anna Maria has a casual air about it, along with great fishing piers and some fun fish houses and bars. Holmes Beach, to the south, is more upscale, while Bradenton Beach, with its beach shops, sometimes borders on tacky but has some historic feel to it as well. Seven miles of beaches edge Anna Maria Island; the best are at Holmes Beach and Bradenton Beach.

GETTING HERE

Rte. 64 (Exit 220 off I-75) intersects with Hwy. 41 and heads across the island's north bridge to Holmes Beach. From the south, take Exit 217 from I-75 follow Rte. 70 to **Hwy. 41**. Turn north on Highway 41, then west on Rte. 684, which takes you across the south bridge. Both bridges connect to **Gulf Drive** (Rte. 789), the island's major thoroughfare.

In Anna Maria, follow **Pine Ave.**, **North Shore Dr.**, and **Bay Blvd.** to find the town's sights. In Holmes Beach, **Marina Drive** takes you away from commercial traffic and along the bay.

In Bradenton Beach, **Bridge St.** is the center of the town's historic district. South of it, **Rte. 789** connects to Longboat Key.

INFORMATION

For local information, contact the **Anna Maria Island Chamber of Commerce**, 5313 Gulf Dr., Holmes Beach, 34217, www. amichamber.com, ☎ 941-778-1541. Hours are Monday-Friday, 9-5.

SIGHTS & ATTRACTIONS

OF HISTORIC OR CULTURAL INTEREST

Small and intimate, the **Anna Maria Island Historical Museum** at 402 Pine Ave., ☎ 941-778-0492, keeps photographs, maps, records, books, a shell collection, a turtle display, and vintage videos preserved in an old ice house. Next to it, the old jail house is a colorful sight. Admission is free; donations are accepted. It's open Monday-Thursday and Saturday, 10-1, June-August; 10-3 the rest of the year. Closed Friday and Sunday.

BEACHES, PARKS & NATURAL AREAS

Bayfront Park, on Bay Blvd. at Anna Maria's north end, rounds the tip of the island Gulf to bay and stays relatively uncrowded. The linear park offers picnic facilities, a playground, recreational opportunities, and a magnificent view of St. Petersburg's Sunshine Skyway Bridge. Open daily, 6 am-10 pm.

In Holmes Beach, **Manatee County Park** on Gulf Drive and Rte. 64 is fun and sunny, with a playground, picnicking, lifeguards, a snack bar, showers, and a fishing pier.

Equally popular **Coquina Beach** lies in Bradenton Beach at the south end of Gulf Dr., and wraps around Gulf and bay. Here, beachers enjoy picnic areas, concessions, boat ramps, good snorkeling, a playground, lifeguards, and lots of shady Australian pine trees.

Across the street, the Coquina BayWalk at the 17-acre Leffis Key Nature Preserve provides a walk among mangroves.

ADVENTURES

■ ON WATER

FISHING

Along with the coast's usual complement of fish, Gulf waters around Bradenton are known as Goliath Grouper Country. The huge fish, formerly know as jewfish, school in great numbers around area wrecks and ledges.

Anna Maria City Pier at the northeast end of Bayfront Park (see above) on Bay Blvd. extends 710 feet into Anna Maria Sound and has food and bait concessions.

Anna Maria Island Pier

Rod & Reel Pier at 875 North Shore Dr. in Anna Maria, ☎ 941-778-1885, has a café and bait shop. Admission for fishing is $2.

In Bradenton Beach, a former bridge forms the T-shaped Bradenton **Beach City Pier** on Bridge St (shown opposite). It reaches into Intracoastal waters and has a restaurant and bait house. Fee for fishing is $1 each for those aged 17 and older. You can walk on the pier for free.

Fishermen also cast off the bridge between Bradenton Beach and Longboat Key.

BOAT RAMPS

On the causeway at the Anna Maria Island end, **King Fish Park** has two public ramps.

On the bay side of **Coquina Beach** (see *Sights & Attractions*, above) on Gulf Drive in Bradenton Beach, you'll find boat ramps and other facilities.

BOAT RENTALS

Rent power and pontoon boats at **Bradenton Beach Marina** at 402 Church Ave., ☎ 941-778-2288. Half-day rates are $210; full day, $275. Gas and tax are extra.

Coastal Watersports at 1301 Gulf Dr., ☎ 941-778-4969, gives free sailing lessons with its rentals, which are $35-$45 an hour for G Cats. It also rents three-seat WaveRunners from $85 an hour and kayaks for $10 an hour.

BOAT CHARTERS & TOURS

Spice Sailing Charters at Galati Yacht Basin in Anna Maria, ☎ 941-704-077, http://charters2. tripod.com, charges $40 each for half-day cruises and $25 for sunset cruises into Tampa Bay and the gulf aboard a 30-foot Catalina. Sailing lessons are also available.

PADDLING

Self-guided tours aboard sit-on-top kayaks depart daily from **Native Rentals**, 5416 Marina Dr. in Holmes Beach, ☎ 941-778-7757. Cost for professional orientation, pickup, delivery, gear, and four hours of paddle time is $24 each.

SNORKELING & DIVING

A sunken sugar barge and a close-to-shore ledge provide fascinating beach dives at Coquina Beach at the south end of Bradenton Beach. Other wrecks and ledges lie 10 to 19 miles from shore. Look for goliath mammoth grouper (formerly known as jewfish).

SeaTrek Divers at 105 Seventh St. N. in Bradenton Beach, www. seatrekdivers.com, ☎ 941-779-1506, leads two-tank, offshore dives

© Gary Humphreys

for $65 each. The store rents diving and snorkeling gear, and teaches PADI certification courses. It is open on Mondays and Wednesday-Saturday, 10-6 (closed on Tuesdays), and Sunday, 9-1.

ON WHEELS

Beach Bum Billy's, 427 Pine Ave. in Anna Maria, ☎ 941-778-3316, rents bikes for $5 an hour, $14 a day. Weekly and month rates and free on-island pickup and delivery are available.

Island Scooters at Silver Surf Resort, 1301 Gulf Dr. N. in Bradenton Beach, ☎ 941-726-3163, rents bikes and scooters. Bicycles rent for $5 an hour, $15 a day, $45 a week.

WHERE TO STAY

ACCOMMODATIONS PRICE KEY		
Rates are per room, per night, double occupancy. Price ranges described for each property often do not take into account penthouses and other exceptional, high-priced accommodations.	$	Up to $75
	$$	$75 to $150
	$$$	$151 to $250
	$$$$	$251 and up

HOTELS & MOTELS

There's much to choose from for lodging on Anna Maria Island. You can rent a home or condo, sequester yourself in historic B&B charm, or stay in the midst of beachdom bustle.

Rod & Reel Motel at 877 N. Shore Dr., ☎ 941-778-2780, www.rod-andreelmotel.com, is tailor-made for fishing folks. Its 10 efficiencies are set on the shores of Tampa Bay, where a nice, long pier accommodates anglers. The compact, 11-unit motel sports bright touches in its landscaping and tiki shelter. $$-$$$

In Bradenton Beach, **Tropic Isle Inn**, 2103 Gulf Drive N., ☎ 941-778-1237 or 800-883-4092, www.tropicisleinn.com, is a pleasant, intimate little place across the street from the beach and with its own pool and patio. The 15 units include guest rooms, efficiencies, and one- and two-bedroom apartments. $$-$$$$

■ INNS/BED & BREAKFASTS

Accommodations on Anna Maria Island leave the realm of chain drone for the individual brightness of small inns and beach rentals. Among the most adorable, **Islands West Resort** at 3605 Gulf Dr. in Holmes Beach, ☎ 877-209-2825 or 941-778-6569, www.

© Island West Resort

islandswestresort.com, names its handful of units after Florida islands and stocks them with everything you need for days at the beach, which lies a short walk away. The one- and two-bedroom villas each have their own décor scheme, plus beach chairs, towels, umbrella, and even a cart to tote them to the sand. $$-$$$

The island's most charming option, **Harrington House B&B** at 5626 Gulf Drive in Holmes Beach, www.harringtonhouse. com, ☎ 888-828-5566 or 941-778-5444, is one of Florida's few beachfront B&Bs. Added to that are its history and casual elegance. The one cottage and each of eight main-house rooms and eight beach-house rooms have their own bath, fridge, TV, antique pieces, and Victorian appointments. A dramatic cut-stone fireplace dominates the sitting room. Guests have use of kayaks and bicycles. $$$-$$$$

■ RENTAL AGENCIES

For families and other large groups, vacation home and condominium rentals can be the smartest way to stay. **Mike Norman Realty**, 3101 Gulf Dr., Holmes Beach, www.mikenormanrealty.com, ☎ 800-367-1617 or 941-778-6696, will send you a catalog brochure listing more than 100 weekly and monthly options as low as $600 a week in summer.

A Paradise at 5201 Gulf Dr., Holmes Beach, ☎ 800-237-2252 or 941-778-4800, www.aparadiserentals.com, lists a wide variety of condos, cottages, and homes on Anna Maria Island starting at $850 a week. Some require a minimum stay of two weeks or a month.

WHERE TO EAT

You'll find a delightful array of beach restaurants, local eateries, fish houses, and dressy dining in the three Anna Maria Island communities.

A great place to go for lunch is **The Sandbar**, beachside at 100 Spring Ave. in Anna Maria, ☎ 941-778-0444, www. sandbar-restaur ant.com. Get a deck table and watch the water world go by while you munch shrimp salad or a seafood sandwich. It's open daily and also serves dinner. Prices for lunch are $8-$15; for dinner, $10-$28.

© The Sandbar

Bradenton & Sarasota

For typical Florida fish-house ambiance and food, try **Rotten Ralph's**, near the pier at 902 S. Bay Blvd. in Anna Maria, ☎ 941-778-3953, www.rottenralphs.com. It straddles a dock within a marina, and serves fried seafood, steamed seafood pots, meat pies, sandwiches, and salads. Sandwich and entrée prices run $5-$18. It's open daily for lunch and dinner.

For fine cuisine in an intimate surfside setting, follow the trail of rave reviews to **Beach Bistro**, 6600 Gulf Dr. in Holmes Beach, ☎ 941-778-6444, www.beachbistro.com. It's open daily for dinner, serving small and large plates of creatively fashioned meat, fowl, and seafood, such as lobsterscargots (chunks of lobster prepared escargot-style), bouillabaisse, and roast duckling with pepper sauce. Main courses range from $37 to $49, with small plate selections that can also serve as entrées for the light eater.

Especially popular for breakfast with a view, **Gulf Drive Café**, 900 Gulf Dr. in Bradenton Beach, ☎ 941-778-1919, also serves home-cooked lunch and dinner at reasonable prices seven days a week. Breakfast (served all day) runs $5-$9; lunch $6-$11 for burgers and sandwiches; and dinner $9-$19 for seafood and continental specialties.

© Beachhouse Restaurant

Enter through a retail souvenir shop and pick a table on the outdoor patio overlooking the beach at **Beachhouse Restaurant** at 200 Gulf Dr. N., ☎ 941-779-2222, www.groupersand wich.com. At lunch, grouper, Cuban, crab cake, and other sandwiches and a few entrées range from $8 to $15. Go for the fresh-catch nightly special or choose something fishy off the regular menu, such as seafood gumbo, stuffed tilapia, or sesame-seared tuna. Entrées range from $15 to $22.

Longboat Key

A lovely, well-heeled island, Longboat Key has little to offer in the way of sights. Its public beaches are unspectacular. It provides panoramic passage between Anna Maria Island and the islands to the south. Its marinas supply water adventure and its bike path offers exercise for scenery-gazers. The superlatives are reserved for its dining. Die-hard shoppers might enjoy browsing the pricey boutiques, but shopping is not covered separately here because the choices in Sarasota and its islands are so much better.

GETTING HERE

Not directly connected to the mainland, Longboat Key can be reached by bridges from its northern and southern neighbors along **Rte. 789**, which here takes the extended name Gulf of Mexico Drive.

INFORMATION

Information is available from **Longboat Key-Lido Key-St. Armands Key Chamber of Commerce** at 6960 Gulf of Mexico Dr., Longboat

Key, 34228, ☎ 941-941-387-9519, www.longboatkeychamber.com. It's open 9-5, Monday-Friday.

SIGHTS & ATTRACTIONS

LOCAL COLOR

Be sure to turn east off the north end of Gulf of Mexico Drive onto Broadway St. and visit **The Village**, Longboat Key's original settlement, where you'll find old-island spirit, the local art center, a couple of great seafood restaurants, and wild peacocks roaming the streets.

ADVENTURES

ON WATER

FISHING

The bridge at Longboat Key's northern end, spanning Longboat Pass toward Anna Maria Island, is a popular fishing spot. For fishing excursions, contact **Spindrift Yacht Services** at 410 Gulf of Mexico Dr., ☎ 941-383-7781. Half-day offshore trips for up to four run $630; bay fishing charters cost $350.

Wolfmouth Charters, 4210 Gulf of Mexico Dr., ☎ 942-755-1632, www.wolfmouthcharters.com, charges $300-$450 for a four-hour fishing or sightseeing charter, $400-$550 for six hours, and $550-$700 for eight hours.

BOAT RENTALS

Cannons Marina at 6040 Gulf of Mexico Dr., www.cannons.com, ☎ 800-566-1955 or 941-383-1311, rents out top-quality fishing boats, skiffs, and deck boats. Half-day rates on runabouts are $130-$290; full day, $180-$385. Deck boats hold up to 12 people and run $250 a half-day, $315 full day. Gas and tax are extra. Cannons also rents tackle, and water skis, and sells bait, tackle, and other supplies. Open daily, 8-5:30.

ON WHEELS

Cyclists slice through the 12-mile-long island's center along the paved bike path on **Gulf of Mexico Drive**. It's a flat, easy, scenic drive, flowered and manicured.

Rent your ride at **Backyard Bike Shop**, 5610 Gulf of Mexico Dr., Ste. 1B, ☎ 941-383-5184. Its selection of mountain, hybrid, beach, road, recumbent, tandem, and BMX bikes rent for $10-$25 for a day, $35-$75 for a week. In season, it's open Monday-Saturday, 10-5, with shortened hours on Wednesday and in summer.

SHOPPING

With renowned St. Armands Key just over the next bridge, serious shoppers head south. If you want to wander out on your bike for some casual window-shopping and gifting, try **Avenue of the Flowers** and **The Centre Shops** along Gulf of Mexico Blvd.

WHERE TO STAY

From beach cottages to grand high-rise resorts, Longboat Key offers it all. Most of its lodging you'll find on the Gulf or the bay, with ready access to adventure.

 Author favorites are indicated with a star.

■ HOTELS, RESORTS & COTTAGES

 The Colony Beach & Tennis Resort at 1620 Gulf of Mexico Dr., ☎ 800-4-COLONY or 941-383-6464, www.colony beachresort.com, is perfect for beach-lovers, tennis-players, and dining aficionados. It boasts 21 soft and hard tennis courts, a beautiful stretch of beach, a small but complete spa, top-rated restaurants (see *Where to Eat*, below), and a complimentary kids' program. Townhouses occupy low-lying buildings with complete amenities and designer décor. Shoulder-season rates, packages, and other room options are available. $$$$

Serious sportsfolk will find bliss at **The Resort at Longboat Key Club**, 301 Gulf of Mexico Dr., www.longboatkeyclub.com, ☎ 888-237-5545 or 941-383-8821. The list of activities is practically endless: one 18-hole and three nine-hole golf courses, a golf school, two tennis centers with 38 Har-Tru courts, bicycles, rafts, sailboats, boogie boards, kayaks, snorkeling gear, an Olympic-size swimming pool, jogging and biking paths, an exercise track, a fitness center, and a kid's club. The 215 guest rooms include club suites and one- and two-bedroom suites. $$$$

If your idea of a true beach vacation involves a little cottage with sand on the floor, check into **Rolling Waves Cottages**, 6351 Gulf of Mexico Dr., ☎ 941-383-1323, www.rollingwaves.com. Its row of eight self-contained cottages exudes charm and relaxation. The 1940s units have been revamped to full modern convenience, only steps away from the beach. $$$

© Rolling Waves Cottages

■ RENTAL AGENCIES

To rent privately owned homes and condos on Longboat Key and neighboring islands, contact **Florida Vacation Connection**, 3720 Gulf of Mexico Dr., www.flvacationconnection.com, ☎ 877-702-9981 or 941-387-9709.

WHERE TO EAT

Dining is an art on Longboat Key. Either you do it sleeves rolled-up with gusto, or with pinkies extended while relishing haute cuisine.

To do the former, visit **The Village** (page 203), which contains two unpretentious restaurants long loved by locals and those visitors who have discovered them. **Mar-Vista Dockside Restaurant & Pub** at 760 Broadway St., ☎ 941-383-2391, www.marvista-restaurant.com, occupies a cozily a-kilter little building that one could almost call a shack. Sit at the bar and tell fishing lies with the locals. Dine outside overlooking the boat dockage or inside at a mismatched assortment of tables. The fish is fresh and fixed in a variety of appealing ways. It's open for lunch ($7-$14) and dinner ($$8-$24) daily.

Nearby, **Moore's Stone Crab Restaurant** at 800 Broadway St., ☎ 888-968-2722 or 941-383-1748, specializes in stone crabs, which are in season only from mid-October to mid-May. Other dishes reflect Southern influences and Florida catches. Main courses are $13-$27. It's open daily for lunch and dinner.

The list of fine restaurants could go on for pages. For the splurge of a vacation (maybe of a lifetime), go to the unique and charming **Euphemia Haye**, 5540 Gulf of Mexico Dr., www.euphemiahaye.com, ☎ 941-383-3633. Local products are prepared in international style with stunning results. The setting is boutique and intimate. Dishes such as Grecian lamb shank and roast duckling are offered, and entrées range from $18 to $44 à la carte. Upstairs in the Haye Loft, the selection of desserts and coffees dazzles the mind and blows the diet. It's open daily for dinner. Reservations are recommended.

The Colony Dining Room at Colony Beach and Tennis Resort, 1620 Gulf of Mexico Dr., ☎ 941-383-5558, www.colonybeachresort. com, also has an impeccable reputation for serving the finest daily, for lunch, dinner, and Sunday brunch. It receives special acclaim for its comprehensive and savvy wine list. The beach reaches up to the walls and their generous windows. Dishes are based on continental classicism, with creative nuances, all executed exquisitely. For lunch you'll pay $9-$19 for salads, sandwiches, and entrées. A la carte dinner prices for dishes such as tempura lobster tails and crispy duck carbonara range from $17 to $39. Dinner reservations are required.

Lido Key & St. Armands Key

GETTING HERE

The northern approach to Lido Key passes through Anna Maria Island and Longboat Key along **Rte. 789**. On Lido Key, Rte. 789 is called **John Ringling Parkway**. At St. Armands Circle, John Ringling Blvd./Causeway forms the western and eastern spokes; **Boulevard of the Presidents** heads south, then jogs into Benjamin Franklin Drive.

From Sarasota's south side, you can get to St. Armands Key, which is tucked into Lido Key's bayside belly, by crossing the John Ringling Causeway (Rte. 780), which branches off Highway 41 (Tamiami Trail) from the mainland. From I-75, take Exit 210 (Fruitville Rd.) or Exit 207 (Bee Ridge Rd.) to **Highway 41** and follow the signs across the John Ringling Causeway.

SIGHTS & ATTRACTIONS

■ BEACHES, PARKS & NATURAL AREAS

Nicest and sportiest of the island's Gulf strip of beaches, 100-acre **South Lido Beach Park** at the south end of Benjamin Franklin Dr., features a wide, beige sand beach

that wraps around Gulf to bay, fitness trails, a bayou for canoeing, volleyball, horseshoes, ball fields, and a shady picnic area. Fishermen enjoy casting into the pass at the tip, where swimming is dangerous.

■ SPECTATOR SPORTS

Sarasota Ski-A-Rees Show takes place at City Island, behind Mote Marine (see below), every Sunday at 2 pm. There is limited bleacher seating. Performers are amateur. Admission is free.

ADVENTURES

■ ON WATER

FISHING

Both passes at Lido Key's polar ends make for a good day of rod-and-reeling. The **New Pass Bridge**, and **Ken Thompson Pier** and **New Pass Pier** on City Island provide vantage points into north-end New Pass. **New Pass Grill & Bait Shop**, 1498 Ken Thompson Pkwy., ☎ 941-388-3050, www.newpassgrill.com, serves angling needs in that neighborhood with huge tanks of fresh bait and a burger stand that's legendary.

For south-end fishing in Big Sarasota Pass, go to **South Lido Beach** (see *Sights & Attractions*, above) at the end of Benjamin Franklin Drive.

Offshore, **artificial reefs** between two and 25 miles from shore attract marine life at New Pass and Big Pass. Contact Sarasota County Parks & Recreation Department for location information, ☎ 941-316-1172.

Tony Saprito Fishing Pier at Ringling Causeway Park accommodates fishermen with a bait concession and other facilities.

Saltwater Sportfishing Guide at 2529 Temple St., www.sarasota-fla-fishing.com, ☎ 941-366-2159 or 941-350-8583 (cell), takes small charters into deep-sea, bay, and backwaters for four to eight hours. Rates range from $260 to $450 for one to four people, depending upon trip length. They pick up at New Pass Bait Shop on Ken Thompson Pkwy.

BOAT RAMPS

Boat-owners will find three public ramps at **City Island** into New Pass, on the east side of Lido Key's north end.

BOAT TOURS

From Mote Marine Aquarium (see *Eco-Adventures*, below), Sarasota Bay Explorers at 1600 Ken Thompson Pkwy., ☎ 941-388-4200, www.sarasotabayexplorers.com, delves into the natural side of Sarasota, which isn't that easy to find these days. Highlights of the naturalist-narrated trip are a close-up view of Rookery Islands and a peek at sea life netted from the waters. Rates are $26 for adults; $22 for children aged four-12 (three and under ride free). You can also purchase combination Mote-cruise tickets. The almost two-hour pontoon cruise departs every day at 11, 1:30, and 4. Custom tours are also available.

SAILING

© Sara-Bay Sailing School

Sara-Bay Sailing School & Charters is based at New Pass Grill & Bait Shop, ☎ 941-914-5132, www.sarabaysailing. com. Basic 12-hour keelboat sailing instruction, ASA certified, starts at $300. Captained charters run $200 (up to four passengers) to $350 (up to six passengers) for a half-day, $300-$500 for a full day. Rent a Catalina 22 for $150 a day, a Cal 24 for $200 a day.

PADDLING

For a guided eco-tour by kayak into Sarasota's backwaters, paddle with **Sarasota Bay Explorers** behind Mote Marine Aquarium, 1600 Ken Thompson Pkwy., City Island, ☎ 941-388-4200, www.sarasota-bayexplorers. Guides teach beginners necessary skills and everyone learns about marine life. Cost for three hours is $50 for adults, $40 for children aged four to 12.

South Lido Beach (see *Sights & Attractions*, above) at the south end of Benjamin Franklin Dr., has a canoe launch and a self-guided canoe trail through **Brushy Bayou**.

■ ON FOOT

At South Lido Beach (see *Sights & Attractions*, above), a 20-minute **nature trail** takes you through woodsy parts into the swampland of Brushy Bayou.

ON WHEELS

The Longboat Key **bike path** crosses the New Pass Bridge and continues for a few miles through Lido Key's northern residential section.

ECO-ADVENTURES

Just north and east of the bridge from Longboat Key on Ken Thompson Parkway, **City Island** holds several eco-attractions for nature enthusiasts. The first, **Sarasota Bay Walk** at 1550 Ken Thompson Pkwy., takes you on a self-guided tour of the bay, estuaries, lagoons, and uplands along boardwalks and shell paths. Admission is free.

Nearby, **Mote Marine Laboratory and Aquarium** at 1600 Ken Thompson Pkwy., www.mote.org, ☎ 800-691-MOTE or 941-388-2451, specializes in the research and rehabilitation of marine mammals. Its original attraction is a 135,000-gallon shark tank, stocked with sharks and other local fish. Twenty-two smaller aquariums, a touch tank, and a touchless tank hold more than 200 varieties of common and unusual species. Other exhibits include an outdoor ray touch tank, a pickled 25-foot giant squid, and an interactive shark theater. Special effects make you feel as though you're under water, let you feel a shark's skin, and show you a shark's anatomy. New in 2005 an Immersion Cinema has families using touch screens on virtual underwater learning adventures.

Manattee with calf.

Three of the facility's research labs are open for viewing. In the Marine Mammal Center, visitors can watch recovering whales, dolphins, manatees, or whatever happens to be the latest guest, in its 55,000-gallon marine mammal recovery tanks. Hugh and Buffett, two manatees born in captivity, charm with their docile demeanor. Sealife encounter boat tours depart from the site (see *Sarasota Bay Explorers*, below). Admission to the aquarium is $15 for adults and $10 for children aged four-12. It's open daily, 10-5.

SHOPPING

Flip-flops and fur coats (yes, in Florida!) intermingle at the spinning wheel shopping district that ranks itself with Rodeo Drive. **St. Armands Circle**, ☎ 941-388-1554, www.starmandscircle.com, was

built as John Ringling had envisioned it, in the shape of a circus ring. The inner park displays some of his Italian statuary, as well as plaques honoring circus illuminati in the Circus Ring Hall of Fame. "The Circle," as locals call it, holds pricey boutiques, upscale chains, art galleries, restaurants, and clubs.

Parking is free (but sometimes scarce) on the street and in a nearby garage. Look for **Wyland Galleries** at 465 John Ringling Blvd., ☎ 941-388-5331, showroom of the well-known namesake's wildlife art.

WHERE TO STAY

If you're looking for Lido Key's beachy action, check into the **Lido Beach Resort** at 700 Benjamin Franklin Dr., ☎ 800-441-2113 or 941-388-2161, www.lidobeachresort.com, center of activity. A total of 222 rooms, kitchenettes, and suites stack up next to Lido's central public beach. Very Florida with its pastel color scheme, it provides two pools, watersports rentals, restaurant and café, and a bar on premises. Accommodations are well furnished and roomy. $$$-$$$$

© Lido Beach Resort

WHERE TO EAT

Dining is centered in St. Armands Circle, where everything is classy or trendy, or both. Catch a snack in a deli or ice cream shop, or sit down to a multi-course culinary celebration.

© Columbia Restaurant

Florida's chain of Spanish-cuisine establishments, **Columbia Restaurant**, has a storefront at 411 St. Armands Circle, ☎ 941-388-3987, www. columbiarestaurant.com. Open daily for lunch and dinner, it serves authentic Spanish-Cuban dishes, such as paella, *ropa vieja*, and pompano *en papillote*. Dinner plates are $16-$25; lunches run $7-$16. Reservations recommended for dinner.

When you're visiting Mote Marine and its neighboring attractions, satisfy hunger pains at **Old Salty Dog** at 601 Ken Thompson Pkwy., City Island, ☎ 941-388-4311, www.theoldsaltydog.com, for a quick casual bite overlooking New Pass between Lido and Longboat keys. You can sit comfortably outdoors even in summer, thanks to a cool breeze, and enjoy a great view of boat traffic. The menu consists of hot dogs, burgers, baby back ribs, fish 'n chips, and such, priced $5-$18. Locals hang out at the ship-shaped bar.

NIGHTLIFE

In a town where nightlife glitters, **St. Armands Circle** contends for a great deal of the action. Its clubs and restaurants host live local rock bands and national artists in an intimate setting.

The most popular clubs include **Tommy Bahama**, 300 John Ringling Blvd., ☎ 941-388-2446; and **ChaCha Coconuts** at 417 St. Armands Circle, ☎ 941-388-3300. Cover charges vary.

Sarasota

GETTING HERE

From I-75, take exits 205, 207, 210 and 213 to get to Sarasota. From north to south, **University Parkway**, **Fruitville Rd.**, **Bee Ridge Rd.**, and **Clark Rd.** (Rte. 72) are Sarasota's big east-west streets. **High-**

way 41 (Tamiami Trail) heads through town close to the bay. It intersects with **Main St.** and **Bayfront Dr.** downtown. Between Highway 41 and I-75, **Tuttle Ave.**, **Beneva Rd.**, **McIntosh Rd.**, and **Cattlemen Rd.** run north to south. Hwy. 301 branches off Highway 41 downtown.

Sarasota County Area Transit (SCAT), ☎ 941-861-5000 or 861-1234, provides public transportation around town. Regular bus fare is 50¢. Monthly unlimited-use passports and discount punch cards are available.

INFORMATION

The Greater Sarasota County Chamber of Commerce at 1945 Fruitville Rd., Sarasota, 34236, ☎ 941-955-8187, www.sarasotachamber.org, has specific information on Sarasota. Hours are 8:30-5, Monday-Friday. You can also contact the **Downtown Association of Sarasota**, 1818 Main St., Sarasota, 34236, ☎ 941-951-2656.

SIGHTS & ATTRACTIONS

Downtown

Downtown Sarasota has a perky waterfront and downtown. Its renowned restaurants, art galleries, clubs, and theaters compose the Theatre and Arts District.

■ PERFORMING ARTS

Most of the action is centered in downtown's Sarasota Theatre and Arts District.

Grand dame of the downtown theater scene, **Sarasota Opera House**, 61 N. Pineapple Ave., ☎ 888-673-7212 or 941-366-8450, is a

beautifully restored historic mission-style building known as the A.B. Edwards Theatre. You can tour the facility Mondays at 10:30 during season (and see the chandelier from the set of *Gone With the Wind*) for $10; advance arrangements required. Sarasota Opera (www.sarasotaopera.org) performs here in February and

March. The troupe, which has been performing for nearly 45 years, stages Puccini, Verdi, Tchaikovsky and other classic operas at night and Saturday and Sunday matinee performances. Tickets are $32-$109.

All your favorite musicals come to stage year-round at **Golden Apple Dinner Theatre**, 25 N. Pineapple Ave., ☎ 800-652-0920 or 941-366-5454, www.thegoldenapple.com. Tickets for dinner and a show range from $33 to $45.

For something more avant-garde, check out **Florida Studio Theatre** at 1241 N. Palm Ave. downtown, ☎ 941-366-9000, www.fst2000.org. It uses its Mainstage and Cabaret theaters as testing grounds for up-and-coming playwrights during the October-June season and a summertime New Plays Festival. A la carte dining is available in the Cabaret. The box office is open daily. No shows on Monday. Cost of tickets ranges from $19-$34.

Based in a movie house in the historic Burns Court District, **Sarasota Film Society**, Burns Court Cinema, 506 Burns Ln., www.filmsociety.org, ☎ 941-955-FILM, presents international films year-round and hosts the Sarasota Film Festival, a 10-day gala event in April. Film tickets are $7.75 for non-members.

■ NATURAL AREAS

Marie Selby Botanical Gardens at 811 S. Palm Ave., www.selby.org, ☎ 941-366-5731, has 15 acres planted with palms, bamboo, hibiscus, tropical food plants, herbs, and other exotic species. It is particularly known for its collection of 5,000 orchids, set in a lush

rainforest environment. The gardens are open daily, 10-5. Admission is $12 for adults, $6 for children aged six-11.

Outlying Areas

■ OF HISTORIC OR CULTURAL INTEREST

At **Sarasota Classic Car Museum**, 5500 N. Tamiami Trail, ☎ 941-355-6228, www.sarasotacarmuseum.org, you can see more than 100 antique and classic cars. A highlight of the museum is the col-

lection of John Ringling's Rolls Royces and Pierce Arrows. Kids enjoy the antique penny arcade, where a nickel can buy them a game. Adult admission is $8.50; seniors, $7.65; children aged 13-17, $5.75; aged six-12, $4. It's open daily, 9:30-6.

THE RINGLING ESTATE

The best of Sarasota's attractions spreads out its circus and arts heritage over 66 bayfront acres. John Ringling left the estate to the state upon his death. It's at 5401 Bay Shore Rd., ☎ 941-359-5700, www.ringling.org. The center's cornerstone is The John and Mable Ringling Mu-

seum of Art, whose 22 galleries specialize in late Medieval, Renaissance Italian, and Spanish religious and other baroque works, including five original Rubens tapestries. A third wing to the museum plus an Education Conservation Complex should be open by the time you visit.

You can also tour Cà d'Zan, Ringling's 30-room Italianate palace (shown here), built in the 1920s at a cost of $1.5 million and renovated recently at 10 times that price; the Museum of the Circus, filled with calliopes, costumes, a scale-model circus, elaborate wagons, behind-the-circus scenes, and other Big Top art and memorabilia; the new in 2005 Tibbals Learning Center, featuring an astounding 3,800-square-foot miniature circus; and estate rose gardens.

Admission fees for entrance into all Ringling Estates attractions are $15 for adults, $13 for seniors, $5 for Florida students and teachers (with ID), and free for children under age five. Admission to the art museum is free for everyone on Monday, by provision of Ringling's will. The complex is open daily, 9:30-6, but the museums are open only 10 to 5.

PERFORMING ARTS

The Ringling tradition lives on through **Circus Sarasota**, ☎ 941-355-9335, www.circussarasota.org, which stages professional performances, in February, under the one-ring Big Top at Fruitville Rd. and Tuttle Ave. Call for show times and dates. Tickets are $8-$30.

FSU Center for the Performing Arts at 5555 N. Tamiami Trail, ☎ 800-361-8388 or 941-351-8000, incorporates elements of a circa-1900 Scottish opera house into one of its two theaters. The professional Asolo Theatre Company (www.asolo.org) is at home in the 500-seat Harold E. and Esther M. Mertz Theatre November-May. The other theater, Jane B. Cook, houses the FSU/Asolo Conservatory for Actor Training, where graduate level students perform with professional actors in an intimate 161-seat setting. Tickets prices vary. Call or visit the website for performance schedule and ticket prices.

Van Wezel Performing Arts Hall at 777 N. Tamiami Trail, ☎ 800-826-9303 or 941-953-3366, www.vanwezel.org, looks like a big purple clam shell on the outside. Inside, the 1,736-seat hall hosts Broadway shows, major classical orchestras, ethnic music, dance, choral music, and the Florida West Coast Symphony.

Van Wezel Performing Arts Hall

> **TIP:** *For up-to-date information on community events, call the 24-hour* **InfoLine** *at* ☎ *941-953-4636, ext. 6000.*

FAMILY FUN

G. Wiz (Gulf Coast Wonder & Imagination Zone) at 1001 Blvd. of the Arts, ☎ 941-906-1851, www.gwiz.org, occupies the Selby Library

Building with more than 85 imaginative and educational learning stations, including a cool outdoor playground. Bring your kids and their creativity, 10-5 Monday through Friday, 10-6 Saturday, and noon-6 on Sunday. Adults pay $9; children aged six-21, $6; children aged three-five, $2.

North of downtown, **Sarasota Jungle Gardens** at 3701 Bayshore Rd., ☎ 941-355-5305, www.sarasota junglegardens.com, is worth a few hours' time to stroll peaceful gardens, watch bird and reptile shows, and look at monkeys, flamingos that you can feed from your hand, swans, wallabies, and other animals. Hours are 9-5, daily. Admission is $12 for

adults; $11 for seniors; $8 for children aged three-12.

In-line skate or skateboard for $5 a day at **Sarasota Skate Park** (☎ 941-373-7932, one block south of Ringling Blvd. between School and East avenues). It opens at noon daily; closing times vary.

■ SPECTATOR SPORTS

Sarasota Polo Club at 8201 Polo Club Ln., east of I-75 off University Pkwy., ☎ 941-907-0000, www. sarasotapolo.com, competes on Sundays at 1 pm from mid-December through Easter. Adult tickets are $10; children under 12 are admitted free.

East of Highway 41, the **Cincinnati Reds** train during March at Ed Smith Stadium, 2700 12th St., ☎ 941-954-4101, www.cincinnatireds.com. Tickets cost $7-$14. In summer, the **Sarasota Reds** take the stadium; ☎ 941-365-5560; tickets are $5-$6.

Buy some dog food (you may even win money!) at **Sarasota Kennel Club** at 5400 Bradenton Rd., ☎ 941-355-7744, where greyhound racing happens at matinees (Monday, Wednesday, Friday, and Saturday) and evening shows every day but Sunday, late November through mid-April. The club also simulcasts greyhound and horse racing from around Florida and other locations year-round, Monday-Saturday, plus hosts Texas Hold 'Em poker. Admission is $1.

ADVENTURES

ON WATER

FISHING

Flying Fish Fleet at Marina Jack in Island Park, www.flyingfishfleet.com, ☎ 941-366-3373, has deep-sea excursions: half-day and sunset ($30-$40 each), six-hour ($47-$52) and all-day ($55-$65). (The low-end rates are for children aged 15 and younger.) The 85-foot boat is fully equipped with restrooms, a snack bar, and a carpeted sundeck. A charter boat is also available.

© Flying Fish Fleet

BOAT RAMPS

To launch your own vessel, use the free ramps on **Sixth St.** at Boulevard of the Arts.

BOAT CHARTERS & TOURS

For dining afloat, **Marina Jack Luxury Cruises** at Marina Jack, Island Park, ☎ 941-365-4232, www.marinajacks.com, is one name you'll want to know. Take a lunch ($32 for adults) or dinner ($52) cruise aboard a 62-foot yacht. Tax and gratuity are extra.

LeBarge Tropical Cruises at Marina Jack, ☎ 941-366-6116, is oh-so islandy, with live entertainment, palm trees on board, an aquarium bar, and your favorite seafood nibbles and exotic cocktails. Daytime cruises ($18 for adults, $13 for children aged four-12) include narration and a bit of nature orientation. Accent is on party for the sunset cruises ($20 for adults only).

PERSONAL WATERCRAFT

Enticer Watersports at Bayfront Park, ☎ 941-366-7245, rents WaveRunners for $55 for a half-hour, $85 and up for an hour, including gas. Kayaks, paddleboats, aqua cycles, and small sailboats are also available.

SAILING

© Enterprise Sailing Charters

Enterprise Sailing Charters also departs from Marina Jack, ☎ 888-232-7768 or 941-951-1833, www.sarasotasailing.com, for two-hour ($35-$40 per person) and day ($60) sails on a 41-foot Morgan.

To rent a sailboat 13- to 19-feet long, head to **Enticer Watersports** at Bayfront Park, ☎ 941-366-7245. Rental rates are $60-$70 for two hours and $240 for four hours on the 19-footer.

Key Sailing, Marina Jack, ☎ 888-539-7245 or 941-346-7245, www.siestakeysailing.com, specializes in dining excursions aboard a 41-foot Morgan Classic. The one-day dolphin cruise includes lunch and beverages for $150 per person. Non-lunch sails range from $45 to $73 per person, depending upon duration.

Bradenton & Sarasota

ON FOOT

Take a walk around **Bayfront Park** for a pleasant form of exercise. It has a nice small-town atmosphere. If you get serious about it, there's a fitness walk and the path followed by the 1996 Olympic torchbearer. Let the kids splash in the interactive water fountain.

Kids splash around the fountains of Bayfront Park on a hot day.

■ ON WHEELS

Bicycle Center at 4084 Bee Ridge Rd., ☎ 941-377-4505, offers pickup and delivery. Mountain bike and beach cruiser rentals run $15 by the day, $40 by the week. It's open 9-6, Monday-Friday; 9-5 on Saturday.

Florida Ever-Glides at 200 S. Washington Blvd., Ste. 11, ☎ 941-363-9556, www. floridaever-glides.com, tours the town by Segway Human Transporter. Morning or afternoon lessons and tours last 2½ hours and cost $61.

SHOPPING

Downtown Sarasota has undergone a recent renovation which turned its historic district into a shopping mall where shops, boutiques, and restaurants occupy vintage buildings. Improvements continue to make the town more walker-friendly. It is best known for

The Gallery, Towles Court

its art galleries, most of which line **Palm Ave**. The first Friday of each month, shops, galleries, and restaurants stay open later for the **Palm Avenue Art Walk**, held 6-9 in the evening. A charming artists' colony called **Towles Court**, ☎ 941-362-0960, www.towles court.com, is tucked away in downtown's southeast corner, off Hwy. 31 between Adams Ln. and Morrill St. It holds "Third Friday" gallery walks from 6 to 10 pm.

Book-lovers won't want to miss **Main Bookshop** at 1962 Main St., ☎ 941-366-7653, www.mainbookshop.com, where discounted books on every subject fill four floors.

Westfield Shopping Town Southgate, 3501 Tamiami Trail, ☎ 941-955-0900, http://westfield.com/southgate/, has Saks Fifth Avenue and other department stores, three restaurants, and a variety of food and clothing shops.

Westfield Sarasota Square, Hwy. 41 and Beneva Rd., ☎ 941-922-9609, www.shopsarasotasquare.com, is one of the region's most complete shopping malls with more than 140 shops and department stores.

WHERE TO STAY

 Author favorites are indicated with a star.

Most of the area's best lodging is on the beaches. Business visitors find chain and mom-and-pop places along Highway 41 around the airport.

ACCOMMODATIONS PRICE KEY		
Rates are per room, per night, double occupancy. Price ranges described for each property often do not take into account penthouses and other exceptional, high-priced accommodations.	$	Up to $75
	$$	$75 to $150
	$$$	$151 to $250
	$$$$	$251 and up

■ HOTELS

The newest grande dame on the Sarasota resort scene rises on the edge of downtown and its bayfront and faces the Hyatt across a buzzing marina. The **Ritz-Carlton Sarasota**, 1111 Ritz-Carlton Dr., ☎ 941-309-2000, www.ritzcarlton.com, carries all the pomp and luxury the name brand has come to represent. Rooms are plush (though less soundproof than one would expect) with marble bathrooms and in-room computers. Grand restaurants and lounges recall the opulent age of John Ringling. There is a large spa facility on property and a private beach club on Lido Key. $$$$.

Hyatt Sarasota at 1000 Blvd. of the Arts, ☎ 800-233-1234 or 941-953-1234, is an option for folks who want to be on the mainland, yet on the water, and can afford luxury. The skyscraper overlooks its marina. Its 294 rooms and 12 suites are tastefully decorated, as are its spacious lobby and waterfront restaurant. Other amenities include lighted tennis courts, a fitness center, swimming pool, and close proximity to the Van Wezel Performing Arts Hall and downtown attractions. $$$-$$$$

■ BED & BREAKFASTS

At the doorstep to downtown's gallery row and with a glorious harbor sunset view, **The Cypress B&B**, 621 Gulfstream Ave. S., ☎ 941-955-4683, www.cypressbb.com, is a sanctu-

© The Cypress B&B

ary of historic and artistic quality. Each of its five individually crafted rooms creates a different mood. Antiques and art pieces decorate. Fresh flowers in the rooms, teatime hors d'oeuvres, bedtime liqueurs, and turndown service with homemade cookies add pampered luxury to the experience. $$$-$$$$

WHERE TO EAT

If you're culinarily adventuresome, plan to spend a lot of time relishing Sarasota's highly competitive dining scene. The prevailing style is cutting-edge creative, but you'll also find top-rate ethnic restaurants, down-home cooking, Old Florida-style oyster bars, and classic continental.

■ DOWNTOWN

Bright and stylish **Bijou Café** at 1287 First St., ☎ 941-366-8111, www.bijoucafe.net, is a favorite for shoppers and theater-goers (it's across the street from the opera house). Its often-changing menu features dishes such as roast duckling and shrimp piri-piri (spicy, Mozambique-style). Lunch, served Monday-Friday, ranges from $9 to $19, and dinner, served daily and à la carte, runs $12-$30 for an entrée only. Reservations are recommended.

Take a tastebud tour of Peru at **Selva Grill**, a new sensation at 1345 Main St., ☎ 941-362-4427, www.selvagrill.com. Start with an authentic seafood ceviche (select from 10 different types), then move onto duck breast with cilantro and beer-infused risotto, roasted lamb rack with mashed purple potatoes, braised venison, grilled tuna with pomegranate vinaigrette, or something equally exotic, creative, and wonderful. Dinner entrées range from $21 to $38.

■ OUTLYING AREAS

For something less budget-busting, look for one of Sarasota's Old Florida-style oyster bars. The best in the genre is **Phillippi Creek Village Oyster Bar**, waterside at

5353 S. Tamiami Trail, ☎ 941-925-4444, www.creekseafood.com.
It's most famous for its combo seafood steamer pots, but the sand-

© Phillipi Creek Village

wiches and other seafood items are
fresh and tasty, too. You can sit inside
the old Southern-style fish house or
creekside on the patio or floating
dock. It's open daily for lunch and dinner. A wide array of dishes cost $5-
$25 and up, depending on market
price.

To escape the rat race on South Tamiami Trail, duck into **Café Baci**,
4001 S. Tamiami Trail, ☎ 941-921-4848, www.cafebaci.net, for fine

but affordable Italian lunch or dinner. Lunch dishes of sandwiches,
crêpes, pasta, veal, chicken, and
seafood run $8-$11. An extended
selection of gourmet dinner offerings
– from osso buco to potato-crusted
escolar (a type of fish) – are priced
$16-$25. Open daily for dinner,
weekdays for lunch. Dinner reservations are accepted.

© Café Baci

Sarasota is also known for its Amish/Mennonite restaurants, operated by members of a local farming community.
Farmhouse goodness prevails in a country atmosphere of
lacy window treatments and stenciled detail. And the price is right.
Sugar & Spice Family Restaurant, 4000 Cattlemen Rd., ☎ 941-
342-1649, is one of the most popular. You're apt to find baked
chicken, beef and noodles, Swiss steak, or barbecue pork ribs as a
daily special. Sandwiches and entrées are $5-$16. Leave room for
pie. The restaurant serves lunch and dinner every day except
Sunday.

NIGHTLIFE

Contrary to what you may have heard about the dearth of nightlife
and culture in Florida's resort areas, Sarasota pulsates with live
music and professional theater (see *Performing Arts*, page 212).

Downtown nightclubs include **Gator Club**, 1490 Main St., ☎ 941-
366-5969, a longtime favorite.

Siesta Key

Technically part of Sarasota, Siesta Key has developed a separate, slightly renegade personality, even compared to the other islands. It breaks from the chain both spiritually and physically – its two bridges connect with the mainland, but not with the islands to the north. Siesta Key's renown was built upon sand – the whitest, finest, softest sand south of Florida's Panhandle. Unlike other West Coast beaches, Siesta Key gets quartz sand. It drifts down from the Panhandle, where the beaches derive from Appalachian Mountain run-off.

Siesta Key's claim to the world's whitest beach has naturally made the island beach-preoccupied. It is quite heavily developed, but still within the boundaries of good taste that Sarasota sets. At its fringes, resorts are non-chain and the wealthy have built up exclusive communities.

Where does all this leave the visitor with a yearning for outdoor excitement? In good standing. Fishing, boating, kayaking, snorkeling, and sports of all sorts are a strong part of this stunningly white beach world hedged by protected bay waters.

GETTING HERE

From I-75, take Exit 205 to get to Siesta Key. Exit 207 takes you to **Bee Ridge Rd.** Turn north on **Highway 41** and west on **Siesta Dr.**, which leads to the north bridge. From Exit 205, head west on **Clark Rd**. (Rte. 72), which changes names to **Stickney Point Rd**. and crosses the south bridge.

On the island's north end, **Higel Ave.** and **Ocean Blvd**. are the main roads into the shopping district. **Beach Rd**. runs Gulf-side, and intersects with **Midnight Pass Rd.**, which travels to the island's south end, intersecting Stickney Point Rd.

INFORMATION

For specific information on the island, contact the **Siesta Key Chamber of Commerce** at 5118 Ocean Blvd., Sarasota, 34242, ☎ 866-831-7778 or 941-349-3800, www.siestakeychamber.com. It's open Monday-Friday, 9-5.

SIGHTS & ATTRACTIONS

■ BEACHES, PARKS & NATURAL AREAS

People cross to Siesta Key mainly for the beach. Shopping and dining are sidelines. Not all of its beaches are created equal, however. **Siesta Key County Beach** on Midnight Pass Rd. at Beach Way Drive is 2,400 feet long and luxuriously wide. Its porcelain-white sands are plush, and a dream-come-true for recreationists. The park contains volleyball nets, tennis courts, a fitness trail, ball fields, a soccer field, playgrounds, lifeguards, and rental and food concessions. For slightly more seclusion, park on the street, rather than at the huge parking lot, or walk to the park outskirts.

For privacy and great snorkeling and fishing, head to the beach's south end, **Point of Rocks**. Parking access is just south of the intersection of Midnight Pass Rd. and Stickney Point Rd. Watch for the #12 access sign near the Siesta Breakers resort.

Although **Turtle Beach**, at the south end of Midnight Pass Rd., lacks Siesta Beach's powdery white sands, it is more secluded. It has a full line of amenities – horseshoes, volleyball, a playground, picnic shelters, and boat ramps. Serious seclusionists hoof it down to adjoining **Palmer Point Beach**, the sands that formed between Siesta and Casey keys when Midnight Pass closed in 1984. It is accessible only by foot or boat, and is a good place to find shark teeth.

ADVENTURES

■ ON WATER

FISHING

Good land points for fishing include the Siesta (north) Bridge and Bay Island; Stickney Point (south) Bridge or seawall; Point of Rocks, south of Siesta Public Beach; and Turtle Beach's pier and seawall at the island's south end on Blind Pass Rd. Turtle Beach Park also has two boat ramps, picnic facilities, a playground, volleyball, horseshoes, and a beach.

CB's at 1249 Stickney Point Rd., ☎ 941-349-4400, www.cbsoutfitters.com, has fishing charters in Sarasota Bay for up to six people. Rates for inshore, offshore, and instructional fly-fishing excursions are $325 for a half-day, $475-$800 for full day. Night snook-fishing trips cost $350. In tarpon season, tarpon charters run $475 each. Rod and reel rentals and fishing licenses are also available. It's open daily, 7-6.

BOAT RENTALS

CB's, 1249 Stickney Point Rd., ☎ 941-349-4400, www.cbsoutfitters.com, rents runabouts, center console boats, pontoons, and deck boats (capacity three to eight) for use in Intracoastal waters. Daily rates are $145-$295; half-day, $95-$225, plus tax and gas. It's open daily, 7-6.

At Siesta Key Marina, **Siesta Key Boat Rentals**, 1265 Old Stickney Point Rd., ☎ 941-349-8880, rents vessels that hold two to 18 passengers. A 15-foot fishing boat with 25hp engine rents for $60 a day. Top of the range is a 22-foot deck boat for $190 a day. Some half-day rates are available.

PADDLING

Siesta Sports Rentals at Southbridge Mall, 6551 Midnight Pass Rd., ☎ 941-346-1797, www.siestasportsrentals.com, rents single kayaks for $13 an hour, $30 a half-day, and $45 a day. Doubles go for $18, $40, and $55. Kayaking tours cost $35 each.

SNORKELING & DIVING

Point of Rocks (see above), on the south end of Siesta Public Beach near Midnight Pass Rd. and Stickney Point Rd., is a favorite spot with snorkelers looking for coral, caves, and marine life.

ON WHEELS

Bikers and joggers use the **path** that runs for 12 miles from Siesta Key's north bridge to Turtle Beach.

Siesta Sports Rentals at Southbridge Mall, 6551 Midnight Pass Rd. , ☎ 941-346-1797, www.sistasportsrentals.com, rents beach cruisers and speed bikes for $5 an hour, $10-15 a day. Tandems, kids' bikes, and two- and four-person Surreys are also available.

WHERE TO STAY

Resorts and condos are packed in tightly at Siesta's mid-section, so you won't have a problem finding a room except at the height of the season. Non-franchised, each place exudes its own sense of style. Some of those with the most to offer are listed here.

HOTELS & MOTELS

Away from the beach, **Banana Bay Club Waterside** at 8254 Midnight Pass Rd., ☎ 888-622-6229 or 941-346-0113, www. bananabayclub.com, is suited to nature lovers. Located on the brink of a quiet lagoon bird sanctuary, it accords guests free use of bikes, canoes, and pool. Its seven guest units are decorated with individual style, and are equipped with full kitchens. Accommodations range from studio apartments to a two-bedroom house. Weekly and monthly rates offer discounts. $$-$$$

Also on Heron Lagoon, **Siesta Key Bungalows** at 8212 Midnight Pass Rd., ☎ 941-349-9025 or 888-5SIESTA, www.siestakeybungalows.com, creates a mellow, charming space for relaxation and meditation. All 10 bungalows have been prettily dressed for tropical convenience. A swimming pool, dock, and free kayak use accommodate the sports-minded. $$-$$$.

■ RENTAL AGENCIES

For longer-term rentals of homes and condos, you are best off working through the **Siesta Key Chamber of Commerce**, 5118 Ocean Blvd., Sarasota, FL 34242, www.siestakeychamber.com, ☎ 888-837-3969 or 941-349-3800. Homes begin at about $3,000 a month and there's a one-month minimum requirement. Condos can be rented for any length of time.

WHERE TO EAT

Casual and seafood are the catchwords of the Siesta Key restaurant trade. Some people drive out here just to eat. English and American casual eats such as fish & chips, custom-made burgers, and other seafood and sandwich favorites are served up at **The Old Salty Dog**, 5023 Ocean Blvd., ☎ 941-349-0158, www.theoldsaltydog.com. You can sit indoors in a pub setting or outdoors amidst Siesta's "downtown" activity. It's open daily for lunch and dinner. Prices range from $5 to $16.

For breakfast, the favorite gathering spot is **The Broken Egg**, 210 Avenida Madera, ☎ 941-346-2750, where you can take a sidewalk table or one inside next to the bakery. Breakfast offerings include omelets, pancakes, quiches, blintzes, muffins, and coffee cake for $5-$10. It also serves lunch; salads, soups, and sandwiches range from $6 to $10. Open daily.

NIGHTLIFE

I find the nightlife of Siesta Key more relaxed and less showy than in Sarasota's other hot spots. Reflecting the island's mix of creativity and wealth, the after-hours scene has a rowdy cast at one end of the scale, refined at the other.

For jazz, check out **Fandango's** at 5148 Ocean Blvd. in Siesta Village, ☎ 941-346-1711, Thursday-Saturday

Nokomis Area

Some may call it the in-between zone, situated as it is between Sarasota and Venice. It encompasses the communities of Osprey, Casey Key, Nokomis, and Nokomis Beach, with a state park and other attractions for the curious and adventuresome visitor.

FLORIDIOM: The tiny suburb of Osprey is named for a large bird of prey sometimes called a fish hawk. Ospreys nest in high trees or atop pole aeries that good citizens build for them. Mom and dad return to their same nest each winter and raise fledglings together.

GETTING HERE

The communities of Osprey and Nokomis lie along **Highway 41** (Tamiami Trail). To get to Casey Key, turn west on Blackburn Point Rd. south of Osprey. To get to the south end at Nokomis Beach, turn west on Albee Rd. south of the town of Laurel. Exits 200 (southbound traffic only) and 195 (northbound traffic only) are the I-75 exits most convenient to the area.

Narrow, twisty **Casey Key Rd.** winds through the island from end to end.

SIGHTS & ATTRACTIONS

▓ OF HISTORIC OR CULTURAL INTEREST

A woman named **Mrs**. **Potter** (Bertha) Palmer exerted nearly as much influence on Sarasota's growth and development as John Ringling. Although she was a well-known name among Chicago socialites at the time, we hear much less about her – except at **Historic Spanish Point** at 337 N. Tamiami Trail in Osprey, ☎ 941-966-5214, www.historicspanishpoint.com. Assembled on the 30-acre estate she once owned back in the dawning days of the 1900s is a collection of local historic structures that includes ancient Indian shell mounds, a pioneer homestead, an old schoolhouse, Mrs. Palmer's restored gardens, a late Victorian home, a reconstructed chapel, and a citrus packing house. Local actors give living history performances on Sundays from mid-January to mid-April. Guided walking tours of about two hours' duration are available Monday-Saturday, 9-5; noon-5 on Sunday. Tram

tours are available by 48-hour advance reservation daily for $3 plus admission. Adult admission is $9; $8 for seniors and Florida residents; $3 for children aged six-12.

■ BEACHES, PARKS & NATURAL AREAS

Experience the natural history of old Sarasota at **Oscar Scherer State Park**, 1843 S. Tamiami Trail, ☎ 941-483-5956, www. floridastateparks.org/oscarscherer. If you camp there, your neigh-

bors will include river otters, alligators, scrub jays, bob cats, and bald eagles. The nearly 1,400-acre park also offers picnicking, a playground, hiking, freshwater swimming, canoe rentals, ranger-led tours, and fishing. Admission fee per car of eight passengers or fewer is $4 per vehicle, $1 for pedestrians and cyclists.

Casey Key at its north end provides a pleasant, winding drive around an exclusive residential neighborhood. At its southern end, bustling Nokomis Beach is resortier and popular with families. **North Jetty Park** tips the island, where a small pass separates it from Venice Beach (see *Venice*, below). This is a good place to get out of the traffic, have a picnic, swim, surf when the waves are up, and catch lots of fish. It has lifeguards and concessions.

From Nokomis, inland on Rte. 72, **Myakka River State Park**, ☎ 941-361-6511, www.myakkariver.org or www.floridastateparks.

org/myakkariver, appeases adventure hunger with camping, canoeing, and 26,000 acres of forest and wetlands. Through it runs 12 miles of one of Florida's designated Wild and Scenic rivers, which forms two lakes within park boundaries and marshes between them. Lower Myakka Lake is part of the 7,500-acre wilderness preserve. Among its rare wildlife are sandhill cranes, bald eagles, and a nesting colony of endangered wood storks. A 25-foot canopy walkway lets you explore at treetop level. Tour the park via tram (winter only, ☎ 941-365-0100), boat, airboat, guided walks, canoe, bicycle, or horse (must provide your own mount). A small visitor's center introduces the park and its wildlife. One trail leads to a boardwalk high in the tree canopy. Admission is $5 per car to enter for the day. The tram tour, which takes you to areas not accessible by car, costs $10 for adults, $5 for children aged six-12, and is free for younger children on laps. (The tram does not run in off-peak periods, so call ahead.) The park is open for day use from 8 to sunset. Boat tours are also available (see below under *Boat Charters & Tours*).

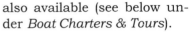

Near the state park at 16405 Myakka Rd., **Crowley Museum & Nature Center**, ☎ 941-322-1000, www.crowleymuseumnaturectr.org, provides a leisurely stroll through time and nature. A boardwalk penetrates swamp habitat with an observation tower overlooking the marsh.

Historic buildings include a turn-of-the-century Cracker home, a sugarcane mill, and a blacksmith shop. The 190-acre complex is open 10-4, Tuesday-Sunday (January-April) and Thursday-Sunday (April-January). Admission is $5 for adults, $3 for children five-12.

ADVENTURES

■ ON WATER

FISHING

The **Intracoastal Waterway** at the narrow south end of Sarasota Bay and around Nokomis and Venice is known as "Snook Alley," because of the abundance of prized snook feeding there.

Cast into bay waters from the **Osprey Fishing Pier** at the west end of Main St.

Locals tell you the best fishing is from the **North Jetty** (see *Sights & Attractions*, above) at the south-end Casey Key Rd. Beach, where a guarded beach and picnic areas give other members of the party something to do. A bait and snack shop is also handy.

Reel Fast Charters at 504 S. Tamiami Trail #7 in Nokomis, ☎ 941-412-0560, www.reelfastcharters.com, charges $425 for four-hour charters, $600 for six hours, and $725 for eight hours.

BOAT RAMPS

You'll find launch ramps at **Captain's Cove** on Blackburn Point Rd.

BOAT CHARTERS & TOURS

Go amphibious on *Just Ducky* on Hwy. 41 in Nokomis, ☎ 941-485-6336. The customized amphibious vessel takes in land and sea sights along Venice's Intracoastal Waterway and streets. Cost is $23.50 for adults, $21.50 for seniors and children older than three.

Take a one-hour narrated tour of Myakka River State Park on Rte. 72, ☎ 941-365-0100, aboard the "world's largest enclosed airboats," *Gator Gal* and *Myakka Maiden*. The boat departs from the park's boat basin three or four times daily. Fare is $10 for adults and $5 for children aged six-12; young children seated on an adult's lap ride free.

PADDLING

Myakka Outpost, inside Myakka River State Park (see above), ☎ 941-923-1120, rents canoes for use along the Wild and Scenic Myakka River and its two lakes. Rates are $15 for two hours, $25 for a half-day, and $40 for a full day. Kayaks rent for $25 a half-day, $50 full day. In winter, it's open Monday-Friday, 9-5; on weekends, 8:30-5. Summer hours (June 1-December 15) are Monday-Friday, 10-4; weekends, 8:30-5.

Oscar Scherer State Park (see *Sights & Attractions*, above) at 1843 S. Tamiami Trail, ☎ 941-483-5956, also rents canoes ($5 an hour, $25 a day, plus tax) and conducts ranger-led canoe trips.

You can join a guided tour or rent a kayak or canoe from **Silent Sports**, 2301 Tamiami Trail in Nokomis, ☎ 941-966-5477. Three-hour kayak rentals cost $24 for a single, $33 for a tandem; $2 for each additional hour. Closed Thursdays.

WATER-SKIING & WAVERUNNERS

Kahunas at 520 Blackburn Point Rd. in Osprey, ☎ 941-486-811 or 800-550-2007, rents Yamaha WaveRunners for $80 per hour.

■ ON FOOT

HIKING

Oscar Scherer State Park (see *Sights & Attractions*, above) at 1843 S. Tamiami Trail, ☎ 941-483-5956, www.floridastateparks.org/

oscarscherer, has more than five miles of nature trails, plus bike paths, which allow you to witness nature and wildlife as you exercise. A one mile-plus nature trail accommodates disabled persons and includes audio speakers and a butterfly observation area. During winter season, rangers lead bird walks.

Myakka River State Park on Rte. 72, ☎ 941-361-6511, is treasured by both bikers and hikers. It offers extensive nature trails, a bird walk, a canopy walkway, and the 39-mile Myakka Trail, a system of loops maintained by the Florida Trail Association. Wilderness backpacking trails cross prairies, hammocks, and pine flatwoods. Bob-cats, bald eagles, sandhill cranes, deer, and wild turkeys inhabit the less traveled areas of the park not accessible to motorists. Six primitive campgrounds lie along the trails. Ask the park ranger for a "Hiking & Biking" map.

HUNTING

Knight Trail Park, east of I-75's Exit 195 off Knight Trail Rd., ☎ 941-486-2350, has an archery course, trap and skeet, a pistol and rifle range, and picnic areas. The park is open to the public Tuesday-Sunday, 8-4:30. Fees are charged per activity. The pistol and rifle range, open Tuesday-Sunday, 9-4:30, costs $6 a day per person.

■ ON WHEELS

At **Myakka River State Park** (see above) on Rte. 72, seven miles of road wind through the park for cyclists, who often incorporate the scenic ride into longer treks along Rte. 72. The park's North Park Drive is preferred for its smoothness and lighter traffic. Backcountry fire-break roads not marked "no bicycling" are available to "dirt bikers." These can be sandy in spots, with areas dug up by feral pigs. Bike rental (☎ 941-923-1120) rates range from $10 for two hours to $30 for a full day.

> *FLORIDIOM: Florida's healthy population of feral pigs, a.k.a. wild boars, descends from Spanish stock brought by early explorers to La Florida, as they called it. They offloaded the hogs from their ships to ensure themselves food on the next visit. The wild animals today are a bane to farmers and a boon to hunters.*

WHERE TO STAY

■ MOTELS

Nokomis Beach has several small lodges geared toward fishing or beaching. **A Beach Retreat** at 105 Casey Key Rd., ☎ 866-BEACH-80 or 941-485-8771, www.abeachretreat.com, addresses the fishing with units on the back bay as well as beach, boat docks, and proximity to North Jetty. Many of its newly redecorated units have kitchens. The property takes up two sides of the road with a prettily fenced small pool, 27 suites and efficiencies, a courtyard, and a deck for barbecuing. $$-$$$$

■ CAMPING

To make campground reservations for **Florida State Parks**, call ☎ 800-326-3521, or visit www.reserveamerica.com.

Two state parks in the area give you the best deal and optimum closeness to nature. At **Oscar Scherer State Park**, 1843 S. Tamiami Trail, ☎ 941-483-5956, www.floridastateparks.org/oscarscherer, campers feel secluded in a huge waterside campground, thanks to the palmettos, pines, oaks, and other native vegetation. Camping rates are $24.20 per night with water and electricity. Pet camping is available.

Myakka River State Park, ☎ 941-361-6511, www.myakkariver.org, is also nice, but tends to feel more closed-in and crowded, especially on weekends. Two family campgrounds contain 76 sites, plus there are five cabins, three group tent sites, and six primitive camp areas. Rates are $22 per night and include water and electricity. Cabins rent for $60 per night for up to four people, $5 per additional person (except for children in a family), maximum of six. Group camping is $4 each per night.

WHERE TO EAT

Pelican Alley, 1009 W. Albee Rd., ☎ 941-485-1893, www. pelicanalley.com, is essentially an Old Florida-style fish house overlooking the Intracoastal Waterway, where preparations are classic and seafood is flopping fresh. Choices range from burgers and fish 'n chips to sushi, shrimp tempura and a deep-fried or grilled seafood platter, priced $7-$11 for lunch and $10-$19 for dinner. For an adventurous meal, try the buffalo shrimp wrap, volcanic style! Open daily for lunch and dinner; closed Tuesdays in summer.

Venice

Venice is the small-town version of Sarasota. It has the same Mediterranean architecture, fun beaches, art galleries, boutique shopping, and seafood restaurants as its big sister, but on a smaller scale. This keeps it less known, more lightly visited, but still as appealing to adventure-driven vacationers. In its past, it has hosted the Kentucky Military Institute, served as winter headquarters for Ringling Brothers Barnum & Bailey Circus, and the Brotherhood of Locomotive Engineers' retirement village, which built a model Italian city there. Above all, Venice is recognized for its **shark-teeth** collecting. Snorkelers and beachcombers search for fossil specimens that wash up from an ancient shark graveyard offshore. Its shark teeth caches, indeed, have given Venice an identity all its own.

Beachcombing is a big draw.

GETTING HERE

Exit 193 or 191 off **I-75** will get you to Venice Ave. **Highway 41** splits when it gets to Venice. Take the business end of it to cross the Intracoastal Waterway onto the island, where you will find the town of Venice proper. Turn west on **Venice Ave**. to head downtown and to the beaches. **The Esplanade** delivers you to Venice's resort district and to **Tarpon Center Dr.**, which goes to the island's northern end beach and jetties. **Harbor Dr**. sightsees residential areas and leads to south-end beaches.

INFORMATION

The **Venice Area Chamber of Commerce** at 597 Tamiami Trail S., Venice, 34285, ☎ 941-488-2236, www.venicechamber.com, can give you information about the location and about shark's teeth. It's open 8:30-5, Monday-Friday. You can also contact Venice Main Street at PO Box 602, Venice, FL 34284, ☎ 941-484-6722.

SIGHTS & ATTRACTIONS

▨ OF HISTORIC OR CULTURAL INTEREST

The historic Triangle Inn's architecture (circa 1926) is the most remarkable display at the **Venice Archives and Area Historical Col-**

lection, 351 Nassau St., ☎ 941-486-2487, which it houses. The unusual three-sided building features Italian Renaissance characteristics. The archives and historic exhibits are open to the public Monday and Wednesday, 10-4. Admission is free.

▨ PERFORMING ARTS

Venice Little Theatre, 140 W. Tampa Ave., ☎ 941-488-1115, www. venicestage.com, claims to be one of the most successful community theaters in the US. Its October-May season brings musicals, comedies, readings, contemporary plays, and children's productions to the stage. Tickets are $10-$22 each; Theatre for Young People tickets are $10.

▨ BEACHES, PARKS & NATURAL AREAS

Venice's pebbly beaches each have their distinct qualities. At heavily visited **Brohard Park** on Harbor Dr., shark-tooth collectors and fishermen converge. The park has picnic facilities, a restaurant, a dog beach with pooch showers, and a fishing pier (see next page).

South of Brohard, **Caspersen Beach** on S. Harbor Dr., ☎ 941-951-5572, has most of the same amenities – picnic areas and dune walkovers – plus a bayside area with playground, bike path, pier, and kayak launch. A stroll south along this beach leads to Manasota Key.

Good shark-tooth collecting is also reported at **Venice Municipal Beach** at Tarpon Center Dr. Divers like this beach for the near off-shore reef, only a quarter of a mile from the beach. Facilities include a picnic area, showers, concessions, and lifeguards.

SHARK-TOOTHING

Equip yourself with a "Florida snow shovel," a screen basket on a long pole, available at local hardware stores for less than $20. (Anything with a screen mesh will work.) Head to Brohard Park or Venice Municipal Beach (see above). Next, sift at water's edge and pull teeth! It's the thing to do in Venice. If you're confused about what you're looking for, stop at the Venice Chamber of Commerce at 597 Tamiami Trail S., ☎ 941-488-2236, and ask for samples and a guide.

Bradenton & Sarasota

■ LOCAL COLOR

South of Venice, spa-goers find their way to a little-known attraction called **The Springs** at 12200 San Servando Rd., Warm Mineral Springs, ☎ 941-426-1692, www.warmmineralsprings.com. Some believe this was the Fountain of Youth that Ponce de León sought. Its 2½-acre lake maintains a temperature of 87E and soothes bathers with a high mineral content. The facility shows its 50-some years of age, but believers find the waters healthful. To enhance the dunk experience, there are massage, acupuncture, and other spa services available. A café sells healthy snacks and juice. The spa and springs are open daily, 9-5. Admission is $20 for adults, $14 for students with ID, $8 for children age 12 and under.

ADVENTURES

■ ON WATER

FISHING

The premier spot for fishing is the **Venice Fishing Pier**. Among the state's longest at 750 feet, it furnishes showers, beach, a bait house, and a restaurant. Admission to the pier is now free.

The **South Jetties** on Tarpon Center Dr. project into the pass toward Casey Key and are equally popular with the casting crowd.

MARINAS & BOAT RAMPS

Crow's Nest Marina, ☎ 941-484-7661, and Fisherman's Wharf Marina at 505 N. Tamiami Trail, ☎ 941-484-9246, serve boaters in the backwaters.

Boat ramps are located at **Marina Boat Ramp Park**, 215 E. Venice Ave., and at **Higel Park** on Tarpon Center Drive.

BOAT RENTALS

Snook Haven, off I-75 at Exit 191, 5000 E. Venice Ave., ☎ 941-485-7221, is a water adventurer's paradise on the banks of the Wild & Scenic Myakka River. Rates for 12- and 14-foot boats (with 6hp engines) start at 27.50-$37.50 for an hour. Pontoon rentals begin at $37.50 for an hour and hold up to nine people. There's also a boat launch and picnic-table dining (see *Where to Eat*, below).

BOAT CHARTERS & TOURS

Terry's River Tours, ☎ 941-255-0400, takes you on a one-hour narrated cruise along the Myakka River, departing from Snook Haven (see above) at 3 Wednesday through Sunday. Cost for adults is $12 plus tax; $6 plus tax for children. Reservations are required and payment is cash only.

PADDLING

For canoeing on the Myakka River and a taste of Old Florida, stop at **Snook Haven** (above). It rents canoes for $21.50 for up to three hours and $32.25 for up to eight hours.

SNORKELING & DIVING

Divers like **Venice Municipal Beach** because there's a reef just a quarter-mile from shore. Fossil-seekers search underwater along the shoreline for shark teeth and other finds, but visibility is often poor. The greatest caches are found in water around 18 feet deep. Offshore, **ledges** and **artificial reefs** harbor marine life out from the jetties at the north end.

SHOPPING

Venice's shopping, like the town itself, is quiet, tasteful, and architecturally pleasing. Turn off Highway 41 onto **West Venice Ave**. An

West Venice Ave

inviting sign heralds your arrival on a date-palm-lined boulevard where shops evoke the Mediterranean and drivers politely stop for crossing pedestrians. Shops, galleries, and restaurants sell the gaudy and the elegant along the avenue and its side streets. South of Venice Ave., **Miami Ave.** is an antique-hunter's paradise.

A block over, **Venice Mall** at 226 Tampa Ave., occupies the former winter quarters of the Kentucky Military Institute. The structure is listed on the National Register of Historic Buildings. Specialty shops fall into formation in a spit-and-polish hall, where historic military displays remember the building's past.

WHERE TO STAY

■ HOTELS & MOTELS

Venice has a small but pleasant selection of hotels, motels, and condominiums. Among its nicest resorts, **Inn at the Beach** at 725 W. Venice Ave., ☎ 800-255-8471 or 941-484-8471, www.innatthebeach.com, has the beach advantage: Venice Municipal Beach lies directly across the street. Clean, modern, and stylish, it offers a small pool and rooms, kitchenettes, or one- and two-bedroom suites. $$-$$$$

© Inn at the Beach

■ BED & BREAKFASTS

Banyan House B&B at 519 S. Harbor Dr., ☎ 941-484-1385, www.banyanhouse.com, is part of Venice's old Mediterranean-fashion neighborhood of the mid-1920s. Distinct elements include a swimming pool that served the community as its first, a Greek goddess fountain under a huge banyan tree, cheery blossoms, a sundeck, a breakfast solarium, a hot tub, and a billiard and fitness room. Each of the five rooms has a private bath and fridge; three of them are efficiencies. The B&B closes July-Aug. and December, but weekly rental apartments are available in a separate structure by the month. $$-$$$

■ RENTAL AGENCIES

The Rental Company of Venice, 236 Tampa Ave. W., ☎ 941-484-7644, www.rentalcompanyofvenice.com, has a repertoire of homes and condos for short-term rental.

■ CAMPING

Venice Campground at 4085 E. Venice Ave., ☎ 941-488-0850, www.campvenice.com, is set under age-old oak trees along the Myakka River. Facilities include security gates, heated swimming pool, shuffleboard, horseshoe, nature trail, fishing, canoe rentals, laundry room, and supply store. It has sites for tents ($43-$47 a night) and RVs ($48-$50), plus rental cabins ($70).

© Venice Campground

WHERE TO EAT

Die-hard fishermen and lots of other hungry folks prefer **Sharky's on the Pier** at Venice Fishing Pier, 1600 S. Harbor Dr., ☎ 941-488-1456, www.sharkysonthepier.com, for its convenience to the fishing and its view of the beach. Lunch features seafood salads, pasta-and-seafood dishes, wraps, and the likes for $8-$15. At dinner, there's

© Sharky's on the Pier

more of the same plus seafood specialties such as seabass in sweet potato crust and macadamia tilapia, ranging from $16 to $25. Outdoors on the deck, the menu is an abbreviated version of the one offered inside, with dishes ranging from $8 to $18. It opens daily.

Swashbuckling, boating types will enjoy **The Crow's Nest Marina Restaurant** at 1968 Tarpon Center Drive on the South Jetty, ☎ 941-484-9551, www.crowsnest-venice.com. Overlooking a yacht marina through tall windows, it is tastefully nautical through and through. The lunch and dinner menus offer seafood prepared flavorfully. It is open daily for lunch and dinner, with price ranges of $7-$15 and $13-$32 respectively. Downstairs, enjoy tavern fare in a pub setting. Reservations are accepted.

While shopping downtown, do lunch with a French accent at **Le Petit Jardin** in the Venice Mall, 218 W. Tampa Ave., ☎ 941-485-4449. Crópes, quiche, filled croissants, French onion soup, and creative salads range from $3.50 to $9.

Snook Haven at 5000 E. Venice Ave., ☎ 941-485-7221, is a country fun kind of place on the Myakka River, where you can paddle a canoe, have some chow, and party to live music. It's open daily for lunch and dinner, with sandwiches and home-style meals ranging from $6 to $18.

Charlotte Harbor

Wide, deep Charlotte Harbor is a place known for pirates and tarpon. The **pirates** are long gone, leaving only their names and sense of adventure upon the islands where they supposedly once maintained their lairs. The **tarpon** are still there, most notably off Boca Grande on Gasparilla Island, one of Charlotte Harbor's islands far removed from the hum of mainstream tourism.

FLORIDIOM: Tarpon (Megalops atlantica) have been around for more than 10 million years. For their sheer size – up to 300 pounds – and valiant fighting efforts, they've been nicknamed "silver king" in these parts. They are the only fish that breathe through an air bladder. They roll at the water's surface to air breathe. Their collective rolling in Boca Grande Pass is an awesome sight, and a heart-racing one for aspiring tarpon hunters. All tarpon fishing these days is done on a catch-and-release basis.

The harbor – the second largest estuarine system in Florida – and its feeders, the Peace and Myakka rivers, section off Charlotte County, which boasts 219 miles of waterfront. The nation's earliest recorded history was written on these coastlines, local historians claim. At Punta Gorda, a park commemorates the landing and wounding of no other than **Juan Ponce de León**, legendary seeker of youth. Downtown Punta Gorda acts slightly metropolitan, having been a major commercial fishing port in a later heyday. Across the Peace, urban sprawl claims smaller communities along the Tamiami Trail. Subdivided by the Myakka River and Charlotte Harbor, a wide peninsula inhabited by golfing communities buffers Gulf barrier islands from the development seen on islands to the north and south.

Charlotte County in general is a hushed location bookended by its more highly touted neighbors. The population is largely retired. You'll notice that the Chamber of Commerce's Visitor's Guide devotes as much space to hospitals as to tourist attractions. What little tourism you do find in its highly residential communities has to do mainly with the great outdoors. Sports opportunities, especially fishing, abound on all the waterfronts. The distance of the region's beaches from main thoroughfares keeps the barrier islands rural and lightly visited. In eastern regions, wildlands have been preserved for sportsmen and nature lovers.

TRANSPORTATION

■ AIRPORTS

Sarasota Bradenton International Airport (SRQ), ☎ 941-359-2770, www.srq-airport.com, and **Southwest Florida International Airport** (RSW) in Fort Myers, ☎ 239-768-1000, www.flylcpa.com, both bring you close to the Charlotte Harbor area. Flights arrive at the two airports from all over the US, from Canada, and from limited international destinations. Major air carriers serving the two airports are listed below.

AIRLINES SERVING SARASOTA-BRADENTON (SRQ) & SOUTHWEST FLORIDA (RSW) INTERNATIONAL AIRPORTS		SRQ	RSW
Air Canada	☎ 888-247-2262	✔	✔
Air France	☎ 800-237-2747	✔	
AirTran Airways	☎ 800-247-8726	✔	✔
Alitalia	☎ 800-223-5730	✔	
American/American Eagle	☎ 800-433-7300	✔	✔
Cape Air	☎ 800-352-0714	✔	
Condor	☎ 800-524-6975		✔
Continental	☎ 800-525-0280	✔	✔
Delta/Comair	☎ 800-221-1212	✔	✔
Frontier Airlines	☎ 800-432-1359		✔
JetBlue	☎ 800-538-2583	✔	✔
LTU International	☎ 866-266-5588		✔
Midwest Express	☎ 800-452-2022		✔
Northwest/KLM	☎ 800-225-2525	✔	✔
Spirit	☎ 800-772-7117		✔
Sun Country	☎ 800-359-6786		✔
United	☎ 800-241-6522		✔
US Airways	☎ 800-428-4322	✔	✔

■ RENTAL CARS & TAXI SERVICE

Rental cars are available at the airports and from locations within the immediate area. Try **Avis**, ☎ 800-331-1212, 941-359-5240 (SRQ), or 239-768-2121 (RSW); **Hertz**, ☎ 800-654-3131, 941-355-

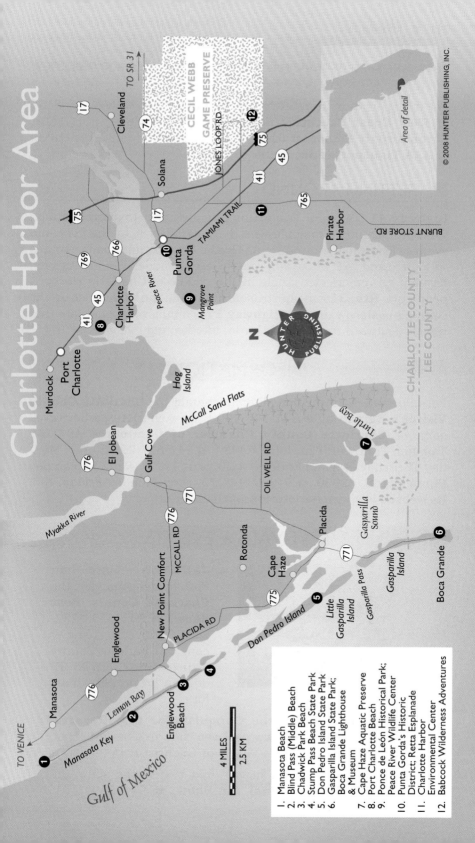

Charlotte Harbor Area

TO VENICE

Gulf of Mexico

Manasota

Manasota Key

Lemon Bay

Englewood

Englewood Beach

New Point Comfort

PLACIDA RD

MCCALL RD

Don Pedro Island

Rotonda

Cape Haze

Little Gasparilla Island

Gasparilla Pass

Gasparilla Island

Gasparilla Sound

Boca Grande

Placida

Turtle Bay

OIL WELL RD

McCall Sand Flats

Hog Island

Gulf Cove

El Jobean

Myakka River

Port Charlotte

Murdock

Charlotte Harbor

Peace River

Punta Gorda

Mangrove Point

TAMIAMI TRAIL

Pirate Harbor

BURNT STORE RD

CHARLOTTE COUNTY

LEE COUNTY

CECIL WEBB GAME PRESERVE

JONES LOOP RD

Solana

Cleveland

TO SR 31

17

74

75

41

45

765

17

766

769

75

45

41

776

771

776

775

771

4 MILES

2.5 KM

Area of detail

© 2008 HUNTER PUBLISHING, INC.

N

HUNTER PUBLISHING

1. Manasota Beach
2. Blind Pass (Middle) Beach
3. Chadwick Park Beach
4. Stump Pass Beach State Park
5. Don Pedro Island State Park
6. Gasparilla Island State Park; Boca Grande Lighthouse & Museum
7. Cape Haze Aquatic Preserve
8. Port Charlotte Beach
9. Ponce de León Historical Park; Peace River Wildlife Center
10. Punta Gorda's Historic District; Retta Esplanade
11. Charlotte Harbor Environmental Center
12. Babcock Wilderness Adventures

8848 (SRQ) or 239-768-3100 (RSW); and **Budget**, ☎ 800-763-2999, 941-359-5353 (SRQ) or 239-768-1500 (RSW).

For transportation from SRQ, call **Diplomat Taxi**, ☎ 941-355-5155 or **West Coast Executive Sedans**, ☎ 941-359-8600; from RSW, **Aaron Airport Transportation**, ☎ 800-998-1898 or 239-768-1898; or **AAA Transportation**, ☎ 800-872-2711.

■ GETTING AROUND

Highway 41 (Tamiami Trail) runs roughly north to south through Charlotte County's major towns. I-75 parallels it to the east and swings closest to it around Punta Gorda. Main county roads – routes 771, 775, and 776 – take you into the area's hidden coastal regions, forming an imperfect triangle in the middle of Charlotte Harbor's peninsula. **Rte. 31** runs north-south through the wilderness on the county's eastern extreme. **Highway 17** is a major thoroughfare that travels eastward from Punta Gorda, intersecting I-75 at Exit 164.

INFORMATION

For information on the overall area, contact the **Charlotte County Visitor's Bureau** at ☎ 941-743-1900; www.charlotteharbortravel. com, or **Charlotte County Chamber of Commerce** at 2702 Tamiami Trail, Port Charlotte, 33952, ☎ 941-627-2222, open Monday-Thursday, 8-5 and Friday 8-4:30; or at 311 W. Retta Esplanade, Punta Gorda, 33950, ☎ 941-639-2222, open Monday-Friday, 8-5. Its website is www.charlottecountychamber.org.

FESTIVALS & EVENTS

★ **JANUARY** – More than 800 boats come for the **Charlotte County Boat Show**, ☎ 941-629-4252, www.fortmyersboatshow. com, at Charlotte County Fairgrounds, 2333 El Jobean Rd. in Port Charlotte.

★ **MARCH** – Watch the **Conquistador Cup Regatta**, ☎ 941-456-5059, www.pgscweb.com, in Charlotte Harbor from Fishermen's Village or Gilchrist Park.

★ **APRIL** – One of the biggest and best in the state, the **Florida International Air Show**, ☎ 941-639-1101, www.fl-airshow.com, features the Thunderbirds and Golden Knights.

★ **MAY** – Boca Grande hosts **Ladies Day Tarpon Tournament**, ☎ 941-964-0568, early in the month. Other tarpon tournaments continue through mid-June. Two redfish tournaments take place in Punta Gorda during the month: **Kid's Cup Redfish Tournament** at Fishermen's Village, ☎ 941-766-8180, www.kidscuptournament.com, and **Oh Boy! Oberto Redfish Cup** at Gilchrist Park, ☎ 941-743-1900, www.redfishnation.com. At Port Charlotte Beach, the **Charlotte Harbor Kayak & Wildlife Festival**, ☎ 941-743-1900, www.pureflorida.com, takes place for two days, with kayak tours, demonstrations, wildlife seminars, and a kayak fishing tournament.

★ **JULY** – Fishermen's Village in Punta Gorda (1200 W. Retta Esplanade) is the site of several water-oriented festivals throughout the year. **Fourth of July Freedom Swim**, ☎ 941-637-1177, is a big event with hundreds of participants and boats crossing the wide mouth of the Peace River between Seahorse Marina in Charlotte Harbor and Fishermen's Village.

★ **DECEMBER** – Lighted boat parades are the quintessential mode for holiday celebrating in Southwest Florida. In Charlotte County, watch early in the month for the **Englewood Lighted Boat Parade**, ☎ 941-475-6882 and the **Peace River Lighted Boat Parade**, ☎ 941-639-3720, www.puntagorda-chamber.com.

Most of the Charlotte Harbor region, with the exception of Boca Grande and Gasparilla Island, provides quite affordable vacationing. Lodging, dining, and attractions are much less expensive than territories on either side of this chapter.

- **Charlotte County Environmental Centers** are free and provide opportunity for hiking, learning, and canoe-launching. There's one south of Punta Gorda and one in Englewood.

- History and enlightenment on a shoestring? Check out **Charlotte County Historical Center**, **Boca Grande Lighthouse Museum**, **A.C. Freeman House**, **Punta Gorda History Park**, the **Railroad Depot** in Punta Gorda, **Blanchard House**, **Ponce de León Historical Park**, and **Peace River Wildlife Center**. All have low or no admission prices. Some request a donation.

- It costs nothing but gas to ride around and appreciate the views. Charlotte Harbor rivals the Everglades for undeveloped and waterfront scenery. The ride to **Boca Grande** and **Englewood Beach**, and along **Burnt Store Marina Rd**. south of Punta Gorda, and **Rte. 31** provide especially pastoral settings. Or drive around **Lake Webb** at Babcock-Webb Wildlife Management Area. Entry fee is $6 per car.

- Itching to snag a flashy tarpon or other prize fish? Fishing charters and rentals are less expensive around Englewood Beach and Port Charlotte than in big-reputation Boca Grande.

Manasota Key/Englewood

The island of Manasota Key is actually a continuation of Venice Beach to the north, but the only way to get from one to the other without leaving the island is by foot.

Although two communities lie on way-off-the-beaten-path Manasota Key, the quieter, more exclusive community to the north is more commonly known as Manasota Key, while the resortier one to the south is called Englewood Beach. In north Manasota Key, homes – mostly palatial – greatly outnumber resorts and other commercial enterprises. **Archaeological digs** have unearthed a rich Amerindian past in Manasota Key. In the present, the entire community is a designated wildlife sanctuary. Its beaches are maintained in a more natural, less developed manner than those in Englewood Beach, a mecca for youthful and cost-conscious vacationers and day-trippers.

Across the bridge from Englewood Beach, the town of Englewood skirts the mainland. It got its start as a vast lemon farm. Today mostly a destination for winter-long golfers and retirees, it's also where beach vacationers go for non-resort services.

The waters that lie between mainland and island – Lemon Bay and Stump Pass – belong to the 7,667-acre **Cape Haze Aquatic Preserve**, a haven for sportsfolk and nature lovers.

Stump Pass

GETTING HERE

Directions can get confusing here, so far from the main thoroughfares. That's what keeps the area so blessedly undiscovered. In addition to the directions that follow, you may want to procure a map.

To approach the area from the north via I-75, take Exit 193 and follow River Rd. to **Rte. 776**. From the south, take Exit 179, head west on Rte. 776, and turn right (north) on **Highway 41**. From Highway 41, turn west on Rte. 776.

Manasota Key has bridges at its north and south ends. The south end bridge is known as the **Tom Adams Bridge**. From Rte. 776 at the north end, take **Manasota Key Rd**. across the bridge. From the south end, turn west on **Beach Rd**. (Rte. 776).

Manasota Key Rd. is the north end's main route. Its name changes to Beach Rd. in the south. **Gulf Blvd.** extends south of the bridge in Englewood Beach. Along it you'll find most of the town's resorts and a secluded beach.

Indiana Ave. (Rte. 776) comprises Englewood's "strip." To get into downtown, head west on **Dearborn Ave**. East of Englewood's north end, **Rte. 776** goes by the name McCall Rd.

INFORMATION

For information on Manasota Key's north end, contact the **Sarasota Convention & Visitors Bureau**, at 655 N. Tamiami Trail, Sarasota, 34236, ☎ 800-522-9799 or 941-957-1877, www.sarasotafl.org, open Monday-Saturday, 9-5; Sunday, 11-3 (during the summer, Sunday hours are noon-2).

To learn more about Englewood Beach and Englewood, contact **Englewood-Cape Haze Area Chamber of Commerce**, 601 S. Indiana Ave, Englewood, 34223, ☎ 800-603-7198 or 941-474-5511, www.englewoodchamber.com. Open Monday-Friday, 8:30-5.

WEEKEND ADVENTURE ITINERARY

- **FRIDAY:** Drive to Manasota Key. Spend morning on Blind Pass or Chadwick Park Beach. Have lunch at Zydeco Grille. In the afternoon, explore the shops and galleries of Olde Englewood Village downtown. Have dinner at Compadre's Mexican Food. Spend night in the Englewood area.

- **SATURDAY:** Do a morning kayak or pontoon nature excursion with Grande Tours. Drive to Boca Grande for lunch at South Beach. Shop in Boca Grande or bicycle and explore the island. Have dinner at PJ's Seagrille. Return to hotel in Englewood.

- **SUNDAY:** Drive to Punta Gorda in the morning. Head to Fishermen's Village for lunch. In the afternoon, hike at Charlotte Harbor Environmental Center or walk the downtown historic district. Have dinner at the Turtle Club and spend the night in Punta Gorda.

SIGHTS & ATTRACTIONS

Manasota Beach

North End

■ BEACHES, PARKS & NATURAL AREAS

Manasota Key's two beaches are developed with services and facilities, but allow you to get away from it all and do some serious beach hiking. Fourteen-acre **Manasota Beach** at 8570 Manasota Key Rd., ☎ 941-316-1172, draws crowds because it is conveniently located where the north bridge makes landfall on the island. Active beachers can hike up to **Casperson Beach** on the south end of connecting Venice Beach, or use the boat ramp facilities across the road on Lemon Bay.

Blind Pass Beach (or Middle Beach) at 6725 Manasota Key Rd., ☎ 941-316-1172, has 63 acres, and is the less used and most natural of the two. It has a boardwalk trail into the mangroves. Both Blind Pass and Manasota Beach offer picnic facilities, restrooms, and other conveniences. Surfers head here when fronts bring in viable waves.

Blind Pass Beach

Englewood Beach

■ BEACHES, PARKS & NATURAL AREAS

Englewood Beach also has two distinct choices for beaches. If you like 'em secluded and natural, head for **Stump Pass Beach State Park**, ☎ 941-964-0375, at the very south end and shown here. Pop-

ular with fishermen as well as sunners, it charges a parking fee of $2 per day ($1 access fee for bikes and pedestrians). **Chadwick Park Beach**, ☎ 941-473-1081, is located squarely where the south bridge meets the Gulf of Mexico. Recent major renovations mean modern buildings, a boardwalk, and – most importantly – a widened beach. Facilities include a pirate playground, basketball, and picnic pavilions. You'll hear locals refer to it simply as "Englewood Beach." The park is open sunrise-sunset; parking is 50¢ an hour.

Englewood

■ OF HISTORIC OR CULTURAL INTEREST

Indian Mound Park on Winson Ave. in downtown Englewood (follow the signs from Dearborn Ave.), preserves an ancient Indian midden mound more than 2,000 years old in a lovely bayside park. Take the short nature trail and have a picnic.

■ PERFORMING ARTS

Fine community theater takes the stage at **Lemon Bay Playhouse**, 96 W. Dearborn in downtown Englewood, ☎ 941-475-6756, www. lemonbayplayhouse.com. Tickets for comedies, dramas, and musicals run $10-$15 during the troupe's September-July season.

ADVENTURES

■ ON WATER

FISHING

The swift waters of Stump Pass flush out a wide variety of saltwater fish. Tarpon is king – the silver king, by name – but mackerel, snapper, grouper, and sheepshead also make worthy trophies.

Try casting from the south end of **Stump Pass Beach State Park** (see *Sights & Attractions*, above) or from a boat in Lemon Bay. Offshore artificial reefs create popular hangouts for the local gill-breathing population. You'll find fishing piers along Beach Rd. on the east side of the drawbridge.

For bait and gear, stop at **Island Court**, 1939 Beach Rd., ☎ 941-474-8236; open daily, 7:30-5. On the bridge to Englewood Beach, **Englewood Bait House**, 1450 Beach Rd., ☎ 941-475-4511, sells bait, tackle, gas, and supplies, plus rents docks and boats. It opens daily 6-6.

Captain Jack's Charters, at the Englewood Bait House (see above), 1450 Beach Rd., ☎ 941-475-4511, takes passengers aboard a party boat for $50 each. Private boat charters are $150 per person.

BOAT RAMPS

At Manasota Key's north end, the county maintains docks and a ramp on the **Intracoastal Waterway**, across the road from Manasota Beach. There are others at **Indian Mound Park** (above) on Winson Ave. in downtown Englewood.

BOAT RENTALS

Rent Carolina Skiffs and pontoons from **Bay Breeze Boat Rentals**, just east of the south (Tom Adam's) bridge to Manasota at 1450 Beach Rd., ☎ 941-475-0733. Skiffs run $109-$135 for a half-day, $149-$210 for full; pontoons, $155-$240 for a half-day, $240-$350 for full. Fuel and tax are extra. Fishing equipment rentals are available. Open daily.

Beach Road Watersports, next to Red Pelican shop at 1350 Beach Rd. on the way to Englewood Beach, ☎ 941-475-9099, rents WaveRunners ($90 for one hour), water bikes and pedal boats ($25 for one hour), and 16-foot skiffs ($90 for four hours, $130 for eight) to 24-foot pontoons holding 12 ($175, $275). It opens daily at 9 and closes at sundown.

BOAT CHARTERS & TOURS

© Island Adventures

Island Adventures Boat Tours at Palm Island Marina in Cape Haze, ☎ 941-408-5138, www.islandadventuresboattours.com, offers private charters for 2½ hours for up to six people. Adventures range from sunset cruises and Boca Grande visits (three hours for $245) to island tours and a sandbar eco-excursion.

PADDLING

Boating, canoeing, and kayaking into **Lemon Bay** affords rich opportunities for wildlife spotting. Manatees, dolphin, ibises, egrets, herons, and a host of other birds hang out here year-round.

Canoeists can launch into Lemon Bay from **Cedar Point Environmental Park** on Rte. 775, ☎ 941-475-0769. It's open Monday-Friday, 9-3. For more information on local waterways, contact the Charlotte County Parks service (☎ 941-625-7529, www.charlottecountyfl.com) for its Blueway Trails guide.

Bikes and Boards at 966 S. McCall Rd., ☎ 941-474-2019, rents single and tandem kayaks at $36 a day. Hours are 10:30-6, daily.

SNORKELING & DIVING

Local waters, though sometimes low in visibility, hold a number of wrecks and reefs worth exploring at depths of 45 to 60 feet. A beach dive from the south end of Manasota Beach takes you to an area known as The Rocks. Snorkelers search for sharks' teeth inshore.

■ ON FOOT

Take a hike on **Manasota Beach** (see *North End Sights & Attractions*, above). It's remote and connects to Venice's Casperson Beach, about 1½ miles to the north. Don't forget to take something to drink and to allow for the added difficulty of walking in sand. Watch for sharks' teeth at the shoreline.

Cedar Point Environmental Park on Rte. 775, ☎ 941-475-0769, www.checflorida.org, has five nature trails, picnic tables, a small playground, and a visitor's center with a kids' touch table. Bald eagles and gopher tortoises live among the 88-acre park's pine flatwoods, oak scrub, salt flats, and mangroves fringing Lemon Bay Aquatic Preserve. Hours are Monday-Friday, 9-3. The park offers guided tours every Saturday and Sunday at 10 in season.

Nature trails explore the mangrove, wetland, and flatwood bayfront environment of 195-acre **Lemon Bay Park**, 570 Bay Park Blvd., ☎ 941-474-3065.

■ ON WHEELS

Cape Haze Pioneer Trail has developed a **rails-to-trails bike path** that parallels Route 771 for 5.5 checked miles. There are four trailheads. Call ☎ 941-627-1628 for a map. When complete, it will connect to the Boca Grande bike path (see page 264).

Four miles of **Beach Rd**. is shouldered with a **bike lane**, which starts in Englewood Beach and ends where the community of Manasota Key begins at the Sarasota County line.

Bikes and Boards, 966 S. McCall Rd., ☎ 941-474-2019, rents, sells, and services bikes. Rental rates are $12-$16 a day, and $39-$59 a week. It also rents bicycle car racks. Open Monday-Saturday, 10:30-6; shortened hours in off-season.

SHOPPING

To discover a hidden stroll of art galleries and other fun boutiques and eateries, head down **Dearborn Street**, Englewood's main street of Route 776, between the two bridges to Manasota Key to Olde Englewood Village.

WHERE TO STAY

■ COTTAGES & RESORTS

Part summer camp, part classic resort, **Manasota Beach Club** at 7660 Manasota Key Rd., ☎ 941-474-2614, www.manasotabeach-club.com, is a family-run, 22-acre complex. You stay in a cottage in wooded, beachy surroundings and eat in the communal dining room. Somewhat exclusive, the club focuses on nature, bird watching, and resting – aside from the tennis courts, pool, kayaking, bocci ball, shuffleboard, basketball, horseshoes, croquet, bicycling, sailing, windsurfing, and charter fishing available. In high season, which runs from February through March, rates include three meals daily. Pre- and post-season rates include modified or no meal plans. $$$$

© Manasota Beach Club

Down at the south end, small condominium resorts, apartments, and mom-and-pop motels rule. Outdoor types will find most of what they need at the sprawling yellow resort community of **Weston's Fish 'n Fun Resort**, 985 Gulf Blvd., ☎ 941-474-3431, www.westonsresort.com. It has apartments on the beach or back bay, tennis, pools, slips, a boat ramp, boat rentals, and a fishing pier. Accommodations range from fully furnished efficiencies to one- to three-bedroom apartments. Weekly and monthly rates are available. $$-$$$

■ RENTAL AGENCIES

To rent a vacation home in the Englewood area, contact **Manasota Key Realty**, 1927 Beach Rd. S., ☎ 800-870-6432 or 941-474-9536, www.englewoodfl.com. It lists condos and homes for weekly, monthly, and longer stays. Many require a minimum stay of a month or longer.

WHERE TO EAT

Downtown Englewood has a growing number of fun restaurants, including **Compadre's Mexican Food** at 498 W. Dearborn St., ☎ 941-475-4010. It's cozy inside, and outside, where there's a band stage and bar, is popular with smokers and party folk (there's live music weekends). Order Mexican favorites from tacos to *chile relleno* and *carne asada* in the $7-$12 range.

At 2639 Placida Rd. in Englewood, **Zydeco Grille**, ☎ 941-473-7479, brings the Big Easy tastes, sounds, and scenes to a stylish dining room and streetside patio. New Orleans-style scroll work decorates the booth-lined dining room and adjacent full bar. Start with the gumbo of the day and dig into some jumbo boiled crawfish or etouffée. It's all homemade good. Open for lunch ($7-$14) and dinner ($14-$25) Tuesday through Saturday.

Gasparilla Island & Out Islands

The island Gasparilla got its name from a pirate of legend. Though pirate Gasparilla's actual existence has been disproved, his renegade spirit still lives on the island, which for decades remained aloof from development. The Gasparilla Inn set the tone back in the 1920s, when it was built to accommodate wealthy northern industrialists who arrived to exploit the deep harbor for phosphate shipping and cast for treasured tarpon in the island town of Boca Grande. Their influence kept the island exclusively wealthy for years, but in recent years, growth has visited Boca Grande and Gasparilla Island, as it has many of Florida's discovered treasures.

Historic Gasparilla Inn

© The Gasparilla Inn

Tethered to the mainland by a long causeway, Gasparilla lies at the crossroads of island personalities. To its north, a string of islands, which through the years have become interconnected, resists the settling effect of attaching to the mainland. To its south begins a lily-pad trail of islands in various stages of naturalness and commercialism.

GETTING HERE

From **Highway 41**, northwest of Port Charlotte, turn west on Rte. 776 (El Jobean Rd) and follow it to **Rte. 771**, which leads you to the island. Toll at the quaint little booth is $4. If arriving by interstate, take Exit 167 and head west on Rte. 776, turn north onto Highway 41 to reconnect to Rte. 776, then proceed as above.

From Gasparilla Island and the Intracoastal towns of Placida and Cape Haze (on Rte. 775), you can find transport to the unbridged, interconnected out-islands of **Little Gasparilla**, **Palm**, and **Don Pedro** (see *On Water*, below).

Boca Grande Limousine, ☎ 800-771-7433 or 941-964-0455, provides connections to all Florida airports. For more grandiose arrivals and departures, call **Boca Grande Seaplane**, ☎ 800-940-0234 or 941-964-0234.

INFORMATION

Contact the **Boca Grande Chamber of Commerce** at PO Box 704, Boca Grande, 33921, ☎ 941-964-0568, www.bocagrandechamber. com. Open Monday-Friday, 9-5.

SIGHTS & ATTRACTIONS

■ OF HISTORIC OR CULTURAL INTEREST

People day-trip to Boca Grande just to wander its main business street (**Park Ave.**) – where a historic depot and theater house small shopping malls – and to gawk at the **mansions** along the Gulf. These are nearly impossible to see from the road in many places, but the island's other intriguing buildings are readily accessible, including the **Gasparilla Inn** at Fifth and Palm streets (see *Where to Stay*, below), the **historic churches** downtown, the pretty-in-pink **Johann Fust Community Library** at 10th St. and Gasparilla Rd., and Tarpon Ave.'s historic **fish-village shacks** (known as Whitewash Alley).

Gasparilla PirateFest

■ NATURAL AREAS

Gasparilla Island State Park, south of Boca Grande on Gulf Blvd., ☎ 941-964-0375, fronts one defunct historic lighthouse and another in use. The plush beach encompasses 135 acres subdivided into three areas – Sand Spur Beach, Sea Grape Beach, and Lighthouse Beach. Facilities include showers, restrooms, picnic tables, and grills. Swimming at Lighthouse Beach is treacherous because of the deep  pass at the island's end, where in summer you can watch tarpon rolling and fishermen trying to lure them. Parking is $2 per vehicle. The park is open daily, 8 until dusk.

Don Pedro Island State Park (shown on next page), ☎ 941-964-0375, www.floridastate parks.org/donpedroisland, occupies 129 acres of unbridged island north of Boca Grande. Access is by boat only. See the *On Water* section below for details on how to get to Don Pedro for a day of isolated picnicking and beaching. Visitors are asked to pay a $1 per person fee.

> **TIP:** *Take a shady, peaceful stroll or bike ride under the awesome tree canopy that lines Banyan St., the area's most-photographed road.*

■ MUSEUMS

The Boca Grande Lighthouse Museum at Gasparilla Island State Park on Gulf Blvd., ☎ 941-964-0375, www.barrierisland parkssociety.org/lighthouse.html, is more than 115 years old. Renovated to Old Florida style, it is open for self-touring and has a mu-

seum that deals with the history of the lighthouse and Boca Grande, Calusa Amerindians, and tarpon. The museum features a hands-on table for kids. Hours are Wednesday-Sunday, 10-4. Hours are sometimes extended in season. A $2 parking fee is required to enter the park. Donations of $1 are requested.

An 80-year-old island institution, **Whidden's Marina** at 190 E. First St. has devoted one of its National Register of Historic Places buildings to house the new and growing Gasparilla Island Maritime Museum, ☎ 941-964-GIMM. The restored fish house holds antique fishing and boating gear, other artifacts, photographs, and displays that tell the story of Boca Grande's maritime heritage. Admission is by donation.

> *FLORIDIOM: The so-called Calusa people inhabited Southwest Florida from Charlotte Harbor to the Everglades, beginning about 2,500 years ago. Spaniards gave them their name, believing their leader to be named Calos. They met Ponce de León with bows and arrows when he dropped anchor in Charlotte Harbor. Excavations of their settlement prove that the Calusa were a war-like, well-developed nation with advanced engineering skills.*

ADVENTURES

■ ON WATER

FISHING

Fishing is practically synonymous with Boca Grande. Once winter's "social season" has ended, tarpon season brings a second influx of

Charlotte Harbor

tourists, the rod-wielding type, from April through July. To learn the ropes about catching an in-your-dreams silver king, hook up with a pro through **The Boca Grande Fishing Guides Association**, ☎ 800-667-1612, www.bocagrandefishing.com, an organization of about 50 local guides.

Capt. Fred Scott, ☎ 941-628-8839, an experienced charter captain, charges $250 for a half-day of trout spincasting or mackerel trolling; $350 for a half-day of tarpon fishing and $600 for a full day. Rates are for six or fewer passengers.

Fishing Unlimited, ☎ 800-4-TARPON, 941-964-0907 or (evenings) 697-1611, www.4tarpon.com, bases tarpon-fishing rates according to tides. A half-tide (three hours) costs $400, full tide (five hours) $600 for six people max. Backwater trips for snook, redfish, trout, and snook cost $350 for a half-day, $500 for a full day. Maximum is three persons. Shark and fly-fishing excursions also available.

Fish for tarpon, snook, and redfish on a fly-fishing charter with Capt. Austin Lowder and **Sea & Stream Outfitters**, ☎ 941-255-4071 (voice mail), 941-697-9966 (home), or 941-815-0254 (cell), www.seaandstream.com. Call for rates on tarpon and other fishing.

An old railroad bridge that pokes into Gasparilla Sound serves as **Gasparilla Pier**. Enter it from the parking lot near Boca Grande Resort complex at the island's north end. Just off the island, where the causeway road meets Rte. 775, you'll find Coral Creek Pier.

Boca Grande Outfitters, 375 Park Ave., ☎ 941-964-2445, www. bocagrandeoutfitters.com, sells light tackle and fly-fishing gear, and offers lessons and seminars in fly-fishing. For guide service, ☎ 941-964-1112.

The little enclave of shops, charters, and food outlets on **Fishery Rd**. in Placida, just south of the Boca Grande Causeway, is a good place to find bait and fishing charters. **Anglers Dream**, ☎ 941-697-7997, www.theanglersdream.com, takes you deep-sea fishing in a 50-foot boat for half- and full-day or night trips. They start at $40 each and include bait, or buy your own at Coral Creek Bait nearby.

BOAT RENTALS

Boca Boat Cruises & Charters, Uncle Henry's Marina, 5800 Gasparilla Rd., ☎ 888-416-BOAT or 941-964-1333, www.bocaboat.com, has powerboats from 17 to 22.5 feet that rent for $160-$260 for a half-day, $220-$360 for a full day. Fishing licenses are available for purchase.

Boaters can put in at the **Placida Public Boat Ramp** at the east end of the Boca Grande Causeway on Placida Rd. (Rte. 771).

BOAT CHARTERS & TOURS

For transportation to **Don Pedro Island State Park** (see *Natural Areas, above*), hop aboard Grande Tours shuttle service, ☎ 941-697-8825, www.grandetours.com, which departs from the Fishery Dock, just south of Boca Grande Causeway, at 10 am. The shuttle leaves Don Pedro at 2:30 pm. Call for dates and schedule. Round-trip cost is $19 each. Grande Tours also does sunset and wildlife tours for $23 each.

Boca Boat Cruises & Charters at Uncle Henry's Marina, 5800 Gasparilla Rd., ☎ 888-416-BOAT, www.bocaboat.com, sets out on luncheon excursions to Cabbage Key ($36), sunset cruises ($25), and charter tours ($325 for a half-day, $550 for all day). Tours take in shelling, shark-toothing, and swimming. Reservations are required.

Capt. Fred Scott, ☎ 941-628-8839, makes charter boat excursions to local islands. Cost for six or fewer passengers ranges from $65 to $150.

PADDLING

Boca Boat Cruises & Charters at Uncle Henry's Marina, 5800 Gasparilla Rd., ☎ 888-416-BOAT or 941-964-1333, www.bocaboat. com, rents single kayaks at $20 for two hours, $30 for a double kayak. It's open daily, 8-4:30.

Charlotte Harbor

Grande Tours, 12575 Placida Rd. in Placida (close to the Boca Grande Causeway), ☎ 941-697-8825, www.grandetours.com, conducts kayak tours starting at $50 each for a 2½-hour eco-experience, $50 for a full moon trip. Introductory, advanced, Greenland-style, and Eskimo Roll kayaking classes are available, plus owner Capt. Marian offers kayak fishing guide service and Kayak Kamp for Kids.

■ ON WHEELS

About a mile after Gasparilla Island's toll booth (only $1 fee for bike riders), the **Boca Grande bike path** begins. It follows an old train route along Railroad Ave., through downtown, and seaside on Gulf Blvd., for a total of seven miles. Golf carts also use the path and are rentable around town.

Bike rentals are available at **Island Bike 'N Beach**, 333 Park Ave., ☎ 941-964-0711, for $7 an hour, $12 for four hours. It's open Monday-Saturday, 9-5, and Sunday 10-4.

■ ECO-ADVENTURES

Get as close to nature as you choose on **Grande Tours** 12575 Placida Rd. in Placida (close to the Boca Grande Causeway), ☎ 941-697-8825. The premier charter company for get-back-to-nature tours, its varied menu ranges from catamaran Sea Life Excursions with seine-netting for hands-on encounters with sea creatures (two hours for $25 per person) to custom charters. Specialty tours are geared toward birding, kids, watchable wildlife, manatees, dolphin, and touring Boca Grande.

SHOPPING

Downtown Boca Grande holds a handful of shops and **galleries** in the historic settings of an old train depot and 1920s **movie theater**. Try **Boca Grande Outfitters**, 375 Park Ave., ☎ 941-964-2445, www. bocagrandeoutfitters.com, for quality fishing gear and outdoor wear.

WHERE TO STAY

 Author favorites are indicated with a star.

ACCOMMODATIONS PRICE KEY		
Rates are per room, per night, double occupancy. Price ranges described for each property often do not take into account penthouses and other exceptional, high-priced accommodations.	$	Up to $75
	$$	$75 to $150
	$$$	$151 to $250
	$$$$	$251 and up

■ INNS & RESORTS

For the ultimate Boca Grande experience, book at **The Gasparilla Inn** on Palm Ave., ☎ 800-996-1913, 941-964-2201, www.the-gasparilla-inn.com. The Vanderbilts, duPonts and their ilk have stayed here for generations. During tarpon season, April through June, the fishing buffs arrive and stay in the inn's cottages, all that's open in the summer. Amenities include an 18-hole golf course, a beach club with swimming pool, restaurants, croquet, and after-noon tea. Rooms are rather simple in this historic, 1920s yellow wood palace. Rates in social season include three meals a day; in tarpon season, break-fast and dinner only. $$$$

© The Gasparilla Inn

The Innlet, nearby at 12th St. and East Ave., ☎ 941-964-2294, www.innletonthewaterfront.com, is more motel-like and adventure-oriented, perched on bayside banks. Accommodations are comfortable with shared porch or balcony, and guests have use of a pool, restaurant, boat ramp, and dockage. Efficiencies have kitchens, plus there's a restaurant on-property. $$-$$$

© The Innlet

A getaway to **Palm Island Resort**, offshore at Cape Haze, ☎ 941-697-4800, 800-824-5412, www.palmisland.com, will cure you of all reality-related blues. The modern, Old Florida-style villas are poised on a wide apron of sand, silky and soothing as baby powder. To many, they are a vision of fantasies unleashed.

© Palm Island Resort

This is not a place for people who need lots of activity, although you can hook up with a number of different tours and charters, or swim and play tennis on the 200-acre property. You arrive by ferry boat from the mainland harbor. The main mode of transportation on the island is golf cart. One- , two- and three-bedroom island villas are available, and there's a minimum two-night stay required. $$$$

■ RENTAL AGENCIES

Grande Island Vacations, ☎ 800-962-3314 or 941-964-2080, www.grandeislandvacations.com, rents condominiums and homes on the island for short-term vacationing.

WHERE TO EAT

Boca Grande is a fun place to go for lunch or dinner in a novel setting. The experience is sure to teach your palate lessons on how seafood should really taste.

South Beach fronts the beach at 777 Gulf Blvd., ☎ 941-964-0765. Sand-between-the-toes casual, it seats guests open-air, inside a screened lanai, or indoors and air-conditioned, near the bar. It's the utmost in beach funky. Daily lunch and dinner prices range from $7 to $13 and $9 to $25 respectively for burgers, salads, and grouper as fresh as it comes. It features weekly all-you-can-eat shrimp or fish nights. Open daily.

If you're looking for a meal-time adventure, hop aboard the **Palm Island Resort ferry** at 7092 Placida Rd. in Cape Haze and take the short, slow ride (fare $2 each) to Rum Bay, ☎ 941-697-0566. Tender baby-back ribs are a specialty; its daily lunch and dinner menus are complete with burgers, salads, chicken wings, fish, and steaks. Prices are $6-$10 for lunch, $7-$20 for dinner. Call ahead for reservations and transportation to the island.

For something slightly more formal, **PJ's Seagrille** in the Old Theatre Building at Fourth and Park avenues, ☎ 941-964-0806, does linen and candlelight for dinner, and also serves lunch. The setting is unfinished wood and aquariums. Lunch will run you $9-$13 for creative sandwiches, salads, and seafood; dinner, runs $22-$49 for changing entrées the likes of char-grilled yellowfin tuna, Key lime chicken, crab cakes, and other innovative, artistically presented delights. The restaurant closes Sunday and August-September. Dinner reservations are recommended.

Port Charlotte & Environs

Port Charlotte grew up on the Tamiami Trail as the area developed into a residential community tuned primarily for retirement. It consists of a strip of highway shopping centers, fast-food restaurants, and smaller branch communities, with no true downtown. It has a few attractions for sightseers, but not a lot in the way of adventure.

GETTING HERE

Exits 167 and 170 take you to town from I-75. **Hwy 41**, a.k.a. Tamiami Trail, runs congestedly through its center. **Kings Highway** (Rte. 769) and **Harbor View Rd**. are major streets to the east of Highway 41. **Edgewater Drive** is a main through-street to the west.

SIGHTS & ATTRACTIONS

■ OF HISTORIC OR CULTURAL INTEREST

Charlotte County Historical Center at 22959 Bayshore Dr., ☎ 941-639-3777, occupies a roomy facility on the waterfront in Charlotte Harbor. It concentrates on local, Florida, and natural history with permanent and changing exhibits. Admission is $2 for adults, $1 for children aged 12 and under. Hours are Monday-Friday 10-5; Saturday 10-3; closed Sunday.

■ BEACHES, PARKS & NATURAL AREAS

The best bet for recreationists is **Port Charlotte Beach** at the end of Harbor Blvd., ☎ 941-625-7529. This man-made beach is central to a variety of facilities and activities, including volleyball, basketball, tennis, horseshoes, a playground, boat ramps, a fishing pier, picnic facilities, canoe and kayak access, bocci, a swimming pool (☎ 941-505-8686), and a kiddy pool. Parking is 50¢ an hour. Admission to the swimming pool complex is $2.50 plus tax for adults aged 17 and over, $1.50 for youths aged three-16. The park is open sunrise-sunset.

■ FAMILY FUN

Putt-putt around the two 18-hole miniature courses at **Fish Cove Adventure Golf**, 4949 Tamiami Trail, ☎ 941-627-5393. Cost is $6.50-$8.50. Hours are 10 am-11 pm, daily. Children aged two-12 can use the bounce house for an extra $2.

ADVENTURES

■ ON WATER

FISHING

There is a fishing pier with bait and tackle concession at the **Port Charlotte Beach recreational complex** on the southeast end of Harbor Blvd., ☎ 941-627-1628. It pokes into Alligator Bay off Charlotte Harbor. The park also has a boat ramp.

The old **railroad bridge** that crosses the Myakka River at El Jobean Park is a popular spot for angling. Known as the Myakka South Fishing Pier, it's located on El Jobean Rd.

Charlotte Harbor Pier juts into the mouth of the Peace River on Bayshore Rd. in the community of Charlotte Harbor, which lies on the northern banks of the river.

For freshwater fishing, try the small lake at **Kiwanis Park** (see *Hiking & Biking*, below) on Donora St. at Victoria Ave.

Tarpon Hunter II in Port Charlotte, ☎ 941-743-6622, offers charters in Charlotte Harbor and backwaters. Specialties include fly and light tackle fishing. Call for rates.

■ ON FOOT

HIKING & JOGGING

Kiwanis Park on Donora St. at Victoria Ave., ☎ 941-624-3057 or 627-1628, has a jogging/fitness trail, a self-guided nature trail, and a lakeside Audubon trail, as well as picnic facilities. It's open daily, sunrise-9.

■ ON WHEELS

The Bicycle Center, 3795 Tamiami Trail, ☎ 941-627-6600, rents a variety of bikes, including beach cruisers, hybrids, tandems, children's bicycles, and adult tricycles. Rentals are available by the day, week, or month. Daily rates begin at $12.

WHERE TO STAY

Port Charlotte offers an inventory of chain hotel lodgings that is expected to grow in the near years to come. A Microtel Inn & Suites, Sleep Inn, Country Inn, and La Quinta will be moving in.

■ CAMPING

East of town, **Riverside RV Resort & Campground**, 9770 SW County Rd. 769 (Kings Highway), ☎ 941-993-2111 or 800-795-9733, www.riversidervresort.com, posts overnight rates of $34-$52 for tents and RVs with full hookup. Canoe rentals are available.

© Riverside RV Resort

WHERE TO EAT

Highway 41 leaves a trail of fast-food and chain restaurants from one end of Port Charlotte to another. For something with more personality, head to Boca Grande or Punta Gorda.

Local places often change hands and names before you can make a return visit. One that gets current acclaim for its steaks is **Cap'n and the Cowboy**, 2200 Kings Hwy., ☎ 941-743-3969. It's open daily (except Monday) for lunch ($4-$11) and dinner ($15-$30).

Punta Gorda

Port Charlotte's neighbor across the river provides a historic counterpart to the newer town's lack of identity. Its history begins with **Ponce de León**, who is believed to have landed and suffered fatal Indian arrow wounds on the shores of Charlotte Harbor at Punta Gorda's western boundary. Within the shelter of the **Peace River**, a turn-of-the-century community cropped up around a deep port and commercial fishing industry. Once a thriving city and resort, Punta Gorda today is a quiet, neighborly community where history is being revived and the wilderness beckons at the side door. In 2004, Hurricane Charley delivered the community a near-fatal blow of its own, but the downtown area is slowly recovering stronger and better than before.

GETTING HERE

Follow **Highway 41** to reach Punta Gorda's heart. Downtown, it's known as **Cross St**. From I-75, take the short drive off of Exit 164. **Marion** (one-way westbound) and **Olympia** (one-way eastbound) avenues are the main streets downtown. **Retta Esplanade** is a scenic riverside route to the north of and paralleling Marion Ave.

SIGHTS & ATTRACTIONS

■ OF HISTORIC OR CULTURAL INTEREST

Explore Punta Gorda's past within its **historic district**, which hugs Tamiami Trail along Nesbit St. and Marion and Olympia avenues. Old commercial buildings have been spruced up for a second life. Sculptures, murals, and old-fashioned street lamps adorn business streets. Take a slow drive along **Retta Esplanade**, absorbing the riverfront scenery on one side and the row of handsome historic homes on the other.

City Hall is one of the town's many historic buildings.

To commemorate Juan Ponce de León's local landing in his quest for youth, **Ponce de León Historical Park**, on the west end of Marion Ave., holds an unpretentious monument, nature observation boardwalk into the mangroves, and lovely waterside picnic area with barbecue grills. Admission is free. It's open daily except Tuesday, dusk-dawn.

ADVENTURES

■ ON WATER

FISHING

Gilchrist Park on Retta Esplanade has a fishing pier that reaches into the wide mouth of the Peace River. For fishing needs, stop at Laishley Marine at 3415 Tamiami Trail, ☎ 941-639-3868. Hours are normally 8-5 daily.

King Fisher Fleet at Fishermen's Village Marina, 1200 W. Retta Esplanade, ☎ 941-639-0969, www.kingfisherfleet.com, has been running fishing excursions for years and years. Rates for deep-sea fishing aboard a 35-footer are $700 per day for up to six persons; for back-bay fishing, $400 per day, $250 for a half-day for up to three. Extra persons pay $50.

BOAT RAMPS

Boat ramps in Punta Gorda are located at **Ponce de León Historical Park** on the west end of Marion Ave., at **Laishley Park City Marina** on Nesbit St., and at **Riverside Park** on Riverside Dr., on Washington Loop Rd., and on **Darst Ave**.

BOAT RENTALS

At **Fishermen's Village**, Holidaze, ☎ 941-505-8888, www.holidaze-boatrental.com, rents boats for periods of two hours to a full day. A 17.5-foot Carolina Skiff costs $50 for one hour, $150 a half-day, and $250 a full day. At the high end of the scale, rent a Cobia for $90 an hour, $300 half-day, or $500 full day. Pontoon boats and jet skis also available.

BOAT CHARTERS & TOURS

At **King Fisher Fleet** at Fishermen's Village Marina, 1200 W. Retta Esplanade, ☎ 941-639-0969, www.kingfisherfleet.com, sightseeing voyage fares begin at $9.95 for a sunset cruise. The menu of other excursions ranges from a 90-minute harbor tour to a full-day trip to Cabbage Key or Cayo Costa, $13-$25 per adult. Children under age 12 board for half-fare. Tax is not included in prices.

■ ON FOOT

HIKING

The **Charlotte Harbor Environmental Center Alligator Creek Preserve** (see above) at 10941 Burnt Store Rd., ☎ 941-575-5435, www.checflorida.org, has three miles of nature trails where marsh rabbits, bald eagles, ospreys, alligators, and pileated woodpeckers dwell amidst the slash pine and saw palmetto. Admission is free. Hours are 8-3, Monday-Saturday; 11-3 on Sunday. Guided walks take place at 10 on weekdays in season.

Follow the **Old Datsun Trail** at Charlotte Harbor Preserve State Park, ☎ 941-575-5861, www.floridastateparks.org/charlotteharbor, the fourth-largest state park in Florida at 30,000 acres.

Charlotte Harbor

HUNTING

Fred C. Babcock-Cecil M. Webb Wildlife Management Area, east of town off Rte. 31, ☎ 941-575-5768, http://floridaconservation.org/recreation/babcock_webb, covers over 79,000 acres populated by doves, quail, deer, and wild hogs. A management stamp is required to enter, and hunters must have licenses. For management stamps, call the county tax collector's office at ☎ 941-637-2150.

The **Cecil M. Webb Shooting Range**, on Tucker Grade at Rifle Range Rd., east of I-75 at Exit 158, is open to the public during daylight hours every day except the fourth Saturday of each month from daylight to 2 pm, when hunter education training is held on-site. For information and rules, contact the Game and Fresh Water Fish Commission's office at ☎ 863-648-3206, http://myfwc.com/huntered/CecilWebb_brochure.pdf.

■ ON WHEELS

Gilchrist Park runs along the river on Retta Esplanade and has bike paths plus picnicking, a huge playground, basketball court, and a tennis court.

■ ECO-ADVENTURES

On the grounds of Ponce de León Historical Park, **Peace River Wildlife Center**, 3400 W. Marion Ave., ☎ 941-637-3830, conducts tours

Gopher tortoise

among orphaned, injured, and recovering animals that are being rehabilitated for release. Annually, some 1,300 patients are admitted, including gopher tortoises, pelicans, and owls. Permanent injured residents include bald eagles and hawks. The center is open Wednesday-Monday, 11-3. Donation requested.

To slip into the bygones of Florida wilderness, enjoy the low-key attractions at **Babcock Wilderness Adventures** off Rte. 31 east of Punta Gorda, ☎ 941-637-0551 or 800-500-5583, www.babcockwilderness.com. A swamp buggy is your chariot through time and the pristine wetlands of 90,000-acre Telegraph Cypress Swamp and Crescent B Ranch. The 90-minute tour shows you an Old-Florida working ranch and settlement, alligators, deer, relocated bison, turkeys, and panthers. You can see the Cracker shack built for the filming of *Just Cause*, which starred Sean Connery, and have lunch at the mess hall. Admission: $17.95 for adults, $10.95 for kids aged three-12. Tours run daily, 9-3 (mornings only in summer), by reservation.

© Babcock Wilderness Adventures

South of town, the **Charlotte Harbor Environmental Center** at 10941 Burnt Store Rd., ☎ 941-575-5435, conducts guided tours around three miles of nature trails, and displays exhibits about local wildlife in its Discovery Center and Bat Center. One trail provides a wildlife observation and bird blind. Admission is free. OPen 8-3, Monday-Saturday; 11-3 Sunday. Guided walks start at 10 on weekdays in season.

SHOPPING

Downtown Punta Gorda is a small, charming place to browse for art and gifts. **Fishermen's Village**, 1200 W. Retta Esplanade, ☎ 800-639-0020 or 941-639-8721, www.fishville.com, has more to offer. It was once the site of a crab packing plant, circa 1940. Today, in a marina-side setting, many of its clothing and gift shops tend toward the nautical and craftsy.

WHERE TO STAY

■ MOTELS

Time-shares at **Fishermen's Village Villas**, 1200 W. Retta Esplanade, ☎ 800-639-0020 or 941-639-8721, www.fishville.com, have a full kitchen and two bedrooms at a reasonable price. Completely renovated following Hurricane Charley in 2004, they overlook the shopping-entertainment mall's courtyard, but are soundproofed. Guests can use the swimming pool, tennis courts, and bicycles. $$-$$$

■ CAMPING

Most of the local RV resorts and campgrounds lie east of I-75 in Punta Gorda's vast wilderness. **Punta Gorda RV Resort** is closer to town, south of Punta Gorda at 3701 Baynard Dr., ☎ 941-639-2010, on Alligator Creek. Facilities in the adults-only park include a rec room, clubhouse, pool and spas, shuffleboards, a boat ramp, a bait shop and convenience store, and docks. Daily rates cost $45 a day. Long-term discounts are available.

One of the east-lying resorts, **Water's Edge RV Resort**, off Exit 161 and Jones Loop Rd., www.watersedgervresort.com, ☎ 800-637-9224 or 941-637-4677, borders a 20-acre fishing lake with tent and RV sites, paddleboat rentals, laundry facilities, a swimming pool and hot tub, a rec hall, wireless Internet access, and a playground. RV sites cost $31-$35 a day.

WHERE TO EAT

Many head to Fishermen's Village, a waterside shopping-dining complex at 1200 W. Retta Esplanade, to find a variety of meal-time options, from deli to sit-down. More discriminating diners prefer downtown's fine Restaurant Row offerings.

The most formal at Fishermen's Village is **Captain's Table**, ☎ 941-637-1177. The setting is tastefully nautical, with lots of pewter, classic sailing ship models, and a great view of the river, especially from the outside deck. Menu items are continental in nature, featuring local fresh fish. Lunch (sandwiches and entrées $9-$13) and dinner (entrées $20-$26) are served daily. Reservations are suggested, especially for dinner.

Below the Captain's Table, **Harpoon Harry's**, at the same address and phone, is more casual and also opens daily for lunch and dinner. Hot sandwiches, salads, steamer pots, and fried seafood baskets range from $6 to $18.

Downtown in the historic district, **The Turtle Club** at 139 W. Marion Ave., ☎ 941-637-9477, www.theturtleclubrestaurant.com, raises the bar (and prices) on local eats with its style of tried-and-true "Gracious Coastal Cuisine." In its handsome setting of vintage brick and dark woods, it's worth the price. Specialties demonstrate deftness with seafood and meat, including the signature Sea Harvest Platter sampler seared on a flat-top grill and finished with lemon buerre blanc, Low Country Shrimp & Smoked Sausage, and blackened scallops. It opens for daily for lunch ($9-$15) and dinner ($16-$30).

Fort Myers & Sanibel Island

here is only one Fort Myers and 90 million people are going to find out, declared **Thomas Edison** in the late 1880s. The genius inventor moved his winter quarters to town after northern chills threatened his health and he discovered a stand of bamboo on a Caloosahatchee riverside plot. The bamboo would come in handy for his experiments in creating a lightbulb. The area's balmy weather would extend his life another 46 years.

As Edison predicted, plenty have discovered Fort Myers, and it has grown into a major city, the hub of Lee County. Bordered by the **Gulf of Mexico**, mottled by islands, and stabbed through by the wide **Caloosahatchee River**, this area is favored by visitors for its quiet, protected waters and proximity to wild and play-happy islands.

Lee County guards some of the West Coast's most precious historical and natural treasures. Edison's winter home and laboratory remain, along with the remnants of a peculiar turn-of-the-19th-century religious cult at **Koreshan State Historic Site**. From more distant times, ancient wetlands survive untouched and protected, along with **Calusa Amerindian mounds**, wooded preserves, barrier islands, fruit farms, fishing communities, and wildlife estuaries. Lee County offers endless possibilities for outdoor activity on land and sea. It has long been held as a model of ecotourism by the state agencies that help other communities and regions develop environmental attractions within their boundaries.

TRANSPORTATION

AIRPORTS

Southwest Florida International Airport (RSW) in Fort Myers, ☎ 239-768-1000, www.flylcpa.com, services this segment of coast, with flights from all parts of the country and to and from Canada, Germany, and limited other international destinations. In 2005, the airport opened a brand new facility that increased terminal gates from 17 to 28. It was the first entirely new terminal to open with post-9/11 security advances. Major airlines servicing this facility are listed below.

AIRLINES SERVING SOUTHWEST FLORIDA (RSW) INT'L AIRPORT

Air Canada . . . . ☎ 888-247-2262 . . . . www.aircanada.com
AirTran Airways . . . . ☎ 800-247-8726 . . . . www.airtran.com
American/American Eagle. . . . ☎ 800-433-7300. . . . . www.aa.com
Cape Air . . . . ☎ 800-352-0714 . . . . www.flycapeair.com
Condor . . . . ☎ 800-524-6975 . . . . www11.condor.com
Continental . . . . ☎ 800-525-0280 . . . . www.continental.com
Delta Air Lines / Comair . . . . ☎ 800-221-1212 . . . . www.delta.com
Frontier Airlines . . . . ☎ 800-432-1359 . . . . www.frontierairlines.com
JetBlue . . . . ☎ 800-538-2583 . . . . www.jetblue.com
LTU International . . . . ☎ 866-266-5588 . . . . www.ltu.com
Midwest. . . . . ☎ 800-452-2022. . . . www.midwestairlines.com
Northwest/KLM . . . . ☎ 800-225-2525 . . . . www.nwa.com
Southwest . . . . ☎ 800-435-9792 . . . . www.southwest.com
Sun Country . . . . ☎ 800-359-6786 . . . . www.suncountry.com
Spirit . . . . ☎ 800-772-7117 . . . . www.spiritair.com
US Airways . . . . ☎ 800-428-4322. . . . . www.usairways.com
United . . . . ☎ 800-241-6522 . . . . www.united.com
USA 3000 Airlines . . . . ☎ 877-872-3000 . . . . www.usa3000airlines.com
WestJet. . . . . ☎ 888-937-8538 . . . . www.westjet.com

TAKE A SIDE TRIP TO KEY WEST

Two modes of transportation provide fast service to Key West: **Cape Air** does business as Continental Connection (☎ 800-525-0280, www.continental.com), flying direct several times a day in under an hour from Southwest Florida International Airport; and **Key West Express** (☎ 888-KEY-BOAT or 239-765-0808; www.atlantisxpress.com) has four-hour (one-way) high-speed ferries departing from two Fort Myers Beach locations.

▨ RENTAL CARS & TAXI SERVICE

Rental cars are available at the airport and other locations throughout the area. Major companies include **Avis**, ☎ 800-331-1212 or 239-768-2121 (airport), www.avis.com; **Hertz**, ☎ 800-654-3131 or 239-768-3100 (airport), www.hertz.com; and **Budget**, ☎ 800-527-0700, 239-768-1500 (airport), or 239-275-6886, www.budget.com.

Several taxi companies provide transportation to and from the airport, including **Aaron Airport Transportation**, ☎ 800-998-1898 or 239-768-1898, and **AAA Airport Transportation**, ☎ 800-872-2711.

GETTING AROUND

I-75 and **Highway 41** (Tamiami Trail) are the major arteries, and they run parallel to each other, north-south. Both connect to Tampa and the East Coast metropolitan area of Miami-Fort Lauderdale.

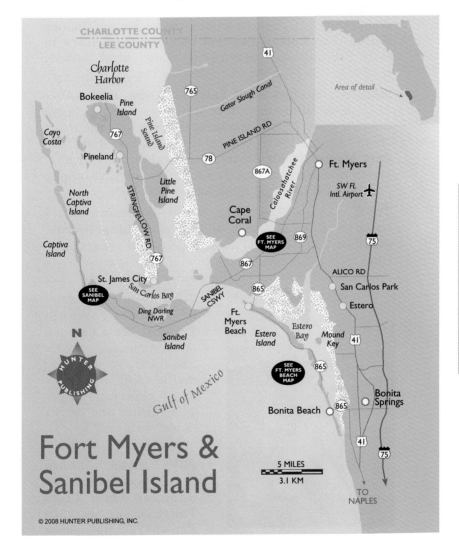

Fort Myers & Sanibel Island

© 2008 HUNTER PUBLISHING, INC.

INFORMATION

Contact **Lee County Visitor & Convention Bureau**, 12800 University Drive, Suite 550, Fort Myers, 33907, ☎ 888-231-6933 or 239-338-3500, www.fortmyerssanibel.com.

FESTIVALS & EVENTS

★ **FEBRUARY** – Like many things in Fort Myers, the town's grandest festival revolves around the memory of Thomas Edison. The **Edison Festival of Light** takes place in early February and features a lighted night parade. ☎ 239-334-2999, www.edisonfestival.org.

★ **MARCH** – **Sanibel Shell Fair and Show**, ☎ 239-472-2155, kicks off the month of March, as it has for more than 70 years. Held at the Sanibel Community House, it showcases sea life, specimen shells, and shell art. The **Fort Myers Beach Shrimp Festival** is held in mid-March and serves up 1,000 pounds of boiled shrimp, a parade, a 5K run, and more, ☎ 239-463-6986.

★ **JUNE** – South Seas Island Resort on Captiva Island hosts the **Caloosa Catch & Release Fishing Tournament** (☎ 239-671-9347, www.caloosacatchandrelease.com), a four-day event that kicks off a four-part series of tournaments throughout the area.

Mango display.

★ **JULY** – Pine Island celebrates **Mangomania Tropical Fruit Fair** ($6 adult admission), ☎ 239-283-4842, www.mangomania.com, a two-day event with food (especially dishes and drinks made with mangoes), music, and a craft fair.

★ **SEPTEMBER** – South Seas Island Resort hosts **Summer Slam Flats Tournament**, ☎ 239-671-9347, www.caloosacatchandrelease.com, an invitation fishing tournament awarding more than $15,000 in cash and prizes, is the third in the Caloosa Tournament Series.

★ **OCTOBER** – Cape Coral celebrates **Oktoberfest**, a two-weekend festival of German music, food and culture, at the German-American Social Club, ☎ 239-283-1400, wwwgasc-capecoral.com.

★ **NOVEMBER – The American Sandsculpting Championship Contest**, ☎ 239-454-7500, www.sandfesti val.com, takes place in early November at four local beach resorts. The **Caloosa Grand Championship** ends the Caloosa Tournament Series at South Seas Island Resort on Captiva Island, ☎ 239-671-9347, www.caloo sacatchandrelease. com.

★ **DECEMBER** – Cape Coral's **Holiday Boat-a-Long** is a decorated boat parade with live entertainment; ☎ 239-573-3123.

BUDGET TIPS

▪ Instead of pricey Sanibel Island, head to **Pine Island** or **Fort Myers Beach** for less-expensive lodging and dining.

▪ Some restaurants serve many of their same dinner dishes at lunch, for a significantly lower cost. Plan a late lunch out and snack or picnic for dinner.

▪ Instead of a fishing charter, book with a Fort Myers Beach **party fishing boat**.

▪ Also in Fort Myers Beach, visit **Ostego Bay Marine Foundation** and **Matanzas Pass Preserve** for free (or a donation).

▪ **Koreshan State Historic Site** charges only $4 for up to eight persons in a vehicle and provides a half-day's worth of sightseeing, hiking, canoeing (rentals at a small extra charge), and picnicking.

- Many local restaurants offer **early-bird dinner** specials.
- The region's historical museums provide bite-sized, budget morsels of education. Check out Sanibel Island's **Historical Village**, **Cape Coral Historical Museum**, and Pine Island's **Museum of the Islands**. Adults are asked to make a small donation.
- At **Sanibel-Captiva Conservation Foundation**, you get your $3 worth and more of nature.
- Take a hike. The trail at **J. N. "Ding" Darling National Wildlife Refuge's Bailey Tract** is free. Admission for pedestrians and cyclists to the main refuge is only $1 ($5 for cars) and there's no charge to enter the Education Center.

Cape Coral & North Fort Myers

North Fort Myers and Cape Coral lie on the north bank of the **Caloosahatchee River**, across from Fort Myers. They are two separate, relatively new communities. Cape Coral is the largest, a growing residential town with interesting family attractions and lots of water around – it claims more canals than the Italian city of Venice. It is gateway to offbeat Pine Island and its complement of unbridged islands.

GETTING HERE

Approaching from the north via I-75 or Highway 41, you will first reach North Fort Myers. To get to North Fort Myers and Cape Coral from I-75, head west along **Bayshore/Pine Island Rd.** (Rte. 78, Exit 143). **Highway 41** takes you directly into North Fort Myers. Head west again on Rte. 78 to reach Cape Coral.

Del Prado Blvd. and **Santa Barbara Blvd.** are Cape Coral's major east-west thoroughfares. Bridges cross to Fort Myers at I-75, Highway 41, Business Highway 41 (Edison Bridge at Fowler St.), Veteran's Parkway/Colonial Boulevard (Midpoint Memorial Bridge/toll), and Cape Coral Parkway/College Parkway (toll).

WEEKEND ADVENTURE ITINERARY

▪ **FRIDAY:** Drive to Pine Island in the morning. Take a half-day fishing charter, sightseeing charter or rental boat to Cayo Costa or Cabbage Key. Have lunch at Cabbage Key Inn or back at Lazy Flamingo in Bokeelia. Drive to Fort Myers to tour the Edison & Ford Winter Estates in afternoon. Have dinner downtown at the Veranda. Spend the night in Fort Myers. Make the lively nightlife scene downtown.

▪ **SATURDAY:** Drive to Sanibel Island in the morning. Kayak the Commodore Creek Canoe Trail into J.N. "Ding" Darling National Wildlife Refuge. Drive to Captiva Island for lunch at the Mucky Duck and hang out on the beach. Drive back to Sanibel in the afternoon and visit the Sanibel-Captiva Conservation Foundation and the Bailey-Matthews Shell Museum. Have dinner at Lazy Flamingo. Spend the night on Sanibel.

▪ **SUNDAY:** Drive to Fort Myers Beach in the morning. Head south to Lovers Key State Park to spend time on the beach. Drive to Bonita Beach for lunch at Doc's Beach House. Drive to Estero to tour Koreshan State Historic Site. Return to Fort Myers for dinner at Bistro 41. Spend the night in Fort Myers.

INFORMATION

Contact the **North Fort Myers Chamber of Commerce**, at 3323 N. Key Drive, Suite 1, North Fort Myers, 33903, ☎ 239-997-9111, www.northfortmyerschamber.org, with questions. Information is available 9-5, Monday-Friday.

For Cape Coral questions, contact **Cape Coral Chamber of Commerce**, PO Box 100747, Cape Coral, 33910, ☎ 239-549-6900 or 800-226-9609, www.capecoralchamber.com. The office is located at 2051 Cape Coral Pkwy. E. and is open 9-5, Monday-Friday.

SIGHTS & ATTRACTIONS

OF HISTORIC OR CULTURAL INTEREST

Learn more about the history of Cape Coral, a young river town created from a vast hunting preserve, at the **Cape Coral Historical Museum**, Cultural Park Blvd., ☎ 239-772-7037. Exhibits include one explaining the natural history of the burrowing owl, a local inhabitant and icon, and a model of an old Cracker kitchen. Hours are 1-4, Wednesday, Thursday, and Sunday. (Closed July and August.) Adults are asked to donate $2.

Look for the overgrown conch shell on Highway 41 in North Fort Myers, and you'll have found **The Shell Factory & Nature Park** at 2787 N. Tamiami Trail, ☎ 239-995-2141 or 800-282-5805, www. shellfactory.com. Admission to most of the attractions is free. The original draw was its bazaar for shells, shell things, and other Florida souvenirs. These days a growing nature park with new life-size dinosaur models is what's new and exciting. It also offers a

bumper boat ride ($5), aquariums, a miniature golf course ($5), Water Wars ($2), the Waltzing Waters lighted fountain shows ($5 for anyone older than 12), and a restaurant. Retail hours are 7-4 Monday-Friday; the nature park is open 10-7. Zoo admission is $8 for adults, $6 for seniors, and $4 for children aged four to 12.

© The Shell Factory

■ BEACHES, PARKS & NATURAL AREAS

Headquarters for fishing types, boaters, and beachers, **Cape Coral Yacht Club**, 5819 Driftwood Pkwy., ☎ 239-574-0815, is a city facility set on the Caloosahatchee River. The public beach is enhanced by a barbecue area, shaded picnic tables, restrooms, outdoor shower, tennis, horseshoes, a heated pool($2.50-$4.50 admission), adult and youth classes and programs, a 620-foot lighted fishing pier, and a free public boat ramp. A large beach pavilion is available for rental. The beach closes at dusk.

■ FAMILY FUN

Many of Cape Coral's attractions are kid-oriented. A favorite for families on steamy summer days, **Sun Splash Family Waterpark** at 400 Santa Barbara Blvd., ☎ 239-574-0557, www.sunsplashwaterpark.com, offers refreshment for all ages. The smallest can splash around shallow pools, climb on an alligator's back (not real, of course), or ride with mom and dad on an innertube. Taller ones will want to stand in line for the speed-demon slides. Lockers, snacks, and gifts are available. Coolers are not allowed in the park, but there is a picnic ground with play equipment outside the gate. Admission is by height: $14.95 for anyone 48 inches or taller; $12.95 for children under 48 inches and older than two; $4.95 for children younger than two, plus tax. Hours vary, and the park is closed in slow seasons. Call ahead for current schedule.

Batting cages, go-carts, bumper boats, miniature golf, paintball, and a video arcade make **Greenwell's Bat-A-Ball and Family Fun Park**, at 35 NE Pine Island Rd., ☎ 239-574-4386, www.greenwells familyfunpark.com, a hit with the kids. It is named after Red Sox baseball player Mike Greenwell, a Cape Coral son. Hours are 10-10, weekdays, and 10-midnight on Friday and Saturday. Admission is per activity. Eighteen holes of mini-golf costs $2.50-$5.50, depending upon age. Go-cart rides cost $3.25 to $5.75.

© Greenwell's

ADVENTURES

ON WATER

FISHING

Cape Coral Yacht Club's (see *Sights & Attractions*, above) 620-foot lighted fishing pier is a popular convergence point for land-bound fishermen. For charter fishing, contact Capt. Ron Smith, ☎ 239-549-9366. He specializes in tarpon fishing and charges $325 for up to four per half-day.

BOAT RAMPS

Boat launching is free at Cape Coral Yacht Club (see page 284).

BOATING SCHOOL

Learn to captain a sailing or power vessel through a live-aboard experience with **Florida Sailing & Cruising School**, based at Marinatown Marina, 3444 Marinatown Lane NW in North Fort Myers, ☎ 800-262-7939 or 239-656-1339, www.swfyachts.com or www.flsailandcruiseschool.com. Classes range from a $40 day course on safe boating to weekend and 12-day sail or power courses at $495-$3,195 each. Combination power and sail courses are also available, all taught aboard well-equipped yachts.

BOAT RENTALS

Mid-Island Marina, ☎ 800-778-2109, www.midislandmarina.com, rents boats at 1510 SE 46th Ln. in Cape Coral, ☎ 239-549-2636. Prices start at $200 for a half-day, $300 a day for a 19.5 fishing boat with 140 hp engine; to $225 and $350 for boats that hold up to eight. Fuel and deposit are additional. Open daily.

HOUSEBOAT RENTALS

Holiday Cruise Yacht Charters, PO Box 101128, Cape Coral, ☎ 239-945-5459, www.holidaycruisehouseboats.com, rents luxury 41- to 44-foot Gibson houseboats for live-aboard water adventures in local waters. Fully furnished and sleeping eight adults, the boats rent starting at $1,600 for three nights, $2,400 for a week.

■ ON WHEELS

BICYCLING

Many of Cape Coral's city streets designate **bike lanes**. Bikers also branch out from town along **rural roadways**. One scenic, low-traffic route on the city outskirts, **Burnt Store Rd.**, connects to Pine Island Rd. northwest of town. It's best on weekends where there are fewer trucks traveling the back road.

Strauser BMX Sports Complex, 1410 SW Sixth Place, ☎ 239-772-4232, has a Bicycle Moto-Cross track, as well as a picnic area, playground, boat ramp, and sand volleyball court.

WHERE TO STAY

Not widely known for its tourism and resorts, Cape Coral offers mostly chain hotels. Visitors to the area tend to stay in Fort Myers or closer to the Gulf front. However, watch for **The Resort at MarinaVillage**, a large resort property within a residential development, due to open in 2008.

WHERE TO EAT

Cape Coral boasts a surprising number of ethnic restaurants – from Italian and Hispanic to Thai and Jamaican.

You can't miss **Iguana Mia's** lizard-green exterior at 1027 Cape Coral Pkwy., ☎ 239-945-7755, www.iguanamia.com. The large dining room is casual, with murals of Mexican scenes. One of the area's most popular Mexican restaurants (there are spinoffs in Fort Myers and Bonita Springs), it serves standard specialties with a few creative variations. Its sour cream chicken is popular. Prices run $6-$13 for main dishes. It's open daily for lunch and dinner.

Décor and food are all about style at **The Joint** at 5785 Cape Harbour Drive, Cape Coral, ☎ 239-542-0123, www.capeharbourmarina.com/thejoint.htm, a new casual harborside marvel. Munch tapas-style on a terrific yellow tomato gazpacho heaped with lump crab, chimichurri beef satay, scallops wrapped in chorizo, wood-roasted "pizzetas," and sandwiches such as grilled kobe sliders and veggie panini. Dine on deck or inside. Lunch and dinner dishes range $8-$14.

Pine Island & Out Islands

You must be a specialty traveler to truly appreciate Pine Island. Only utterly devoted fisherfolk, history buffs, or exotic fruit and fresh seafood connoisseurs need apply.

Don't come here looking for beaches and yuppie bars. Go to neighboring Sanibel Island or Fort Myers Beach if that's what you want.

Beaches do not really exist on Pine Island (there's one man-made beach in St. James City) and that is the very reason it has ducked tourism's inherent damage to island heritage and identity. Tucked between barrier islands and the Cape Coral

mainland, Pine Island hides from hedonistic sun-seekers. Still to-day, as in centuries past, it is about Amerindian villages, farming, and fishing.

Pine Island's south-end **Galt Island** and the separate community of Pineland once held major **Calusa Amerindian** religious centers with elaborate canal systems and sizable shell midden mounds. In the Calusas' wake settled Cuban immigrants who set up fishing camps and began a way of life that continues to this day. In recent years, a ban on net-fishing has changed life somewhat for Pine Islanders. Many have turned to related careers, such as crabbing and charter fishing. **Artists** inspired by the fishermen, their boats, and their way of life have now become more representative of Pine Island occupation.

> *FLORIDIOM: Midden mounds were the earliest compost piles. Native Americans tossed their dinner debris – oyster shells, bird bones, small animal carcasses, and broken pottery on a heap and covered it with soil. These shell mounds revealed to archaeologists important details about how the Calusa lived, work, and ate.*

GETTING HERE

From Highway 41 or I-75, take **Rte. 78**, a.k.a. Pine Island Rd. (Exit 143) heading west. The road shoots straight across the **Pine Island Bridge** (known as the World's Fishingest Bridge) to and through Matlacha, one of the island's four communities, and into Island Center. At **Rte. 767** (Stringfellow Rd.), turn left to reach St. James City, the island's oldest, biggest town, or right to Pineland and Bokeelia.

Pine Island is the departure point for water taxis and charters to the unbridged islands of **Useppa**, **Cayo Costa**, **Cabbage Key**, and **North Captiva**. Light aircraft owners can use North Captiva's 2,300-foot grass airstrip. Few cars run on the island, but visitors can rent golf carts and bicycles.

Cabbage Key operators are also based on Pine Island at Bokeelia. For reservations and information on transportation, ☎ 239-283-2278.

> *FLORIDIOM: Two of Pine Island's five towns have tongue-twister names that are often mispronounced, and probably developed in the first place from mispronunciations and misspellings. Matlacha (MATT-la-shay), historians surmise, derived from an Indian word for defender. Bokeelia (Bo-KEEL-ee-ya) is an Anglicized rendition of the Spanish word boquilla, meaning mouth.*

INFORMATION

Contact the **Greater Pine Island Chamber of Commerce**, PO Box 525, Matlacha, 33909, ☎ 239-283-0888, www.pineislandchamber. org. An information center is located before east of the bridge to Matlacha on Pine Island Rd. It's open Monday-Friday, 9-4; Saturday, 10-1.

SIGHTS & ATTRACTIONS

Pine Island

■ OF HISTORIC OR CULTURAL INTEREST

Turn left on Pineland Rd. for a scenic trip through time-stilled Pineland, a tiny town studded with historic **Cracker shacks** and **Amerindian mounds**. A plaque commemorates archaeological finds, proving the island's importance as a Calusa cultural center.

For a tour into Pineland's Calusa past, make a reservation with **Randell Research Center**, ☎ 239-283-2062, www.flmnh.ufl.edu/rrc, which leads walks along the Calusa Heritage Trail at 13810 Waterfront Dr. on Wednesdays at 10 am from January through April. Otherwise you can browse the 3,700-foot walkway on your own, guided by the detailed and nicely illustrated exhibit signs. Recommended donation is $7 for adults, $4 for children. Land and sea tours and **Calusa Ghost Tours**, ☎ 239-938-5342, www.calusaghosttours.com, by 14-person canoe are also available.

At Phillips Park on Pine Island, **Museum of the Islands**, 5728 Sesame Dr., ☎ 239-283-1525, www.museumoftheislands.com, concentrates on the island's Calusa and fishing heritage with vignettes, portraits, and artifacts. Interpretive headsets and tours are available. Call for current hours. Admission is $2 for adults and $1 for children.

Shells on display

LOCAL COLOR

Artists relish Pine Island for inspiration and seclusion. Take note of the many telephone poles they've decorated throughout the island. Several nationally known artists hide out in the island's backwaters and backwoods. Others hang their shingles in town or sell their work in island galleries.

© Matlacha's Art Gallery

In Matlacha, look for **Matlacha's Art Gallery**, 4637 Pine Island Rd., ☎ 239-283-6453, www.seaweed gallery.com, to find local sculpture and paintings in a whimsical vein. Julia's Arts, at 4574 Pine Island Rd., ☎ 239-283-083, www.juliasarts.com; and **Wild Child Gallery** at 4625 Pine Island Rd., ☎ 239-283-6006, www.wildchild-artgallery.com, deal in more serious realms of fine and decorative art. Bokeelia's sophisticated **Crossed Palms Gallery**, 8315 Main St., ☎ 239-283-2283, carries the works of locals and North Carolinian potters, jewelers, and painters.

ART NIGHT

Every second Friday of the month from November to April, the local galleries host Art Night on the Island from 4-9. Often, the festivities spill into the weekend and island-wide.

Upper Islands

BEACHES, PARKS & NATURAL AREAS

Lee County's unbridged islands may be its most tantalizing feature, especially for adventurers. **Cayo Costa State Park**, ☎ 941-964-0375, www.floridastate parks.org/cayocosta, spreads over two barrier islands with secluded beaches and other treasures.

North Captiva, also referred to as North Cap or Upper Captiva, is a long, skinny island whose park lands contain primitive beachfront with no facilities. The state park's 500 acres at the island's southern end, which was split up by Hurricane Charley in 2004, provide refuge for waterfowl, shore birds, and migrating species (including human). Recreational boaters head here with their suntan lotion and picnics, or boat around to Safety Harbor on the northern lee side for lunch in one of its little restaurants. Home and condo rentals are available on the island (see *Where to Stay*, below). Two new developments are underway on the island: one, a 10-room lodge, another a resident's and visitor's day club for docking, swimming, bowling, dining, and more.

Cayo Costa, to the north, offers more formal beach facilities at its state park on the northern Gulf side. Rustic cabins and tent sites accommodate primitive campers (see *Camping*, below), and picnic tables, grills, pavilions, and showers serve the need of picnickers. Off the beach, hikers can follow trails to an old cemetery and other remnants of a bygone fishing community. Take lots of bug repellent. Bike rentals are

© Cheryl Rolph

Osprey taking off at Cayo Costa State Park

available. There are sheltered moorings on the bay side, with a tram that runs between them and the beach. Johnson Shoals, a sandbar to the north, is a popular stop for shellers. There are also stretches to the south with no facilities, which are favored by lovers of isolation. **Tropic Star Cruise** (see *Boat Charters & Tours*, below) is the official park ferry concession and also rents kayaks and canoes. Admission to the park is $1 per person.

ADVENTURES

ON WATER

Pine Island's lack of beaches keeps away throngs of wildlife-disturbing tourists. The even better news is that it attracts rich sea life to its mangrove inlets, canals, and mudflats – for example, the blue-eyed bay scallop, blue crab, and a wide variety of fish, from the tasty snook to the disdained catfish. Serious fisherfolk will find Pine Island, with its predilection for angling, pure heaven.

Fort Myers & Sanibel Island

FLORIDIOM: The Atlantic bay scallop, Agropecten irradians, has 100 blue eyes and is smaller than the more common larger scallop. Commercial and recreational fishing of the bay scallop, once an important food source in Southwest Florida, has been banned due to pollution.

FISHING

The bridge to Pine Island is known as the **World's Fishingest Bridge**, but the fate of its reputation hangs in the balance as county commissioners draw up plans for a new bridge. Get your supplies, bait, and licenses at **Seven C's Bait & Tackle Shop**, before the bridge in Matlacha, ☎ 239-283-1674.

BOAT RAMPS

Boaters can use the public boat ramp at **Matlacha Park** for free. It's on Island Ave., south of Pine Island Rd. in Matlacha.

BOAT RENTALS

From **Four Winds Marina** at 16501 Stringfellow Rd., Bokeelia, ☎ 239-283-0250, www.fourwindsmarina.com, you can rent a 20- to 22-foot powerboat for $135-$160 a half-day, $200-$225 a full day. You can rent kayaks from **Tropic Star Cruises** at the marina, ☎ 239-283-0015, www.tropicstarcruises.com, for $30 per single for

a half-day, $40 a full day; $40 per double for half-day, $50 a full day. Guided tours and ferry-kayak packages are available.

BOAT CHARTERS & TOURS

You can board a daily **water taxi** to Cayo Costa. Reserve through **Tropic Star Cruises** (at Four Winds Marina, see above), ☎ 239-283-0015, www.TropicStarCruises.com. Tours cost $25 for adults, $17 for kids under age 12. Nature cruises are also available.

PADDLING

The best way to explore Pine Island's unplundered natural pleasures is with the **Gulf Coast Kayak** in Matlacha, 4530 Pine Island Rd., ☎ 239-283-1125, www.gulfcoastkayak.com. It offers day-trips into Matlacha Aquatic Preserve (part of the Pine Island Sound Aquatic Preserve). Average cost for a three-hour nature tour is $45 per person. Call ahead to reserve. Rentals are also available: $30-$40 for a half-day; $44-$55 for a full day.

ON FOOT

Residents and guests of North Captiva most often get around via golf cart. The **trails** make for good hiking along paths covering several miles that lead to preserved state park land.

On **Cayo Costa** (see page 290) six trails cover five miles at the island's wooded north end. One takes you to a **pioneer cemetery**; another follows the **Gulf shoreline**. **Quarantine Trail** recalls the island's former life as a circa-1904 quarantine station. **Cabbage Key** provides a short, marked **nature trail**, perfect for walking off lunch in the Inn.

ON WHEELS

The **bike** path along Stringfellow **Rd**. wends through Bokeelia and St. James City.

ECO-ADVENTURES

Pine Island's backwaters are a great place for spotting manatees, dolphins, and rare birds. **Pine Island Sound Aquatic Preserve** encompasses 54,000 acres of protected submerged land and shoals. The **Pine Island National Wildlife Refuge**, offshore from the island's west side, can be seen only by boat. It consists of a number of keys, including **Big Bird Rookery**, the principal one.

WHERE TO STAY

■ MOTELS

Bridge Water Inn (shown at left) at 4331 Pine Island Rd., ☎ 800-378-7666 or 239-283-2423, www.bridgewaterinn.com, lets you experience Matlacha's fishy side while providing the creature comforts you might be looking for. Its wide wraparound deck accommodates anglers who love nothing better than to step out their door and cast. In addition to eight individually decorated rooms, the owners rent several cottages that are set along the bay. $$-$$$.

In Pineland, **Tarpon Lodge** at 13771 Waterfront Dr., ☎ 239-283-3999, www.tarponlodge.com, occupies a historic sportsman's inn remade into a barebones, fish-fanatic kind of place with an excellent restaurant and fishing charters. $$-$$$.

■ RENTAL AGENCIES

Most visitors to the island rent long-term. Throughout the island you can find rentals, from mobile homes to luxury condominiums. In season, monthly rates are $1,500-$3,300. For information call **Pine Island Realty**, ☎ 800-741-0805 or 239-283-1028 in Bokeelia; ☎ 800-531-5937 or 239-283-0909 in St. James City, www.pine-island.com.

For the ultimate island getaway, escape to North Captiva. You'll find no cars, no pressure, and lots of peace. For home rentals, contact **North Captiva Island Club Resort**, PO Box 1000, Pineland, FL 33945, ☎ 239-395-1001 or 800-576-7343, www.northcaptiva.com.

Rates start at $189 a night for a one-bedroom suite and range on up to six-bedroom homes. Rental rates include use of a golf cart, kayaks, bikes, beach chairs, and umbrellas. Bring groceries and supplies with you, or order them ahead when you reserve. Tennis courts, a fitness center, a pool, a playground, and children's activities are provided. Watersports rentals are available.

CAMPING

Fort Myers-Pine Island KOA in St. James City at 5120 Stringfellow Rd., ☎ 800-562-8505 or 239-283-2415, www.pineislandkoa.com, accommodates tent and RV campers and cabin lodgers. Rates for tent and RV sites change according to season; call or visit the website for current prices. The campground has three on-premises fishing lakes, a tennis court, shuffleboard, a pool and spa, horseshoes, laundry, activities, and its own tour bus to take you to local attractions.

© KOA

At **Cayo Costa State Park**, you can reserve a rustic cabin ($30/night) or set up a tent on the Gulf ($18/night). In season, cabins are reserved a year in advance. Tent sites are less in demand. To reserve a cabin, call ☎ 800-326-3521, or visit www.reserveamerica.com (search by park name). Boaters can anchor bayside in a safe harbor.

WHERE TO EAT

With its fishy preoccupation, the island has a reputation for fresh seafood. Matlacha's fish houses, where fresh oysters, shrimp, blue crab, grouper, snapper, pompano, and scallops are off-loaded for transshipment, are the place to buy. The island boasts a slew of small restaurants using local products, but with a Midwestern, comfort food approach.

MANGO LAND

Mangoes and Pine Island are synonymous. The island hosts a mango festival (see *Festivals & Events*, page 280) in the height of mango season. Exotic fruit farmers also grow guavas, carambolas (star fruit), lychees, longans, and other rare species. You can buy them fresh off the tree from stands along Stringfellow Rd.

Fort Myers & Sanibel Island

If you're looking for the locals' hangout, stop in at **Bert's Bar & Grill** at 4271 Pine Island Rd. in Matlacha, ☎ 239-282-3232. Both locally colorful and waterside scenic, it does a mean basket of wings, in addition to sandwiches, burgers, pizza, and peel-and-eat shrimp. Open daily for lunch and dinner. Sandwiches and dinners range $5.50-$14.

A favorite of boaters and residents is situated on a canal in St. James City. **The Waterfront Restaurant** at 2131 Oleander St., ☎ 239-283-0592, www.waterfrontrestaurant.com, occupies a historic one-room schoolhouse and has indoor and outdoor seating. The all-day menu ranges from grouper sandwiches to shrimp dinners; meals are priced from $6-$22. It is open daily for lunch and dinner.

© The Waterfront Restaurant

⭐ **Lazy Flamingo**, a spin-off from a well-loved Sanibel establishment (see page 324), is at Four Winds Marina in Bokeelia, 16501-B Stringfellow Rd., ☎ 239-283-5959, www.lazyflamingo.com. This one overlooks the harbor and its boats, and is decorated in the chain's typical old shrimp-boat wood and corrugated tin. Open daily for lunch and dinner. Most menu items are priced at $8-$16.

One of the most delightful dining adventures the region has to offer involves island-hopping to somewhere with no cars and lots of character. **Cabbage Key Inn** on Cabbage Key, ☎ 239-283-2278, www.cabbage-key.com, is most popular among tour and recreational boaters. In a historic home built by novelist Mary Roberts Rinehart in the 1930s, diners tape autographed dollar bills to the wall and feast on cheeseburgers, stone crabs, and grouper sandwiches. Open daily for breakfast, lunch and dinner. Prices for lunch are $8-$15; for dinner, $17-$25.

⭐ Lesser known (but building a following) and harder to reach, **Barnacle Phil's** at 4401 Point House Trail in North Captiva's Safety Harbor, ☎ 239-472-6394, is known for its black beans 'n rice – the rage among reclusive stars, such as Henry Winkler, who visit here. It also serves burgers, fish sandwiches, and other casual fare, priced at $6-$23. Open daily for lunch and dinner.

Fort Myers

As the metropolitan hub on this slab of coast line, Fort Myers is home of Southwest Florida International Airport and the new Florida Gulf Coast University. It was settled back in the days when the Caloosahatchee River was the major thoroughfare, plied first by dugout canoes, later by steamboats. It got its "fort" designation during Civil and Seminole wars, which, in their wake, brought its first wave of settlers: soldiers who fell in love with the pleasant climate. Inventor **Thomas Alva Edison** moved his winter quarters here in the late 1880s, which brought other rich and famous types, including automobile manufacturer **Henry Ford**, his next door neighbor, and **Harvey Goodyear**, tire tycoon.

In recent years, the focus of seasonal visitors has shifted to the Gulf front and Fort Myers struggles to keep its downtown alive.

GETTING HERE

Highway 41 becomes **Cleveland Ave.** as it crosses the Caloosahatchee River from the north into Fort Myers. Exits off I-75 lead to the main east-west arteries: **Palm Beach Blvd./Rte. 80** (Exit 141), **Martin Luther King Blvd./Rte. 82** (Exit 138), **Colonial Blvd./Rte. 884** (Exit 136), and **Daniels Pkwy.** (Exit 131). Traveling (roughly) north-south, historic and royal palm-lined **McGregor Blvd.** (Rte. 867) follows the river and its old homes. **Summerlin Ave.** (Rte. 869), **Cleveland Ave.**, and **Metro Parkway** run parallel to the east.

N

HUNTER PUBLISHING

41

75

NORTH FT. MYERS

1

BAYSHORE RD.

12

80

TAMIAMI TRAIL

78

ALT 41

PONDELLA RD.

PALM BEACH BLVD.

EXIT 141

BURNT STORE RD.

TROPICANA PKWY.

HANCOCK BRIDGE PKWY.

75

ORTIZ AVE.

BUCKINGHAM RD.

EXIT 139

PINE ISLAND RD.

2

3

DR. MLK BLVD.

6

7

8

9

10

82

765

78

4

EDISON AVE.

EXIT 138

Matlacha

CAPE CORAL

WINKLER AVE.

EXIT 136

METRO PKWY.

IMMOKALEE RD.

Little Pine Island

DEL PRADO PKWY.

COLONIAL BLVD.

FORT MYERS

13

FOWLER

SIX MILE CYPRESS

CAPE CORAL PKWY.

PAGE FIELD

82

EL DORADO PKWY.

5

CRYSTAL DR.

COLLEGE PKWY.

15

Caloosahatchee River

MCGREGOR BLVD.

CYPRESS LK. DR.

14

DANIELS RD.

EXIT 131

GLADIOLUS

11

75

SHELL PT. BLVD.

SAN CARLOS BLVD.

SUMMERLIN RD.

ALICO RD.

EXIT 128

Southwest Florida Int'l Airport

SANIBEL CSWY.

SAN CARLOS BLVD.

THREE OAKS PKWY.

EXIT 123

SAN CARLOS PARK

BROADWAY

SEE SANIBEL MAP

SEE FT. MYERS BEACH MAP

16

CORKSCREW RD.

ESTERO BLVD.

COCONUT RD.

ESTERO

Sanibel Island

Ft. Myers Beach

75

Estero Island

TAMIAMI TRAIL

OLD 41 RD.

75

HICKORY BLVD.

BONITA BAY BLVD.

ALT 41

BONITA SPRINGS

17

BONITA BEACH RD.

EXIT 116

18

NOT TO SCALE

1. The Shell Factory
2. Cape Coral Historical Museum
3. Sun Splash Family Waterpark
4. Greenwell's Bat-A-Ball & Family Fun Park
5. Cape Coral Yacht Club
6. Edison & Ford Winter Estates
7. Southwest Florida Museum of History
8. Skatium; City of Palms Park
9. Imaginarium
10. Calusa Nature Center & Planetarium
11. Lakes Park
12. Manatee Park
13. Edison Mall
14. Bell Tower Shops
15. Six Mile Cypress Slough Preserve
16. Koreshan State Historic Site
17. Bonita Beach
18. Barefoot Beach Preserve

Fort Myers & Vicinity

Lee County Transit provides public transportation in Fort Myers. Full fare is $1, 50¢ for seniors and youths under age 18, 15¢ transfers. For a schedule, call ☎ 239-533-8726, www.rideleetran.com.

INFORMATION

For information on Fort Myers, contact the **Greater Fort Myers Chamber of Commerce**, PO Box 9289, Fort Myers, 33902, ☎ 800-366-3622 or 239-332-3624, www.fortmyers.org. A **welcome center** is located downtown at 2310 Edwards Dr. and in south Fort Myers at 6900 Daniels Pkwy., Ste. A11. They are open 9-4:30, Monday-Friday.

SIGHTS & ATTRACTIONS

 Author favorites are indicated with a star.

Downtown

■ OF HISTORIC OR CULTURAL INTEREST

Fort Myers' premier attraction remembers its most illustrious citizens. **The Edison & Ford Winter Estates** at 2350-2400 McGregor Blvd., ☎ 239-334-7419, www.efwefla.org, conducts tours of the famous neighbors' river homes, which recently

underwent a $9 million restoration. Walk through Edison's botanical gardens whose rare plants he imported to use in experiments. The 90-minute guided or audio tour includes Edison's winter lab

Edison's laboratory

and a visit to Ford's home. You may even run into Edison, Ford, or one of their contemporaries – portrayed by actors, of course. Afterwards, you are free to browse the museum, which displays many of Edison's 1,093 patented inventions. Admission to all attractions is $20 for adults and 11 for children aged six-12; laboratory and museum only tours are $11 and $4. 50. Special botanical tours are available and the estates host special monthly events for kids and adults.

Nearby in a historic train depot, the **Southwest Florida Museum of History**, at 2300 Peck St. (at Jackson St.), ☎ 239-332-5955, www. cityftmyers.com/museum, displays prehistoric Calusa Amerindian models, graphic depictions, historical IQ games, rare glass and art collections, a circa-1930 private rail car, a stuffed scrub cow, and changing exhibits. It's open Tuesday-Saturday, 10-5. Admission is $9.50 for adults; $8.50 for seniors; $5 for students, free for children under age three.

■ PERFORMING ARTS

Downtown's most aggressive and highbrow attempt at reestablishing itself comes in the guise of **Florida Repertory Theatre**, ☎ 877-787-8053 or 239-332-4488. October through May, the professional company performs comedies, classics, and musicals in the setting of the historic Arcade Theatre at 2267 First St. Tickets cost $215-$34.

■ FAMILY FUN

The Imaginarium: Hands-On Museum and Aquarium, at 2000 Cranford Ave., ☎ 239-337-3332, www.cityftmyers.com/imaginarium, transformed the city's old waterworks into an interactive facility where you can feel a cloud, learn about the world of finance, touch a horseshoe crab, and get blown away by a hurricane. Be sure to check out the gift shop; it has a great collection of nature-oriented toys and books. Museum hours are 10-5, Monday-Saturday, noon-5 Sunday. Admission is $8 for adults, $7 for seniors, and $5 for children aged three to 12.

If you're looking for cool action, head to **Fort Myers Skatium** at 2250 Broadway, next to the City of Palms Park stadium, ☎ 239-461-

3145, www.fmskatium.com. The Skatium is open for public inline and ice skating Tuesday, Thursday, and Friday-Sunday. Call for hours. Regular admission is $5 for adults and $4 for children under age 12, plus $2 for skate rental.

SPECTATOR SPORTS

The **Boston Red Sox** play their spring exhibition game season (March) at City of Palms Park on Edison Ave. at Jackson St., ☎ 877-REDSOX-9 or 239-334-4700, www.redsox.com. Tickets, $10-$44.

Outlying Areas

BEACHES, PARKS & NATURAL AREAS

Lakes Regional Park at 7330 Gladiolus Drive in south Fort Myers, ☎ 239-432-2000, a 277-acre complex, has been re-invented with native vegetation and a birding focus since recent hurricanes. It offers trails, playgrounds, an interactive fountain play area, a climbing wall, picnic areas, paddle-boats, kayaks, and a model train you can ride. You can rent bikes and boats. The train runs 10-1:45, Monday-Friday; 10-3:45, Saturday; noon-3:45, Sunday. Parking costs $1 an hour or $5 a day. Train rides, ☎ 239-267-1905, cost $3 for persons over five years old, $1 for children aged one to five. The park is open sunrise-sunset daily.

Manatee Park (see *Eco-Adventures*, below) rents kayaks for $10 an hour, $30 a day November through March at 10901 Rte. 80, ☎ 239-432-2038, www.leeparks.org. Rentals are available daily 9-3.

> **TIP:** *A **trolley shuttles** people from the mainland to Fort Myers Beach for free. Fare for traveling around the islands is 25¢-35c per passenger.* ☎ *239-275-TRAM.*

PERFORMING ARTS

Broadway Palm Dinner Theatre, at 1380 Colonial Blvd., ☎ 239-278-4422, www.broadwaypalm.com, serves a lavish buffet with professionally performed comedies and musicals. In the main theater, matinees are presented twice weekly, Wednesday or Thursday and Saturday or Sunday, for $43. Evening show prices are $47, Tuesday-Friday (no Tuesday shows May-October); $50 on Saturday. Gratuities are extra. Children aged 12 and under pay $21 for any show. Show-only tickets cost $25. In the 90-seat off-Broadway theater, tickets are $22-$39.

© Broadway Palm Theatre

LOCAL COLOR

© Seminole Gulf Railway

Ride the **Seminole Gulf Railway** from the corner of Colonial Blvd. and Metro Pkwy., (☎ 239-275-8487 or 800-SEM-GULF, www.semgulf.com) into the past and nature's hidden spots. Round-trip excursions on Wednesday, Saturday and Sunday (except Labor Day through Thanksgiving) last 105 minutes and cost $20 for adults, $12 for children aged three-12. Family discounts are available. Special dinner, theater, holiday, and murder-mystery excursions are scheduled throughout the year.

SPECTATOR SPORTS

South of town, the **Lee County Sports Complex**, 14100 Six Mile Cypress Rd., hosts Minnesota Twins spring league action. From April through August, the Miracle Professional Baseball team, member of the Florida State League, competes. For information on Miracles' games, ☎ 239-768-4210, www.miraclebaseball.com. For Twins tickets, ☎ 800-33TWINS or 239-768-4270, www.twinsbaseball.com. Twins tickets start at $10 for standing room only and go up to $35; Miracles tickets run $5 to $8.

ADVENTURES

ON WATER

FISHING

Fishermen cast from the pier at **Centennial Park**, downtown on Edwards Drive near the Yacht Basin. It provides picnic and playground facilities. For freshwater fishing, try **Lakes Regional Park** at 7330 Gladiolus Drive in south Fort Myers, ☎ 239-432-2000 (see page 304).

For **deep-sea** and **backwater fishing charters** or boat rentals, it's best to head out to the islands.

Meet at the Punta Rassa ramp across the causeway from Sanibel Island for excursions with **SoulMate Charters** with Capt. Rob. Modys, ☎ 239-851-1242, www.soulmatecharters.com. A half-day charter for one to three people is $325; for six hours, $375 ($400 for tarpon fishing); and full-day, $450 ($500).

BOAT RAMPS

Boaters can launch their vessels into the bay from Punta Rassa, just before the Sanibel Causeway on Summerlin Rd.

BOAT CHARTERS & TOURS

In Fort Myers, you are more apt to find sightseeing tours. **J.C. Cruises** departs from the Fort Myers Yacht Basin, ☎ 239-334-7474 or 334-2743, www.modernsurf.com/jccruises. Excursions aboard the 600-passenger, three-decker paddlewheeler **Capt. J.P.** last from three hours to a day and tour the Caloosahatchee River, the Gulf, and Lake Okeechobee. Lunch and dinner buffet cruises are also offered. Tickets cost $19-$83 for adults, $10-$14 for children. J.C. also offers nature tours about a 49-passenger motorized catamaran.

PADDLING

For freshwater kayaking, you can rent at **Lakes Regional Park**, 7330 Gladiolus Dr., ☎ 239-432-2000, for a rate of $10 an hour ($15 for a double). Paddleboats are also available for about $20-$25 hourly.

Ace Performer Windsurf, Kayak & Sailboat Shop, 16340 San Carlos Blvd., ☎ 239-489-3513, www.ace performer.com, rents single kayaks for $40 a half-day, $50 a day; and tandem kayaks for $75 a half-day; $100 full day. They also offer a weekly rate of $250 for either a tandem or a single.

SNORKELING & DIVING

Fort Myers and vicinity have their share of dive operators. Because of the normal murkiness of local waters and lack of natural offshore reefs, dive trip leaders often take you out of the region for open-water dives.

To inquire about lessons and equipment, call **Underwater Explorers Diving Center & School**, at 12600 McGregor Blvd., ☎ 239-481-4733.

WINDSURFING

For your windsurfing needs, visit **Ace Performer Windsurf, Kayak & Sailboat Shop**, 16342 McGregor Blvd., ☎ 239-489-3513, www.aceperformer.com. You can get lessons for $100 an hour or rent a board for $50 an hour, $75 a half-day, and $100 all day. Kitesurfing lessons are also available. Best local windsurfing and kitesurfing conditions are along the **Sanibel Causeway**, and Ace makes deliveries there.

ON FOOT

Short trails loop through the woods at **Calusa Nature Center**, 3450 Ortiz Ave., ☎ 239-275-3435, www.calusanature.com (see *Sights & Attractions*, above). Admission to the trails is included in the price of museum admission.

Centennial Park (see *Fishing*, above) has a short fitness trail, plus picnic pavilions, and a fishing pier. It's the site of open-air concerts and special festivals.

Boardwalks meander one mile through wetlands ecology at 2,200-acre Six Mile Cypress Slough Preserve, Six Mile Cypress Pkwy. at Penzance Crossing, ☎ 239-432-2004. It's open daily, 8 to sunset. Guided walks are offered throughout the year at 9:30, daily, and are free. Parking costs $1 per hour (maximum of $5).

ON WHEELS

A stretch of **bike path** along **Daniels Pkwy**. reaches from Summerlin Ave. to the airport. Another path follows **Linear Park**, a length of recreational area fronting a canal parallel to Metro Parkway, between Colonial Blvd. and Six Mile Cypress Pkwy. The Summerlin path leads to the Sanibel Causeway, which you can cross to connect with island paths (see *Sanibel & Captiva Islands*, below).

Lakes Regional Park (see page 304) at 7330 Gladiolus Drive in south Fort Myers, ☎ 239-432-2000, has extensive bike trails, along with its other facilities. Parking costs $1 an hour or $5 a day. The park rents Surrey bikes and is open sunrise to sunset, daily.

ECO-ADVENTURES

Aboard a 49-passenger pontoon boat, **J.C. Cruises,** ☎ 239-334-7474 or 334-2743, www.modernsurf.com/jccruises, goes manatee-

(November-April) and dolphin-spotting. Cost is $17 plus tax for adults, $10 for kids under age 12. Call for schedules.

On the east side of town, manatee-sighting cruises up the Orange River are the popular thing. Contact **Fort Myers Manatee World**, at Coastal Marine Mart, Rte. 80 at I-75, Exit 141, ☎ 239-693-1434, www.manateeworld.com. Adults pay $18; children aged 12 and younger, $9.

Small and homey, **Calusa Nature Center and Planetarium** at 3450 Ortiz Ave., ☎ 239-275-3435, www.calusanature.com, offers a two-mile wildlife trail, a Seminole Amerindian village, butterfly house, and a native bird aviary. Snakes, tarantulas, alligators, and bees are among the more than 100 live animals. Staff demonstrate snake and

alligator behaviors daily. The planetarium uses telescopes and astronomy lessons in its presentations. Museum and trails open 9-5, Monday through Saturday; 11-5 on Sunday. Call or visit the website for planetarium show information and times. Adult admission to the museum, trails and planetarium is $8; children aged three to 12, $5.

Garter snake

Manatee Park, at 10901 Rte. 80, opposite the Florida Power and Light plant, ☎ 239-690-5030, www.leeparks.org, features a manatee-viewing deck on the Orange River with special polarized filters, a hydrophone that lets you eavesdrop on the manatees, manatee exhibits, a canoe launch, and interpretive programs in season. It serves as a rescue and release site for rehabilitated injured manatees being returned to their native environment. The park is open daily, 8-sunset, October-March; 8-8, April-September. For current recorded information, call the Manatee Viewing Update Line, ☎ 239-694-3537. Parking costs $1 an hour; $5 maximum per day.

SHOPPING

For air-conditioned shopping, head to **Simon's Edison Mall** on Cleveland Ave. at Colonial Blvd., ☎ 239-939-5464, www.simon.com. Anchor stores include Macy's, Dillards, Sears, and JC Penney.

Other more specialized shopping centers take advantage of Southwest Florida's balmy climate and palmy landscaping. Near Edison on Cleveland Ave., **Page Field Commons** features discount and major retail outlet stores. At exclusive **Bell Tower Shops**, on S. Cleveland at Daniels Parkway, ☎ 239-489-1221, you'll find Saks Fifth Avenue and a variety of upscale boutiques. Near Sanibel on Summerlin Blvd., **Sanibel Tanger Factory Outlets**, ☎ 888-471-3939 or 239-454-1974, www.tangeroutlet.com, offers a collection of factory outlet and other bargain shops.

WHERE TO STAY

For the most part, hotels in Fort Myers are chains geared toward business travelers.

Upscale and fitness-conscious, **Sanibel Harbour Resort & Spa**, 17260 Harbour Pointe Dr., ☎ 239-466-4000 or 800-767-7777, www.sanibel-resort.com, boasts first-class spa and exercise programs and facilities. A canoe trail right on the property allows adventurers an intimate encounter with nature in the mangroves. Full service, the resort offers condo and concierge-club accommodations, several dining options, bars, swimming pools, excellent kids' program, boating tours, watersports rentals, a bayside beach, and fishing pier. Rooms, suites, and condos, more than 400 in all, come in various sizes and prices. Packages available. $$$$

© Sanibel Harbour Resort & Spa

WHERE TO EAT

Downtown Fort Myers has an excellent selection of restaurants whose reputation is based on fine cuisine or waterfront location. Local seafood typically dominates the menus.

■ DOWNTOWN RESTAURANTS

At **The Veranda**, a downtown landmark at 2122 Second St., ☎ 239-332-2065, seafood comes accented Southern-style. In a historic Victorian-decorated home and its garden courtyard, diners enjoy fresh corn muffins with pepper jelly and creative entrées, such as pan-seared grouper with blue and citrus hollandaise or tournedos of beef in smoky sourmash whiskey sauce. Leave room for the peanut butter fudge pie. Entrées are $20-$32. Lunchtime brings in the local business community for sandwiches, salads, and entrées in the $8-$11 range. It's open Monday-Saturday for dinner; Monday-Friday for lunch. Dinner reservations recommended.

FLORIDIOM: Grouper is a large deepwater fish with mild meat that lends itself to culinary versatility. Sadly, populations are becoming depleted and seasons are limited. Fried grouper sandwiches are a Florida restaurant staple.

OUTLYING AREAS

A favorite on the seafood scene, **Shrimp Shack**, www.shrimpshack. net, has two locations in Fort Myers and now one in Cape Coral. The original is located on Metro Pkwy. at the corner of Daniels Rd., ☎ 239-561-6817; the second occupies Royal Palm Square at 1400 Colonial Blvd., ☎ 239-277-5100. Enjoy your shrimp, grouper, clams, catfish, and more, either hand-breaded and fried, broiled, or blackened for lunch and dinner. Hush puppies come along no matter what preparation you choose. A medley of finger foods and some meat dishes provide other options. The two outlets serve lunch ($6-$9) and dinner ($10-$17) daily.

Bistro 41, at Bell Tower Shops, Daniels Pkwy. and Cleveland Ave., ☎ 239-466-4141, www.bistro41.com, makes a cutting edge statement with a bright, minimalist atmosphere and eclectic dishes such as meatloaf with veal gravy and Yucatán pork. Pay attention to the day's specials. It's open Monday-Saturday for lunch and daily for dinner. Lunch salads, plates, and sandwiches run around $10-$12; dinner entrées range from $13-$30.

Seafood is at its best and freshest at **Blue Pointe Oyster Bar & Seafood Grill** at Bell Tower Shops, Daniels Pkwy. and Cleveland Ave., ☎ 888-456-DINE, www.bluepointerestaurant.com. For lunch and dinner, folks prefer the porch, but the handsome wood-and-tile dining room with its cobalt accents and exposed ductwork makes a pleasant choice as well. Start with a sample platter of oysters from three U.S. locales or the Salt & Pepper Tuna or gazpacho with shrimp. Order sandwiches such as grilled salmon BLT or entrées such as parmesan-crusted lemon sole day-long. Lunch sandwiches and entrées range $8-$16, dinner $8-$30.

NIGHTLIFE

Downtown slowly blooms into a hip nightlife scene as the sun sets. Throughout the year, street parties enliven the cobblestones. Pub crawlers make the rounds to **Patio 33**, at 33 Patio de Leon, ☎ 239-337-3357, www.patio33.com; **Brick Bar & Sky Bar** at 2224 Bay St. above **Harold's on Bay** restaurant, ☎ 239-332-7425; and the **Cigar Bar/Fat Cats Drink Shack**, 1502 Hendry St., ☎ 239-337-4662.

Sanibel Island

Sanibel & Captiva Islands

Alluring names with an exotic ring, the sister islands of Sanibel and Captiva sound like adventure. Legend has it they were named by a Spanish pirate called **Gasparilla**. Whether or not the old legend holds water, the water holds plenty of opportunity for outdoor recreation, from voracious shelling to tarpon fishing and 'gator-spotting. As much nature preserves as resort islands, Sanibel and Captiva provide prime wildlife experiences.

GETTING HERE

From Southwest Florida International Airport or Exit 131 off I-75, head west on **Daniels Parkway** for about 10 miles. Turn left on **Summerlin Rd**. (Rte. 869) and continue for about 10 miles to cross the **Sanibel Causeway** ($6 toll for most vehicles).

Turn right at the four-way stop sign at **Periwinkle Way** to get to Captiva Island. Turn right four miles later onto **Tarpon Bay Rd.**, then left onto **Sanibel-Captiva Rd**. Drive about eight miles and cross the **Blind Pass** bridge.

Sanibel Island has two main roads that more or less parallel each other. Periwinkle Way is the main business route. Gulf Drive roves along the resorts, beaches, and homes at water's edge. It is segmented into East, West, and Middle Gulf Drive. **Sanibel-Captiva Rd.**, known as San-Cap, connects the two islands at the Blind Pass bridge. On Captiva, the road becomes Captiva Dr., a narrow, twisty, scenic drive.

INFORMATION

Contact the **Sanibel-Captiva Islands Chamber of Commerce** for more information: PO Box 166, Sanibel, 33957, ☎ 239-472-1080, www.sanibelcaptiva.org. You'll find its information center on the right side shortly after the causeway ends; it's open Monday-Saturday, 9-7; Sunday, 10-5.

SIGHTS & ATTRACTIONS

 Author favorites are indicated with a star.

Sanibel Island

■ OF HISTORIC OR CULTURAL INTEREST

 Bailey-Matthews Shell Museum, at 3075 Sanibel-Captiva Rd., ☎ 888-679-6450 or 239-395-2233, www.shellmuseum. org, is the only one of its kind in the US. It underlines

 Sanibel's reputation as a top shell-collecting destination. It employs nature vignettes, games, and artistically arranged displays to demonstrate the role of shells in ecology, history, art, economics, medicine, religion, and other fields. One of the most popular displays is the collection

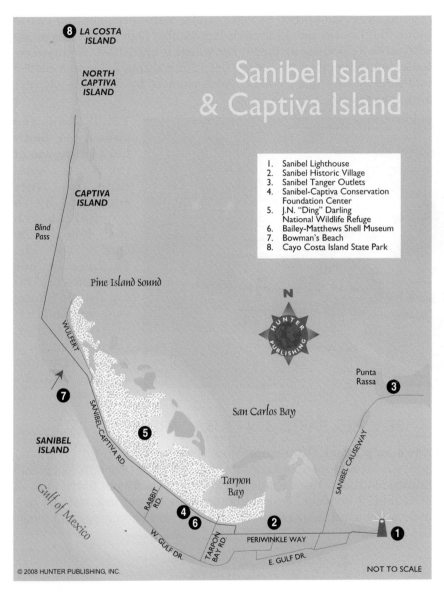

8 LA COSTA
ISLAND

NORTH
CAPTIVA
ISLAND

Sanibel Island
& Captiva Island

1. Sanibel Lighthouse
2. Sanibel Historic Village
3. Sanibel Tanger Outlets
4. Sanibel-Captiva Conservation
   Foundation Center
5. J.N. "Ding" Darling
   National Wildlife Refuge
6. Bailey-Matthews Shell Museum
7. Bowman's Beach
8. Cayo Costa Island State Park

CAPTIVA
ISLAND

Blind
Pass

Pine Island Sound

WULFERT

N

HUNTER
PUBLISHING

Punta
Rassa

3

SANIBEL-CAPTIVA RD.

7

San Carlos Bay

SANIBEL
ISLAND

5

SANIBEL CAUSEWAY

Gulf of Mexico

RABBIT RD.

Tarpon
Bay

4
6

W. GULF DR.

TARPON BAY RD.

2

PERIWINKLE WAY

1

E. GULF DR.

© 2008 HUNTER PUBLISHING, INC.

NOT TO SCALE

Fort Myers & Sanibel Island

donated by the late actor Raymond Burr, who helped establish the museum. Kids can play in the Children's Science Lab. Hours are daily, 10-5. Admission is $7 for aged 17 and older; $4 for children aged five-16.

Nearer to Sanibel's shopping and restaurant district, the **Sanibel Historical Village and Museum**, at 950 Dunlop Rd., ☎ 239-472-4648, has been a catch-all for the island's vintage homes and buildings, beginning with a pioneer Cracker house that serves as a historic museum. Additions include a 1920s post office, historic general store, tea house, cottages, and a turn-of-the-century island home that houses an old French-cut Sanibel Lighthouse lens along with other lighthouse artifacts. The village is open 10-4, Wednesday-Saturday, November to June; 10-1, June through August; closed mid-August through October. Admission is by donation ($5 per adult suggested).

You'll find the circa-1884 **Sanibel Lighthouse** at the island's eastern tip, surrounded by a popular beach that curves from Gulf to bay side. Facilities include restrooms, a fishing T-dock, nature trail, and an interpretive station. Currents make it dangerous to swim at the island's southern tip.

■ BEACHES, PARKS & NATURAL AREAS

Bowman's Beach, to the north on Bowman's Beach Rd., is the island's most secluded and arguably best shelling beach. It has picnic tables, restrooms, and shade trees. Parking is $2 per hour. Like all of Sanibel's beaches, it is maintained in its natural state, which means the sand is ungroomed (great for beachcombing) and facilities are basic. Open 7-7.

Captiva

Captiva shines more for its watersports opportunities than its tourist attractions. It's a lovely island worth driving around and stopping for lunch, if you do nothing else.

■ OF HISTORIC OR CULTURAL INTEREST

While exploring, peek in at **Chapel-By-the-Sea**, at 11580 Chapin St., a charming country-style church close to the beach. Next to it, early settlers rest in a small cemetery. Stop and look for free anytime during the day.

ADVENTURES

ON WATER

FISHING

The **Sanibel Lighthouse Beach T-Dock**, Sanibel Causeway, and bridge between Sanibel and Captiva attract fishermen praying for snook, tarpon, sheepshead, and snapper to grab their hook.

For bait, tackle, and fishing licenses, stop at the **Bait Box**, 1041 Periwinkle Way, ☎ 239-472-1618, open 7-6 daily, 7-8 in summer.

Several competent and knowledgeable fishing guides are headquartered at **Sanibel Marina**, 634 N. Yachtsman Dr., ☎ 239-472-2723. Rates for up to four people are $350 for a half-day, $700 for a full day. Rates for six people are $400 and $470. Guides are available for sightseeing charters to the upper islands.

BOAT RENTALS

For your boat rental needs on Sanibel, go to **The Boat House** at Sanibel Marina, 634 N. Yachtsman Dr., ☎ 239-472-2531. It rents powerboats from there for use in Intracoastal waters only. Rates for 21-foot vessels are $132.50 for a half-day, $212 for a full day; for a 20-foot deck boat, $159 half-day and $235 full day. Fuel is additional.

To captain your own vessel, contact **Sweet Water Boat Rentals** at 'Tween Waters Inn Marina on Captiva Dr., ☎ 239-472-6336. It rents 19-foot center-console boats holding up to six passengers for $160 a half-day, $275 a full day. Tax and fuel are additional.

Jensen's Marina, also on Captiva at Twin Palm Resort, ☎ 239-472-5800, www.gocaptiva.com, offers a variety of rental boats, from a 16-foot skiff for $100 per half-day, $145 per day; to a 24-foot pontoon for $190 per half-day, $275 per full day. It also provides water taxi service to the upper islands for $185-$325 round trip, or $125 per hour for up to six people. Guides are available for charters.

Adventures in Paradise in Port Sanibel Marina, ☎ 800-472-SAIL or 239-472-8443 or 437-1660, rents 19- to 20-foot Grady White powerboats and 23-foot deck boats for $225 per half-day, $375 per full day.

SAILING CHARTERS & INSTRUCTION

© New Moon Sailing

For an adventure under sail, **New Moon**, at 'Tween Waters Inn Marina, ☎ 888-472-SAIL or 239-395-1782, www.newmoonsailing.com, conducts excursions and teaches classes. Reserve in advance. Three-hour charters for up to six to the upper islands cost $350. Sailing instruction for kids is available.

Offshore Sailing School at South Seas Island Resort Marina, ☎ 239-454-1700 or 800-221-4326, www.offshore-sailing.com, was founded by Olympic and America's Cup sailor Steve Colgate. It is internationally known for its sailing course and club. Sailing instruction begins at $125 for two hours per person, minimum of four people required. Private, big-boat, and three- to seven-day courses are available.

Captiva Kayak Co. & Wildside Adventures at McCarthy's Marina, 11401 Andy Rosse Ln., Captiva Island, ☎ 239-395-2925 or 877-395-2925, www.captivakayaks.com, rents trimarans starting at $25 per hour.

PADDLING

The islands offer various canoeing and kayaking adventures. In 1998, *Canoe & Kayak Magazine* named Sanibel Island as one of the top 10 paddling destinations in North America, based primarily on trails through and from J.N. "Ding" Darling National Wildlife Refuge.

Tarpon Bay Explorers, 900 Tarpon Bay Rd., ☎ 239-472-8900, www.tarponbayexplorers.com, rents canoes and kayaks for exploring the backwaters of "Ding" Darling, where you can spot alligators, manatees, roseate spoonbills, ibises, and other birds. It also conducts guided ecology kayaking tours of the refuge. Tarpon Bay Explorers is open every day, 8-5; 8-4 in summer. Canoe and kayak rentals cost $20-$30 for two hours, $10-$15 each additional hour. Basic

© Tarpon Bay Explorers

guided tours cost $30-$40 for adults for two hours and free paddle time.

You can rent kayaks and canoes for $20-$30 for a half-day, at **Castaways Marina**, 6460 Sanibel-Captiva Rd. on Sanibel at the bridge to Captiva, ☎ 239-472-1112, www.castawayssanibel.com; or **'Tween Waters Marina**, at 15951 Captiva Dr., ☎ 239-472-5161, www.tween-waters.com.

For guided open water kayaking, contact **Captiva Kayak Co. & Wildside Adventures** at McCarthy's Marina, 11401 Andy Rosse Ln., Captiva Island, ☎ 877-395-2925 or 239-395-2925, www.captivakayaks.com. Two-hour tours in the bay range $35-$45 for adults, $25-$35 for teens and children. You can also rent kayaks independently starting at $15 an hour for a single. All varieties of kayaks are available, including those for fishing, with rudders, and with sails. Demos cost $20 per hour, lessons $35 per hour.

SNORKELING & SCUBA

Because of low visibility, island waters don't attract snorkelers and divers in great numbers, except for one specific sort: the **sheller**. By snorkeling off the sandbar that fronts island beaches, collectors find the great variety and numbers of shells for which Sanibel especially is famous.

> **THE LAW:** To collect live shells around Sanibel Island, you must, by law, be offshore more than a half-mile from the mean high tide mark and have a valid fishing license.

Wrecks and other man-made reefs help restock waters with fish for the benefit of divers and fishermen alike. More than a dozen artificial reefs lie within a 15-mile radius of Sanibel and Captiva. One of the largest is the **Edison Reef**, created from the rubble of a former mainland bridge. It was built less than 15 nautical miles from the Sanibel Lighthouse in 42 feet of water. Closer to home, the **Belton Johnson Reef**, about five nautical miles off Bowman's Beach, was named for a well-known island fishing guide. A yellow and white marker shows the location of the reef, constructed of concrete culverts. Other popular sites include the **Redfish Pass Barge**, less than a nautical mile from Redfish Pass between Captiva and North Captiva, in 25 feet of water, and the **Doc Kline Reef**, a popular tarpon hole less than eight nautical miles from the Sanibel Lighthouse.

On Captiva, you can rent snorkeling equipment starting at $10 for four hours from **YOLO Watersports** at 11534 Andy Rosse Ln., ☎ 239-472-1296 or 866-YOLO-JIMS, www.yolo-jims.com.

SHELLING TOURS & CHARTERS

Sanibel Island ranks among the world's best shelling destinations. Because, unlike the other Gulf coast barrier islands, Sanibel takes an east-west heading, it better intercepts the diverse shells that arrive from the Caribbean Sea. For generations, serious and casual collectors have gathered on Sanibel shores to do the so-called "Sanibel Stoop" as they look for shells. Shelling is equally good on all beaches, best after a storm and in winter. Bowman's Beach (see *Sights & Attractions*, above) is more secluded, so its shells are less picked-over.

> **THE LAW:** The State of Florida enforces a law prohibiting the collection of live shells on Sanibel Island. This includes sand dollars and starfish. Captiva and the rest of Lee County limits collection of live shells to two per person, per day.

Many charter and tour boat operators conduct shelling excursions to the upper islands, particularly to Johnson Shoals off Cayo Costa (see page 290).

SHELLING TOURS

Any boating excursion that puts you on the beach could be considered a "shelling tour." Plenty of them can be found between Charlotte Harbor and Ten Thousand Islands. Some are actually called shelling tours, indicating that shelling is the main purpose, and that along with the boat trip comes someone with a certain amount of expertise in finding and identifying shells. The truly shell-bent, those often referred to as "the hard-cores," don't wish to gang-shell. They don't need someone telling them the difference between a coquina and a conch. They don't mind paying the extra money for someone to take them to where the shelling is best that day – away from the crowds and tour boats – and to guide them to exactly where the shells are. Pick your shell tour according to your level of shelling and budget.

Opposite: Sand dollars and shells © Bruce Coleman/Dreamstime

On Captiva Cruises' **Cayo Costa Beach and Shelling Tour**, ☎ 239-472-5300, www.captivacruises.com, knowledgeable captains talk about the different shells passengers will find. After the captain's instructional talk, shellers scatter on the beach to see what they can find and return to show off their discoveries and ask questions. Three-hour tours cost $35 for adults, $20 for children; all-day tours are $45 and $25.

Captain Mike Fuery, ☎ 239-466-3649, www.sanibel-online.com/fuery, at 'Tween Waters Marina, has been operating shelling charters for decades and has learned exactly where to find them and when. This is a serious sheller's tour for about four people. He charges $200 for three-hour tours for up to four people.

WATERSPORTS

YOLO Watersports at 11534 Andy Rosse Ln. on Captiva, ☎ 239-472-1296 or 866-YOLO-JIMS, www.yolo-jims.com, gives parasail rides for $59 to $69, depending on height, and rents WaveRunners for $65 a half-hour, $95 an hour per WaveRunner. An upper island excursion costs $195 for two hours.

ON FOOT

One of the best **nature trails** on the islands takes you along four miles of natural habitat at **Sanibel-Captiva Conservation Foundation** (see *Sights & Attractions*, above) at 3333 Sanibel-Captiva Rd., ☎ 239-472-2329, www.sccf.org.

Along "Ding" Darling Refuge's (see *Eco-Adventures*, below) two-mile **Indigo Trail**, you can see ospreys, herons, hermit crabs, and alligators. It leads to the **Cross-Dike Trail**. The **Shell Mound Trail** is another popular one. Naturalists lead guided hikes focused on plants and Calusa Indian heritage in season. For an extended hike, do the paved **Wildlife Drive**, 4.5 miles long (eight miles to loop back to the Education Center), through the refuge. Pedestrians pay a $1 gate fee. At **Bailey Tract**, a portion of "Ding" Darling located off Tarpon Bay Rd., south of Periwinkle Way, almost two miles of trails take visitors past freshwater forms of wildlife, with no entrance fee.

© Cindy Anderson/USFWS

Indigo Trail

ON WHEELS

Sanibel's 23-mile **bike path** takes you around the island's main streets and back woods. Joggers, strollers, and inline skaters also use the shared-use paved trail. It leads to J.N. "Ding" Darling National Wildlife Refuge's **Wildlife Drive**, a nice paved road shared with one-way traffic. It loops back to point A via the bike path for a total of eight miles. You can rent bikes from **Billy's Bikes & Rentals**, 1470 Periwinkle Way, ☎ 800-575-8717 or 239-472-5248, www.billysrentals.com, open daily, 9-5. Bikes start at $5 for two hours. Tandems, surreys, and recumbent bikes are available.

Wildlife Drive

Captiva has no bike path and the narrow roads are dangerously contorted. To get around the "downtown" area, rent a bike from **YOLO Watersports** at 11534 Andy Rosse Ln., ☎ 239-472-1296 or 866-YOLO-JIMS, www.yolo-jims.com, for $8 for four hours, $12 for eight hours, and $16 for 24 hours. It's open 9-5, daily.

ECO-ADVENTURES

Sanibel's prime nature attractions lie on Sanibel-Captiva Rd. The most prominent is **J.N. "Ding" Darling National Wildlife Refuge**, ☎ 239-472-1100, www.fws.gov/dingdarling. It takes up about half

of the island with its 6,300 acres of wetlands and other habitat. Denizens of the haunting Everglades-like refuge include American alligators, manatees, pelicans, roseate spoonbills, great blue herons, ospreys, river otters, bobcats, and about 230 species of birds, 50 types of reptiles and amphibians, and 32 different mammals. Wildlife Drive takes you around the area, and you can climb the observatory tower for an osprey's-eye view, but it's best to follow the short trails into the mangroves or see the refuge by canoe or kayak (see *On Water*, below). You can catch an interpretive tram from **Tarpon Bay Explorers**, 900 Tarpon Bay Rd., ☎ 239-472-8900; $12 for adults and $7 for children aged 12 and under. Call for a schedule. Otherwise, admission to the refuge is $5 per car or $1 per cyclist or walk-in. It's open daily, except Friday, from sunrise to sunset. Admission to the refuge's interactive education center is free. The education center is open daily.

Nearby, you can take a longer nature hike and learn more about native critters and ecology at the **Sanibel-Captiva Conservation Foundation Center** at 3333 Sanibel-Captiva Rd., ☎ 239-472-2329, www.sccf.org. Interactive teaching tools include a touch tank, a pliable life-sized manatee that children can climb, an alligator's jawbone, and a mangrove vignette. The center hosts guided walking and boat tours. The center is open weekdays, 8:30 to 3. December-April it also opens Saturdays, 10-3. In the off-season, it closes at 3 and is closed on Saturdays as well. Admission is $3 for visitors 17 and older.

C.R.O.W. (Clinic for the Rehabilitation of Wildlife), 3833 Sanibel-Captiva Rd., ☎ 239-472-3644, www.crowclinic.org, replicates natural habitat to make comfortable its special patients – birds, bobcats,

raccoons, rabbits, and other critters brought from near and far to mend and be reintroduced. Education programs take place weekdays at 11; and from November-April also at on Sunday at 1. Visitors aged 13 and older are asked to make a $5 donation.

Operators on Sanibel and Captiva conduct group tours to local places of interest on the high seas. Some are nature-oriented, others head to beaches and upper islands to fish or picnic. These provide an affordable option for getting out on the water. **Adventures in Paradise** in Port Sanibel Marina, shortly before the bridge to Sanibel, ☎ 239-472-8443 or 437-1660, www.adventureinparadiseinc.com, uses its pontoon boat for backwater fishing, sealife encounters, and sunset cruises. Costs are $20-$55 for adults, $15-$35 for children older than three. Trolley transportation to the cruise departure point across the causeway is provided from several island resorts.

The **Sanibel-Captiva Conservation Foundation** (see *Sights & Attractions,* above) at 3333 Sanibel-Captiva Rd., ☎ 239-472-2329, www.sccf.org, narrates interpretive nature and dolphin-watch tours, cooperating with **Captiva Cruises**, ☎ 239-472-5300, www.captivacruises.com. They depart from South Seas Island Resort Marina. The 150-passenger *Lady Chadwick* also runs shelling and luncheon tours to the upper islands, including Useppa Island, a private club on an island where Zane Grey, Hedy LaMarr, and other stars of the 1920s came to fish for tarpon. With up to 40-foot shell mounds, it claims some of the highest elevation on the coast. Excursion fees are $20-$45 for adults, $10-$25 for children aged 12 and under.

© Captiva Cruises

SHOPPING

Not known as a great shopping mecca, Sanibel and Captiva are recognized for their art galleries – many of them dealing in wildlife renderings – and shell shops.

For shells and shell gifts, try **Showcase Shells** at Heart of the Islands Center, 1614 Periwinkle Way, ☎ 239-472-1971; or, for great prices, Sanibel Seashell Industries, at 905 Fitzhugh St., ☎ 239-472-1603, www.seashells.com.

Among the islands' many fine galleries are **Tower Gallery** at 751 Tarpon Bay Rd. on Sanibel, ☎ 239-472-4557, featuring the wildlife depictions of local artists; and **Jungle Drums** at 11532 Andy Rosse Ln. on Captiva Island, ☎ 239-395-2266, which shows the wildlife work of local and national artists.

WHERE TO STAY

▓ SANIBEL ISLAND

From simple beach cottages to big-name destination resorts, the islands have practically infinite possibilities. Prices in general are somewhat steep, but most resort units are equipped with kitchens, which saves on dining costs.

Sanibel's largest, most full-service resort, **Sundial Beach Resort**, 863 E. Gulf Dr., ☎ 239-472-4151 or 866-565-5093, www. sundialresort.com, specializes in family accommodations, with

kitchen-equipped suites and a top-notch kids' recreation program. Amenities include restaurants, 12 tennis courts, eco-center with touch tank, beach, watersports and bicycle rentals, five heated swimming pools, and 10 Jacuzzis. One- and two-bedroom condos also available. Ask about packages. $$$-$$$$

For something small and laid-back on Sanibel, **Seaside Inn**, at 541 E. Gulf Dr., ☎ 239-472-1400 or 866-565-5092, www. sanibelcollection.com/seaside_inn, is a charming old-island property on the beach with a swimming pool and 32 modern studios, suites, and cottages. Each has some kitchen facilities. Continental breakfast is included in the rates. Guests are welcome to use facilities at Sundial Beach Resort, above. $$$-$$$$

The Castaways, 6460 Sanibel-Captiva Rd., ☎ 239-472-1252 or 800-375-0152, www.castawayssanibel.com, spreads from Gulf to bay at Sanibel's north end. With its full-service marina and beach-cottage style, it provides equal doses of beach relaxation, and adventure opportunity. It also has a swimming pool. Cottages are old but well-kept, with one to three bedrooms. $$$-$$$$

Closest to "Ding" Darling Refuge, **West Wind Inn** at 3345 W. Gulf Dr., ☎ 239-472-1541 or 800-824-0476, www.westwindinn.com, clusters around the beach in four two-story buildings prettily decorated with Mediterranean-style embellishments. Low-key and ultra-casual, it makes a stay fun with its

© West Wind Inn

lively pool bar, restaurant, butterfly garden, tennis courts, and tiki hut for fish and shelling cleaning. $$$-$$$$.

■ CAPTIVA ISLAND

© Twin Palm Cottages

Jensen's **Twin Palm Cottages & Marina** at a curve in Captiva Dr., ☎ 239-472-5800, www.gocaptiva.com, is one of Captiva's most affordable lodging options and is specifically designed for the fishing aficionado with bayside docks, fishing charters, boat rentals, and bait supplies. Its 14 charming one- and two-bedrooms cottages are historic and cheerful. $$$-$$$$

Bay to Gulf on Captiva, **'Tween Waters Inn** at 15951 Captiva Dr., ☎ 239-472-5161, 800-223-5865, www.tween-waters.com, has rooms, efficiencies, apartments, and historic cottages, some of which have been renovated with inviting, homey trappings. There are restaurants, a lively bar, a swimming pool, and a full-service marina. Packages available. $$-$$$$

About a fourth of Captiva Island is occupied by **South Seas Island Resort**, ☎ 239-472-5111 or 800-965-7772, www.southseas.com, a spacious beach resort perfect for families. Pick whatever type of lodging best suits your requirements: hotel room, suite, villa, cottage, or home. Recreational opportunities are virtually endless, including a marina with rentals and guides, fishing dock, nine-hole golf course, fitness center, 19 swimming pools, 18 tennis courts, a brand new spa, watersports rentals and lessons, excursion cruises, and 2½ miles

© South Seas Island Resort

Fort Myers & Sanibel Island

© South Seas Island Resort

of well-maintained beach. There are also several restaurants and lounges accessible only by guests. The resort underwent a major overhaul after 2004's hurricane season and is beginning to blossom under new ownership that takes it in a casual luxury direction. A free resort trolley transports you around the 330-acre property. $$$-$$$$

RENTAL AGENCIES

Furnished homes, most of them on a beach or golf course, are available to rent throughout Sanibel (one-month minimum) and Captiva (one-week minimum). Agencies offer condominiums at lower prices and with only a one-week minimum required on Sanibel. Contact **Sanibel Accommodations** at 2341 Palm Ridge Rd., ☎ 239-472-7133 or 800-237-6004, www.sanibelaccom.com.

WHERE TO EAT

Seafood is the main course at Sanibel restaurants. Many feature a new Florida style that incorporates elements from New Orleans, the Caribbean, the Deep South, and the Pacific Rim. Most are casual.

SANIBEL ISLAND

Boat in or drive to Sanibel Marina for a nautical view and casual screened-porch atmosphere at **Gramma Dot's Seaside Saloon**, at 634 N. Yachtsman Dr., ☎ 239-472-8138. "Saloon" is a bit of a misnomer as the bar serves only beer and wine. Specialties on its lunch (entrées $8-$15) and dinner ($9-$29) menus include curried lobster salad, mesquite grilled grouper, coconut shrimp, fried oysters, and the best key lime pie around.

Lazy Flamingo, 6520 Pine Ave., ☎ 239-472-5353, is a neighborhood hang-out. The menu concentrates on seafood and finger foods. The grilled grouper sandwich is a sure bet; ask for a Caesar salad instead of fries, if you're so inclined. There are two restaurants bearing the name. The original one at Blind Pass, where Sanibel ends, is favored by locals. The newer one at 1036 Periwinkle Way, ☎ 239-472-6939, occupies a building shaped like a ship's bow. Both are can't-miss-'em pink. They open daily for lunch and dinner. Items are priced at $8-$16.

CAPTIVA ISLAND

Boaters like **The Green Flash**, 15183 Captiva Dr., ☎ 239-472-3337, www. greenflashcaptiva.com, for its docks. All its guests love the view overlooking the bay from on high. Open daily for lunch and dinner, serving sandwiches and seafood ($7-$13 for lunch dishes, $14-$30 for dinner entrées). Try the Green Flash Sandwich or Grouper "Café de Paris."

© The Green Flash

Keylime Bistro, 11509 Andy Rosse Ln., ☎ 239-395-4000, www. captivaislandinn.com, serves breakfast, Sunday jazz brunch, lunch, and dinner daily in a lively indoor-outdoor setting with live music. Start dinner with a key lime martini. Sesame-seared tuna or Chicken Voodoo (blackened) over angel hair pasta, make good entrée selections, which range $13-$26. Breakfast/brunch ($5-$13) and lunch ($5-$10) are equally creative – crab cake Benedict with key lime hollandaise, huevos rancheros, grilled salad, and grilled fish sandwiches.

The Mucky Duck, 11546 Andy Rosse Ln., ☎ 239-472-3434, www. muckyduck.com, is a must-do. Go early, put your name in, and spend the hour-or-so wait on the beach right outside the door. Sunsets here are spectacular. The menu covers seafood in sandwiches and fine dishes, plus a smattering of English specialties. The restaurant is open daily except Sunday for lunch and dinner. Lunches are $4-$15; dinners $17-$26.

NIGHTLIFE

For music and dancing, try Sanibel's **Jacaranda**, 1223 Periwinkle Way, ☎ 239-472-1771, or Captiva's **Crow's Nest Lounge** at 'Tween Waters Inn (see *Where to Stay*, above), ☎ 239-472-5161.

Don't miss the **Nascrab Races** at 'Tween Waters' Crow's Nest Lounge every Monday night at 6 and 9 (go early for a ringside seat). It's the island's best entertainment.

Fort Myers Beach

This resort town on Estero Island has a reputation for fun. It attracts a value-conscious clientele, including families and college students on spring break. Shrimping is a major industry, which brings seafood-lovers to its reasonably priced restaurants. Watersports enthusiasts also find plenty of reasons to visit.

Activity on the island centers around so-called **Times Square**, the intersection where the high bridge meets Estero Boulevard. The area slowly upgrades into an attractive pedestrian mall that features beachy shops, casual sidewalk eateries, sunset celebrations, and access to the fishing pier and main public beach.

TRANSPORTATION

From Fort Myers' Southwest Florida International Airport or Exit 131 on I-75, follow **Daniels Parkway** west 10 miles to **Summerlin Rd**. (Rte. 869). Turn left and follow Summerlin until you reach **San Carlos Blvd**. (about seven miles) and turn left. Continue to the island's **Matanzas Pass High Bridge**. After the bridge, you'll reach **Times Square**, a busy intersection at the core of beach activity. A right turn takes you to the quieter north end. Turning left leads you through the island's commercial district and southward to Lovers Key and Bonita Beach before reconnecting to the mainland.

■ AROUND TOWN

Fort Myers Beach has a **trolley** that shuttles people to and from the mainland for free. Fare to travel around the island and to Bonita Beach is 25¢-50c per passenger, and there are dozens of stops along Estero Blvd. (look for the signs). ☎ 239-275-TRAM.

INFORMATION

For specific information on Fort Myers Beach, contact or stop in at The **Greater Fort Myers Beach Area Chamber of Commerce** at 17200 San Carlos Blvd., Fort Myers Beach, 33931, ☎ 800-782-9283 or 239-454-7500, www.fortmyersbeach.org. Open weekdays, 8-5; Saturday, 10-5; Sunday, 11-5.

1. Bowditch Point Regional Park
2. Lynn Hall Memorial Park
3. Fort Myers Beach Pier
4. Ostego Bay Marine Foundation
5. Lovers Key State Park

NOT TO SCALE

SIGHTS & ATTRACTIONS

BEACHES, PARKS & NATURAL AREAS

Fort Myers Beach's biggest draw is its beaches. The main one, **Lynn Hall Memorial Park** on Estero Blvd. in the commercial district features a free fishing pier, a small playground, picnic tables, grills, restrooms, and a bathhouse. Hours are 7 am-10 pm. Parking is limited and metered. Restaurants, bars, and shops line the beach. Several public beach access points lie to the south along Estero Blvd. Park only in marked areas. Cars are frequently towed for illegal parking.

Bowditch Point Regional Park (shown at right), at the north end of Estero Blvd., ☎ 239-765-6794, is quieter than Lynn Hall. Facilities include showers, restrooms, changing rooms, picnic tables, grills, a small playground, and hiking paths.

ADVENTURES

ON WATER

FISHING

Fish for free from the **Fort Myers Beach Fishing Pier** at Lynn Hall Memorial Park (see above) at the center of activity in Fort Myers Beach. You'll find bait and snack shops. Or cast off the bridge that connects the island's south end to Lovers Key.

Fort Myers Beach's **fishing party boats** provide a less expensive option than private charters and rentals. At **Getaway Deep Sea Fishing**, Getaway Marina at 18400 San Carlos Blvd., ☎ 239-466-3600 or 800-641-3088, www.getawaymarina.com, a 90-foot boat takes you to deep water for grouper, mackerel, snapper, and other offshore catches. All-day rates are $65 for all; reservations requested. For half-day trips from 9-3, rates are $42, $30, and $20; no reservations necessary.

BOAT RAMPS

Boaters can use the free boat ramps at **Lovers Key** State Park (see *Eco-Adventures*, below).

BOAT RENTALS

Rent a boat at **Fish-Tale Marina**, 7225 Estero Blvd., ☎ 239-463-3600, www.fishtalemarinagroup.cc. A four-person skiff runs $95 and rates go up to include Grady White fishing boats for $135-$360 for a half-day, $200-$475 for a full day, depending on boat size. Deck and pontoon boats rent for $125-$225 half-day, $200-$320 full day. The marina opens daily, 8-4:30 pm.

BOAT CHARTERS & TOURS

© Big M Casino

Big M Casino at Moss Marine, 450 Harbor Ct., ☎ 888-373-3521 or 239-765-PLAY, www.bigmcasino. com, departs from Snug Harbor restaurant and takes daytime brunch and dinner gambling cruises daily. Cost is $10-$20. Buffet dining is also available. No passengers under age 21.

Nature Recreation Management at ☎ 239-314-0110, www.nature recreationmanagement.com, conducts one-hour eco-, shelling, and sunset tours departing from Lovers Key State Park. Cost is $20 for adults, $8 for children aged three through 12. Fishing charters are also available.

PADDLING

The **Great Calusa Blueway** paddling trail started up in these waters. The first 50-mile segment begins at San Carlos Bay Preserve and extends south through Estero Bay to Mound Key Archaeological State

Park (see page 338) and the Imperial River. Another 30-plus miles heads north to Fort Myers' Bunche Beach and on to Sanibel Island and the upper islands.

You can rent canoes and kayaks at a concession at **Lovers Key State Park** (shown here), for use in local estuaries and bay waters, where dolphin

Fort Myers & Sanibel Island

and other wildlife abound. Contact Nature Recreation Management at ☎ 239-314-0110, www.naturerecreationmanage ment.com. Rentals for a single kayak begin at $20 for a half-day, $30 for a full day.

PARASAILING

For high adventure on the **Caloosahatchee**, contact Ranalli Parasail at **DiamondHead Resort** on Fort Myers Beach, 2000 Estero Blvd., for reservations, ☎ 239-565-5700 or 542-5511, www.ranalli parasail.com. It gives rides daily, 9-6, for $50-$70 for heights of 600 to 1,200 feet. Call in advance for reservations and free parking.

OTHER WATERSPORTS

You can book a Jet Ski tour to see dolphins, or head skyward by parasail with **Holiday Water Sports**, located at Pink Shell Beach Resort, 250 Estero Blvd., ☎ 239-765-4FUN, and **Best Western Beach Resort**, 684 Estero Blvd., ☎ 239-463-6778. Sailboat, kayak, paddleboat, and WaveRunner rentals available, with lessons. Dolphin WaveRunner tours last 1½ hours and cost $125 for two people.

ON WHEELS

To rent just about anything on wheels – from strollers to Harleys – see the folks at **Fun Rentals**, 1901 Estero Blvd., ☎ 239-463-8844. Bike rentals start at $12 for two hours, with rates for up to seven days. Scooters start at $35 for two hours, $65 for a day.

Nature Recreation Management at ☎ 239-314-0110, www.nature recreationmanagement.com, rents bikes for use in Lovers Key State Park for $10 a day.

ECO-ADVENTURES

Peek into aquariums, a touch tank, and other exhibits focused on local sea life at **Ostego Bay Marine Foundation**, 718 Fisherman's Wharf (turn north of the high bridge), ☎ 239-765-8101, www. ostegobay.org. Three-hour working waterfront tours are available Wednesdays starting at 9, for a $15 donation. It's open Wednesday-Friday, 10-4 and Saturday, 10-1. Admission is free.

Matanzas Pass Preserve at the end of Bay Rd., ☎ 239-432-2127, provides a quiet respite from the bustle of Fort Myers Beach with a short loop trail, boardwalks through mangroves to the bay, and a historic cottage filled with artifacts and exhibits. The preserve is open daily; the cottage, Wednesday and Saturday, 10-2. Admission is free; donations are accepted.

For wildlife and fewer crowds, head south and cross over the bridge to Lovers Key. **Lovers Key State Park**, ☎ 239-463-4588, www.florida stateparks.org/loverskey/, is a lovely estuary. The Travel Channel has listed the park as Florida's most romantic beach on its list of "Florida's Top-10 Beaches." Admission to the 712-acre park is $5 per vehicle with up to eight passengers, $3 for single passengers, and $1 for extra passengers, bicyclists, and pedestrians. It includes a round-trip mini-tram ride from the parking lot to the southernmost beach. Facilities include free boat ramp, outdoor showers, restrooms, picnic tables, grills, canoe and kayak rentals, and food concessions in season. Open 8-sunset, daily.

WHERE TO STAY

HOTELS, MOTELS & RESORTS

Hotels, resorts, and condominiums line the shore for the entire nine-mile length of Fort Myers Beach.

Fort Myers & Sanibel Island

ACCOMMODATIONS PRICE KEY		
Rates are per room, per night, double occupancy. Price ranges described for each property often do not take into account penthouses and other exceptional, high-priced accommodations.	$	Up to $75
	$$	$75 to $150
	$$$	$151 to $250
	$$$$	$251 and up

The only Fort Myers Beach resort that is a true destination in itself, **Pink Shell Beach Resort**, 275 Estero Blvd., at the island's quieter north end, ☎ 888-222-7465 or 239-463-6181, www.pinkshell.com, spreads Gulf to bay. Recently rebuilt with modern beachfront towers, it features a new spa, Octopool, restaurants, a fishing pier, a kids' activity program, boat docking, and tennis courts. $$$-$$$$

© Pink Shell Beach Resort

At the island's south end, activity quiets down to an easy pace of beaching and playing in the water. **The Outrigger Beach Resort**, at 6200 Estero Blvd., ☎ 239-463-3131 or 800-749-3131, www.outriggerfmb.com, is casual and unstructured, with an on-site café, a pool, a sundeck, a lively bar, and watersports concessions. Rooms and efficiencies available. Ask about special packages. $$-$$$$

© Santa Maria Harbour Resort

The boating crowd likes **Santa Maria Harbour Resort**, 7317 Estero Blvd., ☎ 800-765-6701 or 239-765-6700, www.sunstream.com, for its 36-slip harbor ($1 per foot per day docking fee), its proximity to the good fish of Estero Bay Aquatic Preserve and Fish-Tale Marina next door, and its like-home one- to three-bedroom condos. Housekeeping costs extra. $$$-$$$$.

WHERE TO EAT

Head to Fort Myers Beach for fresh seafood at good prices with great water views.

For a taste of authentic Greek food in an open-air milieu near the beach, try **Plaka I**, at 1001 Estero Blvd., ☎ 239-463-4707. This long-time beach fixture serves breakfast ($4-$11), lunch ($7-$15), and dinner ($11-$15) daily in a casual beachside atmosphere inside and out.

Boaters, those who love eating by the marina, and anyone in the island spirit will rejoice in the casual, open-air Caribbean vibes at **Parrot Key Caribbean Grill**, Salty Sam's Marina, 2500 Main St., ☎ 239-463-3257, www.myparrotkey.com. It's located on San Carlos Island, before you get to the high bridge and Fort Myers Beach's Estero Island. Go for lunch or dinner, in the $8-$25 range, and order something tropical such as habanero wings, chicken sandwich with kiwi-strawberry-mango barbecue sauce, filet au poivre with a brandy-mango demi-glace, or fried oysters with Creole mustard. Stay for a good-time party. Wednesday evenings is Nascrab Races, with live hermit crabs.

Anthony's on the Gulf, at 3040 Estero Blvd., ☎ 239-463-2600, specializes in Italian dishes served in a modern, vaulted ceiling, indoor-outdoor setting with an elevated view of the beach. Pasta, veal, seafood, beef and chicken entrées are $17-$30. It serves dinner daily.

NIGHTLIFE

Fort Myers Beach parties day and night. Hot spots include **The Bridge**, 708 Fisherman's Wharf, ☎ 239-765-0050; **Jimmy B's Beach Bar**, 1130 Estero Blvd., ☎ 239-463-6158, www.beachcomber stpetebeach.com (click on Dining & Lounges); **Outrigger Beach Resort**, 6200 Estero Blvd., ☎ 239-463-3131, ext 150; **Dockside Sports Pub**, 1130 First St., ☎ 239-463-9510; and **Smokin Oyster Brewery**, 340 Old San Carlos, ☎ 239-463-3473.

> **DAYLIFE:** *You don't have to wait until the sun goes down to party on Fort Myers Beach. On weekends and weeklong in season, people whoop it up hours before the sun sets. Many find themselves a bar headquarters and set up their beach party outside. Popular beach party spots include the **Junkanoo** at Anthony's on the Gulf restaurant, 3040 Estero Blvd., ☎ 239-463-6139, and **Lani Kai**, at 1400 Estero Blvd., ☎ 239-463-3111. Beach bars often prohibit coolers on their waterfront. Some serve food (usually inexpensive) as well as drink.*

The Bridge Restaurant, 708 Fisherman's Wharf, ☎ 239-765-0050, puts on a Sunday reggae dock party that draws boaters and motorists for an afternoon and evening of island-style music and casual fun. It's the best in island partying, and it's free.

San Carlos Park & Estero

Florida Gulf Coast University recently debuted in the vicinity of South Fort Myers/San Carlos Park a blossoming area. At its southern fringe lies Estero. Just recently an old, quiet community offering opportunities for outdoor activity, its close proximity to the university has spawned a sudden proliferation of business, most notable two shopping centers that will be part of a residential and a resort complex.

GETTING HERE

The communities of San Carlos Park and Estero straddle **Highway 41** south of Fort Myers proper.

SIGHTS & ATTRACTIONS

■ OF HISTORIC OR CULTURAL INTEREST

© Lowell Gehman

Koreshan State Historic Site, US 41 at Corkscrew Rd., ☎ 239-992-0311, www.floridastateparks.org, put Estero on the map. Contained within a park, the site has restored a commune established in 1893 by a religious cult that settled on the banks of the Estero River. Under the tutorship of Dr. Cyrus Teed (who adopted the Hebrew name Koresh), members of Koreshan Unity believed the earth lined the inside of a hollow globe that looked down into the solar system. Teed and his followers envisioned an academic and natural "New Jerusalem." They planted exotic crops and vegetation and built a theater, one of several reconstructed buildings on the site. Besides exploring bygones, you can picnic, camp, walk the short nature trail, boat, fish, and canoe in the park. Day-use hours are 8-sunset. Admission is $4 per vehicle of eight passengers or less, $3 for single drivers, $1 for extra passengers, pedestrians, and cyclists.

© John Udick

■ SPECTATOR SPORTS

The Florida Everblades, Southwest Florida's professional ice hockey team, plays its October-April season at the Germain Arena, 11000 Everblades Pkwy. in Estero, off I-75 (Exit 123) at Corkscrew Rd., ☎ 239-948-7825, www.floridaeverblades.com. Tickets cost $11-$33.

ADVENTURES

■ ON WATER

PADDLING

Koreshan State Historic Site (see above), rents aluminum canoes for the four-mile trip through the park's wildlife asylum for $5 plus tax per hour, $25 plus tax per day. There is also a boat ramp in the park.

Across the street from the park, you can rent better quality vessels at **Estero River Outfitters**, 20991 S. Tamiami Trail, ☎ 239-992-4050, www.esteroriveroutfitters.com. Three-hour rentals cost $22.50-$27.50 for canoes, $17.50-$42.50 per person for kayaks. There is a boat ramp on the river, and the outfitters also sell bait and tackle. Open every day, 7-6.

© Lowell Gehman

Fort Myers & Sanibel Island

■ ON FOOT

Nearly eight miles of trails wrap through **Estero Bay State Buffer Preserve**, ☎ 239-463-3240. Parking is off W. Broadway, just north of Koreshan State Historic Site. Four trails (three of them loops) travel through 1,245 acres of scrub and pine flatwoods, salt marshes, and salt flats along the Estero River. Open sunrise to sunset.

Cool off on a hot day on the indoor ice-skating rinks at **Germain Arena** at 11000 Everblades Pky., off I-75 at exit 123, ☎ 239-948-7825, www.germainarena.com. Besides open skating sessions ($6 admission, $3 skate rental), you can sign up for classes in figure skating, hockey, and more.

WHERE TO STAY

■ HOTELS

The glamorous newcomer to this booming area, **Hyatt Regency Coconut Point** at 5001 Coconut Rd., ☎ 800-554-9288 or 239-444-

1234, www.coconutpoint.hyatt.com, makes a shocking high-rise statement at the edge of an estuary that once belonged to fish

camps. With its 27-hole golf course, deluxe watsu spa, two restaurants, dazzling water features, nature tours, and kids' program, the hotel provides it all. To get to the beach, however, you must take a boat to a private island. $$-$$$$.

© Hyatt Hotels

CAMPING

Koreshan State Historic Site (see above), US 41 at Corkscrew Rd., ☎ 239-992-0311, has 60 tent and RV sites with electricity that rent for $24.42 per night, including tax, for up to eight people.

SHOPPING

Brooks Brothers, Bass, Reebok, and nearly 250 other stores and restaurants make **Miromar Outlets** at I-75, Exit 123, ☎ 239-948-3766, www.miromar.com, the hottest factory outlet mall in the region. Open Monday through Saturday 10-9 and Sunday 11-6, it entertains with its Spectacular Musical Waters, kiddy play area, family lounge, food court, and interactive water fountain.

Two more major malls opened in the Estero area in 2007: **Coconut Point** on Tamiami Trail at Coconut Rd., www.coconutpointretail.com, and **Gulf Coast Town Center** at I-75 and Alico Rd., ☎ 239-267-5107, www.gulfcoasttowncenter.com, which includes a Bass Pro Shops outlet.

WHERE TO EAT

My favorite part of Tarpon Bay at **Hyatt Regency Coconut Point**, 5001 Coconut Rd., ☎ 800-554-9288 or 239-444-1234, is the ceviche bar, where raw fish is marinated in a variety of ingenious sauces from sweet to fiery. If you have room left after sampling there, the crispy-fried whole red snapper is a work of art. Or try the goat cheese-crusted snapper or bacon-wrapped grouper for novel seafood interpretations. It opens daily for dinner (entrées $24-$35). Sit inside the faux fish shack or on the porch overlooking the lagoon.

Bonita Springs & Bonita Beach

Once a fertile tomato-growing and fishing community, Bonita Springs is trading in farm land for grand residential communities these days. Tourism does not figure as importantly here as it does in neighboring towns, which keeps it a bit more low-key and natural. Fishing and boating possibilities abound, mainly from Big and Little Hickory islands, home of Bonita Beach. Other small, uninhabited islands attract wildlife and those seeking to spy upon them.

GETTING HERE

Bonita Springs bills itself as "Gateway to the Gulf" because its exit off I-75 (#116) comes closer to the beach than the other exits. Just follow **Bonita Beach Rd.** to its end, for about eight miles, to find the sands. Close to toney Naples, Bonita Springs has in recent years seen neighborly influence bleed north, especially in developments along Highway 41.

Highway 41, or Tamiami Trail, runs along the western edge of the town of Bonita Springs. **Old 41 Rd.** penetrates the town center.

To reach Bonita Beach from Bonita Springs, turn west off Highway 41 onto Bonita Beach Rd. and follow it to the bend at the public beach, where it becomes **Hickory Blvd.** This is Bonita Beach's main thoroughfare. Resort services lie at the north and south end of the approximately three-mile-long island.

> **NOTE:** *You can also get to Bonita Beach by a more scenic route from Fort Myers Beach (however, in winter, traffic moves very slowly during rush hours): Follow Fort Myers Beach's **Estero Blvd**. south to Lovers Key along Rte. 865. Here, the road becomes lightly traveled and bordered only by greenery and park facilities. Watch the sky for ospreys, frigates, and other birds. Continue about three miles over another bridge to Bonita Beach's Hickory Blvd.*

INFORMATION

You can get more information on Bonita Springs and Bonita Beach through **Bonita Springs Area Chamber of Commerce**, 25071 Chamber of Commerce Dr., Bonita Springs, 34135, ☎ 239-992-2943 or 800-226-2943, www.bonitaspringschamber.com. Its welcome center is open hours weekdays, 8:30-5 and Saturday (in season only), 9-2.

Fort Myers & Sanibel Island

SIGHTS & ATTRACTIONS

■ OF HISTORIC OR CULTURAL INTEREST

Offshore **Mound Key** is an unexploited island of special interest to bird watchers and archaeologists, who believe it was once an important ancient Native American headquarters. Digs now probe it for secrets of the past, many preserved within 30-foot-high shell mounds. A segment of the island is designated **Mound Key State Archaeological Site**, an arm of Koreshan State Historic Site (see page 334). Charter tours in the area take you there to do your own exploring, but artifact collecting is strongly discouraged.

■ BEACHES, PARKS & NATURAL AREAS

Bonita Beach has top-notch recreational beaches. At **Bonita Beach Park**, on Hickory Blvd. at Bonita Beach Rd., ☎ 239-949-4615, you'll find sheltered picnic tables, a bathhouse and boardwalks, handicap access, lifeguards, a food stand, a Hobie Cat sailboat concession, and other watersports rentals and restaurants nearby. Parking costs $1 per hour; the lot fills early in season. North of the main beach, along Hickory Blvd., 10 access points offer limited facilities and free parking.

The turnoff to **Barefoot Beach Preserve**, ☎ 239-3254-4000, is near main beach parking on Bonita Beach Rd. Its 342 acres contain a coastal hammock, 8,200 feet of beach, and low dunes. Facilities include changing rooms, showers, restrooms, nature interpretation stations, and snack bar. Hours are 8-sunset. Parking is $6 a day.

■ SPECTATOR SPORTS

Attend matinees or night races for $2 each (children under age 12 admitted free with parent or guardian) at **Naples-Fort Myers Grey-**

hound Track, 10601 Bonita Beach Rd., ☎ 239-992-2411, www. naplesfortmyersdogs.com. Trackside dining is available. Call for current race times.

ADVENTURES

ON WATER

FISHING

Big Hickory Fishing Nook Marina, 26107 Hickory Blvd., ☎ 239-992-3945, can take care of all your fishing needs: bait, tackle, fuel, equipment repair, fishing charters, and rental boats. It's open daily.

Hickory Bay Charters, ☎ 239-947-3851, operates out of Big Hickory Marina. Custom trips for one to six people costs $250-$350 for a half-day. Sightseeing and shelling tours are also available.

BOAT RAMPS

You can launch your boat into the **Imperial River**, with access to the Gulf, at a ramp off Highway 41, just north of Bonita Beach Rd.

BOAT RENTALS

Big Hickory Marina, 26107 Hickory Blvd., ☎ 239-992-3945, rents skiffs, open and center console fishing boats, and pontoons. Rates range from $60-$165 a half-day, $90-$250 a full day. Tax and fuel are additional.

Bonita Boat Rentals at Bonita Beach Resort Motel, 26395 Hickory Blvd., ☎ 239-992-2137, www.bonitabr.com, rents 22-foot pontoon boats that hold up to 12 people for $65-$70 for two hours, $105-$115 for half-days, $170-$185 full days (fuel and tax not included). It sells live bait and tackle and rents rods for $8 half-days, $12 full days.

Rent pontoons, deck boats and fishing boats for back bay use only from **Bay Water Rentals**, 5124 Bonita Beach Rd. SW, ☎ 239-495-0455 for half days ($145-$305) or full ($245-$405). Rates include fuel and oil.

BOAT CHARTERS & TOURS

For fishing, sightseeing, cocktail, and picnic cruises, contact **Capt. Ed Fischl charter boats** at Bonita Bay Marina, Highway 41 and Bonita Bay Blvd., ☎ 239-566-6510, www.captainedscharterboats. com. Two-hour sightseeing and cocktail charters start at $160 for up to four people. Four-hour backwater fishing starts at $325. Group lunch and dinner cruises to local restaurants are available.

■ ON WHEELS

A **bike path** runs the length of Bonita Beach, nearly three miles long, and connects to another at its south end, which leads to Vanderbilt Beach.

Naples Cyclery, at 27820 S. Tamiami Trail, ☎ 239-949-0026, rents bikes, recumbents, surreys, and kids equipment starting at $5-$10 for two hours. Surreys rent for $15-$20 for one hour. Daily, weekly, and other rates are also available.

Bonita Bike & Baby, ☎ 239-947-6377, delivers rental bikes. Rates run $8 a day for kids' bikes to $14 for adult multi-speed bikes. Call Monday-Saturday, 9-5.

SHOPPING

The **Highway 41** corridor has become a prime shopping venue in Bonita Springs. The Mediterranean-style **Promenade** in Bonita Bay presents an array of fashionable jewelers, clothiers, and restaurants arranged around courtyards, streams, and waterfalls.

WHERE TO STAY

Representative of the Naples influence, the **Trianon Hotel** at Bonita Bay, 3401 Bay Commons Dr., ☎ 239-800-859-3939 or 948-4400, www.trianon.com, is a spin-off of a boutique hotel in Old Naples. Created in the likeness of European luxury inns, it is richly decorated in marble and fine fabrics. Guests have access to a pool bordering a lake and a restaurant overlooking it, a lounge with fireplace, and complimentary continental breakfast. $$-$$$$

Hard-core fishing types will like the convenience of **Bonita Beach Resort Motel** at 26395 Hickory Blvd. on Bonita Beach, ☎ 239-992-2137. Situated on the back bay with fishing docks and boat rentals, it's also convenient to the beach, a short walk away. The efficiencies and apartments all come with a fully equipped kitchen. $-$$

WHERE TO EAT

A spin-off of a fashionable Naples restaurant, **Chops City Grill**, Hwy. 41 at Brooks Grand Plaza in Bonita Springs, ☎ 239-992-4677, gets its name from its fine cuts of meat and its Asian influence. Sushi, teriyaki roasted sea bass, Asian barbecue pork porterhouse, and banana-coconut spring rolls demonstrate utmost creativity and care. Open for dinner nightly, entrées range $18-$30.

For a taste of the Caribbean, try **Toucan Grille** at 4480 Bonita Beach Rd., ☎ 239-495-9464, www.toucangrille.com, all up done in rattan, wicker, bamboo, and bright tropical colors. Its offerings of coconut shrimp, jerk chicken, and chili-rum-glazed salmon make an easy-to-enjoy island statement. At happy hour, the bar stools fill with local business people. At lunch, salads and sandwiches run $9-$12; dinner entrées are $8-$25.

Big Hickory Seafood Grille and Marina, 26107 Hickory Blvd., ☎ 239-992-0991, www.bighickorygrille.com, inserts a fine dining experience into an old-Florida fish shack setting at the edge of a marina. The menu, too, combines old and new Florida cuisine: One section is devoted to "Cracker style" fried seafood baskets, another to scrumptious creations such as banana-crusted grouper with a creamy banana liqueur sauce. One menu caters to lunch and dinner crowds with "sammiches" and entrées ranging from $9 to $27. Several nightly specials continue along the creative streak and Lobster Night happens twice weekly. It opens daily for lunch and dinner, except for Mondays in summer.

The essence of casual Florida waterfront dining, **Doc's Beach House**, 27908 Hickory Blvd., ☎ 239-992-6444, www.docsbeach house.com, hugs the wide sands at Bonita Public Beach. Beachers grab a burger at a seat outside or in the lower level, with its own bar and sports TV. Upstairs is air-con-

© Doc's Beach House

Fort Myers & Sanibel Island

ditioned with an overview of beach goings-on through walls of windows. Open daily for breakfast ($4-$11) and lunch and dinner (sandwiches, salads, and entrées, $4-$25).

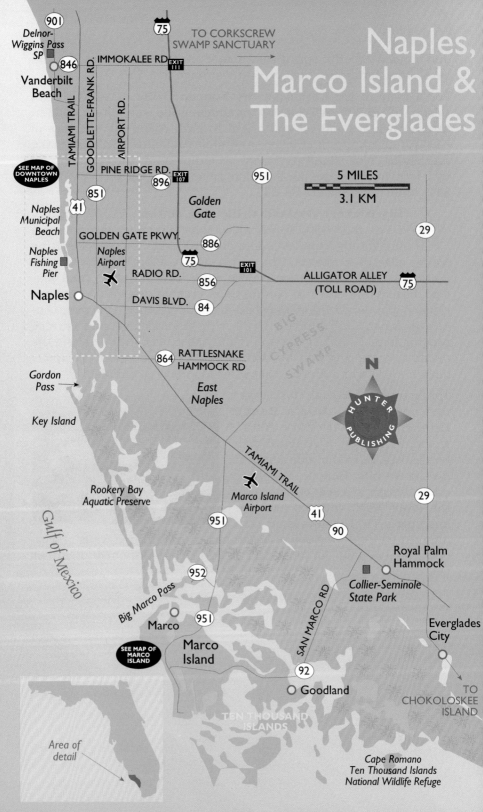

Naples & The Everglades

ollier County puts the "wild" in Florida's "West." It set the stage for gun-slinging outlaws, plucky mosquito-slapping pioneers, and prosperous adventure-seekers. The former took cover in the Everglades'

nearly impenetrable, wet wilderness. Pioneers and visitors settled in around Naples, Marco Island, and the largest of the Ten Thousand Islands. Here, they tried to eke a living from bountiful sea life, year-round crops, and often a shady deal here or there. They invented swamp buggies – plodding, big-wheeled vehicles – so they could travel the Everglades' outback. They poled flatboats across the **River of Grass** and around the mangrove-clotted **Ten Thousand Islands**. They created a new way of life in these parts, a new life that thrived on adventure.

Naples eventually rose above the crudeness of pioneer settlement to make a stance in the ultra-civilized world. As an outpost for people of means looking to get away – completely away – from it all, it developed along exclusive lines etched in wetland muck. Contrast defined Naples and its surroundings: pearlescent beaches and alligator-infested swamps, dapper neighborhoods and thatched Amerindian villages, Mercedes and swamp buggies.

The contrasts remain in this land at the end of Florida's West Coast. The wild juxtaposes with the refined at Naples' doorstep. Adventure still lures, especially in the past decade as Naples resorts, once considered snooty, urge their privileged guests into the rich muck of the Everglades, where life thrives at its rawest and most basic.

TRANSPORTATION

AIRLINES

The closest major airport is **Southwest Florida International Airport** (RSW) in Fort Myers, ☎ 239-768-1000, www.flylcpa.com. Taxi services will transport you to Naples in under an hour and to Marco Island in just over an hour.

AIRLINES SERVING SOUTHWEST FLORIDA (RSW) INT'L AIRPORT		
Air Canada	☎ 888-247-2262	www.aircanada.com
AirTran Airways	☎ 800-247-8726	www.airtran.com
American/American Eagle	☎ 800-433-7300	www.aa.com
Cape Air	☎ 800-352-0714	www.flycapeair.com
Condor	☎ 800-524-6975	www11.condor.com
Continental	☎ 800-525-0280	www.continental.com
Delta Air Lines / Comair	☎ 800-221-1212	www.delta.com
Frontier Airlines	☎ 800-432-1359	www.frontierairlines.com
JetBlue	☎ 800-538-2583	www.jetblue.com
LTU International	☎ 866-266-5588	www.ltu.com
Midwest	☎ 800-452-2022	www.midwestairlines.com
Northwest/KLM	☎ 800-225-2525	www.nwa.com
Southwest	☎ 800-435-9792	www.southwest.com
Sun Country	☎ 800-359-6786	www.suncounty.com
Spirit	☎ 800-772-7117	www.spiritair.com
US Airways	☎ 800-428-4322	www.usairways.com
United	☎ 800-241-6522	www.united.com
USA 3000 Airlines	☎ 877-872-3000	www.usa3000airlines.com

Small commercial flights come into **Naples Municipal Airport**, ☎ 239-643-0733, www.flynaples.com, usually shuttles and commuter flights from other Florida ports. Carriers servicing this airport include **Delta Connection**, ☎ 800-221-1212, www.delta.com.

■ RENTAL CARS & TAXI SERVICE

From the airport you can rent a car through **Avis**, ☎ 239-643-0900 or 800-331-1212; **Budget**, ☎ 800-527-0700; and other agencies.

For local taxi service, contact **Checker Cab**, ☎ 239-455-5555; **Naples Taxi**, ☎ 239-643-2148; or, for Marco Island, **A-Action**, ☎ 239-394-4000.

■ GETTING AROUND

Highway 41, also known as the Tamiami Trail, runs through the center of Naples (Ninth Street), then heads southeast to the Everglades. It ends at Miami. **I-75** runs parallel to the east and north of Highway 41, connecting with **Alligator Alley**, which requires a toll of $2.50 and ends at Fort Lauderdale.

WEEKEND ADVENTURE ITINERARY

■ **FRIDAY:** Drive to north Naples. Spend the morning at Corkscrew Swamp Sanctuary. Take a picnic lunch to Delnor-Wiggins Pass State Park and spend the afternoon on the beach and fishing. Have dinner at Bha! Bha! Persian Bistro and stay the night in North Naples or Vanderbilt Beach.

■ **SATURDAY:** Visit the Conservancy of Southwest Florida's Nature Discovery Center or The Naples Zoo in the morning. Have lunch at Riverwalk at Tin City and spend the afternoon shopping and sightseeing in Old Naples. Take a sunset cruise and have dinner at Zoe's. Spend the night downtown Naples.

■ **SUNDAY:** Drive to Everglades City. Take a boat or kayak tour of Ten Thousand Islands. Have lunch at Rod & Gun Club. In the afternoon, bicycle around Chokoloskee Island and W.J. Janes Scenic Memorial Drive or take a nature hike at Collier-Seminole State Park. Spend the night at the Ivey House B&B or camp out in Collier-Seminole State Park.

FESTIVALS & EVENTS

★ **JANUARY** – The **Goodland Mullet Festival**, ☎ 239-394-3041, www.goodland.com/buzzard.htm, is a hometown event that draws a small crowd to eat fish and Indian fry bread, and to dance the "Buzzard Lope," a goofy, high-energy step invented by event promoters.

★ **FEBRUARY** – Early in the month, Everglades City hosts the **Everglades Seafood Festival**, ☎ 239-695-4100, www.evergladesseafood.com, which features music, an artisan fair, and lots of seafood.

★ **MAY** – The **Great Dock Canoe Race** headquarters is The Dock at Crayton Cove restaurant, ☎ 239-263-9940, www.greatdockcanoerace.com.

★ **OCTOBER**– Three times yearly (October, January, and March) the nationally televised **Swamp Buggy Races**, ☎ 239-774-2701 or 800-897-2701, www.swampbuggy. com, take place in Naples at Florida Sports Park on Rte. 951. The October event kicks off the season with a parade and mud-dunking of the Swamp Buggy Queen.

FLORIDIOM: Swamp buggies are vehicles adapted to the Everglades' marshy terrain. Speedy, souped-up versions add the thrill of race-car action to this event.

BUDGET TIPS

■ Collier County's small museums provide quick lessons at bargain prices. Admission to **Collier County Museum** and **Museum of the Everglades** is by donation ($2 for adults suggested). Adults pay $3 for admission into **Smallwood Store Museum**, seniors $2.50, children under 12 are admitted free when accompanied by an adult.

■ Enjoy the region's good nature by foot for next to nothing. **CREW Marsh Trail System** and The Conservancy of Southwest Florida's **nature trails** are open free to the public. **Fakahatchee Strand**, **Big Cypress Preserve**, and **Florida Panther Refuge** also have free boardwalks and trails into local habitat.

■ You can often find new designer threads for less than half-price at local **consignment shops**. Naples' consignment shops are considered some of the best bargain shopping in the state.

INFORMATION

Greater Naples Marco Everglades Convention & Visitors Bureau at 3050 N. Horseshoe Blvd. #218, Naples 34104, ☎ 239-403-2379, 800 688 3600, www.paradisecoast.com, disseminates information on the entire region covered in this chapter.

Naples

"Walter, this is the most beautiful place in America. Let's build a town here," said Senator John Williams to publisher Walter Haldeman from the deck of their chartered schooner, according to legend. With a toddy of Kentucky bourbon, they toasted their deci-

Opposite: Old Naples

sion to move their families from Louisville to the wilderness that was then Naples. The year was 1885.

Touted as the town "where roses bloom in December," young Naples had died on the vine itself by 1890. Haldeman, publisher of the *Louisville Courier-Journal*, bought the town from partners. Naples later flourished with an influx of wealthy winterers and the support of Barron Collier, builder of the Tamiami Trail.

Perched on plush sands at the edge of Florida's primeval Everglades, meticulously manicured Naples today transcends its wild setting like a diamond in the rough. In fact, the only rough many visitors to this cultural oasis ever see is the one that sets them back two strokes on the seventh fairway. For along with Naples' reputation for outland poshness comes its claim for most golf holes per capita of any statistically tracked city in the US.

Waterfront homes are common in Naples.

But it wasn't always that way. Naples' high-brow, high-rent status came about primarily in the past two decades, after The Ritz-Carlton came to town. Not long ago, it was Florida's roughest neighborhood, roughest in the sense of unsettled and adventure-conducive. As gateway to the Ten Thousand Islands and the Everglades, it attracted well-to-do sportsfolk along with unsavory characters taking cover in the land of great erasure. Naples still holds some of that undiscovered mystique, along with its polished image of glamour resorts, pricey shopping, top-shelf restaurants, an active arts scene, and finely barbered golf courses.

TRANSPORTATION

Highway 41, or the Tamiami Trail, is Naples' main thoroughfare, known also as **Ninth St.** in town. From I-75, take Exits 105 and 107 and head west to reach North Naples; Exit 101 gets you eventually downtown and to south Naples.

Other main roads that run parallel to Highway 41 to the east are (west to east) **Goodlette-Frank Rd.** (Rte. 851), **Airport-Pulling Rd.** (Rte. 31), and **Livingston Rd.** East-west trunks are **Immokalee Rd.** (846) at the north edge of town, **Vanderbilt Beach Rd.**, **Pine Ridge Rd.** (896), **Golden Gate Pkwy.** (886), **Radio Rd.** (856), and **Davis Blvd.** (84) in town; **Rattlesnake Hammock Rd.** (864) is at the southern extreme. **Central Ave.** divides north from south numbered avenues mid-town. **Gulfshore Blvd.** provides a winding, scenic drive along the Gulf and its mansions.

■ AROUND TOWN

Naples Trolley Tours, ☎ 239-262-7300, www.naplestrolleytours. com, transports you around town for a two-hour narrated lesson on 100 points of interest, with free re-boarding. It runs daily beginning at 8:30 am. Cost: $20 for adults, $10 for children aged four to 12. Just look for signs indicating its many stops.

INFORMATION

For information, visit or contact the **Naples Area Chamber of Commerce Visitors Center** at 895 Fifth Ave. S., Naples, 34102-6605, open Monday-Friday, 9-5, ☎ 239-262-6141, www.napleschamber. org, 2390 Tamiami Trial N., Naples 34103.

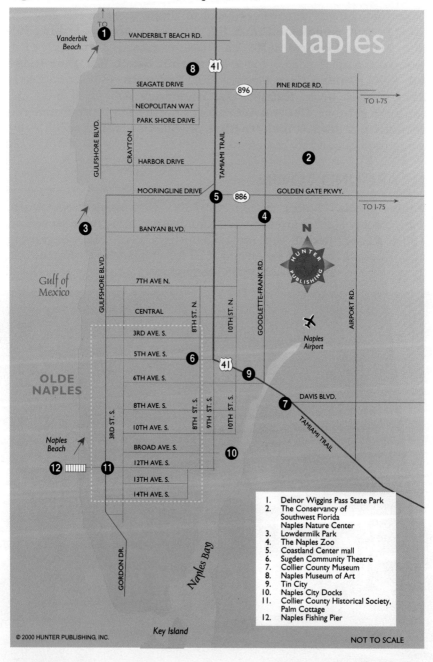

1. Delnor Wiggins Pass State Park
2. The Conservancy of Southwest Florida Naples Nature Center
3. Lowdermilk Park
4. The Naples Zoo
5. Coastland Center mall
6. Sugden Community Theatre
7. Collier County Museum
8. Naples Museum of Art
9. Tin City
10. Naples City Docks
11. Collier County Historical Society, Palm Cottage
12. Naples Fishing Pier

© 2000 HUNTER PUBLISHING, INC.

Key Island

NOT TO SCALE

SIGHTS & ATTRACTIONS

 Author favorites are indicated with a star.

Downtown

Unlike most Florida cities these days, Naples has kept its heart and soul contained in its downtown section. Historic neighborhoods have been remade into fashionable shopping centers in Old Naples.

▨ OF HISTORIC OR CULTURAL INTEREST

In Old Naples, **Palm Cottage** at 137 12th Ave. S., ☎ 239-261-8164, www.napleshistoricalsociety.org, demonstrates pioneer building methods and lifestyles. Made from local cypress, Florida pine, and tabby mortar, a sort of cement made from seashells, it has hosted visiting celebrities such as Hedy Lamarr and Gary Cooper. Today it houses the Collier County Historical Society. In 2007, the historical society opened a historic garden next to the site. The cottage is open 1-4 Tuesday-Saturday in season (November-April) and Wednesday-Saturday the rest of the year. Admission is $6 for adults for a guided tour of the cottage, $8 for the cottage and gardens.

In its four-acre historical park, **Collier County Museum**, at 3301 Tamiami Trail E., ☎ 239-774-8476, www.colliermuseum.com, chronicles the region's adventurous past. Cleanly displayed exhibits make time travel easy. Take in a Seminole Indian village, a classic swamp buggy you can climb onto, an archaeological lab stuffed with stuffed stuff, a 1926 cottage for hands-on discovery, native Florida gardens, a giant tree sloth skeleton, and a steam locomotive, plus new indoor vignettes and artifacts. Hours are 9-5, weekdays. $2 donations are suggested.

PERFORMING ARTS

Sugden Community Theatre, the latest darling of the fashionable Fifth Ave. South scene, hosts an October-through-May season of comedies and dance musicals in its two theaters, presented by The Naples Players community theater group. The theater is located at 701 Fifth Ave. S., ☎ 239-263-7990, www.naplesplayers.org. Tickets cost generally $10 for students, $20-$35 for adults.

BEACHES, PARKS & NATURAL AREAS

© Marc Ryckaert

The district's most distinguished landmark, **The Naples Fishing Pier**, ☎ 239-213-3062, extends 1,000 feet into the Gulf (more on page 356). It is the longest free-access pier in the state, and makes for a nice sunset stroll and a great place from which to cast. It juts out from the public beach on Gulf Shore Blvd. at 12th Ave. S. and is open 9-sunset. Parking is metered. More beach access points with parking lie to the north and south.

The city's most popular beach, **Lowdermilk Park**, is located along Gulf Shore Blvd. at Banyan Blvd., ☎ 239-213-3029. The play-full park has 1,000 feet of sandy beach, outdoor showers, volleyball, a playground, two gazebos, a shaded pavilion, picnic tables, and a concession stand. A special beach access, accessible restrooms, and free use of special wheeled surf chairs accommodate disabled users. Park hours are 9-5.

Pristine, white-sand beaches are big attractions.

◼ FAMILY FUN

Part botanical garden, part zoo, **The Naples Zoo**, formerly Caribbean Gardens, 1590 Goodlette Rd., ☎ 239-262-5409, www.napleszoo.com, takes an environmental and educational approach to showing off monkeys, tigers, and other animals rare and exotic. A boat ride takes visitors to Primate Island. Trails pass Alligator Bay, rare cats, kangaroos, and playground areas. Shows and demonstrations involve lions, 'gators, tigers, birds, hyenas, and kinkajous. Admission is $15.95 for adults and $9.95 for kids four-15, plus tax. The park is open daily, 9:30-5:30 (ticket office closes at 4:30).

Outlying Areas

■ OF HISTORIC OR CULTURAL INTEREST

Dale Chihuly's dazzling red glass chandelier and lighted sea-reminiscent ceiling are the showpieces of the **Naples Museum of Art** at the Philharmonic Center (see listing below), 5833 Pelican Bay Blvd., ☎ 800-597-1900 or 239-597-1900, www.thephil.org. The modern, elegant facility holds 15 galleries of traveling and permanent exhibits, including the works of modern Mexican masters and American miniatures. Admission is $6 for adults, $3 for students, free for children aged 5 and under. The museum opens Tuesday through Saturday, 10 to 5, and Sunday, noon to 5 November through April. May through October, it closes at 4 and is closed completely August through Labor Day.

■ PERFORMING ARTS

For a plunge into Naples' warm cultural climate, check with the **Philharmonic Center for the Arts** at 5833 Pelican Bay Blvd., ☎ 800-597-1900 or 239-597-1900, www.thephil.org. The 85-piece Naples Philharmonic is based at "The Phil" and the Miami City Ballet performs there three times a year. It hosts audiences of up to 1,425 for Broadway productions, touring orchestras, chamber music, and children's shows. Its art galleries host changing exhibitions and a permanent exhibit of stage set miniatures.

■ BEACHES, PARKS & NATURAL AREAS

For a beachfront away from mid-town's bustle, relax, fish, and hike at **Delnor-Wiggins Pass State Park**, at Rte. 846 (Immokalee Rd.) and Gulf Shore Drive N., ☎ 239-597-6196. An observation tower gives you a treetop view of the park's two waterfronts: the Gulf of Mexico and Vanderbilt Channel, the latter of which separates the island from the mainland and affords boating opportunities. Fishing is great in the swift pass waters; but don't swim there. Besides a boat ramp and fish-cleaning station, you'll find picnic facilities, bathhouses, lifeguards, and lots of natural vegetation and beach. In summer, the park hosts Turtle Walks – educational beach programs about nesting loggerhead sea turtles. The park is open daily, 8-sundown, and costs $5 per vehicle for two-eight passengers, $3 for a single occupant in a vehicle; $1 for pedestrians and bikers.

FLORIDIOM: The finicky wood stork (Mycteria americana) acts as a barometer for the health of local wetlands. The unmistakable, large bird – also know as Ironhead for the coloring of its neck, face, and bill – will nest only when the water table is deep enough so it may feed, but not too deep so that the fish are dispersed over a large area. If conditions aren't just so, it won't nest that year.

East of downtown, the new and still developing **Naples Botanical Garden** at 4820 Bayshore Dr., ☎ 239-643-7275, www.naplesgarden.org, goes from natural habitat on its nature trail to formal gardens, and the Pollinators Pavilion, where you'll find butterflies, lorikeets, Madagascar geckoes, and hummingbirds.

LOGGERHEAD TURTLES

They rise from the sea every summer, weighing 200 or so pounds each, dragging their awkward, sea-designed bodies ashore to lay 100 ping-pong-ball-sized eggs. They come in the dark of the night and leave only tractor-tire trails as signs of their tearful labor. Then they disappear, never to see their spawn. Sixty days later, the baby loggerhead turtles (*Caretta caretta*) that have survived fire ants and raccoons scurry to the sea to begin their ancient-ongoing ritual of life. Patrollers up and down the coast fence in loggerhead nests and help along the hatchlings in a life fraught early with danger.

■ FAMILY FUN

Families find fun away from the beach at **King Richard's Amusement Park**, 6780 N. Airport Rd., ☎ 239-598-1666, www.kingrichardspark.net. Rides and activities include bumper boats, batting cages, video and other electronic games, go-carts, a kiddie train, an interactive water play area, and an 18-hole miniature golf course. In season, it is open 11-9, Sunday-Thursday; 11-10, Friday-Saturday. The water play area opens noon-6, weather permitting. Tickets cost $5 per amusement, $28.50 for six tickets, and $54 for 12. A full-day's admission (available at peak times) costs $25.95.

Naples & the Everglades

ADVENTURES

ON WATER

Naples City Docks at 10th Ave. S. on the bay, ☎ 239-434-4693, is headquarters for water-bound action. You'll find rentals and charters at **Port-O-Call Marina**, off Hwy. 41 E., and nearby at Tin City, 1200 Fifth Ave.

FISHING

Naples' charters take you to **Rookery Bay** (see *Marco Island*, below) and **Ten Thousand Islands** for the best backbay fishing. Some go into deep waters or haunt the passes. From land, piers and passes offer best access to fish congregations, including snook, trout, sheepshead, ladyfish, trout and snapper.

Naples Fishing Pier at 12th Ave. S., ☎ 239-213-3062, in the heart of Old Naples, is Florida's longest free-access fishing pier, extending 1, 000 feet into the Gulf. Facilities include bait shop, cleaning tables, snack bar, restrooms, and shower. There is metered parking. Open 9 to sunset.

Lady Brett 45, at Tin City on Hwy. 41, ☎ 239-263-4949, www. tincityboats.com, departs twice daily for half-day fishing trips aboard a 45-foot powerboat. Fish in deep water about 12 miles from shore. Cost is $60 per adult, $50 per child under age 12. Tax is not included in prices.

For half-day bay water excursions, climb aboard the *Captain Paul* 34 at the same location and for the same prices.

If fly-fishing is your thing, contact Capt. Tom Shadley at **Mangrove Outfitters**, 4111 E. Tamiami Trail, ☎ 239-793-3370, www.mangrove-outfitters.com. He conducts classes in fly-tying on Tuesday evenings in season, 7-9 (no reservations required; $5 for supplies), and holds casting clinics by prior arrangement. Guided trips are $550 for full day, $350 for half-days, and take you to the Everglades, Rookery Bay, Pine Island Sound, Estero Bay, and other local backwaters.

Opposite: Ten Thousand Islands

BOAT RAMPS

Boat owners can launch their vessels into Vanderbilt Channel at **Delnor-Wiggins Pass State Park** (see *Outlying Sights & Attractions*, above) at 11100 Gulf Shore Dr. N., ☎ 239-597-6196. There's an entry fee into the park. A free ramp is located at Cocohatchee River Park off Vanderbilt Dr. The park has picnic tables and a playground.

BOAT RENTALS

Naples Water Sports at Port-O-Call Marina, off Hwy. 41 E., ☎ 239-774-0479, rents 21-foot deck boats for $250 half-days and $350 for full days; gas and tax extra.

BOAT CHARTERS & TOURS

Sweet Liberty docks at the City Dock at 880 12th Ave. S., ☎ 239-793-3525, www.sweetliberty.com. The 53-foot sailing catamaran departs daily for shelling, sightseeing, dolphin watch, and sunset trips. Cost is $27-$38 for adults, $15 for children, plus tax. Call ahead for reservations.

© *Sweet Liberty*

Most famous for its dolphin watch cruises, **Double Sunshine**, at Tin City on Hwy. 41, ☎ 239-263-4949, www. tincityboats.com, is a two-decked vessel that departs five times daily for 1½-hour narrated sightseeing, sunset, and dolphin excursions. Cost is $28 per adult, $14 per child under age 12. Tax is extra. Reservations suggested.

The Naples Princess, at Port-O-Call Marina off Hwy. 41, ☎ 239-649-2275, www.naplesprincesscruises.com, is the premier dinner cruise vessel in the area. Its excursions are $25-$49 per person, plus tax, gratuity, and port charge. Cruises include a Naples Bay buffet lunch cruise; mid-afternoon or sunset sightseeing; sunset cruise with hors d'oeuvres; and sunset dinner buffet on the Gulf. Call ahead for times and to make reservations.

The Conservancy of Southwest Florida, Merrihue Drive at 14th Ave. N., ☎ 239-262-0304, www.conservancy.org, leads free 45-minute on-site boat tours through mangrove forest. Fare is covered with admission to the Nature Discovery Center.

WAVERUNNERS

Explore Naples' waters on a 2½-hour tour of mansions and mangroves with **Naples Water & Land Tours**, Charter Club Resort, ☎ 239-793-7529, www.napleswatertours.com. Rates are $50 for adults, $25 for kids under age seven.

SNORKELING & DIVING

Diving on the West Coast appeals to die-hard divers only, because of low visibility and lack of natural reefs. However, local operators teach scuba courses, usually taking students out of the region for open-water dives. For information and supplies in Naples, contact **Scubadventures**, 971 Creech Rd. at Seabreeze Plaza on Hwy. 41 N., ☎ 239-434-7477.

ON FOOT

HIKING

Five miles of **hiking trails** intertwine with pine flatwoods and oak and palm hammock terrain at the edge of **CREW Marsh Trail System** on Corkscrew Rd. (Rte. 850), 19 miles east of I-75 Exit 123,

☎ 239-657-2253. The five miles of three loop trails are open free to the public daily during daylight hours. A 12-foot observation tower overlooks the marsh. Free guided tours are offered the second Saturday of each month, October-May. In summer, the trails are soggy, but it's a good time to see animal tracks, so grab your galoshes.

At **The Conservancy of Southwest Florida**, Merrihue Drive at 14th Ave. N., ☎ 239-262-0304, www.conservancy.org, naturalists take you on a free guided hike through a sub-tropical hammock. You can also hike the two trails unguided for free.

SHELLING

Avid shellers comb local beaches; the most devoted head to **Key Island**, a barrier island at the mouth of the Gordon River at Naples' south end, largely owned by local conservation agencies and the state. Local charters will take you there. You'll also hear the island referred to as Keewaydin Island.

ON WHEELS

Naples lays out a start-and-stop loop of metropolitan **bike paths**. One favorite route of local cyclists runs through **Pelican Bay**, a huge development at the north end of town with a 580-acre nature preserve.

Clint's Bicycle Shoppe of Naples at Pelican Bay, 8789 Tamiami Trail N., ☎ 239-566-3646, rents bikes by the week or month only. A beach cruiser rents for $30 a week and $65 a month. It is open Monday-Friday, 10-6; Saturday, 10-4.

To rent all sizes and styles of bikes – including Surreys by the hour, day, and longer – visit **Naples Cyclery** at Pavilion Shopping Center, 813 Vanderbilt Beach Rd., ☎ 239-566-0600. Single bike rentals start at $5 for two hours. Delivery is available.

ON HORSEBACK

Trail rides, Western riding lessons, and hayrides are all on the agenda at **M&H Stables**, 2920 Newman Dr. in East Naples, ☎ 239-455-8764, www.mhstables.com. Cost for trail rides is $40 for one hour. Lessons are $50 an hour.

ECO-ADVENTURES

The **Conservancy of Southwest Florida's Naples Nature Center**, Merrihue Drive at 14th Ave. N., ☎ 239-262-0304, www.conservancy. org, occupies about 20 acres of mangrove and hammock habitat where you can tour the Nature Discovery Center, a serpentarium, a wildlife rehabilitation facility, and nature trails. Free boat tours (with paid museum admission) of the mangrove waterway are available. The facility also offers off-site nature hiking, canoe, and boat tours. Canoe and kayak rentals are available for use in the Gordon River, which runs through the property. Rental rates start at $15 per vessel for two hours. The facility is open 9-4:30, Monday-Saturday and, from November to April, 12-4 on Sunday. Museum admission is $7.50 for adults and $2 for children aged three-12.

In Naples' outlying areas, the wilds encroach. To the north, one of the nation's most important birding and wildlife sites hides off the beaten path, 21 miles east of Hwy. 41 off Immokalee Rd. at 375 Sanctuary Rd. **Corkscrew Swamp Sanctuary**, ☎ 239-348-9151, www. corkscrew.audubon.org, operated by the National Audubon Society, comprises 11,000 pristine acres, two miles of boardwalk that cross wetlands inhabited by rich plant and marine life, alligators, deer, otters, and wild hogs. The sanctuary is most famous for its 700-acre stand of bald cypress trees – the largest pure, unmixed forest of the specimen found anywhere in the world. More than 500 years old, the trees grow up to 130 feet tall, forming a natural, moss-hung cathedral ceiling. They are the nesting habi-

tat of choice for the endangered wood stork. The Blair Audubon Center, a national prototype, features Swamp Theater, a virtual trip down the boardwalk. The sanctuary is open daily, April 11-September 30, 7 am-7:30 pm; October 1-April 10, 7-5:30. Admission is $8 for adults, $6 for full-time college students, and $4 for children aged six-18.

SHOPPING

Naples' renowned shopping has spread throughout the city, in old restored downtown areas and new, fashionable shopping plazas. Art galleries are abundant, as are jewelry, antique, home decor, and fashion shops and boutiques. The town's posh shopping centers are known for their one-of-a-kind shops.

For the best in window shopping, head to Old Naples' **Fifth Avenue South** and **Third Street South Plaza** and **the Avenues**, or to the new, spectacular plazas: **The Village of Venetian Bay**, at Gulfshore Blvd. N. and Park Shore, and **Waterside Shops** at Pelican Bay, Seagate Drive and Tamiami Trail N. Part of the Third Street South Plaza center, **Gallery Row**, includes some of Naples' finest art shops. The plaza also boasts the world's first street concierge, who helps arrange transportation for packages and makes store recommendations.

More touristy, but also more affordable, are **Old Marine Waterfront Marketplace** at

Gallery Row

Tin City, 1200 Fifth Ave. off Highway 41 S., and **Dockside Boardwalk**, 1100 Sixth Ave. S. You'll find nice wildlife-themed shops at both.

At the core of new Naples on Tamiami Trail at **Fleischmann, Coastland Center**, ☎ 239-262-2323, www.coastlandcenter.com, occupies more than 950,000 square feet, making it Naples' largest and only enclosed, climate-controlled shopping center. The mall's 150 stores include a full array of shopping options, from major department stores to small specialty shops, including a children's play area. Valet parking is available.

To buy the unaffordable at more affordable prices, vie for the cast-offs of the rich at upscale **consignment** shops, of which there are a wealth. Some of the best include **Conservancy Upscale Resale Shoppe**, 732 Tamiami Trail N., ☎ 239-263-0717, open Monday-Friday, 10-4, and Saturday, 10-2; **New To You Consignments**, 933 Creech Rd. and Hwy. 41, ☎ 239-262-6869, open Monday-Saturday, 10-5; and **Encore** at 3105 Davis Blvd., ☎ 239-775-0032 and at 28 10th St., ☎ 239-262-5558, open Monday-Friday, 10-4, Saturday 10-2. The shops sell clothing, furniture and decorative items.

Dockside Boardwalk

WHERE TO STAY

Naples lodging doesn't come cheaply, as a rule, although it does have its off-ramp chains and older motels for budget travelers.

ACCOMMODATIONS PRICE KEY		
Rates are per room, per night, double occupancy. Price ranges described for each property often do not take into account penthouses and other exceptional, high-priced accommodations.	$	Up to $75
	$$	$75 to $150
	$$$	$151 to $250
	$$$$	$251 and up

■ DOWNTOWN

Great for all manner of sportslovers, **Naples Beach Hotel & Golf Club**, at 851 Gulf Shore Blvd. N., ☎ 800-237-7600 or 641-261-2222, www.NaplesBeachHotel.com, lines the beach at the heart of Old Na-

© Naples Beach Hotel & Spa

ples. The 135-acre resort is especially popular with golfers. It also offers extensive watersports, a pool, tennis courts, and a fine kids' program. Complete with restaurants, bars, shops, and spa and fitness center, the hotel has accommodations in Old Florida-style buildings and high-rises. Packages available. $$$-$$$$

Stay right on the bay for some of Old Naples' most reasonable prices at **Cove Inn**, 900 Broad Ave. S., ☎ 800-255-4365 or 239-262-7161 www.coveinnnaples.com. Situated at Naples City Dock, it's close to boating activity and waterfront restaurants. It has its own pool and coffee shop. Units range from rooms to two-bedroom apartments. $$-$$$$

On Fifth Avenue South, new boutique hotels recall European city hotels. Closest to the action, **Inn on Fifth**, 699 Fifth Ave. S., ☎ 888-403-8778 or 239-403-8777, www.innonfifth.com, can't be missed with its ochre exterior and ever-bustling Irish pub shipped directly from Dublin. Rooms and

© Inn on Fifth

suites overlook Fifth Ave.'s activity and the Sugden Theatre next door, but keep the noise out. A rooftop pool complex, spa, and fitness center complete the amenities. $$$-$$$$

In a less-trafficked neighborhood a couple of blocks away, **Trianon Hotel Old Naples**, 955 Seventh Ave. S., ☎ 877-482-5228 or 239-435-9600, www.trianon.com, boasts spacious rooms and suites done up in Old World good taste. Buffet breakfast is included in rates. There is also a lounge and swimming pool. $$$-$$$$

VANDERBILT BEACH

Vanderbilt Beach, the Gulf-side community at Naples' north side, has several fun beach resorts in different price ranges.

© La Playa Beach Resort

LaPlaya Beach Resort, 9891 Gulf Shore Dr., ☎ 800-237-6883 or 239-597-3123, www.laplayaresort.com, exudes a privileged Florida air. Rooms are tropical-style gorgeous and the beach is wide and beckoning. Its spa, fitness center, acclaimed restaurant, and rocky waterfall pool complex put it in the boutique category, although it has nearly 200 rooms. $$$$

The Ritz-Carlton, 280 Vanderbilt Beach Rd., ☎ 239-598-3300 or 800-241-3333, is the grande dame of Naples hotels. Book there if you want a splurge on the wild side, because aside from its inherent good manners, the Naples Ritz has a nature-loving proclivity that starts with its mangrove preserve and ends with its eco-tourism concierges. $$$$

RENTAL AGENCIES

For private condo, cottage, or home rentals, contact **ResortQuest**, ☎ 800-GO-RELAX, www.resortquest.com. Weekly and monthly rates are available.

WHERE TO EAT

Naples has a well-deserved reputation for its restaurants, which come in all varieties, but are heavy on fine, eclectic cuisine. Downtown, Fifth Ave. S. is a bustling promenade of boutiques and sidewalk cafés. The Third Street South district keeps up with its own fine offerings, old and new.

NAPLES

Perhaps the best thing about **Randy's Fishmarket Restaurant** at 10395 Tamiami Trail N., Naples, ☎ 239-593-5555, www.randysfish marketrestaurant.com, is the famous key lime pie, but never doubt the freshness of the fish. Daily fish market offerings supplement extensive lunch and dinner menus devoted to seafood classics. Lunch entrées range from $7 to $14, dinner $15 to $37. A casual, colorful setting.

Naples & the Everglades

Tin City

Feel a part of the boating and fishing scene as you dine waterside on the docks at **Riverwalk at Tin City**, 1200 Fifth Ave., ☎ 239-263-2734, www.riverwalktincity.com. Boats pull up and fishermen ready their crafts as diners munch open-air on seafood specialties with a tropical spark. Open daily for lunch and dinner, serving salads, sandwiches, and entrées such as lobster pot pie and mojito pork porterhouse in the $14-$25 range.

One of the oldest favorites, **The Dock** at Crayton Cove, 845 12th Ave. S., ☎ 239-263-9940, www.dockcrayton cove.com, sits outside on Naples Bay and attracts swarms in season. It's very casual, but you'll find a lot of Naples' wealthy population gracing its wooden tables. The menu gives you a little of the old mixed with a bit of the new, selections the likes of Cuban barbecued ribs, blue corn-crusted snapper, and fish & chips. It's open daily for lunch and dinner. Sandwiches and entrées are $10-$25.

For a taste of Naples' cutting edge, try **Zoe's**, downtown at 720 Fifth Ave. S., ☎ 239-261-1221, www.zoesnaples.com. Décor is chicly bistro and the dishes run the gamut from seafood to premium steaks. Its wine offerings, many offered by the glass, are stellar. This is the kind of place where you order your wine and then pick your courses to complement it. Open daily for dinner, its entrées run $23-$38. Reservations recommended.

Close to another shopping front, at 1300 Third St. S., **Ridgway Bar & Grill**, ☎ 239-262-5500, www.ridgwaybarandgrill.com, dabbles in New American cuisine in all its wonderful varieties. Keep it easy and order a burger or crab and lobster roll, or go for the gusto with lamb stew, mustard and herb-glazed lamb rack, or pan-roasted shrimp with fried green tomatoes. Fine cuisine, but don't expect the service to match. Make sure to leave room for Ridgway's famous homemade desserts. Lunchtime sandwiches and specialties the likes of chicken pot pie and quiche Lorraine range from $10 to $16. Dinner entrées run $16 to $36. Dinner reservations recommended.

If you crave authentic Spanish cuisine, you'll be pleased with **Meson Olé**, 2212 N. Tamiami Trail at Oaks Plaza, ☎ 239-649-6616. It has your typical "gringo" expectations – enchiladas, tamales, and burritos. (Salsa that tastes canned is a disappointment with the chips.) Its greatest strength, however, lies in the unexpected, such as mussels in salsa verde, Castilian garlic soup, and sole with mushrooms and artichoke hearts. Serving lunch and dinner daily, it charges $8-$17 for lunch entrées; $10-$21 for dinner.

For a hearty breakfast to jump-start your day of adventure, try **Skillets** at 4170 N. Tamiami Trail, ☎ 239-262-3788; or 5461 Airport Rd., ☎ 239-566-1999, www.goodbreakfast.com. Omelets and frittatas come with delicious hash browns baked with sour cream. Or go for potato pancakes, Belgian waffles, crêpes, eggs Benedict, or Irish oatmeal, priced $4-$9. Salads, wraps, and panini offer something different on the lunch menu, in the $6-$9 range.

VANDERBILT BEACH

For a true tastebud thrill, venture to **Bha! Bha! Persian Bistro**, a one-of-a-kind culinary experience at the Pavilion shopping center, 847 Vanderbilt Rd., ☎ 239-594-5557, www.bhabhapersianbistro.com. It specializes in traditional and innovative Persian cuisine served in a modern Turkish setting. California, Italian, and Oriental styles influence the classics. The intriguing scope includes such novelties as duck *fesenjune* (braised in orange saffron stock with pomegranate-walnut sauce), chicken *isfahan* (with eggplant, provolone cheese, and garlic saffron sauce), and mango ginger shrimp. Lunch sandwiches and entrées range from $8 to $19; dinner selections, $18-$25. Open daily. Reservations accepted for dinner.

For the utmost in top-scale dining, make your reservation at **Artisans in The Dining Room** at The Ritz-Carlton, 280 Vanderbilt Beach Rd. , ☎ 800-241-3333 or 239-598-3300, www.ritzcarlton.com/en/Properties/Naples. From the fine art gracing the walls to the master-piece multi-course meals with such intrigue as trio of foie gras with peaches and Sauternes sorbet, bamboo-steamed Dover sole, and lobster risotto, you'll experience tiptop Naples haute.

© Ritz-Carlton

NIGHTLIFE

The streets of Old Naples hop, skip, and jump with lively music pouring from pubs and bars. The scene is dressier than your typical pub crawl. The new **Sugden Theatre** on Fifth Ave. S. (see page 352) brings a certain class to the clientele, who afterward hit **McCabe's Irish Pub** at Inn on Fifth, 699 Fifth Ave. S., ☎ 239-403-7170; **Zoe's**, 720 Fifth Ave. S., ☎ 239-261-1221, **Yabba Island Grill**, a Caribbean-inspired celebration at 711 Fifth Ave. S., ☎ 239-262-5787; and any number of local cafés and bistros with convivial bars and live music.

Marco Island

Floating offshore in the middle of nowhere, Marco Island is surprisingly developed. Outdoors lovers may at first be put off by its skyscraping row of beachfront resorts and condos, but upon closer inspection you'll find the island thoroughly steeped in water-bound sports. As chief among the Ten Thousand Islands stretching to the

south, Marco Island provides great opportunities for serious fishermen, bird watchers, and outdoors folk in general.

Away from its glamour front, you'll find charming time-stilled communities, waterfront fish houses, and thriving marinas. Here is a civilized departure point for deep adventure in the Everglades.

TRANSPORTATION

Marco Island consists of several communities. The least known, **Isles of Capri**, is a series of interconnected islands at Marco's northern threshold. It has been developed for residential use, but boaters also like to dock at its waterfront restaurants. You can't get to Isles of Capri from Marco Island proper, but must turn off Rte. 952 onto Capri Blvd. before Marco (watch for signs). Capri Blvd. continues through the community.

To get to Marco Island proper from Highway 41 or I-75, take **Rte. 951** (Exit 101). Two bridges span the bay waters known as Marco River to reach the island. The main

Opposite: Marco Island Beach

high bridge (S.S. Jolley Bridge) lies at the island's north end and gets you closest to Olde Marco and the island's resort area. (Talk is of making the Jolley a toll bridge.)

The south-end bridge is a better access if you're approaching from the east along Highway 41 or if you want to get straight to Goodland, the fishing community at that end of the island. Turn southwest off Highway 41 onto Rte. 92 to cross the south bridge.

Collier Blvd. (Rte. 951) crosses the north bridge and continues through the island's commercial section and along the Gulf front. **Crossroad Bald Eagle Dr.** (953) heads north-south to Olde Marco and mid-island. It connects to San Marco Dr. (92), which crosses the south bridge.

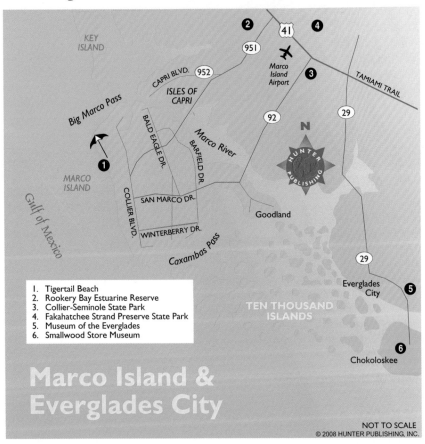

1. Tigertail Beach
2. Rookery Bay Estuarine Reserve
3. Collier-Seminole State Park
4. Fakahatchee Strand Preserve State Park
5. Museum of the Everglades
6. Smallwood Store Museum

Marco Island &
Everglades City

NOT TO SCALE
© 2008 HUNTER PUBLISHING, INC.

■ AROUND TOWN

The **Marco Island Trolley Tour**, ☎ 239-394-1600, makes stops throughout the town of Marco, and issues passes for one-day re-boarding. A complete island tour – thorough and delivered with a sense of fun – takes nearly two hours. Cost is $25 for adults, $12 for children under age 12. Look for signs indicating its numerous stops.

A speedy ferry boat transports guests from Marco Island to Key West for day or one-way trips. Contact **Key West Express** at Rose Marco River Marina, ☎ 888-KEYBOAT or 239-394-9700, www.seakey westexpress.com. Day-trips cost $128 for adults, $118 for seniors, and $50 for children aged six to 12. The boat departs at 9 am and arrives in Key West at 12:30 pm; leaves Key West at 6 pm and docks in Marco at 9:30 pm.

INFORMATION

For more information, contact the **Marco Island Area Chamber of Commerce**, 1102 N. Collier Blvd., Marco Island, 34145, ☎ 239-394-7549 or 800-788-6272. Hours are Monday-Friday, 9-5; in season it is also open on Saturday, 10-3.

SIGHTS & ATTRACTIONS

OF HISTORIC OR CULTURAL INTEREST

Marco Island's rich Calusa culture and archaeological finds of it provide the focus for **Key Marco Museum** at the corner of Bald Eagle Dr. and Waterway Dr., with a branch in Shops at Olde Marco on Palm Dr., ☎ 239-389-1572, www.themihs.org. The Olde Marco branch holds most of the Calusa exhibits, while the other concentrates on the island's early modern settlement and development. The local historical society has plans to move and expand its displays into one larger facility. For now, visit Monday-Friday 9-4. Admission is free.

BEACHES, PARKS & NATURAL AREAS

One of the area's most vital attractions sits at Marco Island's doorstep. **Rookery Bay Environmental Learning Center** at 300 Tower Rd. off Rte. 951, ☎ 239-417-6310, www.rookerybay.org, sits at the edge of 110,000 acres of prime wilderness that looks much the way it did before this rough-and-tumble land was settled. The center opened in 2003 with aquariums, interactive exhibits, a mangrove model,

Red-shouldered hawk

viewable science labs, wildlife art exhibits, and educational programs. It has plans for nature trails, a footbridge, a boardwalk, and kayaking. The center is open 9-4, Monday-Saturday; closed Saturday in the summer. Admission to the nature center is $5 for adults, $3 for children aged six-12.

Two public accesses allow visitors onto Marco Island's beautiful sands and one has no facilities. Hence, **Tigertail Beach**, Hernando Dr., ☎ 239-642-0818, is a popular place. Go early in nice weather to

find a parking spot. Or take the trolley there. If you walk to the north end, away from the parking lot, you can find solitude. Facilities include a food concession, picnic tables, sailboat and personal watercraft rentals, volleyball, restrooms, playgrounds, and showers. Its hours are 8-sunset. Parking is $5 per car.

▓ LOCAL COLOR

The neighboring residential community of **Isles of Capri** has no strong tourist attractions, but does offer visitors a nice variety of restaurants. The time-stilled fishing village of **Goodland** makes a pleasant drive-around and stop for lunch (see *Where to Eat*, page 378).

ADVENTURES

▓ ON WATER

FISHING

Marco's fishing preoccupation is self-evident. Several marinas offer charters, rentals, docking, bait and tackle shops, and other facilities. They include **Rose Marco River Marina** at 951 Bald Eagle Dr., ☎ 239-394-2502; **Cedar Bay Marina** at 705 E. Elkcam Circle, ☎ 239-394-9333, www.cedarbaymarina.com; and **Walker's Coon Key Marina** at 604 Palm Ave., ☎ 239-394-2797.

Fishing charters concentrate on the fish-full waters of Marco Islands' many waterways. Rookery Bay is a favorite, especially in winter. Gordon and Caxambas passes have a reputation as hot summer fishing spots.

Sunshine Tours out of Rose Marco River Marina, ☎ 239-642-5415, www.sunshinetoursmarcoisland.com/aboutus.htm, takes fishermen aboard a 32-foot boat with bathroom for offshore excursions ($475 for half-day, $900 for full day). Backwater fishing and shelling trips cost $55 for three hours ($45 for children under age 10). For current local fishing information, call the Fishing Hotline, v239-642-8888.

Captains John and Pam Stop at Stop's Marine in Goodland's Calusa Marina, ☎ 239-394-8000, w w w . s t o p s m a r i n e charters.com, run backwater fishing adventures lasting 2½ hours for $50 per person, $40 for children under age 10. For private half-day charters, the cost is $300 for up to four, $50 for each additional person up to six. Tax is extra.

BOAT RAMPS

Marco Island's only public boat ramp, on Roberts Bay at the island's south end, is accessible from **Caxambas Park** on S. Collier Ct. Restrooms, bait, and fuel are available.

BOAT RENTALS

For fishing or island-hopping, rent a center-console, pontoon, or deck boat at **Rose Marco River Marina**, 951 Bald Eagle Dr., ☎ 239-394-2502, www.marcoriver.com. Half-day rates range from $150 for a center-console to $200 for a deck boat; $200 to $260 for full day.

Cedar Bay Marina at 705 E. Elkcam Circle, ☎ 800-906-2628 or 239-394-9333, www.cedarbaymarina.com, rents center-console fishing boats, bow riders, and deck and pontoon boats that hold up to 12. Rates are $195 to $210 for a half-day, $260 to $285 for a full day.

BOAT CHARTERS & TOURS

For all varieties of personalized water adventures into Ten Thousand Islands – sightseeing, shelling, fishing, snorkeling, dolphin spotting, and nature tours – connect with **Captains John and Pam Stop** at Stop's Marine in Goodland's Calusa Island Marina, ☎ 239-394-

8000. Modes of transportation include a 26-foot luxury vessel and a 25-foot center-console boat. Rates start at $40 per person ($25 for children under age 12) for a three-hour Everglades eco-tour. Call between 7 am and 9 pm for reservations.

© Sail Kahuna

Known famously for its sailing cruises aboard a 42-passenger catamaran, **Sail Kahuna** at Rose Marco River Marina, 951 Bald Eagle Drive, ☎ 239-642-7704, www.sail-kahuna.com, also runs shelling trips. Three-hour sailing excursions for dolphin-watching, sightseeing, sunset, and shelling cost $35-$45 for adults, $28-$35 for seniors, half price for children aged 12 and under.

Marco Island Water Sports, at Marriott's Marco Island Resort, ☎ 239-642-2359, www.marcoislandwater sports.com, rents Hobie Cats for around $25 an hour. The shop runs 2½-hour eco-shelling and 90-minute sunset champagne cruises into Ten Thousand Islands for $49 adults and $39 children under age 12.

The Marco Island Princess, at Rose Marco River Marina, ☎ 239-642-5415, www.naplesprincesscruises.com, is the premier dinner cruise vessel in the area. Its excursions are $25-$49 per person, plus tax, gratuity, and port charge. Cruises include a Naples Bay buffet lunch cruise; mid-afternoon or sunset sightseeing; sunset cruise with hors d'oeuvres; and sunset dinner buffet on the Gulf. Call ahead for times and to make reservations.

PADDLING

From Isles of Capri, you can set off for nature kayak tours from **Saltwater Sports**, 231 Capri Blvd., ☎ 239-394-9557, www.saltwatersports florida.com. Three-hour wildlife tours run $55 per person. Rentals include free delivery on Marco Island. Three-hour rentals are $30 for a single kayak, $45 for a double; six-hour rentals are $45 and $55. Weekly rates and kayak fishing tours available. Open daily.

SNORKELING & DIVING

The **Baja California**, a Honduran freighter torpedoed 80 miles from shore in 1942 by a German U-boat, supplies a fish-fraught destination for local diving charters.

See the *Naples* section for other charters.

OTHER WATERSPORTS

Marco Island Ski & Water Sports operates out of Marriott's Marco Island Resort, ☎ 239-642-2359, www.marcoislandwatersports.com. It provides 10- to 15-minute parasail rides and rents WaveRunners and leads WaveRunner excursions to the Ten Thousand Islands. Parasailing costs $80 each; WaveRunner tours are $130 per machine; rentals run $75 for a half-hour, $130 for an hour.

Learn to waterski, wakeboard, and kneeboard on a charter with **Waterski Marco Island**, ☎ 239-825-7015, www.waterski marcoisland.com. An hour charter for up to six people costs $130 and includes instruction, refreshments, and equipment use, including tubes.

ON WHEELS

Bike paths run along Collier Blvd., Marco Island's resort road, Rte. 92, and in other parts of the island. At **Scootertown**, 845 Bald Eagle Dr., Marco, ☎ 239-394-8400, bike rental rates begin at $5 for one hour for a single-speed with foot brake or BMX kid's bike. Speed, hybrid, recumbent, and road bikes rent for $6-$14 for one hour. Daily rates range from $10 to $40. Multiple-day rates are available. Open Monday-Saturday, 9-6; Sunday, 10-4.

WHERE TO STAY

Marco Island proper lays out a strip of high-reaching resorts and condos along its crescent beach. This is the Marco Island most know about. To find something less Miami Beach-ish, head to the north end of the island.

© Marriott Hotels

Marriott is the monarch of Marco beach resorts. Its **Marco Island Resort and Golf Club** at 400 S. Collier Blvd., ☎ 800-GET-HERE or 239-394-2511, www.marcoisland marriott.com, is a large property offering all manner of outdoor activities. It has its own playgrounds, more than three miles of beach, and a great program for kids. For big kids, there are watersports rentals, a shopping arcade, an off-property golf course, tennis, a spa and fitness center, and new waterfalls pool with slides. Guests have several dining options. The resort also organizes tours to the Everglades and other nearby attractions. Rooms and suites available. $$$$

The natty newcomer to the Marco beach resort scene, **Marco Beach Ocean Resort** at 480 S. Collier Blvd., ☎ 800-778-9122 or 239-393-1400, www.marcoresort.com, stacks up 103 one- and two-bedroom

suites above its covered parking floors and a tasteful lobby. The suites are equally well-decorated and smartly planned with huge bathrooms and handy kitchens. A complete spa, fitness center, beach club, pool, and restaurant are all squeezed into the resort's compact space. Golfing and tennis privileges are available 10 minutes away. $$$$

© Marco Beach Ocean Resort

At the island's north end, in Olde Marco, **The Boat House Motel**, 1180 Edington Place, ☎ 800-528-6345 or 239-642-2400, www. theboathousemotel.com, provides a more secluded, boating-oriented option. The operation rents bicycles, paddleboats, WaveRunners, pontoons, and fishing boats, and offers docking to boat owners (no boat trailer parking or launch facilities). It is situated on the Marco River, with a wood deck and pool stretching along the water. Condo rentals available. $$-$$$

© The Boat House Motel

■ RENTAL AGENCIES

For private condo, cottage, or home rentals, contact **ResortQuest**, ☎ 800-462-4403, www.resortquest.com. Weekly and monthly rates are available.

WHERE TO EAT

Restaurants are rife on Marco Island, everything from the utmost casual to tiptop elegance. Seafood reigns, particularly stone crab claws, a Florida delicacy encased in a rock-hard shell – hence the name. They are in season from mid-October to mid-May and can be quite costly, depending upon availability. To keep restaurant tabs down, try them as an appetizer, prepared steamy hot or iced with drawn butter or tangy mustard sauce.

To obtain a sense of Marco Island's salty demeanor, savor the seafood and seaside atmosphere of **Snook Inn** at 1215 Bald Eagle Dr., ☎ 239-394-3313. It fronts the Marco River, and has a lively outdoor chickee bar. Those who can't watch boat traffic from a window can peer into an aquarium. The food is typical Old Florida-style – beer-battered grouper, breaded shrimp, plus steaks, chicken and a salad bar, entrées ranging from $10 to $23. Lunches are $9-$14. The restaurant is open daily.

For a brush with island tradition, dine grandly at **Olde Marco Island Inn**, 100 Palm St., ☎ 239-394-3131, www. oldemarcorestaurant.com. Built in 1883, it has been restored to its original gracious Southern style. Its six rooms display distinctive personalities – from fully formal to veranda-style. The menu puts local seafood to creative use with Victorian touches. For dinner ($20-$29), try scallops Saint Jacques, pork porterhouse, or prime rib. It opens daily for dinner; reservations are accepted.

Sale e Pepe at Marco Beach Ocean Resort, 480 S. Collier Blvd., ☎ 239-393-1600, invokes the grandeur of a Renaissance palazzo indoors; outdoors the elevated terrace overlooks Gulf and beach. The setting is perfect for the restaurant's brand of authentic, earthy Italian goods. The menu at Sale e Pepe (salt and pepper in Italian) spells out dishes in Italian and glowing prose: grilled lamb chops with sautéed wild mushrooms, pan-seared yellowfin tuna with caramelized onions and whole grain mustard sauce, fettucine with Maine lobster, and grilled lamb chop with wild mushrooms. Expect to pay $23-$34 for à la carte entrées. It serves breakfast, lunch, and dinner daily; reservations recommended for dinner.

© Marco Beach Ocean Resort

Naples & the Everglades

GOODLAND

A long-time landmark of the waterfront dining scene, **Old Marco Lodge Crab House** at 401 Papaya St., ☎ 239-64-CRABS, www.oldmarcolodge.com, is as unfancy as its seafood is fresh. The bartender makes a tasty Bloody Mary and the kitchen pumps out crab dishes, lobster tails, shrimp, and fish in all the traditional and some delightfully imaginative ways. Extensive selections on the all-day menu include crab cakes, stuffed Florida lobster tail, coconut shrimp, grouper Oscar, seafood Alfredo, steaks, sandwiches, and a load of fun starters. Eat indoors or out. Entrées start at $8 for sandwiches and go up to $30 for seafood platters. Open daily for lunch and dinner.

Well-loved by locals and boat-in guests, **Little Bar** at 205 Harbor Dr., ☎ 239-394-5663, www.littlebarrestaurant.com, outdoes its modest name with lots of dining space, some on a screened porch dockside, some in a room decorated with the remains of a historic boat, some in rooms paneled with oak pipe organ pieces. Cuisine goes beyond Old Florida-style with tropic flair, featuring everything from frog legs and stone crab to kielbasa and kraut, grouper Sicilian, and filet mignon. The wine list is impressive and the beer is served in frosted mugs. Lunches are $6-$15; dinners $13-$25, depending on the market price of fish. Little Bar serves lunch and dinner daily; reservations suggested for dinner.

ISLES OF CAPRI

Isles of Capri is known for its casual waterfront chickee restaurants. Its most popular, **Backwater Nick's**, got lost in 2005's Hurricane Wilma, but a couple of similar places remain. Fishmarket-fresh seafood adds the pizzazz to **Capri Fish House Restaurant** in the bright yellow building at 203 Capri Blvd., ☎ 239-389-5555, www.caprifishhouse.com. Its requisite thatched-roof bar has more character and is a more popular setting than the pastel-painted, sealife-decorated dining room and porch. Lunch and dinner menus are comprehensive. Sandwiches, salads, pasta dishes, and fried seafood baskets range from $7 to $13 at lunchtime. Dinner entrées, which range from $15 to $25, include fried platters, plus more creative fare such as grouper baked with tomatoes and artichoke hearts or jambalaya, as well as filet mignon and duck a l'orange. Open daily.

© Capri Fish House

Everglades City &
Chokoloskee Island

At Naples' back door lies Florida's proudest possession, the Everglades. This vast region was saved from the ravages of man's greed by the writings of **Marjorie Stoneman Douglas**, though it still teeters on the brink of destruction. The federal government has embarked upon a \$237-million project to restore the Everglades to a closer-to-original state. The second-largest national park, after Yellowstone, its appeal is subtler than that of most national parks, so it often gets ignored.

These massive wetlands – home of the endangered **Florida panther** and **American crocodile** – cover 2,200 square miles and shelter more than 600 types of fish and 300 bird species. Its land of Ten Thousand Islands holds one of the largest mangrove forests in the world; its shores support pine and hardwood hammocks and strands, cypress stands, and wetland prairies.

The best-known Everglades features are its **mangrove islands** and its so-called **River of Grass**, the slowest-moving river in the world. Both are fertile wildlife incubators. The region puts on the best bird show around, hosting wood storks, white pelicans, roseate spoonbills, ospreys, sanderlings, frigates, great white herons, tri-color herons, bald eagles, and other species both rare and common. In the water, dolphin come to feed, mullet jump, manatees mow the sea grasses, and alligators ogle. This is also the home of more reclusive animals, most notably the seriously endangered Florida panther, along with the Florida black bear, white deer, and bobcat.

THE FLORIDA PANTHER

 The Florida panther, *Felis concolor coryi*, is actually a sub-species of the cougar and relative to the mountain lion. Tawny in color, it distinguishes itself from its cousins with a kinky tail and cowlick – a result of inbreeding. In recent years, biologists have introduced a Texas sub-species to enhance the dwindling population and remedy other undesirable qualities caused by inbreeding. The animals, which require a wide range, prefer the relatively undisturbed habitat of the Everglades, where they feed on raccoons, rabbits, birds, and even larger prey, such as deer, hogs, and alligators.

Here is a whole different world from the kingdom of Florida beyond. This world holds Florida's heart. If it stops beating, so will the arteries that lead out of it. So will a wealth of wildlife.

The best way to explore the 'Glades is by water, but some hiking and biking opportunities also exist. To base your exploration on this side of the Everglades, you will want to head to one of the major camping areas, or to the slightly redneck island towns of Everglades City and Chokoloskee Island, both of which are steeped in a history of adventure. Everglades City began as a company town, headquarters for Barron Collier's road-building project, Tamiami Trail, in the early 1920s. Chokoloskee Island, inaccessible by car until 1955, was a rough-and-tumble outpost for early settlers, fishermen, outlaws, and the Amerindians who traded with them.

FLORIDIOM: The term Everglades has two frames of reference. Generically, it refers to the type of environment that spreads from Naples to Miami, Lake Kissimmee to Cape Sable, including the 721,000 acres of nearby Big Cypress National Preserve. Specifically, it means that territory bought by the United States Park Service in the 1940s, and protected to this day against development.

GETTING HERE

To penetrate the Everglades from the West Coast, you can approach from either **Highway 41** or from Exit 80 off the stretch of I-75 known as **Alligator Alley** ($2.50 toll). The exit takes you down Rte. 29, a narrow, lightly traveled road from which you get snapshot glimpses of what awaits ahead.

Everglades City lies near the juncture of Highway 41 and Rte. 29. To get to **Chokoloskee Island**, follow the signs in Everglades City that direct you to turn right at Captain's Table. After driving around the circle that is the town hub, you'll head south across the **Chokoloskee Causeway**.

> SCENIC DRIVE: The drive along Tamiami Trail (Highway 41) between Naples and Everglades City's Rte. 29 is one of stark wilderness. The prairie-like fields you think you are seeing are actually a shallow waterway, the famous River of Grass. Only an occasional hardwood hammock, Seminole village, and airboat concession break its interminable stretch. Watch the waterways closely, especially in winter, for protruding alligator snouts and tire-tread backs.

EVERGLADES TRANSPORTATION TRIVIA

The Everglades gave birth to two unusual modes of transportation, adapted to its shallow, swampy waters. **Swamp buggies** are modified Jeep-like vehicles built to hold anywhere from two to a crowd. They were developed by early 'Glades hunters and today are used widely for touring wetlands. **Airboats** (shown here) are fast, shallow-draft, noisy boats that zip across the water's surface. Environmentalists detest them almost as much as Wave Runners. Although not exclusive to the Everglades, pontoon boats –  flat, shallow-draft vessels – are popularly used in the area's skinny waters. They allow passage where V-shaped hulls deny it.

INFORMATION

Contact **Everglades Area Chamber of Commerce**, PO Box 130, Everglades City, 34139, ☎ 239-695-3172, www.florida-everglades. com/chamber. It has a welcome station-store at the corner of Hwy. 41 and Rte. 29; it's open daily, 9-4.

For information about Everglades National Park, write Information, **Everglades National Park**, 40001 State Rd. 9336, Homestead, 33034-6733, call ☎ 305-242-7700, or check online at www.nps.gov/ ever.

The Gulf Coast Visitor Center is located on Rte. 29, a half-mile south of Everglades City, ☎ 239-695-3311. It is open daily, 8 or 9-5:30.

SIGHTS & ATTRACTIONS

OF HISTORIC OR CULTURAL INTEREST

The islands are slowly developing from their historic past into tourist sites. Located in the historic former wash house for Barron Collier's company operations, **Museum of the Everglades**, downtown Everglades City at 105 W. Broadway, ☎ 239-695-0008, www.colliermuseum.com, preserves the lore and history surrounding the monumental task of building a road, Tamiami Trail, across the swampy, mosquito- and alligator-infested Everglades in the early 1920s. It also deals with the region's fishing and Seminole Indian heritage. The tiny, growing museum is open Tuesday-Saturday, 10-4. Admission is free or by donation ($2 suggested for adults).

The first and main historic attraction in Chokoloskee is **Smallwood Store Museum** at 360 Mamie St., ☎ 239-695-2989. Not so long ago, the barn-red building served as an Indian trading post. It remained a store and post office until it closed in 1974, and part of it retains the general store atmosphere while one room is given to exhibits on the Everglades' pioneer days. Its most sensational claim and homespun yarn centers around the gundown of outlaw Ed Watson, subject of a best-selling novel by Peter Matthiessen, *Killing Mister Watson*. The museum's best feature is the view from the back porch, overlooking Ten Thousand Islands and the scene of the crime. The store is open 10-5 daily, December-April; 11-5, May-December. Adults pay $3 for admission, seniors $2.50, children under age 12 are admitted free when accompanied by an adult.

ADVENTURES

■ ON WATER

You can spend several hours in the water here without seeing another boat or other sign of humanity. With all that water, water everywhere, **Ten Thousand Islands National Wildlife Refuge** and **River of Grass** afford the aqua-inclined opportunities unparalleled anywhere in Florida. It is recommended that you explore the area in cool weather, late October through March, to avoid the battalions of mosquitoes. Boating requires a shallow draft and local knowledge of the labyrinthine waters. For first-timers, it's best to hire a guide.

Great white egret

BOAT RENTALS

Outdoor Resorts of Chokoloskee Island, ☎ 239-695-2881, rents boats for $125 a day; canoes, $35; kayaks, $45. Half-day rentals are also available.

BOAT CHARTERS, TOURS

For sightseeing tours of Ten Thousand Islands, you can find private charters or hop aboard two available group tours. **Everglades National Park Boat Tours**, located on the Chokoloskee

Causeway, Rte. 29, ☎ 800-445-7724 or 239-695-2591, conducts naturalist-narrated tours through Ten Thousand Islands and its teeming bird and water life. Tours depart daily every 30 minutes, 9-4:30 or 5, depending upon what time the sun sets. They last about 1½ hours. Reservations are not accepted. Cost is $26.59 for adults and $13.25 for kids aged five-12. A Wilderness Tour into the mangroves and Turner River lasts one hour and 45 minutes and costs $35 for adults, $17.50 for kids aged 12 and younger.

AIRBOAT TOURS

Airboats can load you up with only one other person or a boatfull. You won't have to look very far to find someone who will take you sightseeing in this uniquely Floridian fashion. Some add alligator shows and other land-borne attractions to the trip. If you don't like noise and wildlife exploitation, try another mode of exploration.

Because it has raised seats and is the only tour that has permission to enter the grasslands, **Speedy Johnson's Airboat Rides** on Begonia St. in Everglades City, ☎ 800-998-4448 or 239-695-4448, is one of the best choices. Like most of the competition, it charges $37.50 per adult for a one-hour tour; children aged three to 10 pay $22.50. And also like others, it feeds the raccoons and alligators (marshmallows, no less) to insure that passengers experience wildlife, thus causing the animals to lose their fear of people and natural instincts for hunting.

Combine land and water exploration with an expedition from **Everglades Wildlife Safari**, a half-mile west of Rte. 29 on Hwy. 41, ☎ 877-695-2820. Small airboat-only tours begin at $35 for adults, $20 for children for about a half-hour. Combination airboat and bus safaris are $60 and $35.

PADDLING

By canoe and kayak, you can reach the region's most hidden places. Strike out on your own or follow a guided tour through the Ten Thousand Islands' 100-mile **Wilderness Waterway canoe trail**. Canoeists must register with park rangers. You can paddle portions of the trail; the entire length (ending up in Flamingo) takes at least a week. Designated docks provide tent-camping landings.

For canoe rentals, call **Everglades National Park Boat Tours** at ☎ 800-445-7724 or 239-695-2591. Canoe rentals cost $25.44 for one day, including tax. Longer rentals and shuttle service to Flamingo (the Everglades East Coast access) and Hwy. 41 are available. The facility is open daily, 8-4:30. Reservations are recommended from December through April.

National American Canoe Tours (NACT)/Everglades Rentals & Eco-Adventures, ☎ 239-695-4666, www.evergladesadventures. com, has its headquarters at the Ivey House B&B in Everglades City (see *Where to Stay*, page 389). It rents canoes and kayaks and leads guided day tours and adventures from one night to seven nights into the Everglades. Quality, fully outfitted kayak rentals range from $25-$45 for a half-day, $35-$65 for a full day, depending on the size and sophistication of the vessel. Canoes rent for $25 a half-day; $35 for the first full day. Guided all-day trips are $119 each, including equipment and lunch. Overnight camping trips are available and include a night's stay at Ivey House.

> **TIP:** *A list of canoe rentals, outfitters, and recommended gear, plus necessary charts, guidebooks, and complete information are available from the **National Park Service**, Everglades National Park, 40001 State Road 9336, Homestead, FL 33034-6732, www.nps.gov/ever.*

You can rent canoes at **Collier-Seminole State Park** (see *Sights & Attractions*, above), 20200 E. Tamiami Trail, ☎ 239-394-3397, www.

floridastateparks.org/collier-seminole, for use on the **Blackwater River**, with access to Ten Thousand Islands (filed float plan required). In winter (December-April), guides lead three-hour canoe trips into the park's wilderness preserve (reservations necessary). Primitive overnight camping in the preserve is available to canoeists. Canoe rentals are $5 an hour, $25 a day, plus tax.

ON FOOT

The seven-mile trail at **Collier-Seminole State Park**, 20200 E. Tamiami Trail, ☎ 239-394-3397, www.floridastateparks.org/collier-seminole, ribbons through pine flatwoods and cypress swamp. Plus you can walk a self-guided 45-minute board trail to experience life in a salt marsh. Guided walks are conducted December through April.

Rangers lead swamp walks into **Fakahatchee Strand Preserve State Park** (shown below), ☎ 239-695-4593; call for schedule and reservations; the tours are limited to 15 people. On your own, you can trample your way along old dirt logging roads and see rare orchids and bromeliads. This is a rugged adventure for the committed devotee or experienced botanist. Expect to get wet – up to your waist if you're truly adventurous.

ON WHEELS

A 3.5-mile **mountain bike trail** is open at **Collier-Seminole State Park**, 20200 E. Tamiami Trail, ☎ 239-394-3397, www.floridastate parks.org/collier-seminole. It travels through cabbage palm hammock and runs close to swamp habitat.

FLORIDIOM: A Florida hammock is not always something you can lounge in with a glass of iced tea. The Amerindian word describes a rise in land where hardwood trees grow. Mound-shaped, they're known as domes; linear, they're strands.

Bike paths traverse Everglades City and cross the causeway to Chokoloskee Island. **W.J. Janes Memorial Scenic Drive** branches off Rte. 29 north of Everglades City to lead you along a gravel-paved road into Fakahatchee Strand (see next  page). Its forest of royal palms, cypress trees, orchids and bromeliads provides pristine scenery and bird habitat. Stillness is the drive's greatest asset; you feel completely removed from the everyday world.

IN THE AIR

To see the Ten Thousand Islands from cloud-level, go **flight-seeing** with **Wings** 10,000 Island Aero-Tours, Everglades City Airport, ☎ 239-695-3296. Prices start at $30 per person, with three or four people for a 20-minute flight. Closed during summer.

ECO-ADVENTURES

Collier-Seminole State Park at 20200 E. Tamiami Trail, ☎ 239-394-3397, is one of the most newcomer-friendly ways to access the Everglades environment. The park covers more than 6,423 acres, of which 4,760 is wilderness mangrove preserve. You have options to camp, picnic, hike, bike, canoe, and boat around the encompassing area to become better acquainted with the plants and animals that dwell in the pinelands, salt marsh, and cypress swamp. It features a

Naples & the Everglades

wildlife interpretation center inside a structure replicating Seminole War blockhouses and a historic walking dredge that was used to build Tamiami Trail out of the alligator-infested muck. Mosquito-swatting is the favorite sport between May and November. Other times, folks enjoy the pontoon boat tour along the Blackwater River, canoeing, and hiking. Entrance to the beautifully maintained park, open sunrise to sunset, is $4 per car of up to eight passengers or $2 per vehicle with single occupant. Admission by bike, by foot, or per extra passenger is $1.

Fakahatchee Strand Preserve State Park, ☎ 239-695-4593, protects a 74,000-acre stretch of Big Cypress Swamp, but offers limited access. At **Big Cypress Bend**, west of Everglades City on Hwy. 41, you can follow a 2,000-foot boardwalk to sample Everglades environment. Another access,

Fakahatchee Strand Preserve State Park

W.J. Janes Memorial Scenic Dr., connects to Rte. 29 north of Highway 41. Along the gravel-paved route, you may see wild turkeys, black bears, deer, and rare birds among cypress and native royal palms. Fakahatchee Strand boasts the state's largest population of the reclusive, endangered Florida panther, cypress forest, and the largest stand of royal palms and largest concentration and variety of orchids in North America. It is the setting for Susan Orlean's book *The Orchid Thief*, which inspired the movie *Adaptation*, starring Meryl Streep and Nicolas Cage. No admission fee.

WHERE TO STAY

HOTELS & MOTELS

The islands are known for their RV parks more than any other type of lodging. They do have several inexpensive motels, including some located in RV parks. One of the largest, best maintained of these is **Outdoor Resorts** of Chokoloskee Island, ☎ 239-695-2881 (motel) or 695-3788 (RV resort). It has what's important to vacationers in these parts: a marina, boat rentals, a bait and tackle shop, and guide service for fishing and touring. Pull into one of 283 full-service sites or stay in the motel. Either way, you can take advantage of the resort's three pools, health spa, lighted tennis and shuffleboard courts, and restaurant. Site use for two people runs $69 a day year-round (monthly rates available). Motel efficiency and rental trailers are $85 (and are also offered by the week). Boat and canoe rentals available.

Aside from the camping resorts, Everglades City boasts a cottage resort that has gained attention for its historic, Southern charm. The **Rod and Gun Club** at 200 Broadway, ☎ 239-695-2101, offers nothing fancy but is a complete escape from the real world. It boasts famous guests through the years, from Burl Ives to Sean Connery. Cottages are basic, perhaps in need of a bit of repair, but loved by a devoted following. There's a pool and restaurant (see *Where to Eat*, below) on premises, plus docking and other boating amenities. $$

BED & BREAKFASTS

Outdoor enthusiasts find **Ivey House B&B**, 107 Camellia St. in Everglades City, ☎ 239-695-3299, www.evergladesadventures.com or www.iveyhouse.com, to their liking. The hostelry (shown below) has rooms and cottages in a lodge-like, historic building and a newer section that encircles a swimming pool. The old rooms have shared baths. A breakfast buffet is included in the rate. Ivey House offers guided tours into the Ten Thousand Islands by canoe, kayak, or boat, and rents equipment.$-$$

CAMPING

Big Cypress National Preserve on Hwy. 41, ☎ 239-695-1201, www. nps.gov/bicy, contains six camping areas, some primitive, some with hookups, some free, others with fees in the winter season. Monument Lake Campground has the most facilities of those close to Everglades City including restrooms, drinking water, cold showers, and free access to a dumping station. It is open September-mid-April. Tent and RV sites are $16 a night.

Five miles east of Rte. 29 on Hwy. 41, **Big Cypress Trail Lakes Campgroun**d, ☎ 239-695-2275, lets you camp by tent or RV in Big Cypress National Preserve, a magnificent sanctuary adjacent to Everglades National Park. Tent sites cost $14 per night. Two RV campers pay $18 per night, electric and water included. Weekly and monthly rates available.

Collier-Seminole State Park, 20200 E. Tamiami Trail, ☎ 239-394-3397, www.floridastateparks.org/collier-semi-nole, has 137 sites for tent- and RV campers in two separate campgrounds, plus canoeing and hiking trails. Sites without electricity and water hookups cost $18 per night plus tax. Reservations are accepted at ☎ 800-326-3521, www.reserveamerica.com.

WHERE TO EAT

This part of Florida more closely approximates Southern culture than any other area of the Southwest coast. Accents are twangy and food typically fried. Frog legs, stone crab, blue crab, and grouper appear on most menus.

Everglades Seafood Depot, 102 Collier Ave., Everglades City, ☎ 239-695-0075, serves standard Everglades fare – blue crab, shrimp, oysters, and freshly made hush puppies – plus some tropical specialties, in a historic depot building overlooking the water with a touch of class. Open daily for breakfast, lunch, and dinner. Lunch sandwiches, salads, and fried entrées run $6-$11. Expect to pay $11-$20 for most dinner entrées; $2-$7 for pancakes and egg specialties at breakfast.

With its tin roof, columned front porch, cypress-lined lobby and mangrove view, the venerable **Rod and Gun Club**, 200 Broadway, Everglades City, ☎ 239-695-2101, firmly grasps its Southern roots. Inside the lobby, an alligator hide stretches along a wall behind a copper-topped center fireplace. Built circa 1889 as a home that grew into an inn for hunters, fishermen, and yachters, it once entertained presidents and dignitaries within its pecky cypress walls. Today, the Rod and Gun Club still feeds intrepid sportsfolk who arrive by boat or car. The main dining room feels like a sportsman's lodge, wooded and clubby. A screened porch dining room invites leisurely dining. Sample Dixie-Florida fare: fried fresh fish, steamed shrimp in beer, frog legs, honey-fried crispy chicken, stone crab, and key lime pie. It's open daily for lunch ($11-$17) and dinner (entrées are $19-$25). No credit cards accepted.

Appendix

RECOMMENDED READING

ENVIRONMENT

Campbell, George R. *The Nature of Things on Sanibel*. Sarasota: Pineapple Press, 1988. 174 pp, illustrations, index.

Douglas, Marjory Stoneman. *The Everglades: River of Grass*. St. Simons, GA: Mockingbird Books, 1947. 308 pp.

WATERSPORTS

Hidden Florida, 8th Edition. Berkeley: Ulysses Press, 2003. 592 pp, maps, index.

Lenfestey, Tom. *A Gunkholer's Cruising Guide to Florida's West Coast,* 11th Edition. St. Petersburg: Great Outdoors Publishing, 2000. 156 pp, nautical charts, illustrations, index.

O'Keefe, M. Timothy, and Larry Larsen. *Fish & Dive Florida and The Keys*, Larsen's Outdoor Publishing, 1992. 192 pp, photos, index.

Trupp, Phil. *Diver's Almanac: Guide to Florida & the Keys*. Triton Publishing, Inc., 1990. 236 pp, color maps and photos.

Young, Claiborne S. *Cruising Guide to Western Florida*, 6th Edition, Pelican Publishing, 2003.

LAND SPORTS

Oswald, Tom. *Bicycling in Florida.* Sarasota: Pineapple Press, 1999. 144 pp, black-and-white photos, maps.

WHERE TO STAY & EAT

Walton, Chelle Koster. *The Sarasota, Sanibel Island & Naples Book*. Berkshire House Publishers, 2007. 320 pp, black-and-white photos, maps, index.

HISTORY

Beater, Jack. *Pirates & Buried Treasure.* St. Petersburg: Great Outdoors Publishing, 1959. 118 pp, illustrations.

Bickel, Karl A. *The Mangrove Coast: The Story of the West Coast of Florida.* New York: Coward-McCann, 1942. 332 pp, photos, index.

Briggs, Mildred. *Pioneers of Bonita Springs (Facts and Folklore).* Florida, 1976. 100 pp, photos.

Board, Prudy Taylor, and Esther B. Colcord. *Historic Fort Myers.* Virginia Beach: The Donning Publishers, 1992. 96 pp, photos, index.

Brown, Loren B. "Totch." *Totch: A Life in the Everglades.* University Press of Florida, 1993. 269 pp, photos.

Captiva Civic Association. *True Tales of Old Captiva.* 1984. 353 pp, photos.

Dormer, Elinore M. *The Sea Shell Islands: A History of Sanibel and Captiva.* Tallahassee: Rose Printing Co., 1987. 273 pp, illustrations, index.

Jordan, Elaine Blohm. *Pine Island, the Forgotten Island.* Pine Island: 1982. 186 pp, photos.

Gonzalez, Thomas A. *The Caloosahatchee: History of the Caloosahatchee River and the City of Fort Myers Florida.* Fort Myers Beach: Island Press Publishers, 1932. 134 pp.

Grismer, Karl H. *The Story of Fort Myers.* Fort Myers Beach: Island Press Publishers, 1982. 348 pp, photos, index.

Grismer, Karl H. *The Story of Sarasota.* Tampa: The Florida Grower Press, 1946. 376 pp, photos, index.

Jahoda, Gloria. *River of the Golden Ibis.* New York: Holt, Rinehart & Winston, 1973. 408 pp, illustrations.

Marth, Del. *Yesterday's Sarasota.* Miami: E.A. Seemann Publishing, Inc., 1973. 160 pp, photos.

Matthews, Janet Snyder. *Edge of Wilderness: A Settlement History of Manatee River and Sarasota Bay.* Sarasota: Coastal Press, 1983.

Matthews, Janet Snyder. *Journey to Centennial Sarasota.* Sarasota: Pine Level Press, 1989. 224 pp, photos, index.

Matthews, Janet Snyder. *Journey to Horse and Chaise.* Sarasota: Pine Level Press, 1989. 394 pp, photos, index.

Newton, James. *Uncommon Friends.* New York: Harcourt, Brace, Jovanovich, 1987. 368 pp.

Pacheco, Ferdie. *Ybor City Chronicles.* Gainesville: University Press of Florida, 1994. 301 pp, illustrated.

Peeples, Vernon. *Punta Gorda and the Charlotte Harbor Area*. Norfolk: The Donning Co., 1986. 208 pp, photos, index.

Pizzo, Anthony P. *Tampa Town 1824-1886*. Miami: Hurricane House, 1968. 89 pp, illustrations.

Schell, Rolfe F. *De Soto Didn't Land at Tampa*. Fort Myers: Island Press, 1966. 96 pp, illustrations.

Schell, Rolfe F. *History of Fort Myers Beach*. Fort Myers Beach: Island Press, 1980. 96 pp, photos, index.

Tebeau, Charlton W. *Florida's Last Frontier: The History of Collier County*. Coral Gables: University of Miami Press, 1966. 278 pp, photos, index.

Weeks, David C. *Ringling: The Florida Years, 1911-1936*. Gainesville: University Press of Florida, 1993. 350 pp, photos, annotated, index.

Zeiss, Betsy. *The Other Side of the River: Historical Cape Coral*. Cape Coral, 1986. 206 pp, photos, index.

■ FICTION/LITERATURE

Hudler, Ad. *All This Belongs To Me*. New York: Ballantine Books, 2006, 252 pp.

Lindbergh, Anne Morrow. *Gift from the Sea*. New York: Pantheon, 1955, 142 pp, illustrations.

MacDonald, John D. *The Empty Copper Sea*. New York: Fawcett Gold Medal Books, 1978, 245 pp.

Matthiessen, Peter. *Killing Mister Watson*. New York: Random House, 1990, 372 pp.

Matthiessen, Peter. *Lost Man's River*. New York: Vintage Books, 1998, 560 pp.

Newton, James. *Uncommon Friends*. New York: Harcourt, Inc., 1987, 368 pp.

White, Randy. *Captiva*. New York: Berkley Publishing Company, 1996. 319 pp.

White, Randy. *Heat Islands*. New York: St. Martin's Press, 1992. 307 pp.

White, Randy. *Sanibel Flats*. New York: St. Martin's Press, 1990. 307 pp.

White, Randy. *Shark River*. New York: Berkeley Prime Crime Books, 2001. 302 pp.

White, Randy. *Ten Thousand Islands*. New York: G.P. Putman's Sons, 2000. 320 pp.

White, Randy. *Twelve-Mile Limit*. New York: Berkeley Prime Crime Books, 2002. 356 pp.

Index